C through DESIGN

George E. Defenbaugh, Jr.

Richard Smedley

Franklin, Beedle & Associates
Publishers
8536 S. W. ST. HELENS DRIVE, SUITE D
WILSONVILLE, OR 97070
(503) 682 - 7668

FRANKLIN, BEEDLE & ASSOCIATES INCORPORATED
8536 S. W. ST. HELENS DRIVE, SUITE D
WILSONVILLE, OR 97070

Printed in the United States of America

Library of Congress Cataloging-in-Publication Data

Defenbaugh, George E., 1951-
    C through design / George E. Defenbaugh, Jr., and Richard Smedley.
        p.   cm.
    Bibliography: p.
    Includes index.
    ISBN 0-938661-10-8
    1. C (Computer program language)   I. Smedley, Richard, 1954-
II. Title.
QA76.73.C15D43 1988
005.13'3--dc19   88-11222
                                                          CIP

Dedications

To my wife, Kristie, and our children,
John Mark and Christine

G. D.

To my wife, Cleta, and my daughter, Misty

R. S.

Acknowledgements

We would like to extend our heartfelt thanks to the following individuals and groups. Without their help, encouragement and suggestions this book would not have ever been published:

Michael Clancy (University of California, Berkeley); *Tom Scharnberg* (Tarrant County Community College); *Jeff Carruth* (North Texas State University); *James Edmondson* (Santa Barbara City College); *Lalchand Shimpi* (Keene State College); *Jack Lloyd* (Montgomery College); *Julius Z. Nadas* (Loop College); and *Carl Penziul* (Corning Community College) read and critiqued the manuscript. We appreciate very much their willingness to share thoughts and insights regarding C and teaching.

Deb Shaw, Don Singleton and *Neal Walters* who reviewed a draft of the entire manuscript, *Rich Hardy* and *Dennis Warren* who reviewed individual chapters, and *Terry Kite* and *David Schornack* who provided research assistance. Thanks also to *Mark Davidson* for the use of his laser printer.

Tony Krehbiel and *Janet Stieben*, Chairpersons at Tulsa Junior College, who graciously allowed us to use the draft versions of this book as we taught classes in their departments. And we appreciate the students in those classes as they endured reading the material as it was being written.

And finally, *Sheryl Rose*, our manuscript editor, from whom we learned so much about grammar, punctuation, and clear expression.

The support and encouragement of our familes and co-workers kept this project from failing during the long hours of typing and programming. This book really belongs to our wives and kids, who wholeheartedly granted us the time away from them to write it.

Finally, *Jim Leisy*, our publisher, deserves an extra expression of thanks for his belief in our writing abilities, his confidence that this effort would succeed, and his devotion to the entire effort.

Preface

This book is intended to be used as a textbook for a college level programming class on the C language. The focus of the book is to integrate problem analysis and design with solid programming skills. The exercises are not discipline specific, and therefore suitable for both computer science majors, and also business majors who emphasize or have a minor in computer applications or management information systems.

It is estimated that 80% of commercial computer programs developed for mini and micro computers today are written in C. Although often associated with UNIX, C is also availabile in IBM's System Application Architecture (SAA) environment. C incorporates the features of speed and hardware access with the convenience of a high-level language environment. The current ANSI standard version of C is versatile and powerful, while being much safer and more productive than assembly language.

However, good program and system design practices are also an important part of all programming activities. We wrote this book with the following features in mind:

ANSI Standard C

This book presents 'standard' C, i.e., code that compiles cleanly with a compiler that meets the ANSI C standard. This standard, and its identical counterpart in the ISO C standard, is the right vehicle for teaching the language. After students learn how to write programs in 'standard' C they can begin exploring the particular nuances of specific compilers and host environments.

Abundant Example Programs

Over 90 example programs illustrate the topics in each chapter. In addition, complete, working programs are developed fully, from design to program output, at the end of each chapter.

Sound Programming Techniques

This book is filled with **Antibugging Notes** (that stress traps to be avoided), and **Quick Notes**, that emphasize important points to be remembered. The chapter review programs underscore the specification, design, programming, and testing process. Although the C language is often associated with programs that are difficult to read, clear, well-documented programming techniques are presented in this book.

Equal emphasis on UNIX and MS/PC-DOS

When operating system specifics are discussed within the text, both UNIX and MS/PC-DOS particulars are covered. Separate appendices explain the specifics of these two system environments. Other appendices are included for two very popular implementations of C, Borland's Turbo C and Microsoft's Quick C.

Strong emphasis on modularity

Modern day languages, including C, have the capability to isolate data and organize code into separate modules. This book emphasizes the use of local data along with functions to implement modular programming concepts. Functions are presented early, and structured programming concepts are demonstrated.

Immediate introduction to programming

Programming is an active discipline, and requires much practice to master. Chapter 2 covers sufficient basic language concepts to enable students to write complete programs. As each chapter covers particular concepts in detail, those topics are added to the review program and chapter exercises. Students are expected to begin writing programs early in the course, and to practice the topics covered in each chapter.

Separation of arrays from pointers

The presentation of arrays emphasizes that it is not necessary to understand pointers in order to use an array. Many aspects of arrays are demonstrated and explained before pointers are introduced. The chapter on pointers completes the discussion by explaining the similarities and differences between arrays and pointers.

Instructor's Guide

An Instructor's Guide for this book is available. It contains notes and further explanations on selected topics, sample tests, overhead transparency masters, additional exercises, and answers to all exercises. All programs, headers files, and sample test data shown in the text are also provided on disk to those who use the Instructor's Guide.

□ *Chapter 1*

Briefly discusses C and its importance as a modern, mid-level programming language. A general discussion of the programming development cycle wraps up this chapter with specifics on algorithm implementation using pseudocode.

□ *Chapter 2*

Introduces the language in sufficient depth and detail so that students can immediately begin writing simple programs. The chapter stresses the use of functions and modular programming techniques, which helps orient the student toward the use of C in a 'structured' environment.

☐ *Chapter 3*

Begins a detailed discussion of the language. The various aspects of constants, variables and basic aggregate types (strings) are presented. Two review programs at the end of this chapter provide complete code that exemplifies the manipulation of the various data types.

☐ *Chapter 4*

Explains the rich collection of C operators and the rules for using them to construct expressions. Numerous examples are given, as well as a section explaining how to avoid both common and subtle pitfalls often encountered when writing expressions and statements.

☐ *Chapter 5*

Presents program control flow with detailed discussions of each of the looping constructs that are available. Numerous examples are given along with guidance for the appropriate use for each construct. Emphasis is placed on modular program organization.

☐ *Chapter 6*

Discusses functions, return type and argument prototyping, calling conventions, formal parameters and actual arguments, and commonly encountered problems that occur when using functions. Recursive versus iterative techniques are contrasted along with suggestions where each is appropriate.

☐ *Chapter 7*

Demonstrates character input and output along with a detailed explanation of other commonly used standard library functions that perform I/O. The chapter review program presents a generic, maskable data entry function that can be used for safe and dependable data input.

☐ *Chapter 8*

Defines and explains scope, storage duration, and storage classes. These topics are often overlooked or given cursory treatment, but this chapter presents a clear and organized explanation of the various terms.

☐ *Chapter 9*

Presents arrays in detail, including definition, initialization, and manipulation of both single and multi-dimensional varieties. Arrays are taught separately from pointers, since they can be used without an understanding of pointers.

☐ *Chapter 10*

Begins with a basic definition of pointers and their direct relationship to physical memory locations. Illustrations are included, along with detailed explanation and examples of how pointers provide a facility for concise, fast code. Complex issues such as void pointers, pointers to functions and pointer arrays are given thorough treatment.

□ *Chapter 11*

Introduces the aggregate types of structures and unions. Particular emphasis is given to data structures that describe linked lists and binary trees.

□ *Chapter 12*

Illustrates basic disk file input and output, including text and binary files, commonly used standard library functions, and error handling and recovery techniques. Programs are presented that parse a free-form text file, build a disk file of structures, and update random files containing both single characters and structures. The chapter review program illustrates all of the techniques presented in the chapter.

□ *Chapter 13*

Discusses the C preprocessor with particular emphasis on macros and the **#define** directive. Directives that perform stringizing and token-pasting are illustrated, and conditional compilation is demonstrated. The two chapter review programs epitomize all the techniques shown throughout the entire book.

□ *Appendices & Index*

Appendices supplement the chapters, and may be referenced as needed. An in-depth index has also been included.

Contents

Special Features

Antibugging Notes

Quick Notes

Tables

Figures

1

Introduction, Program Design and Problem Solving

Any book on a programming language should begin with a review of the history of the language and a short synopsis of its features. This chapter will put the C language into perspective and discuss the factors that shaped its development. In recent years, great attention has been given to the techniques used to design computer programs and well-written code. Therefore, this chapter will also view the computer as a "problem-solving" machine and computer programs as the "fuel" necessary to drive that machine, focusing attention on program design and development tools. The techniques discussed will encompass the concepts of structured programming and top-down design principles.

After studying this chapter, you will be able to do the following:

1. Understand the forces that shaped the first versions of C.

2. Understand the major features and weaknesses of C as a modern development language.

3. Understand the importance of the ANSI C standard.

4. Define structured programming and explain its advantages.

5. Recognize how top-down thinking is applied to program design and why it is important in a modern programming environment.

6. Design programs using pseudocode.

7. Define the term *algorithm* and explain how it relates to program design.

1.1   Early Influences on the C Language

The C language has its roots in ALGOL, one of the first block-structured computer languages. Many languages, including Pascal, ADA, and MODULA, have a common ancestor in the ALGOL of the 1960s. Immediately preceding C, and also derived from ALGOL, were CPL, BCPL, and finally the B language, first implemented by Ken Thompson at Bell Laboratories.

During the 1960s and 70s (and in many cases still today) an operating system was written in the assembly language of the particular machine on which it was required to function. It usually takes more effort and training to write and maintain programs written in assembly language than it does to use most higher level languages (like BASIC, COBOL, FORTRAN, etc.). The people at Bell Labs were aware of this, and in an effort to create an operating system written in a high-level language, Dennis Ritchie developed the C programming language. Ritchie and colleague Ken Thompson then used C in their implementation of the new operating system, which co-worker Brian Kernighan suggested be named UNIX.

The PDP-11 computer, which had better addressing modes than its predecessor, was a key factor in the creation of C. Prior to the PDP-11 it was felt that hardware could not support the additional overhead of an operating system written in any language other than assembly. With the PDP-11's improved performance the first significant versions of the UNIX operating system written in C became available. Some parts of the C language still retain the influence of this hardware, and it is not just a coincidence that C expressions like (*to++ = *from++) reduce to a very few PDP-11 machine instructions. Today, as much as 95 percent of some versions of UNIX are written in C, with the rest in assembly language.

Anyone can successfully learn and be productive using the C language without knowing anything about UNIX, although the converse is not true (i.e., it's hard to learn UNIX in depth without eventually learning C). Whichever computer brand, vendor, and operating system you use, the C language should stand or fail on its own merits. It is a successful language, and a person can be successful using it, without having to rely upon the frequent association between C and the UNIX operating system.

1.2   C as a Modern Development Language

The popularity of a particular computer language is almost as transient as clothing fads or car styles. In the 1970s Pascal was the rage. Many people thought that Pascal would be the dominant computer language of the century. Today Pascal is primarily used as a teaching language, although the low cost of Turbo Pascal has created a market all its own. COBOL, initially sponsored by the government but now firmly entrenched in business data processing, has not grown into new areas of use. Nor did PL/I become universally accepted even though IBM strongly promoted it. It didn't replace both FORTRAN and COBOL, as many initially proclaimed would happen. ADA, another government committee creation (like COBOL), will certainly be used for military and government data processing, but has not yet been widely accepted by civilian and commercial institutions. It's size and complexity weigh heavily against it, especially in the micro computer area.

C, in contrast to all these, seems to be taking the computer world by storm. Few have any illusions that it will replace any other computer languages, but programmers and developers are continuing to find new applications where C is the language of choice. This is understandable when we review some of the characteristics that have contributed to its popularity: small size, good portability, and wide application.

C also has a few specific characteristics that are not appreciated by all programmers. First, it is an extremely literal language. Most C compilers do not "question" the programmer as to whether a particular line of code is appropriate. If the compiler understands the syntax of the expression, then the code will be compiled. This puts more responsibility on the programmer to write correct code. In exchange, the programmer gets a powerful tool with fewer restrictions than most languages. This trade hints at the second distinguishing feature, which is that C makes little attempt to hide the underlying hardware from the programmer. A person can quickly learn and use C for simple programming tasks without ever really understanding what is happening "underneath" the language and inside the machine. Many students are, and indeed should be, content to leave their understanding at this point. To utilize the power and potential of the language, however the programmer should, for example, learn the underlying internal format of a string, and master what really happens when a pointer is incremented.

In summary, C, like assembly language, will do almost anything a person could want. It lets the programmer decide whether something is judicious or imprudent. This flexibility and power are two of the main reasons for using and mastering C, while also being a main source of frustration for many students.

1.3   Basic C Language Features

From this overview of features we should be able to formulate a good picture of C in relation to other computer languages. The following points are not always considered desirable in a programming language, but they are part of C, and they will affect our programming, either to enhance it or to provide potential stumbling blocks which we must overcome.

1. Small size—There are fewer syntax rules in C than in many other languages, and it is possible to write a top-quality C compiler that will operate in only 256K bytes total memory. There are more operators and combinations of operators in C than there are keywords (i.e., there are few keywords), and an emphasis on programmer flexibility has resulted in an absence of restrictions.

2. Solid standard—The ANSI C standard provides an even better opportunity than before to write C code that will transfer from one computer to another with a minimum of changes. Not all areas of confusion in the language have been corrected, however, and because C interfaces efficiently with machine hardware many programs will always require some revision when they are moved to a different environment. The committee that developed the standard adopted as guidelines some phrases which collectively have been called the "spirit of C". Some of those phrases are:
   a. Trust the programmer.
   b. Don't prevent the programmer from doing what needs to be done.
   c. Keep the language small and simple.

Further, the international community was consulted to insure that ANSI (American) standard C would be identical to the ISO (International) standard version. Because of these efforts, C is the only language that effectively deals with alternate collating sequences, enormous character sets, and multiple user cultures.

3. Rich syntax—C provides
   a. 15 precedence levels for operators
   b. local variables for block-structured programming
   c. call by value for subroutine data privacy
   d. pointers for efficient and robust data access
   e. subroutines with a variable number of parameters
   f. bit operators for maximum hardware manipulation
   g. multiple exits from a subroutine
   h. optional multipass compile for flexible program organization
   i. external libraries for powerful extensibility

4. Flexible structures—All arrays in C are single-dimensional. Multi-dimensional arrangements are built from combinations of these one dimensional arrays. Arrays and structures ("records") can be joined in any manner desired, creating data base organizations that are limited only by the programmer's ability.

5. Side effects—A side effect in a language is an unexpected change to a variable or other item. This primarily occurs in "weakly typed" languages, those that allow great flexibility and freedom in manipulating data. For instance, the assignment operator, = , can appear more than once in the same expression. This feature, which can be used to a programmer's advantage, means that expressions can be written that have no clear and definite value. To have restricted the use of the assignment and similar operators, or to have eliminated all side effects and unpredictable results, would have removed from C much of its power and appeal as a high-level assembly language.

1.4   The Program Development Cycle

A computer program is a set of instructions that tells the computer what steps to take in solving a particular problem. The computer executes each instruction without question. The extent to which the problem is solved correctly depends on the program designer rather than the computer. The program itself may be written in any language, Pascal, BASIC, Assembler, C, and so forth, and must be translated into the native language of the machine on which it is to run before execution can begin. The design and implementation of the computer program follows a general list of steps known as the *program development cycle*:

1. Define the problem to be solved.

2. Identify the general steps needed to solve the problem.

3. Design the computer program using development tools such as pseudocode and flowcharts.

4. Translate the pseudocode/flowcharts into the computer language desired.

5. Implement the program on the machine. This step may involve compilation, assembly, module linkage, etc.

6. Test and debug the completed program. Repeat the previous steps as many times as necessary until the program functions correctly.

The first three steps are where many programmers spend the least time. Ironically, this is where the programmer should spend the most time. A well-designed and efficiently coded program requires careful planning in these formative steps. We will focus our attention in this chapter on these first three steps, leaving the last three as the subject of the rest of this book.

1.5   Problem Definition and Program Objective

Computers are problem-solving machines; however, they cannot provide solutions to ill-defined problems. To illustrate, consider the following problem statement:

> Write a program to generate prime numbers. A prime number is one like the numbers 2, 3, 5, 7, etc.

Our stumbling block here is the problem statement itself. Insufficient information is given to begin design of the program. Several questions arise: How many prime numbers? What are the common properties of prime numbers? What should be the first prime number generated by the program?

We are not quite sure where to begin, since the problem definition itself is ill-defined. A redefinition of the program objective is in order:

> Write a program to sequentially generate all prime numbers between 0 and 1000. A prime number is an integer (counting number) that is divisible only by 1 and the number itself. By definition, the first prime number is 2.

Now that all our previous questions have been answered, the design phase of our program can begin.

To aid in the general process of problem definition, the list of questions in Figure 1.1 may be of help.

---

1. What is the primary objective of the program?
2. What are the secondary objectives of the program, if any?
3. What output is expected and do range restrictions apply?
4. What input is needed and do range restrictions apply?
5. What special restraints apply to the primary and secondary objectives?

Figure 1.1 Questions for Program Design

Answering these questions of the prime number problem gives us the following answers:

1. The primary objective is the generation of prime numbers.

2. There are no secondary objectives.

3. The output should be all prime numbers between 0 and 1000.

4. No input is needed.

5. "Prime number" must be defined precisely.

Although Figure 1.1 is not intended to be a comprehensive guideline, it will provide a fundamental starting point for program objective definition.

Quick Note 1.1   Program objective

The first step in program design is to describe the objective of the program accurately and precisely.

1.6   Outlining the Program Steps with Pseudocode

Once the program objective has been clearly defined, it is time to rough out the program itself. Although there are many tools and techniques available for this purpose, the primary aid we will utilize in this text is pseudocode. A couple of nice features of pseudocode are (1) there are no hard and fast rules for how to write pseudocode and (2) the resultant program can be readily translated into the working code of the desired language. Pseudocode is a combination of language-like control flow constructs and English statements. The structure of the program itself shares a one-to-one correspondence with the structure of the pseudocode; poorly defined sections are represented by English statements in the pseudocode. To illustrate, consider the following program objective:

Write a program that adds two numbers and returns the result to the user. The user should be allowed to enter the two numbers to be added or to exit the program. Display the answer in the form **a** + **b** = **c** where **a** and **b** are the numbers to add and **c** the result.

Pseudocode for this problem might be written as follows:

```
begin main
    < inform user how to exit the program >
    response = 'Y'
    while (< response is 'Y' >)
        < get 'a' from the user >
        < get 'b' from the user >
        c = a + b
        < display 'a + b = c' >)
        < ask if user wishes to continue; valid response is 'Y' or 'N' >
    endwhile
end main
```

Note how pseudocode frees us from the details of language-specific syntax yet allows us to develop the flow and organization of the program. The < > symbols are used to denote details of the program that aren't clear at this stage of development. As we code the program in a specific language, we will expand these statements as we encounter them.

Although pseudocode is free-form in nature, we will endeavor to be consistent in this text with our own rendition of this development tool. The following pseudocode "rules" will be applied:

Pseudocode "Rules"

Control Constructs

The following outlines the pseudo-control flow constructs:

---

if( )/endif

```
        if (condition 1)
            . . .

        [else if(condition 2)]
            . . .

        [else if(condition 3)]
            . . .
```

[else if(condition n)]
  . . .

[else]
  . . .

endif

---

while( )/endwhile

while(condition)
  . . .

endwhile

---

do/while( )

do
  . . .

while(condition)
enddo

---

switch( )/case

switch(constant)
  case constant__value 1:
   . . .

  [case constant__value 2:]
   . . .

  [case constant__value n:]
   . . .

  [default:]
   . . .

endswitch

Note: the [] characters indicate optional portions of the construct.

All of the above constructs can be directly translated to C code.

Functions

Functions in C are like subroutines or procedures in other languages. Functions will be identified with the general form:

```
begin function__name(arguments...)
    <body of the function>
    [return([<value>])]
end function__name
```

General Pseudocode Statements

The < > symbols will be used to enclose English-like statements that describe operations whose specific translation to C code is not explicitly known at the time of writing the pseudocode. They are primarily used to "bury" the details of the operation to be performed so that the logic of the pseudocode becomes evident.

Pseudokeywords

The following pseudokeywords are used to indicate general input/output (I/O) operations in the pseudocode:

Pseudokeyword	Operation
print	console output
input	console input
write	output to external storage device
read	input from external storage device

Indentation

Indentation will be used to indicate the nesting order for all loops and logical blocks.

Variables/Data Types

Variables used in the pseudocode may or may not be identified since it is not always evident where variables are needed before the actual code is written. Known variables will be identified with a name and a general data type. The following data types apply:

Data Type	Equivalence
integer	short, int, long
character	char, byte
float	float, double
string	char array, ASCII null terminated
adt	Abstract Data Type The data type is used to describe complex data constructions such as tree nodes, list elements, record structures, graph nodes, etc.

The rules can be modified as desired. The important thing to remember when writing pseudocode is to try to be consistent. Pseudocode should be easy to read and should represent the programmer's intent.

1.7   Algorithms and Problem Solving

An *algorithm* is a series of steps that provide a solution to a specific problem—a recipe, in simpler terms. For example, suppose we are given the following task:

> Write a program that determines if a given integer is divisible by 3 without actually dividing the number by 3. Print TRUE if the number is divisible by 3 and FALSE if it is not.

What we need is a good algorithm. A trick that many children learn in grade school goes as follows:

1. Add up all the digits in the number.

2. If the result is not a single digit, repeat step 1 using the previous result obtained.

3. If the resulting number is 3, 6, or 9, the original number is evenly divisible by 3.

Note how the algorithm is described entirely in English statements organized step by step. Often, the algorithm will be translated to pseudocode after we are confident that it will indeed provide a solution to the problem at hand. Applying this to our algorithm yields:

```
begin divisible__by__3(number)
    result = number
    while (<result has more than one digit>)
        new__result = 0
        while(<there are more digits to process>)
            new__result = new__result + <result digit>
            <next result digit>
        endwhile
        result = new__result
    endwhile
    if (<result is equal to 3, 6, or 9>)
        return(TRUE)
    else
        return(FALSE)
end divisible__by__3
```

The next step in our program design would be to write pseudocode for the main code itself, utilizing **divisible__by__3()** where necessary.

Volumes of books have been written on the subject of algorithms, including standard algorithms for sorting and searching, data structures such as trees, stacks, and queues, and analysis of the algorithms themselves. In this book we will draw from this knowledge where appropriate and develop our own algorithms where necessary.

Quick Note 1.2   Algorithm Definition

An algorithm is nothing more than a step-by-step procedure used to solve a problem.

1.8   Structured Programming and Top-Down Design

The concepts of structured programming and top-down design are so interrelated that we present them together in this section. Structured programming is a philosophy rather than a principle of program implementation. Ask any two programmers for a definition of structured programming and there will likely be two entirely different answers. In this text we present our own view of the subject and illustrate how the underlying philosophy is applied using top-down design principles.

Essentially, *structured programming* encompasses a "box-within-a-box" approach to program development. The program itself is viewed in logical units of code. To illustrate, consider the following program objective:

Write a program that displays a table of square root values starting with an integer **a** and ending with an integer **b**. The user should be allowed to input both **a** and **b**.

Pseudocode for the program might look like this:

```
begin main()
    integer a, b
    get_inputs()
    do_table(a, b)
end main

begin get_inputs()
    <get 'a' from user>
    <get 'b' from user>
end get_inputs

begin do_table(a, b)
    while (<a is less than or equal to b>)
        print(a)
        print(square_root(a))
        a = a + 1
    endwhile
end do_table

begin square_root(number)
    return(<square root of the number>)
end square_root
```

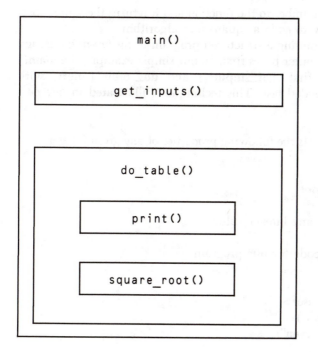

Figure 1.2 Pictorial Representation of main()

Figure 1.2 shows a pictorial representation of **main()**. The main line code, **main()**, controls two *subroutines* (or *functions* as they're called in C), passing input(s) as necessary and receiving output from each. Note that **main()** does not need to know how **get_inputs()** and **do_table()** work, only what input is expected and what output will result. Both functions act as "black boxes":

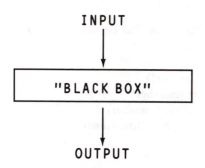

Such a scheme of program design allows the programmer to write code in a modular fashion, coding and debugging each module separately. Although it may not have been obvious at the time, most people have used the "black box" principle in other computer languages. For example, most languages provide a square root function. Simply hand a number to the function and it returns the square root. Few programmers know how to code a square root algorithm.

The approach to programming a structured program using *top-down design* techniques means coding the outer boxes first. In our simple example, the **main**() function would be coded first, **get_inputs**() and **do_table**() next, with **square_root**() and **print**() coded last. This technique is illustrated in our next example:

Write a program that prints the following properties of any given integer:
1. Even or odd
2. Number of digits
3. Divisible by 3 or not

Allow the user to enter any integer value.

To begin, let's write pseudocode for our program:

```
begin main()
    <get number from user>
    if (<number is even>)
        print("number is even")
    else
        print("number is odd")
    endif
    <calculate digits>
    print(<number of digits>)
    if (<number divisible by 3>)
        print("number is divisible by 3")
    else
        print("number is not divisible by 3")
    endif
end main
```

Upon careful examination of our pseudocode, we see that certain portions of the code could be written as subroutines, namely:

<get number from user>	get_number()
<number is even>	is_even(number)
<calculate digits>	num_digits(number)
<number divisible by 3>	divisible_by_3(number)

Therefore we rewrite the pseudocode to yield:

```
begin main( )
    number = get_number( )
    if (is_even(number))
        print("number is even")
    else
        print("number is odd")
    endif
    digits = num_digits(number)
    print(digits)
    if (divisible_by_3(number))
        print("number is divisible by 3")
    else
        print("number is not divisible by 3")
    endif
end main
```

At this point we simply write *dummy* functions for each subroutine:

```
begin get_number( )
    return(123)
end get_number

begin is_even(number)
    return(TRUE)
end is_even

begin num_digits(number)
    return(3)
end num_digits

begin divisible_by_3
    return(TRUE)
end divisible_by_3
```

We then code the **main( )** function, inserting calls to each dummy subroutine. This allows us to test and debug the main-line code before proceeding. We code and debug each function separately, returning to the pseudocode when necessary. We may find that one or more of the functions themselves require their own subroutines, which would be approached in a like manner. This method of approach to program design has been proven to be very productive and produces easily read and maintained code.

Quick Note 1.3   Top-Down Design

Top-down design means writing programs in a systematic fashion, from the general to the specific.

At this point we should define the term *antibugging*. Basically, *antibugging* means "defect avoidance", as opposed to *debugging*, which means "defect removal". The difference in emphasis may seem slight, but is an important concept if we are to successfully implement programs.

Barry Boehm's studies (see bibliography) concluded that the cost of removing program bugs after system implementation can be as much as 200 times the cost to remove the same bugs during requirements definition or design. While careful coding will not correct design mistakes, it can help make programs reliable and "bulletproof" (impossible to accidentally kill). Throughout this text we will include Antibugging Notes and Quick Notes. Following these notes will help us write programs which achieve "bulletproof" stature. Antibugging Notes will emphasize a particular pitfall or trap to avoid, while Quick Notes will recap and condense the major points of the surrounding material.

1.9   Function Design Philosophy

Quite often in the course of program design the programmer is faced with decisions regarding function (subroutine) design. There may even be questions as to whether a logical block of code should be placed in a separate function or simply retained in the main line code. Think beyond the application at hand and determine whether other programs could benefit from this newly written subroutine. Is the function highly specific to the application? Can it be generalized for use by other applications? Remember that C is an extensible language: subroutines (functions) can be written once then used as often as desired in other programs. To aid in the decision-making process we offer the following general guidelines for writing modular programs:

Modularity Guidelines

1. Strive for generalization. Write functions that serve their purpose in the application at hand, but are general enough to be used in other applications. Although generalizing a function may present more work initially, the extra effort will pay off in later applications.

2. Move logical blocks of code from the main program to separate functions if that will enhance the readability and clarity of the application.

3. Keep functions as simple as possible, and short. Don't write functions that perform several nonrelated tasks in the same block of code.

4. Document every aspect of the program carefully, especially generalized versions of functions that can be used by other applications. Remember that functions should always be viewed as "black boxes."

When the principles and guidelines presented in this chapter are used, less time will be spent "fighting with the code" and more time thinking about program design and efficiency. Programs will become more clear and readable, which can only mean increased productivity.

1.10 Exercises

* 1. Write pseudocode for the following program:

   Write a program that plays a game of checkers with the user. The user should be allowed to enter a move and then the program responds with its own move. The program should check for jump situations and respond accordingly. It should also strive to reach the king's row of its opponent.

2. Write pseudocode for the following program:

   Write a program that tracks weather data including temperature, humidity, rainfall (in inches), and barometric pressure. The user should be allowed to enter a date and the current readings. The program should store the daily information on disk and be able to print average readings over any time period.

3. What is wrong with the following problem statement? Explain.

   Write a program that can be used to predict which team will win a football game. The program should give correct predictions most of the time. If the program doesn't know who will win, it may guess.

4. Write algorithms for each the following:
   a. Filling a car with gas at a self-serve station.
   b. Having a birthday party.
   c. Designing and writing a computer program.

5. Describe in your own words what is meant by top-down program design. What advantages does this tool offer the programmer?

6. It has been said that structured programming means not using the **goto** statement in programs. Where do you suppose this idea came from? Explain.

* indicates an advanced exercise

2

A Working Overview of the C Language and Functions

We discussed the history and characteristics of C, and gave an overview of basic program design concepts and terms. This chapter begins the definition of the language itself and presents a working overview of C. Here we will show how to write simple but complete C programs.

Many instructors struggle with the problem of how to present material in a programming class. Often we find that to begin writing even a trivial program it's necessary either to cover topics that are best explained later, or to assume knowledge on the part of the student. The purpose of this chapter is to equip students to write C programs while we develop the concepts that will be introduced here. We'll assume that no one knows anything about C or any other computer languages. In subsequent chapters a more formal definition of C will be developed, and we'll revisit the topics we've presented here, developing each more fully.

After studying this chapter, you will be able to do the following:

1. Identify the three major portions of a C program.

2. Utilize the `#define` and `#include` preprocessor directives.

3. Define global character and integer data.

4. Recognize and code a function.

5. Use the `if` and `while` statements for simple decision making and looping.

6. Perform basic input from the keyboard and output to the screen.

2.1   Components and General Structure

A C program has three primary parts:

1. Preprocessor directives

2. Data

3. Code

C is sometimes referred to as a "write-only" language, meaning that some C programs are difficult to read. This usually reflects more on the coding techniques of the programmer than it does on the language itself. But we admit that, as a language, C is terse and compact. Even veteran data processing professionals have had difficulty learning the syntax of C, so don't be concerned if the structure and components of a C program are not "intuitively obvious" to you at first glance.

For the purposes of this working overview we will consider a C program to be contained in one text file. This means that we will not write the program in two different text files, compile them separately, and link them together. Using multiple source files is a common practice, but in this chapter all references to a C program will be taken in the context of one source file.

Figure 2.1 illustrates a small but complete C program that contains each of the three items mentioned above: preprocessor directives, data, and code. Refer to this figure often while we explain in more detail the main parts of a C program.

```
/*
** complete.c - A Small but Complete C Program
*/
                              /* The #include is the preprocessor directive */
#include <stdio.h>         /* and 'pulls' in predefined source file lines */


                                     /* SIGNON is a string constant */
                                     /* BUF_SIZE is an integer constant */
#define SIGNON "Welcome to the world of C programming,"
#define BUF_SIZE 81
```

(program continued on next page...)

```
main()                            /* C programs always begin execution here */
{                        /* this brace indicates the beginning of main() */
   char first_name[BUF_SIZE];    /* define a character array of size 81 */
                    /* the next line invokes clear_buffer(), a function */
                                   /* (really just a subroutine) */
   clear_buffer(first_name);      /* which is defined a few lines down */
                              /* this printf() displays a message */
   printf("Please enter your first name\n(80 characters or less): ");
                    /* this scanf() reads a string from the keyboard */
   scanf("%s", first_name);
                              /* this is a printf() with arguments */
   printf("%s %s\n", SIGNON, first_name);
                              /* the return statement is optional */
   return;                    /* and returns to the operating system */
                              /* if it is returning from main() */
}                             /* this brace ends the main() function */

clear_buffer(buffer)                    /* our subroutine is defined here */
char buffer[];         /* this line declares the data type for 'buffer' */
{              /* this brace begins the definition of clear_buffer() */
   int sub = 0;              /* define an integer with an initial value */
                        /* this integer will be used as a subscript */
   while (sub < BUF_SIZE)              /* while starts a loop until the */
      {                       /* test in parens is no longer true */
      buffer[sub] = 0;       /* put a binary zero in the buffer character */
      sub = sub + 1;                   /* add one to the subscript */
      }
                              /* the return statement is optional */
   return;                    /* and returns to the caller, i.e., main() */
}                   /* this brace ends the definition of clear_buffer() */
```

Figure 2.1   A Small but Complete C Program—`complete.c`

The output of this program would be:

```
Please enter your first name
(80 characters or less): Myname
Welcome to the world of C programming, Myname
```

2.1.1   *Preprocessor Directives*

C compilers perform the conversion of C source code into machine language instructions in phases, the first of which is a *preprocessor*. Some compilers implement the preprocessor as a separate phase, while others combine it with the syntax editor into a single phase. Regardless of how the phases are arranged, the preprocessor is always the first part of the compiler to process the C source code and it changes (not permanently) the source file each time the program is compiled.

The preprocessor can best be described as a smart text editor. *Directives*, which control the preprocessor, begin with a pound sign (#) and are followed by a control word, with #define and #include being the most frequently used directives. The pound sign often appears in the first column of an input line. This is not required by the ANSI Standard, however, and spaces can be coded before the # if indentation is desired.

The preprocessor does not do anything to the source code that could not be done with a text editor program. Of course, the text editor would be making permanent changes to the source file. But changes made by the preprocessor are in effect only during the current compilation process and are not saved as permanent changes in the source file. Most compilers do however provide the ability to send the output from the preprocessor to another file so that the changes can be made permanent. This technique is also useful as a debugging aid if preprocessor directives are not being processed as anticipated.

Quick Note 2.1   The preprocessor does not know C

The preprocessor does not know C. It is only a smart text editor. It does not permanently change the source file unless conscious and explicit steps are taken to replace the original C source file with the output of the preprocessor.

2.1.1.1   #define

The #define directive is often difficult for many students to understand. They try to find examples from other high-level languages to help them grasp what the #define directive does, but good examples are very hard to locate and often the process causes further misunderstanding. For example, #define is not the same as COMMON data in FORTRAN. It does, however, bear a very close resemblance to the EQU statement in many versions of assembly language. This should not be suprising given the history of C and how it is often used as a high-level assembler.

To fully appreciate the power and flexibility of #define we need to remember that all definitions created with the #define are handled by the preprocessor. This means that when the C compiler actually begins compiling, it cannot tell whether the C source code it reads has ever been processed by the preprocessor or whether the code was typed in by the programmer. For example, if the following preprocessor directive appears at the top of a program:

```
#define  ONE   1
```

then everywhere the characters ONE appear (except inside another word like EVERYONE) they will be replaced by the character 1. This replacement takes place before the compiler syntax checking and analysis begins, so the same thing could be accomplished by editing the program and substituting 1 for the appropriate occurrences of the characters ONE. No piece of data is created to store either the item ONE or the digit 1. The substitution occurs only in the C program source after it is read by the preprocessor and before it is passed to the compiler

In Figure 2.1, we encountered two #define preprocessor directives,

```
#define SIGNON "Welcome to the world of C programming,"
```

and

```
#define BUF_SIZE 81
```

Both of these directives cause the preprocessor to replace every occurrence of SIGNON and BUF_SIZE with "Welcome to the world of C programming," and 81, respectively, just as if they had been typed into the source file. After preprocessing, the statements,

```
char first_name[BUF_SIZE]
printf("%s %s\n", SIGNON, first_name);
while (sub < BUF_SIZE)
```

would become,

```
char first_name[81]
printf("%s %s\n", "Welcome to the world of C programming,", first_name);
while (sub < 81)
```

before being passed along to the compiler.

Another frequently used feature of the preprocessor is to create *macros*. A macro is defined by providing an argument along with a #define directive. For instance, if we define the macro INT like this:

```
#define INT(x, y)    int x = y;    /* no space between INT and the '(' */
```

then we can code

```
INT(my_int, 10)
```

and we will get

```
int my_int = 10;
```

Macros can reduce the amount of code that must be written while making programs easier to read and maintain.

Frequently students are confused about where and when to use semicolons. Semicolons are associated with C syntax and play no direct part in directives, which are interpreted by the preprocessor. Therefore, no semicolons are required for any preprocessor directive, and none have been shown here. If a semicolon is coded as part of a preprocessor directive, it will be either passed along to the compiler (if used on #define) or it will generate an error (if used on #include).

Quick Note 2.2   #define does not reserve storage

#define definitions do not reserve storage in the final compiled program. The substitution of the #define item into a program occurs before the compiling phases begin, and affects the source program for that compilation only.

2.1.1.2   #include

The #include directive is easier for many students to grasp than #define because there are numerous parallels in other languages. Basically #include merely copies another text file into the current source file at the point where the #include directive is found. Like #define, it acts as if the current source file had been edited and a text editor was used to copy in the include file before passing it to the compiler. The advantage of putting part of the program into another file and having it included automatically is readily seen when we consider that the same set of C language statements may need to be used in each file of a set of single source files. By placing the statements in an *include file* (as it is customarily called), we eliminate any possibility that the individual source files will be using different sets of statements. Similarly, any change to the include file will be reflected in the source files after each is compiled again. Include files are also sometimes referred to as "header files".

The include file can be stored in numerous places. Typically there is one directory or subdirectory that holds all frequently used include files, a directory which we might call the *primary system location*. These files are usually those that end in .h. Most of these files came with the compiler, but there might also be other include files that are used so often that they are considered to be as indispensable as the compiler's.

The location of the included file can be identified by placing either double quotes, "", or angle brackets, <>, around the file name. If a file name is entered without indicating the complete path to where the file resides, then the double quotes and angle brackets might locate different files. The difference is that using the double quotes will cause the preprocessor to look for the include file first in the same directory where the C program doing the including is found. (The C program being compiled is called the "including file.") Some people call this directory the "working directory." If angle brackets are used, the preprocessor looks in the primary system location and does not look in the directory where the including program is located. Thus, double quotes can be used to surround an include file name when it is the same as that of a file residing in the primary system location. This allows the primary system include files to be "overridden" and others substituted as replacements.

As an example, consider the `#include` directive in the program `complete.c`:

```
#include <stdio.h>
```

This directive instructs the preprocessor to find a file called `stdio.h` and include its contents in the source file at the point where the `#include` occurs. We could just as easily have coded,

```
#include "stdio.h"
```

which would still include the file. The difference lies in where the preprocessor will find the file and how it is to perform its search. The angle brackets will cause the preprocessor to look first in the primary system location, while the double quotes will make it look first in the working directory, the place where the including file is located.

Quick Note 2.3 Double quotes vs angle brackets in `#include`

Double quotes ("") surrounding include file names cause the preprocessor to look first in the same directory as the including file. Angle brackets (<>) do not, but limit the preprocessor's search for the include file to the primary system location.

2.1.2 Data

In all programming languages data has two primary forms: variables and constants. While the particular forms of each of these are numerous, in this section we will concentrate only on two: characters and integers. Other forms of data will be introduced later in the book.

2.1.2.1 Variables—Characters, Integers, and Arrays

Variables are data items that can change while the program runs. They can be data items of any type, i.e., characters, integer numbers, floating point numbers, or strings of characters. Variables are created once and given a name, then the name is used each time the variable is needed. C is very different from other languages that automatically create a variable the first time the variable name is used. In contrast, C requires that each variable be explicitly defined before the variable is used. Also, in other languages the symbols used in the name may indicate what type of data the name represents. This is not true in C (unless something is implied in the name about the type of data).

In C variables can only be created (defined) two places in a program: completely outside any function, or immediately after the opening brace of a block of code, which includes the opening brace of a function. This section discusses the second type of variables, those created after any opening brace. Both `main()` and `clear_buffer()` are the functions in Figure 2.1, and `first_name` and `sub` are the variables created after the opening braces of those functions.

Variable names belong to a group called *identifiers*. Also belonging to this group are the names of functions. Identifiers can be composed of letters, numbers, and underscores (_), and the maximum number of characters allowed in a name depends on the compiler. Many older compilers allow only six, but the ANSI standard specifies that the first 31 characters are significant. Only letters and underscores are allowed for the first character, but if an underscore is used for the first character it can unintentionally cause a conflict with a system routine of the same name. Therefore, use letters as the first character of variable names. Also, it is a good idea to use data names that are long enough to be meaningful.

The following are valid C variable names:

```
first_name_and_last_name
abc123def
this_is_variable_1
SUM
sum
```

Note that `SUM` and `sum` would be different variables since C is a case-sensitive language. Also, we've used underscores to enhance the readability of the variable names. Using underscores like this is good programming practice and helps create code which is more easily maintained later.

Let's refer back to the two variables defined in Figure 2.1:

```
char first_name[BUF_SIZE];
int  sub = 0;
```

These statements form the definitions of the two variables `first_name` and `sub`, with the type specifiers `char` and `int` appearing before the variable names themselves. In the first instance, 81 items of storage space of type character are set aside for the variable `first_name` because `first_name` is an *array of characters*, and the matching square brackets after the name enclose the size of the array. An array of characters is needed to hold the name which is typed in. The C language stores a sequence of characters in an array of characters. Use a character array when a group of characters, like a name, address, input line from the computer terminal, and so on needs to be stored.

Arrays in C are similar to arrays in other computer languages: an ordered sequence of items, with each item called an *element*. Arrays are referenced by specifying the array name followed by matching square brackets a that contain a subscript. The subscript is either a constant or variable that specifies the particular element being referenced.

One potentially confusing fact is that the subscript of the first element in every array in C is zero, not one. This is different from many languages, and means that the expression

```
first_name[0] = 'a'            /* referencing the first array element */
```

will place the character a into the first character of the array first_name, while the expression

```
first_name[BUF_SIZE - 1] = 'z'
```

will place z into the last character of the same array.

This second example illustrates that the maximum size of a subscript is the number one less than the defined size of the same array. This means that although the expression

```
first_name[BUF_SIZE] = 'z'
```

is syntactically correct and will both compile and execute, it is logically incorrect and will yield incorrect and potentially disastrous results. This expression will cause the z to be placed outside the array boundaries. There is no checking for this type of condition in the C language. (Remember "trust the programmer"?)

Antibugging Note 2.1   Referencing outside the bounds of an array

The maximum valid subscript for the array name[20] is 19, not 20, since the range of subscript values is 0 through 19. While using 20 as a subscript value will compile and execute, it may cause the program to fail. Check for all such references in programs during testing.

Look at first line of the function clear_buffer(). The variable sub has a type specifier of int, indicating that sub is an integer. A variable must always have its *data type* specified, and this is done by placing a data type keyword immediately before the variable name when the variable is defined. Remember to use a variable in a manner in keeping with its defined data type. For instance, if a variable has been defined as a floating point number, it should not be used in integer calculations.

Although we did not use a character variable in our program, we could create one by writing

```
char an_initial;
```

which would define the variable `an_initial` as a character. This means that it would hold a single character, like `a` or `9`. Had we written the example program to ask for initials rather than a name we might have used character variables rather than a character array.

Finally, a variable can be given an initial value when the variable is defined. For example, in Figure 2.1 the variable `sub` was explicitly initialized when it was defined because we wrote:

```
int sub = 0;
```

2.1.2.2   *Constants—Characters, Integers, and String Literals*

Constants are data items that don't change when the program runs. Like variables, they can be any type: characters, integer numbers, floating point numbers or strings of characters. They can either be specified each time they are needed, or created once and given a name. Names should be given to constants by using the `#define` preprocessor directive rather than placing the constant data into a variable.

Character constants are specified by enclosing one character inside two single quote marks (`''`). Writing `'A'` gives a character constant whose value is an uppercase A. `'1'` gives a character constant whose value is the ASCII character 1 in character form. Note that specifying 1 as a character is not at all the same as expressing it as a number. As a number 1 is in a form that can be used immediately in arithmetic expressions without conversion. By specifying it as a character the internal representation of the digit is completely different than if it were specified as a number. As a character it can be displayed on a CRT screen or sent to a printer. If it were in internal numeric form this could not be done unless a conversion took place. Although we did not use any character constants in Figure 2.1, here are some examples:

`'A'`	This is a capital A expressed as a character constant.
`'a'`	This is a lowercase a.
`'5'`	This is a character `'5'`, not the number 5 expressed as a numeric value.

We mentioned that names can also be given to constants, and that the `#define` directive should be used to do this. The value of giving a name to a constant is if the constant is used more than once in a program and may have to change, then only the `#define` directive must change. In the following examples of named character constants remember that the capital letters in the name are important, i.e., the name `LETTER_C` is not at all the same as the name `letter_c` or `Letter_C'`. By naming the constant the name can be used wherever the constant itself would have been written.

```
#define LETTER_C      'C'
#define CHARACTER_1   '1'
```

Numeric constants can be decimal, octal (base 8), or hexadecimal (base 16), although they are usually written as normal decimal numbers. For instance, the numeric constant 0 was used in Figure 2.1 when we wrote:

```
buffer[sub] = 0;
```

Be very careful when writing decimal numeric constants and do not place a leading zero on the constant. Doing so will cause it to be interpreted as an octal (base 8) rather than decimal number. For instance, 17 is really seventeen, while 017 is fifteen (1 times 8 plus 7 times 1).

Numeric constants, like character constants, can be given names, as we show here when we define the name MAX_INT to represent the value 65535:

```
#define MAX_INT 65535
```

We created one decimal numeric constant in Figure 2.1 when we wrote:

```
#define BUF_SIZE 81
```

In Figure 2.1 this sequence of characters

```
"Welcome to the world of C programming,"
```

is not a character constant. It is a *string literal*, which can also be called a string constant. In C a string literal is always enclosed in double quotation marks, in contrast to the single quotation marks used for characters. We gave the string literal the name SIGNON by writing:

```
#define SIGNON "Welcome to the world of C programming,"
```

so that everywhere SIGNON appears in the program the string literal would be substituted.

2.1.2.3   *Local versus Global Data*

Many programming languages have variables that can be accessed from anywhere in the program. In C this type of data is said to be *global*. Global data is defined outside of any function (e.g., before main()), and is visible and can be used anywhere in the program after the point where it is defined. This means that if a variable is defined (remember, outside of any function) on line 50, it can be used on lines 51 through the end of the same file. It cannot be used on lines 1 through 49.

In our example program complete.c we used no global data. The variables first_name and sub were both defined immediately after the opening brace of a function, and therefore were visible only within their respective functions. They are *local* variables.

We encourage the use of local data. While global data is easy to use, it also leaves the program open to problems caused by unsuspected changes made to global data items. This is because every part of a program has access to all global data defined prior to the point where the data is being referenced. However, sometimes a data item needs to be used throughout the program; making that item a global piece of data is one way to meet that need. The other is to pass a data item explicitly to each place where the item is needed.

If the variables found in complete.c were made into global data items, then the variable definitions would have to be moved from immediately after the opening brace of each function to above main(), like this:

```
char first_name[BUF_SIZE];
int sub = 0;
main()
{
    ...
```

Doing this makes both of these variables visible while within both the main() and clear_buffer() functions.

Quick Note 2.4   Visibility of global data

Global data is visible (and can therefore be used) from the point of definition through the end of the same source file.

Antibugging Note 2.2   Restricting the use of global data

Global data is less safe to use than local data, and will expose a program to problems caused by unsuspected changes to the global data items.

This next program, Figure 2.2, illustrates the data definitions we have discussed. The comments in the program explain each data item, and note that the program does not contain any executable statements. It is merely a set of data definitions that are never actually used. The purpose of the program is to illustrate placement and coding techniques for constants and variables.

```
/*
**  data.c - Various Data Definitions
*/

#define  LETTER_A   'A'                      /* a defined character constant */
#define  CHAR_STR   "This is a character string constant"
```

(program continued on next page...)

```
#define   DECIMAL_NUMBER_9  9        /* a defined decimal numeric constant */
#define   OCTAL_NUMBER_9    011      /* a defined octal numeric constant */
#define   HEX_NUMBER_19     0x13     /* a defined hex numeric constant */

char a_char;          /* definition of global character variable 'a_char' */
int  an_int;          /* definition of global integer variable 'an_int' */
                      /* neither was given an explicit initial value */

char an_initialized_char = 'Z';       /* definition of global character */
                                      /* variable with initial value */
int  an_initialized_int  = 1;         /* definition of global integer */
                                      /* variable with initial decimal value */

int  int_array[5]; /* definition of integer array of 5 undefined values */

main()                        /* the one required function in all C programs */
{
    int a_local_variable;             /* a variable local only to main() */
}
```

Figure 2.2 Various Data Definitions—`data.c`

2.1.3 *Functions*

One of the more confusing things about the C language is how to recognize a function. All functions defined in a C program have at least three parts:

1. A name.

2. A pair of parentheses, `()`, which designate the formal parameter list. The parentheses are not optional, but there may not be a formal parameter list coded inside the pair.

3. A pair of braces, `{}`, which designate the block of code that is the body of the function. The function body may be empty, but the opening and closing braces are still required.

Let's look at some examples of functions. We'll be referring back to these during the subsequent discussion, so keep a finger on this page. We'll also use some coding techniques that we haven't described yet. We'll discuss these techniques shortly, so don't be confused if all the functions are not clear and obvious.

```
A. void do_nothing()          /* void means no return value is expected */
   {
       return;                /* don't do a thing except return */
   }
```

```
B.  int round_number(nbr_to_rnd)        /* round number up to an even value */
    int nbr_to_rnd;
    {
        if ((nbr_to_rnd & 1) != 0) {              /* if bitwise AND with 1 */
            return(++nbr_to_rnd);          /* is not equal to zero then add */
        }
        else {                          /* 1 before returning, else */
            return(nbr_to_rnd);       /* just return the value that was sent */
        }
    }
C.  void upper(str)                      /* convert a string to uppercase */
    char str[];
    {
        int sub;                          /* create a local variable */
        for (sub = 0; str[sub] != '\0'; sub++) {  /* use library function */
            str[sub] = toupper(str[sub]); /* toupper() to change each char */
        }
        return;                          /* in the array str[] to uppercase */
    }
D.  int max_of_n1_or_n2(n1, n2) /* determine the maximum of two integers */
    int n1, n2;                                  /* and return the result. */
    {                                       /* If they are equal, return 0 */
        int temp = 0;       /* create a local variable with zero initially */

        if (n1 > n2) {                        /* see if n1 is greater than n2 */
            temp = n1;                      /* if so, put n1 into temp */
        }
        else if (n1 < n2) {                  /* if n1 is less than n2 then */
            temp = n2;                        /* put n2 into temp */
        }
        return(temp);                        /* send the value in temp back */
    }
```

2.1.3.1   *Function Names*

Function names must follow the same rules as variable names, meaning that letters, numbers, and the underscore character can be used to make the names. Be very careful however not to begin function names with an underscore character, an action that could confuse many compilers.

The primary or highest level function has already been given a name, which is main(). The name of main() can't be changed, but almost any names desired can be used for the other functions in the program. Be careful not to use names that match any names of the functions supplied with the compiler. Doing so will mean that the vendor-supplied functions can never be accessed. Refer to the documentation which came with the compiler to determine all the names of the vendor supplied functions. While there is a basic set of functions defined in the ANSI standard, each vendor is free to add additional functions.

A function can not be defined inside another function. Neither can function definitions overlap, which means that the definition of a second function cannot start before the closing brace of the first one. Functions can be called (invoked) in almost any possible manner, including recursively, but they can only be defined sequentially.

Function definitions can appear in a C program in any order desired, although traditionally the highest level function (`main()`) occurs first, followed by subordinate functions in some logical order. This traditional approach is just the opposite of that used by some languages where the primary function must occur last after all subordinate function definitions have been scanned by the compiler.

In summary, a function can be recognized by finding symbols in the following sequence:

```
function_name()
{
}
```

Remember that a function name has no characteristics which distinguish it from a variable name. Begin learning to look for names in conjunction with the parentheses and braces.

In the previous function examples we can identify four function names. They are:

```
do_nothing
round_number
upper
max_of_n1_or_n2
```

Two of the function names were preceded by the data type specifier `int`, while two were preceded by `void`. These type specifiers were used to indicate the *return type* of the function. They signify the type of data to be referenced in the `return` statement. The `void` return type indicates that no data will be returned from the function. The type `void` has been added to the language with the recent ANSI C standard and is not available in older compilers.

Quick Note 2.5   Functions in a C program

A C program is composed of one or more functions of which one and only one must be named `main()`.

2.1.3.2   *Formal Parameters of a Function*

The *formal parameters* of a function are the names within the parentheses when the function is defined. They identify the data items passed to the function by the piece of code that calls or invokes the function. In contrast to many other languages C is primarily a *call by value* rather than a *call by reference* language. (We can, however, create a call by reference situation when needed.) The term call by value means that when a function is called and passed data, a duplicate copy of the data is sent to the function, not a *pointer* or reference to where the original copy of that data is stored. This is similar to giving someone a copy of a letter rather than the original letter itself. Call by value insulates the caller from any effect should the function change the data that was passed to it. Call by value is one way to avoid the problem that arises when code buried deep in the program changes something that should not be changed.

While formal parameters appear inside the parentheses when the function is defined, *actual arguments* appear inside the parentheses when the function is called or invoked. We will use either parameter or argument depending on whether the function is being defined or invoked, respectively.

Formal parameters can be coded in two ways; we'll describe the older style in this chapter since it is compatible with most compilers. In the older style the formal parameter names must appear in two places. First, they must be coded inside the parentheses. Second, they must appear, preceded by an associated data type, immediately after the parentheses and before the opening brace of the function body. In example A, `do_nothing()` has no formal parameters specified. This is perfectly acceptable and illustrates that a function need not receive any arguments from the caller. This means that no arguments were used when invoking `do_nothing()`. The parentheses are left empty.

Example B, `round_number()`, receives a copy of an integer value from the caller. It does not receive the address of that integer. We do not know what this variable is named in the calling block of code, but the formal parameter name (the name which the copy of the integer is called in `round_number()`) is `nbr_to_rnd`. The integer that will be sent to this function will most likely be different each time the function is called. If it weren't, there would be very little need for a function.

Example C, `upper()`, receives the name of a character array from the caller and converts the characters in the array to uppercase letters. This function, just like `round_number()`, does not need to know which names will be used when it is invoked, but the array is named `str` in this function.

Example D, `max_of_n1_or_n2()`, is requested by the caller to return the greater of two integers or to return 0 if they are equal. Once again, `n1` and `n2` may not be the same names that will be used when the function is actually called.

2.1.3.3   *Local Data in Functions*

In contrast to global data which is defined outside any function, data can also be defined immediately after any opening brace. An opening brace designates the beginning of a block, and since a function is nothing more than a block of code, an opening brace is used to indicate the beginning of the function.

Data defined immediately after any opening brace is often referred to as *local data*. By placing the definition of a data item inside the function block we remove the ability of any other function to see or use that data. It doesn't matter whether the other function called us or whether we intend to call it. Therefore it doesn't matter if the names we give to local data items conflict with names already chosen for use elsewhere in the program. If a local data item has the same name that was already given to a global data item, then any reference to the name will reference the local data item rather than the global one.

Like other items already mentioned, these terms are often not used according to their precise definitions. For instance, the term *automatic* also describes local data. The problem is that the terms local and automatic both are valid descriptions of data, but they describe completely different qualities. Local is a description of visibility or scope, while automatic describes the storage duration or storage class of the same item. Don't be confused if either or both of the terms are used to describe data defined inside a block of code.

Some programmers consider local data difficult to use, and they maintain that it is easier to use global data. Reducing the use of global data (in exchange for local) means defining all the data interfaces between the functions in the program. It usually also means developing a different way of thinking about programs. A program can no longer be viewed as one large pool of data and instructions, but rather as a group of modules that are separate and distinct one from another. This is similar to the way in which the program itself is viewed by the host operating system. Errors decrease and programmer efficiency increases as we begin to think about programs in modular fashion. For instance, we reduce the number of cases where data is changed unexpectedly because of instructions buried deep in the code. Most well-written C programs combine a judicious mix of global and local data.

Be careful to distinguish between local data and the formal parameters used in function definitions. Confusing the two is a common error made by beginning C programmers. In Figure 2.3 the function definition for `find_string()` is correct. Note the positions of the function name, the formal parameters, and the opening brace of the function. Also observe that `shorter_one` is a variable local to the function `find_string()`. It is defined after the opening brace of the function, while the declarations of `str1` and `str2` occur before.

```
/*
** fndstrng.c - An Illustration of Function Definitions
*/

#include <stdio.h>
#include <string.h>                    /* contains strncmp() prototype */
```

```
int find_string(char *, char *);        /* older style function prototype */

main()
{
   printf("find_string returned a %d\n", find_string("one", "xoney"));
}

/*
** find_string()  Finds strings inside other strings
*/

int find_string(str1, str2)     /* see if str1 is contained inside str2 */
char str1[], str2[];                 /* the formal parameters, 2 strings */
{
   int shorter_one = strlen(str1);
   while (strlen(str2) >= strlen(str1)) {       /* compare string lengths */
      if (strncmp(str1, str2, shorter_one) == 0) {   /* compare strings */
         return(1);               /* return 1 if one string is found inside */
      }                                              /* the other */
      ++str2;                     /* bump variable telling where we look */
   }
   return(0);                     /* return 0 if we didn't find the string */
}
```

Figure 2.3 An Illustration of Function Definitions—`fndstrng.c`

If by mistake the first three lines of `find_string()` had been coded in this order:

```
int find_string(str1, str2)
{
char str1[], str2[];          /* these shouldn't be here! */
```

we would get an error message when trying to compile the program. The compiler would not find definitions for the formal parameters `str1` and `str2`, and further, would encounter local data definitions for two strings that have no size at all!

Quick Note 2.6   Where data can be defined

Data can only be defined outside of any function, including `main()`, or immediately after the opening brace of a block.
Data defined outside of all functions is considered to be global, while data defined inside a function or other block is local to that function or block.

2.1.3.4   *Function Invocation*

While in one function, such as main(), the method of invoking another function is to code the other function name followed by parentheses and then a semicolon. Any arguments that are passed to the function being called are coded inside the parentheses. After the function being called finishes, control returns to the statement after the one that did the invocation.

Here are some examples of function invocation which use the functions from above:

```
do_nothing();              /* call 'do_nothing()', a function that has no */
                           /* arguments and returns nothing */

char string[] = "abcdefg"; /* create an example character string */
upper(string);             /* then convert the string to uppercase */
                           /* no result is returned */

                           /* call a function, 'max_of_n1_or_n2()' */
                           /* with integers 'moms_age' and 'dads_age' */
                           /* which are defined elsewhere, and */
int bigger;                /* place return value in 'bigger' */
bigger = max_of_n1_or_n2(moms_age, dads_age);
```

Note that in each of these function calls we have been careful to place a semicolon, ;, after the function invocation. If we had not done this the compiler would become confused and give us an error message. Forgetting the semicolon is a common error that many beginning C programmers make. Also note that we have carefully matched the number of arguments in the function call to the number of formal parameters in the function definition. This is a critical point, since too few or too many arguments will cause unexpected (and often disastrous) results.

2.1.3.5   *Function Return Values*

The final topic to consider on the subject of functions is the return statement. A function has value within a C program. This means that not only can the function perform any operation desired, but also the function name takes on a value at the completion of the function execution. This value can be placed into another variable, printed out, or used in many of the ways that any other variable is used.

The *return statement* is the method of associating a value with the function name and thereby returning the value back to the calling statement. The default type of value that a function returns is integer, but functions can be specified to return almost any type of data.

If a return statement is not present or has no expression coded immediately after it, then the function returns no value. If a value is expected, then the result is unpredictable. Parentheses are typically used to surround the return statement expression, although they are not required.

Consider these examples of functions that return a value:

```
A. int power(base, exp)                /* calculate base to the exp power */
   int base, exp;
   {
       int saved_base = base;                        /* save the base */
       while(exp > 1) {              /* allow only positive exponents */
           base = base * saved_base;
           exp = exp - 1;
       }
       return(base);                        /* return the computed value */
   }


B. string_length(str)                /* determine the length of a string */
   char str[];
   {
       int sub;                    /* make a local variable for a subscript */
       for (sub = 0; str[sub] != '\0';) { /* loop till binary zero found */
           ++sub;
       }
       return(sub);                /* return the loop count (string length) */
   }
```

To the left of the function name in the power() function in example A we see a type declaration. This type declaration identifies to the compiler what data type power() will return, which happens to be an integer value. Note that for the string_length() function in example B we did not include the return type. As stated earlier, integer or int, is the default return type of any defined function unless otherwise identified, so the return type of string_length() is int.

2.1.4   *Statement Structure and Program Control*

In order to begin writing simple C programs right away (please do!) a few more tools are needed. First we'll cover the concepts of operators, expressions and statements. Then we'll discuss some of the most frequently used statements that allow you to manage the flow of control in a program.

2.1.4.1   *Operators, Expressions, and Statements*

Arithmetic in C is very similar to algebra. The assignment expression

```
        ┌───────the assignment operator separates sides of an assignment expression
        │
        ▼
a = b + 3
```

means "add 3 to the variable b and place the result in the variable a". The value of b is not altered as the expression is performed. The single equal sign is the *assignment operator* in C; it separates the left and right sides of the *assignment expression*. The right side is evaluated, then the result of the evaluation is placed into the left side of the expression. The symbols + (add), - (subtract), * (multiply), and / (divide) all mean the same thing in C expressions as they do in algebra and other computer languages.

The following are examples of different arithmetic expressions which also utilize the assignment operator:

```
y = x * 2 - y   /* multiply x by 2, subtract y, and put result in y */

z = y - x / 2 + x       /* divide x by 2, subtract from y, add x, and
                           place result in z */

z = x / y * z   /* divide x by y, multiply by z, and put result in z */
```

Parentheses may be used to alter the normal sequence of evaluation of the operators in an expression. For instance, we can take the expressions above and add parentheses to make the expressions entirely different:

```
y = x * (2 - y)         /* subtract y from 2, multiply by x, and put
                           the result in y */

z = (y - x) / 2 + x     /* subtract x from y, divide by 2, add x and
                           put the result in z */

z = x / (y * z)         /* multiply y times z, divide x by that temporary
                           result, then put the final result in z */
```

The order in which arithmetic operators are evaluated follows the normal rules of algebra: multiplication and division are done before addition and subtraction. If an expression contains two multiplication (or both multiplication and division) operators, the order of evaluation is left to right. When addition and subtraction appear together they are evaluated just like multiplication and division, also left to right.

It is not necessary to use the assignment operator in order to have an arithmetic expression. This, for example,

```
(x + 3)
```

is a valid arithmetic expression. In more complex situations there are many uses for arithmetic expressions that do not include an assignment operator. If it is not present then no permanent changes are made to any data, and only temporary or intermediate results are computed.

Adding a semicolon at the end of an expression makes it into a statement. If we have two expressions we can either make them into two statements or we can separate them with a comma and place a semicolon after the last expression to make one statement. For instance, here are two simple assignment expressions combined into one statement:

```
y = 1, z = 3;              /* two expressions combined into one statement */
```

The expressions just as easily could have been separated into two statements like this:

```
y = 1;
z = 3;
```

2.1.4.2   *The* if *Statement*

The if statement in C works like similar statements in most other languages. The general format is:

```
if (expression to be tested) {
    statement to be done if the expression is true;
}
else {
    statement to be done if the expression is not true;
}
next statement after the if;
```

The purpose of the if statement is to divide the flow of control in the program based on the result of evaluating the expression to be tested. If the result of the evaluation is true, then the statement to be done if the expression is true is executed. Likewise if the expression is not true then the statement to be done if the expression is not true is executed. Regardless of which statement is done the next statement after the if is always executed.

There are a few things about the if statement that are important to understand:

1. The parentheses surrounding the expression to be tested are required, but a semicolon should not be included inside the parentheses. The semicolons after the two statements to be done... are required however.

2. The else and its associated statement for the false condition are optional. Leave them out entirely if they are not needed.

3. There is no semicolon after the right parenthesis which ends the test expression. If a semicolon is placed there it effectively terminates the if statement, even if a statement to be done if the expression is true; is included. An incorrectly placed semicolon like this can cause very confusing results.

4. Unless braces are used (as we'll show in an example) only one statement can be placed in either the true or false legs of the if.

Here are some examples of if statements, our first example being:

```
int age = 10;
if (age == 10) {
    printf("The variable 'age' is equal to 10");
}
else {
    printf("The variable 'age' is not equal to 10");
}
```

This example tests the variable age. If it is equal to (==) 10, then the message,

```
The variable 'age' is equal to 10
```

is printed. Otherwise (else), the message,

```
The variable 'age' is not equal to 10
```

is printed. This example illustrates clearly that the double equal operator, ==, is used in C to test for equality. The single equal operator, =, is not used for this purpose, a significant difference from other languages. The = operator is reserved solely for assignment purposes in C. Further, the != operator means not equal, and should be used when testing for the lack of equality is more clear.

Our second example is:

```
int age, answer;
printf("Please enter your correct age: ");
scanf(" %d", &age);
printf("\n");
printf("Have you revealed your true age (0 for NO/ 1 for YES)? ");
scanf(" %d", &answer);
printf("\n");
if (answer == 1)
   {
   printf("Sorry to hear that,\n");
   printf("you are really that old.\n");
   }
else
   {
   printf("What's the problem?\n");
   printf("Are you embarrassed about your age?\n");
   }
```

In this example, we must use braces ({}) to group together statements under the if and else portion of the construct. What would be the output of this program, given various possible responses from the user?

2.1.4.3   *The* while *and* for *Statements*

The while and for statements are very, very similar. The general format of the while statement is:

```
while (expression to be tested)
   {
   statements done inside the loop;
   }
next statement after the loop;
```

The general format of the for statement is:

```
for (initial expression; expression to be tested; increment expression)
   {
   statements done inside the loop;
   }
next statement after the loop;
```

The purpose of these statements is to initiate loops. The loops only execute if the expression to be tested is true in each case, and the loops continue to execute until the expression to be tested is false.

For both of these statements remember that:

1. The parentheses surrounding the expression to be tested are required, but a semicolon should not be included inside the parentheses of the while statement. Semicolons are needed, however, after each statement done inside either loop.

2. There is no semicolon after the right parenthesis for either statement. If a semicolon is placed there, it effectively terminates the while or for, even if statements done inside the loop; are included. An incorrectly placed semicolon like this can cause very confusing results.

3. Unless braces are used, only one statement can occur immediately after the keyword while or for. This one statement then forms the complete body of the while or for.

The initial expression of the for statement is always done before the expression to be tested is checked, even if the result of the test is false and the body of the for statement is not to be executed. The increment expression however is only done after the body of the for statement is executed, and before the expression to be tested is checked again. Since these statements are not required for the while statement, they can be placed wherever desired.

The while statement is very useful in situations where the number of loop iterations is not known in advance. These situations are called *indeterminate loops*. Consider this example of a function:

```
strlen(str)
char str[];
{
    int index = 0;
    while (str[index] != '\0') {
        index = index + 1;
    }
    return(index);
}
```

This function determines the length of a character string by looking at each character to see if it is a binary zero (the ASCII NUL character). Obviously the function strlen() does not know the length of str in advance or it would simply return the result immediately. In our example index is incremented until we encounter a binary 0, at which time index then contains the length of the string.

On the other hand, the for statement is often used when the number of loop iterations is known in advance. These situations are called *determinate loops*. This code fragment, for example:

```
int otr_loop;
for (otr_loop = 1; otr_loop <= 4; otr_loop = otr_loop + 1) {
    int inr_loop;
    for (inr_loop = 1; inr_loop <= 5; inr_loop = inr_loop + 1) {
        printf("%d ", otr_loop * inr_loop);
    }
}
```

would produce this output:

```
1 2 3 4 5 2 4 6 8 10 3 6 9 12 15 4 8 12 16 20
```

The inner loop, `for (inr_loop ...` executes five times for each iteration of the outer `for (otr_loop ...`. Note that `inr_loop` is reinitialized to a value of 1 after each outer iteration. We've also used braces to block the code together under each `for`. If we did not do this the output would be quite different.

The `for` statement can be substituted (with minor changes to the program) anywhere the `while` is used, and any loop that can be coded with a `while` statement can also be coded with a `for`. The choice of which to use is largely a matter of style and personal preference. We will make liberal use of both in this book.

2.1.5   *Input and Output*

All input and output in a C program is done by using functions. Most of these functions have been given standard names so that they are easily recognized. The output function, `printf()`, will be frequently frequently. The input function, `scanf()`, should only be used until we can provide a replacement. Soon we will provide a function to bring ASCII data into a program so that it can be converted to any form needed.

2.1.5.1   `printf()`

The `printf()` function is not very efficient, but it is extremely easy to use. It can send data of almost any type to the standard output file, usually associated the CRT tube or monitor connected to the computer's system unit.

The `printf()` function has one required argument followed by one or more optional arguments. The required argument is known as a *control string*, and can contain both normal text characters and conversion characters. The normal text characters are printed just as they appear in the string. The conversion characters begin with a percent sign (%) followed by a particular character that means something to the conversion. The first conversion character found in the control string is paired with the first of the arguments that follow the control string. Obviously if a conversion character is placed in the control string you must also provide a corresponding argument. The compiler determines how long the control string can be, and how many conversion characters it can contain.

Because we just discussed character and integer data, it is appropriate to demonstrate the conversion characters for those types of data. The conversion character %c will print one character, and %d will print one integer. The following `printf()` command prints "The letter c is the 3rd letter in the alphabet" (the double quotes do not print):

```
printf( "The letter %c is the %drd letter in the alphabet", 'c', 3);
```

The %c is matched up to the c, and the %d is matched up to the 3. The commas between the parts of the `printf()` are very important, as is the semicolon following the closing parenthesis. Most compilers give various error messages if these are not present.

The statement:

```
printf("This printf() function has no conversion characters");
```

is also a valid `printf()` statement. Note that the conversion characters are not always required.

We should mention one other conversion character because we have used it in some of our examples and code fragments. The %s conversion character is matched to strings, like this situation which uses a string literal:

```
printf("%s", "This printf() function has one conversion character");
```

If conversion characters are used in the control string but there are not enough arguments to match each conversion character to the correct argument then unpredictable results will occur. The `printf()` function will attempt to find something to replace the conversion character with as the character is expanded, and without enough arguments it is unlikely that what it finds will be correct or make sense. This type of error is often identified by a display of gibberish on the screen, along with harmless but amusing noises coming from the machine's speaker.

2.1.5.2   scanf()

The `scanf()` function is both a blessing and a curse to the C language. While it provides a simple, immediate way for beginning C programmers to get data into their programs, it is also temperamental and unreliable. We are presenting `scanf()` here only because we want you to be able to write programs quickly that both accept data from the keyboard and also write data back out to the screen. Using `scanf()` allows you to write these programs while you learn more reliable functions for bulletproof data input.

```
/*
** scanfer.c - An Illustration of scanf()
*/

#include <stdio.h>

int day, month, year;
char first, middle, last;

main()
{
    printf("Enter the current date in the form MM/DD/YY: ");
    scanf(" %d/%d/%d", &month, &day, &year);
    printf("Enter your initials in the form F M L: ");
    scanf(" %c %c %c", &first, &middle, &last);
    printf("%d/%d/%d\n", month, day, year);
    printf("%c %c %c\n", first, middle, last);
}
```

Figure 2.4 An Illustration of `scanf()`—`scanfer.c`

As an example of the `scanf()` function, consider the code in Figure 2.4. In both cases here, `scanf()` is expecting data entered to match the control string exactly. In other words, in the first call to `scanf()`, the user must enter data as follows,

1. an integer

2. a '/' character

3. an integer

4. a '/' character

5. an integer

6. a carriage return to terminate the `scanf()`

And in the second function invocation, `scanf()` expects the following,

1. a character

2. a ' ' (space) character

3. a character

4. a ' ' (space) character

5. a character

6. a carriage return to terminate the `scanf()`

If you enter any other characters (or data types) then unexpected results will occur. The leading space immediately after the opening double quote and before the %c and %d conversion characters is a safeguard to help scanf() work correctly. Not every use of scanf() requires this space, but to leave it out can sometimes cause scanf() to misbehave. Had we not placed it in front of the %c our example would not have worked correctly each time. To include it doesn't cause a problem.

From this example we see that scanf() is very similar to printf(). Both require a control string that contains conversion characters, and both have a number of optional arguments following the control string. There should be the same number of optional arguments as there are conversion characters. The %d and %c are used in the same manner as with the printf() function. The new symbol used in Figure 2.4 is the &, which indicates the address of the variable immediately following it. This symbol is used because scanf() needs to know where to place the input data, in contrast to printf(), which needs to have a copy of the data itself.

If we did not provide enough or the right kind of optional arguments to match the conversion characters to the correct optional argument, unpredictable results will occur. In this case, however, the error is much more serious than with printf() because scanf() uses the additional arguments to determine where to put the data coming from standard input. The scanf() function will put that input data somewhere, and without a correct address it just might put it on top of something important. An error made with the printf() function might cause gibberish to appear on the screen, but this same mistake made with scanf() could make the program crash.

One additional problem often encountered with scanf() occurs when students try to use it in conjunction with various other character input functions such as getc(), getch(), getchar(), gets(), and so on. The typical scenario is that scanf() is used to input various data types that would otherwise require conversion from characters to something else. Then the programmer tries to use a character input function such as getchar() and finds that getchar() does not work as expected. The problem occurs because scanf() sometimes does not read all the data that is waiting to be read, and the waiting data can fool other functions (including scanf()) into thinking that input has already been entered. To be safe, if you use scanf() in a program, don't also use other input functions in the same program.

2.2   Programming Style

The subject of programming style takes us far from the C language and jumps right into an emotional and personal topic for many programmers. There are probably as many answers to the question of how a C program should look as there are people to ask. We will present a traditional, somewhat middle-of-the-road style which can be modified as desired. Always remember, however, that most classroom and work environments probably already have established C coding standards. The suggestions presented here are merely guidelines.

2.2.1 *Using Uppercase and Lowercase*

C, unlike many other languages, is *case sensitive*. This means that the name hours is not the same as Hours, which in turn is not the same as HOURS. Some computer science experts dislike case sensitivity because they see the uppercase/lowercase issue as unnecessarily complicating and confusing the language. They suggest that all names spelled with the same letters should mean the same thing. We, however, think that case sensitivity adds an additional opportunity to distinguish names one from another.

It is tradition that certain elements of a C program be coded in lowercase, and others in uppercase. Traditionally C programmers have not used mixed case, such as HoursEmpWorked, but most experienced C programmers do make liberal use of underscores to separate parts of names.

Names created through a #define are usually coded in uppercase, like this:

```
#define  HOURS_WORKED  0
```

Likewise, variables defined as part of the program and which reserve storage are placed in lowercase, like this:

```
int  hours_worked  =  0;
```

There is, of course, no firm requirement that these rules for the use of uppercase and lowercase be followed, but it is always safer to stick to traditional coding methods. Doing so allows programs to be read and understood by more individuals.

2.2.2 *Braces and Semicolons*

Tradition again has provided some examples of where the opening and closing braces are normally coded in a C program. The difference between the two is primarily in the placement of the opening brace and the indentation. Some styles are:

```
1. identifier() {
   }

2. identifier()
   {
   }

3. identifier()
     {
     }
```

Some people mix them, like this:

```
function()
{
   while() {
   }
}
```

Whichever style is chosen, try to be consistent. Because there is so much disagreement about which style is best, you will see all styles in this book, partially because the two authors themselves have different preferences! Remember that brace positioning rules and guidelines established in the classroom or work environment take precedence over personal choice of style.

For all the functions presented in this chapter (and also the examples immediately above), note that neither the formal parameter list (designated by parentheses) nor the body of the function itself (designated by braces) has a semicolon coded immediately afterward. Sometimes it appears that there are no logical rules governing where and when to use semicolons in conjunction with braces. Of course this is not true. The problem occurs because braces are used to block off two entirely different things: data and code. We have seen how the brace defines a block of code called a function, and how braces are used to block a group of statements together inside if and while statements. Later in the book we will see how braces are used to group data items together when initializing certain types of variables.

Quick Note 2.7   Using semicolons with braces and blocks

Semicolons do not need to follow the closing brace when defining a block of code. The block of code can be an entire function or a group of statements inside an if or while statement.

2.2.3   *Indentation and Tabs*

C programmers have contributed to the myth that C programs are hard to read by writing programs that are unnecessarily terse, lacking sufficient comments, and poorly spaced and indented. It is possible, however, to write well-documented and indented code which will make C programs as easy to read as those of any other language.

Traditionally, three spaces have been used for each level of indentation. (This choice has nothing to do with the compiler since all C compilers completely ignore spacing and line boundaries found in the source program.) Three spaces have been widely accepted among C programmers as readable and workable, but this does cause some problems on certain machines when the source code is displayed on a CRT screen or sent directly to a printer. The problem occurs because many text editor programs used to write C source code insert a tab character instead of three blank characters when the tab key is pressed. This is done primarily to save space on the disk media. The default tab width for many CRT screens and printers is eight characters. Therefore, if C source code containing tab characters is displayed directly on the screen or sent to the printer without alteration, the program displays or prints much wider than it would if it were edited with the text editor program.

If a text editor is being used that allows the insertion of tab characters instead of multiple spaces, be sure to find out whether or not this is happening. Be especially careful of tabs being placed in long strings of text where that text is surrounded with double quotes, such as in the long literal strings in a `printf()` function. A tab character inside the double quotes probably will not give the desired display or printed output.

Another consideration is whether to use a space before or after a comma. Our suggestion is to use one space after a comma and one space before and after all operators, like this:

```
printf("I have %d %c's", 3, 'a');
a = b + c;
```

Regardless of the chosen indentation style, remember that indentation has nothing to do with the correct execution of the program. Statements might line up in the most beautiful manner, but a missed or superfluous semicolon can cause completely unintended results. The compiler doesn't care about indentation, only that the syntax is correct. Develop good indentation habits now and use them advantageously, but don't let them take the place of sound logic and good programming techniques.

Antibugging Note 2.3   Indentation

Remember that indentation has absolutely nothing to do with how the syntax of the language is interpreted. Double check programs to make sure that the indentation does not mistakenly imply something about the flow of control which isn't really there.

2.2.4   Comments and Spacing

A comment begins with a slash-asterisk (`/*`) and ends with the first asterisk-slash (`*/`) combination found next. Comments can appear almost anywhere—on a line by themselves, on the end of a line, or started on one line and ended on another. Lines with nothing on them at all can also be used for spacing and formatting the C program. All these parts of a C program—extra spacing, comments and indentation—do not slow down the compiling process the slightest because everything except the actual C language portion of each program is discarded just as soon as the program is read by the compiler.

A problem to watch for when using comments is that comments cannot be nested. This means that /*...*/ can not be used to surround other comments. The preprocessor directive #if can be used to accomplish this, a technique we will discuss in the chapter on the preprocessor.

Where to add comments is a subject that often generates as much discussion as how to indent. Consider the following examples of how comments might be coded (we used extremely short variable names to accommodate all the comment coding styles, and to illustrate a potential problem):

A.
```
/* i, an index for looping */
int i;

/* loop until i is greater than 20 */
for (i = 0; i <= 20; ++i) {
/* loop until j is equal to 40 */
   for (j = 0; j < 40; ++j) {
         .
         .
         .
```

B.
```
int i;                                        /* i, an index for looping */

for (i = 0; i <= 20; ++i) {        /* loop until i is greater than 20 */
     for (j = 0; j < 40; ++j) {        /* loop until j is equal to 40 */
         .
         .
         .
```

C.
```
int i;                                        /* i, an index for looping */

                                              /* loop until i is greater than 20 */

for (i = 0; i <= 20; ++i) {

                                              /* loop until j is equal to 40 */

     for (j = 0; j < 40; ++j) {
         .
         .
         .
```

In these identical code fragments we have used different styles of commenting. Example A contains comments on separate lines, left justified with the code. Example B contains comments on the same lines as the code, and all comments are either aligned on the same column or at the right edge. This style takes the least vertical space, but has some limitations because the use of long variable names doesn't leave much room for comments on the same line. We like to limit the length of the program's lines to the width of the CRT screen. Had we used names like outer_loop_count rather than i we would have quickly run out of space. In this case a choice of commenting style might encourage us to make an unfortunate choice for variable names. Example C is similar to B, but with comments placed on separate lines. It leaves the full screen available for code, but also takes more vertical space and requires time to align the comments. Readability should be the primary requirement when choosing or mixing these commenting styles.

Quick Note 2.8   Comments and looking pretty

A program must not only work correctly, it should also look pretty. Looking pretty has nothing to do with how a program works, but everything to do with its being readable and accepted by others. Do not code as did the summer intern who worked for one of the authors and wrote `dog[pig] = cat`.

2.2.5   *Short Function Length*

Long, rambling sections of code are more difficult to understand than short, "to the point" pieces. The structure of the C language supports a coding style that encourages modularity and brevity when writing functions (i.e., the "pieces" of a program). Functions are easy to use. All that is required to call one is the name of the function followed by a list of the data items to be passed.

A good rule to follow is that function length should be limited to the number of lines that can appear on a terminal screen, or the size of a printed page. This approach is flexible, and we recognize that those who comment liberally (an excellent habit) will be put to some disadvantage. A good compromise might be that comments appearing above the function name or opening brace could be excluded from the requirement that they appear on a terminal screen, but included on one printed page. The point is, use these suggestions to help avoid incidents like that which one of the authors encountered when he had to decipher another programmer's `do` loop that covered 10 pages of code.

2.3   Self Check

These statements are True or False. The answers are given at the end.

1. The three parts of a C program are preprocessor directives, data, and code.

2. Preprocessor directives begin with the & character.

3. Preprocessor directives must begin in column 1.

4. The `#define` directive reserves storage in the final executable program.

5. `#include` can use either double quotes or angle brackets to surround the file name.

6. Variable names in C can be as long as the compiler will allow.

7. To conform to the ANSI standard a compiler must allow at least 31 characters to be used to form a unique variable name.

8. The type of a data item is coded after the name, as in `my_char_data char (5);`.

9. Variable names should not be used to hold data that is truly constant.

10. The definition `int my_int = '1';` correctly defines an integer with a value of 1.

11. Global data can be seen from anywhere in a program, even within the same source file before it is defined.

12. Semicolons are not used after the closing brace that identifies the end of the body of a function.

13. Formal parameters are coded when a function is invoked.

14. C is considered a call by value language.

15. Arithmetic in C uses essentially the same operators as algebra.

16. The `else` portion of an `if` statement is required.

17. The `while` statement continues executing until the expression being tested is false.

18. The `return` statement is not required when writing a function.

19. It's okay to begin variable names with an underscore character.

20. The `%i` character is the conversion character for an integer in the `printf()` function.

21. The `scanf()` function expects the input to occur exactly as shown in the control string.

22. Items defined with the `#define` directive traditionally use uppercase characters, which means that the same name can not be created as a variable using lowercase characters.

23. Indentation is important to and respected by the compiler when it evaluates the logic of the program.

24. The opening brace delimiting a function can be placed on the same line as the function name.

25. The ANSI C Standard allows nested comments.

Answers

1. T 2. F 3. F 4. F 5. T 6. T 7. T 8. F 9. T 10. F 11. F 12. T 13. F
14. T 15. T 16. F 17. T 18. T 19. F 20. F 21. T 22. F 23. F 24. T 25. F

2.4   Review Program—Multiplication Flashcards

In this chapter we have developed the C language to a sufficient degree to allow you to begin writing simple programs. You should realize that programming, like any acquired skill, requires practice above all. Designing and writing programs is the best means of learning any programming language. Another important aid is studying code written by others. At the end of each chapter we will present examples of complete C programs, giving the associated pseudocode and rationale behind our approach for each. You should study these examples carefully, investigate alternative approaches, and ensure that you understand each detail of the examples.

At the end of each example we will present a section called Points to Study, which will list important principles we are illustrating. Pay particular attention to these after studying the example.

□ *Design Specifications*

1. Write a multiplication flashcard program that covers all integer multiples from 0 to 12. The flashcard should be presented in the form,

a X b = ?

where a and b are integer values within the range of 0 to 12.

2. The program should include two simple functions,
   a. int correct__answer(a, b)

   where,

       a, b: **integers to multiply**

   The return value represents the correct answer to a X b.
   b. int rand0__12()

   which is a function that returns a random integer in the range of 0 to 12

3. The program should include provisions for terminating the session at the user's request.

4. The program should display the number of correct versus incorrect answers before terminating the flashcard session.

☐ *Program Design*

Let's begin the design phase of our program by writing pseudocode for the main function:

```
begin main()
    num_correct = 0
    num_wrong = 0
    print(<program title>)
    print(<inform the user how to exit by typing '999' for answer>)
    while (<user does not wish to exit>)
        a = rand0_12()
        b = rand0_12()
        print ("a X b = ?")
        <get 'ans', the user's answer>
        if (ans == correct_answer(a, b))
            print ("That is correct!")
            num_correct = num_correct + 1
        endif
        if (ans != correct_answer(a, b))
            if (ans != 999)
                print ("Sorry. That is incorrect!")
                print ("Correct answer is <correct_answer(a, b)>")
                num_wrong = num_wrong + 1
            endif
        endif
    endwhile
    print ("Number correct is <num_correct>")
    print ("out of a total of <num_correct> + <num_wrong>")
end main
```

And then the two support functions we need:

begin rand0__12()
    < return a pseudorandom number between 0 and 12>
end rand0__12

begin correct__answer(a, b)
    < return result of a multiplied times b>
end correct__answer

☐ *Design Implementation*

Approaching the task of coding our main function in a top-down fashion, we write
and test the `main()` function first, leaving the details of the other two functions,
`correct_answer()` and `rand0_12()`, until later.

```
/*-----------------------------------------------------------------------
flash.c
Multiplication flashcard program
Generates random problems of the form:

    a X b = ?

where  0 <= a, b <=12
------------------------------------------------------------------*/
#include <stdio.h>

#define MAGIC_NBR_M  55535           /* 'magic' numbers for random */
#define MAGIC_NBR_B  6521            /* number generator */

#define UPPER_LIMIT 12               /* maximum random number we want */

#define QUIT 999                     /* program exit signal */

unsigned int seed = 65535;           /* seed value for random number */
```

(program continued on next page...)

```
main()
{
   int var_a;                             /* program local variables */
   int var_b;
   int num_right = 0;
   int num_wrong = 0;
   int ans = 0;                           /* initialize 'ans' to a known */
                                          /* value to avoid possibility that */
                                          /* 'ans' is already 999 */
   printf("MULTIPLICATION FLASHCARD PROGRAM\n");
   printf("--------------------------------\n\n");
   printf("Type %d for answer to exit\n\n", QUIT);

   while (ans != QUIT)                    /* while user wishes to continue */
      {
      var_a = rand0_12();                 /* whip up a problem */
      var_b = rand0_12();
      printf("\n%d X %d = ?", var_a, var_b);
      scanf("%d", &ans);
      if (ans == correct_answer(var_a, var_b)) /* if user got it right */
         {
         printf("That is correct!\n"); /* give pat on the back */
         num_right = num_right + 1;     /* and credit, also */
         }
      if (ans != correct_answer(var_a, var_b)) /* if user got it wrong and */
         {
         if (ans != QUIT)                 /* and doesn't wish to quit, */
            {
            printf("Sorry. That is WRONG!\n"); /* condolences */
            printf("Correct answer is %d.\n", correct_answer(var_a, var_b));
            num_wrong = num_wrong + 1; /* and credit, also */
            }
         }
      }
/*
 give statistics to user
*/
   printf("\nNumber correct = %d\n", num_right);
   printf("out of a total of %d.\n", num_right + num_wrong);
   return;
}

/*-------------------------------------------------------------------------
 correct_answer(i, j)
 DUMMY TEST VERSION - returns a constant value for test purposes
 --------------------------------------------------------------------------*/
int correct_answer(i ,j)
int i, j;
{
   return(9);                             /* constant value for test */
}
```

```
/*-----------------------------------------------------------------------
 int rand0_12()
 DUMMY TEST VERSION - returns a constant value for test purposes
------------------------------------------------------------------------*/
int rand0_12()
{
    return(3);                          /* constant value for test */
}
```

Study the dummy functions `correct_answer()` and `rand0_12()` carefully. Note that we have written functions that return specific, constant values in order to test our main logic. After we are satisfied, we proceed to write the functions, testing after the completion of each one. A sample run from our dummy test version of the flashcard program might look like this:

```
MULTIPLICATION FLASHCARD PROGRAM
--------------------------------

Type 999 for answer to exit


3 X 3 = ?10
Sorry. That is WRONG!
Correct answer is 9.

3 X 3 = ?9
That is correct!

3 X 3 = ?6
Sorry. That is WRONG!
Correct answer is 9.

3 X 3 = ?999

Number correct = 1
out of a total of 3.
```

Now that we're convinced that the main line code works correctly we proceed to code the functions `correct_answer()` and `rand0_12()`. The function `correct_answer()`, is trivial. We immediately code,

```
/*-------------------------------------------------------------------
 correct_answer(i, j)
 Return the result of i * j
-------------------------------------------------------------------*/
int correct_answer(i ,j)
int i, j;
{
    return(i * j);                         /* this is just i times j */
}
```

Note that we do not need intermediate variables to return the value of an expression like i * j. We simply code the expression within the parentheses, forcing its value to be the return argument.

The function `rand0_12()` is somewhat more difficult to code and we must refer to a good book on fundamental algorithms (see Bibliography). We find that there are several, so we choose one that looks promising, the linear congruential method. We will not detail every aspect of this particular algorithm here, only a brief description. This algorithm generates pseudorandom numbers by recycling previously obtained numbers with the following formula,

```
r = (r * b + 1) modulus m
```

where,

```
r:          a pseudorandom number, with an initial 'seed' value
m:          a large integer
b:          an integer smaller than m, usually 1 digit less;
            b, expressed in decimal, should end in the sequence...21
modulus     the modulus (integer remainder) operator, '%' in C
```

Without elaborating on this algorithm, suffice it to say that it works and has been thoroughly tested. The actual randomness of the numbers generated depends on our choice of b and m. We chose both arbitrarily and they seemed to work fairly well. One other point. To assure that `rand0_12()` returns integers in the required range, we will take the result r and apply the modulus operator again to obtain the desired integers,

```
return value = (r = (r * b + 1) % m) % 13
```

Now, coding the function yields,

```
/*-------------------------------------------------------------
 int rand0_12()
 Return a pseudorandom integer in the range of 0 to UPPER_LIMIT.
 This function uses the linear congruential method to generate
 the returned random integer.
 -----------------------------------------------------------*/
int rand0_12()
{
    return((seed = (seed * MAGIC_NBR_B + 1) % MAGIC_NBR_M) % UPPER_LIMIT + 1);
}
```

We chose to use the name s e e d for the variable r in our equation since it describes what r really is—a seed to be used by subsequent pseudo-random number generation in our program. Other variable names from the pseudocode may also have been changed to more clearly describe the purpose of the variable(s) in the program. This is a decision that each programmer must make for each program, i.e., whether to expand on the pseudocode or to use the same names in the program as were used in the pseudocode. If a variable is of significant importance to the correct functioning of the program, then the name should be as descriptive as possible. If it is no more important than are i and j in c o r r e c t _ a n s w e r ( ) function, then little is gained by using a long variable name.

Note that UPPER_LIMIT, MAGIC_NBR_B,and MAGIC_NBR_M are already included as #define preprocessor directives in our program (we cheated). Don't be overly concerned as to why we chose the particular values we did.

All that remains now is to insert the two functions (which have been tested independently) into our program, compile, link, and do a sample run. The completed program would look like this:

```
/*-------------------------------------------------------------
 flash.c
 Multiplication flashcard program
 Generates random problems of the form:

    a X b = ?

 where  0 <= a, b <=12
 -----------------------------------------------------------*/
#include <stdio.h>

#define MAGIC_NBR_M  55535         /* 'magic' numbers for random */
#define MAGIC_NBR_B  6521          /* number generator */

#define UPPER_LIMIT 12             /* maximum random number we want */
```

(program continued on next page...)

```
#define QUIT 999                          /* program exit signal */

unsigned int seed = 65535;                /* seed value for random number */

main()
{
   int var_a;                             /* program local variables */
   int var_b;
   int num_right = 0;
   int num_wrong = 0;
   int ans = 0;                           /* initialize 'ans' to a known */
                                          /* value to avoid possibility that */
                                          /* 'ans' is already 999 */
   printf("MULTIPLICATION FLASHCARD PROGRAM\n");
   printf("-------------------------------\n\n");
   printf("Type %d for answer to exit\n\n", QUIT);

   while (ans != QUIT)                    /* while user wishes to continue */
      {
      var_a = rand0_12();                 /* whip up a problem */
      var_b = rand0_12();
      printf("\n%d X %d = ?", var_a, var_b);
      scanf("%d", &ans);
      if (ans == correct_answer(var_a, var_b)) /* if user got it right */
         {
         printf("That is correct!\n"); /* give pat on the back */
         num_right = num_right + 1;     /* and credit, also */
         }
      if (ans != correct_answer(var_a, var_b)) /* if user got it wrong and */
         {
         if (ans != QUIT)                  /* and doesn't wish to quit, */
            {
            printf("Sorry. That is WRONG!\n"); /* condolences */
            printf("Correct answer is %d.\n", correct_answer(var_a, var_b));
            num_wrong = num_wrong + 1; /* and credit, also */
            }
         }
      }
/*
 give statistics to user
*/
   printf("\nNumber correct = %d\n", num_right);
   printf("out of a total of %d.\n", num_right + num_wrong);
   return;
}
```

```
/*-------------------------------------------------------------------
 correct_answer(i, j)
 Return the result of i * j
-------------------------------------------------------------------*/
int correct_answer(i ,j)
int i, j;
{
   return(i * j);                        /* this is just i times j */
}

/*-------------------------------------------------------------------
 int rand0_12()
 Return a pseudorandom integer in the range of 0 to UPPER_LIMIT.
 This function uses the linear congruential method to generate
 the returned random integer.
-------------------------------------------------------------------*/
int rand0_12()
{
   return((seed = (seed * MAGIC_NBR_B + 1) % MAGIC_NBR_M) % UPPER_LIMIT + 1);
}
```

□ *Program Output*

```
MULTIPLICATION FLASHCARD PROGRAM
--------------------------------

Type 999 for answer to exit


2 X 3 = ?6
That is correct!

4 X 5 = ?20
That is correct!

10 X 7 = ?70
That is correct!

4 X 6 = ?26
Sorry. That is WRONG!
Correct answer is 24.

12 X 1 = ?12
That is correct!
```

(program continued on next page...)

```
2 X 3 = ?7
Sorry. That is WRONG!
Correct answer is 6.

8 X 5 = ?999
Number correct = 4
out of a total of 6.
```

Of course, it's not very fancy, but it works just fine. Study this program carefully and make sure that you understand all its aspects.

Points to Study

1. #define directives and how they are used. Note how #defines help enhance program readability and maintenance. For example, the program exit signal, 999, could easily be changed at a later date by modifying one #define directive and recompiling/linking the program.

2. Syntax of the printf() and scanf() library function calls. Note the & (address of) operator used with ans in the scanf() call.

3. Syntax of the flow-control constructs used, while and if.

4. The function invocations for correct_answer() and rand0_12(), the context in which they are invoked, and their formal parameter definitions. Note that the formal parameter declaration names for correct_answer(), i and j, do not match the argument names, var_a and var_b.

5. Variable definitions used.

2.5   Exercises

1. Write a short program that does the following:
   a. Requests a character from the user via the keyboard (use scanf()).
   b. "Flips" the case of the character; if the character is uppercase, make it lowercase and vice versa.
   c. Prints the resulting converted character.

2. Investigate uses for the printf() library function by coding printf() function calls for the following:
   a. Input
   ```
   #define I 'i'
   int i = 10;
   ```

Program Output

```
i = 10
i + 2 = 12
i / 2 = 5
```

b. Input

```
#define ALPHABET "ABCDEFGHIJKLMNOPQRSTUVWXYZ"
#define NUMBER_LETTERS 26
#define ID "English"
```

Program Output

Any English child knows the 26 letters of the English alphabet. They are,

```
ABCDEFGHIJKLMNOPQRSTUVWXYZ
```

c. Suppose that anthropologists discovered a community of people called Mathematicians who used an alphabet that looked like this,

```
<>,+-/*.%1234567890
```

What changes would be necessary to 2.b to print the following statement,

```
Any Mathematician child knows the 19 letters of the Mathematician
alphabet. They are,

        <>,+-/*.%1234567890
```

* 3. Code a function called `leap_year()` which takes as its argument an integer representing a year such as 1987 and returns an integer to the caller. The return value is interpreted as follows:

Return Value	Meaning
0	Year is not a leap year
1	Year is a leap year

Use the following algorithm (expressed in flowchart form):

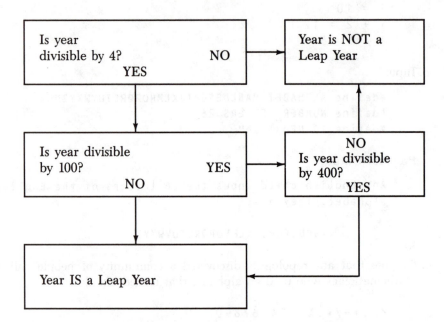

* 4. Write a program to print all the possible combinations of the characters w, x, y and z. For example, four possible combinations would be,

wxyz
zwxy
yzwx
xyzw

5. Write #define preprocessor directives for the following:
   a. the message "hello there" to be used in printf()
   b. the lowercase letter b
   c. the decimal number 2750
   d. the hexadecimal number 0xff7f
   e. the color red coded as the octal number 04

6. Write printf() function calls for the following:

   a. int j = 2750

      printf() output:

          j = 2750

   b. #define MSG "This is a message brought to you by #define."

      printf() output:

          This is a message brought to you by #define.

c. `char s[] = "This is a string of characters known as a string in C."`

   `printf()` output:

   `This is a string of characters known as a string in C.`

d. `#define MSG_PART1 "There are "`
   `int letter_cnt = 26`
   `#define MSG_PART2 " letters in the alphabet."`

   `printf()` should produce the message,

   `''There are 26 letters in the alphabet.''`

7. Given an integer n, the factorial of n is defined as,

   `n! = n * n - 1 * n - 2 * . . . * 1`

   For example,

   `4! = 4 * 3 * 2 * 1`
   `   = 24`

   Write a function that calculates the factorial of a number and returns the result. Restrict n to be less than or equal to 8 and include an error check in your function.

8. Identify the errors in the following example program:

```
/*
**   a c program containing many errors
/*

#include 'stdio.h'

#define OPENING_MSG "This is a program containing common errors that
"
#define OPENING_MSG2 "beginning C programmers make."
#define REQUEST 'How many errors do you think are in this program? '
#define REQUEST2 "Enter your best guess: "
#define WRONG "No. I'm afraid that is not correct. "
#define RIGHT "You guessed correctly!"
#define FACT "There are "
#define FACT2 "errors in this program."
#define ACTUAL_ERRORS
```

(program continued on next page...)

```
main()
{
   int your_guess;

   printf("%s%s%s\n", OPENING_MSG, OPENING_MSG2);
   printf("%s%s", REQUEST, REQUEST2)
   scanf("%c", your_guess);
   if (guessed_right(your_guess))
      {
      printf("%s\n", RIGHT);
   else
         printf("%s\n", wrong);
   printf("%s%d%s", FACT, ACTUAL_ERRORS, FACT2);
   return;
}

guessed_right(someones_guess)
{
   int someones_guess;
   if (someones_guess == ACTUAL_ERRORS)
      return(1);
   return(0);
}
```

9. Write the correct answers to the following equations, given x = 2, y = 8, and z = 3:
   a. x + y + z
   b. x * y + x * z
   c. x * (y + x) * z
   d. y / (x + z − 1) * z
   e. (x + y) * z − 1

10. What is wrong, if anything, with each of the following code fragments?

   a.
   ```
   char c;
   printf("Please enter your response (y or n): ");
   scanf("%c", c);
   ```

   b.
   ```
   #define ANSWER char
   printf("Please enter your response (y or n): ");
   scanf("%c", &ANSWER);
   ```

   c.
   ```
   char get_response()
   char c;
   {
      printf("Please enter your response (y or n): ");
      scanf("%c", &c);
      return(c);
   }
   ```

11. Type in the Review Program, `flash.c`, using your text editor. Next, compile, link and run the resulting executable program.

* indicates advanced exercises

2.6   Pretest

☐ *Multiple Choice*

Circle one correct answer to each of the following questions:

1. What would be the output of the following `printf` statement?

```
printf("%s\n %d", "The value is", 5);
```

    a. The value is 5
    b. The value is
       5
    c. The value is   5
    d. None of the above

2. What would be the output from the following code fragment?

```
if (i < 6)
   {
   printf("i is less than 6");
   }
else
   {
   printf("i is greater than or equal to 6");
   }
```

    a. i is less than 6
    b. i is greater than or equal to 6
    c. no output at all
    d. i is less than 6
       i is greater than or equal to 6
    e. can't say

3. A string in C is
    a. a string of bytes
    b. a string of integers
    c. a string of bytes terminated by a '\0' character
    d. a string of bytes terminated by a '0' character

4. What would be the result of the expression

```
i + j * (k + 2) * l
```

given that i = 2, j = 4, k = 3, l = 0?
a. 16
b. 30
c. 22
d. 2

5. Which C identifier name is written incorrectly?
a. 2_of_a_kind
b. _a_system_routine
c. a_very_very_long_name
d. aNameWithUpperCaseLetters

6. Which of the following statements is not true?
a. A function can return any fundamental data type.
b. A function cannot have more than four formal parameters.
c. A function may or may not return a value.
d. A valid variable name is a valid function name.

7. What would be the output produced by the following code fragment?

```
int i = 3;

while (i > 0)
   {
   printf("%d\n", i);
   i = i - 1;
   }
```
a. 321
b. 3
  2
  1
c. 3210
d. 3
  2
  1
  0

8. Which code fragment is not written correctly?
a. {
```
   while (5 != 0)
       printf(" ");
   }
```

```
b. {
    int i = 0;
    while (i != 0)
        i = i - 1;
    }
c. {
    while (5 != 0)
        int i = 0;
    }
d. {
    printf(" ");
    while(5 != 0)
        ;
    }
```

9. Given the following function call, what is scanf expecting the user to input?

```
scanf("%d %c, %d", &i, &char, &j);
```

    a. an integer
       a character
       an integer
    b. an integer
       a space
       a character
       a space
       an integer
    c. an integer
       a space
       a character
       a comma
       a space
       an integer
    d. none of the above

10. Which of the following is not a valid function?

```
a. func1(a)
   {
   int a;
   printf("%c", a);
   return;
   }
b. func1(a)
   int a;
   {
   printf("%c", a);
   return(a);
   }
```

```
c. func1()
   {
   int a;
   printf("%c", a);
   return(a);
   }
d. func1()
   {
   int a;
   return(a);
   }
```

3

Constants and Variables

I n chapter 2 we looked at a complete C program and discussed some of its important characteristics. Even while we begin covering the language in depth you can begin writing simple programs. This chapter will explain some of the components of the C language which make up expressions: constants and variables. In chapter 4 we will discuss the various operators that can be used with the variables and how variables, constants and operators can make up different expressions.

After studying this chapter, you will be able to do the following:

1. Code and use constants in your program.

2. Identify correctly written variable names.

3. Describe the size and use of different variable types.

3.1   Constants

A *constant* is a piece of data whose value does not change during the execution of a program. According to the ANSI standard the C language has four fundamental types of constants:

1. character

2. integer

3. floating point

4. enumeration

All other constants are derived from one of these basic types. For instance, strings are built by combining characters together, and hence are not a fundamental type. We'll discuss each of these in detail except enumeration constants (enum), which will be covered in the section on enumeration variables.

3.1.1   *Character Constants*

A *character constant* is just what its name describes, a constant that represents a single character. It can be formed by either a single character or an escape sequence.

Certain characters cannot always be coded directly into a program (a newline inside a string literal, for example). However, *escape sequences* provide a way to enter into a program those characters that either cannot be typed directly from the keyboard, or that must be represented by a symbol rather than the physical character itself. For instance, the sequence \0 is used to create the NULL value, or binary zero. An escape sequence is coded as more than one character, but it represents only one character in memory.

In either case, whether the character itself or an escape sequence representing the character is entered, single quote marks surround the character constant. The exception to using the single quotes is when an escape sequence is used inside a string literal.

ANSI Escape Sequence	Name	Effect
\a	bell	Sounds the alarm or beeps the speaker
\b	backspace	Moves the cursor back one position
\f	form feed	Used in printing to advance the paper
\n	newline	Line feed (moves to the next line)
\r	carriage return	Moves cursor to beginning of the line
\t	horizontal tab	Default of 8 characters on the IBM/PC
\v	vertical tab	Seldom if ever used
\'	single quote mark	Surrounds character constants
\"	double quote mark	Surrounds string literals
\?	question mark	The literal question mark character
\\	back slash	Two backslashes end up making one
\ddd	octal character	Makes an octal, not a decimal number
\xdd...	hexadecimal character	Older compilers may allow only \xdd

Table 3.1 Escape Sequences

The ANSI standard escape sequences are shown in Table 3.1. We will illustrate through examples some of these escape sequences. We will also show selected cases where we might utilize the hexadecimal (hex) forms, but we will not cover the octal forms since the format of an octal constant is so similar to one in hex.

\n—*line feed*

This escape sequence is probably the most frequently used of all. It is also called the *newline sequence*. Program output frequently consists of a sequence of "logical lines" which are produced on some output device. The standard library function printf() produces output on the standard output file (normally the display), but does not include automatic provision for the creation of these logical lines. For example, coding

```
printf("This is the first line.");
printf("This is the second line.");
```

would produce,

```
This is the first line.This is the second line.
```

which is probably not at all what we intended to produce. To create two lines of output we need to embed \n in the first string, like this:

```
                                    ┌──── this becomes a line feed character
                                    └┐
printf("This is the first line.\n");
printf("This is the second line.")
```

which would produce two separate lines of output. This escape sequence, along with any combination of it or others, can appear numerous times, embedded at various locations within the string.

Note that coding \n is not the same as placing an actual line feed inside the character constant. While the \n will become a line feed when the constant is sent to an output device, it is still just \n inside the source code of the program.

Why was this output not produced?

```
This is the first line.
                        This is the second line.
```

This output would be in keeping with the precise definition of a line feed, but the actual observed effect is that the cursor is also returned to the left edge of the screen (the action of the carriage return character). The reason that both actions occur is because a translation takes place upon output and the single line feed character becomes both a carriage return and a line feed. We'll study more about this when we discuss input and output.

\r—*carriage return*

Sometimes when output appears on the display it needs to replace other output that has already appeared before it on the same row. The solution is to use the

\r, which causes only a carriage return. For instance, suppose we wish to devote a certain section of the display to status information (error messages, command lines, etc.). Consider the following example display layout:

```
     0          10         20         30         40
     01234567890123456789012345678901234567890
     ---------------------------------------------
0    ¦
1    ¦
2    ¦
3    ¦
4    ¦
5    ¦
6    ¦
7    ¦
8    ¦
9    ¦    <status information to appear on this line>
```

A suitable algorithm for the status line would be,

1. Position the cursor on the tenth line (numbered from zero).

2. Print 40 spaces to clear the line.

3. Print status information, with possible carriage return but no line feed.

Let's code a simple function, one that contains the function locate() (locate() is used to position the cursor—we'll assume that it works just fine). Our function could look something like this:

```
status(status_string)
char status_string[];
{
    locate(10, 0);            /* position cursor on row 10, column 0 */
    printf("                                        %c", '\r');
    printf("%s", status_string);                                    └┘
}                                                          └──────── carriage return
```

This function implements our simple algorithm and illustrates how \r might be used. Note that our function depends on status string conforming to line 3 of our algorithm. In practice, we might also include code to identify incorrect strings, or clearly state the responsibilities of the caller in comments in the function.

\t —horizontal tab

The actual effect that results from using this escape sequence depends on how the output device interprets the tab character. Many display monitors (CRTs) and printers have default tab settings of every eight positions.

The tab character, \t, is useful when we wish to display information in columns. For example, suppose we wish to write a program to produce a simple decimal—> binary—> hexadecimal conversion table. The statement to output a line of data might be coded as follows:

```
printf("%d \t %s \t %x \n", dec_num, bin_num, hex_num);
```
- the newline character escape sequence, \n
- conversion character for a hexadecimal integer
- the tab character escape sequence, \t
- conversion character for a string
- the tab character escape sequence, \t
- conversion character for a decimal integer

An example line of output from this statement might look like this:

```
155     10011011        9b
```

Remember that the exact spacing depends on many things, so don't count the spaces in our sample output.

\'—single quotation mark

This escape sequence is needed in rare instances like the following:

```
#define SINGLE_QUOTE '\''
printf("A single quotation mark looks like this - %c", SINGLE_QUOTE);
```

which would produce the output,

```
A single quotation mark looks like this - '
```

The escape sequence is needed since coding

```
#define SINGLE_QUOTE '''
```

would cause the first two single quotation marks to form ' ', an empty character constant, leaving the last orphan single quote to produce a compile error message.

\"—the double quotation mark

The double quotation mark normally indicates the end of a string literal. Therefore, to express it within a string requires the \" escape sequence. For example,

```
printf("The double quote mark (\") is used to enclose C strings.");
```

would produce the output,

```
The double quote mark (") is used to enclose C strings.
```

whereas,

```
printf("The double quote mark (") is used to enclose C strings.");
```

code that produces as error

would produce a compile error message.

\\—*escape character*

Another frequent error occurs when trying to output the backslash character itself, as in this example:

```
printf("The escape character is \.");
```

The problem here is that \. will be interpreted as an escape sequence. But since \. is not a valid escape sequence the consequences of executing this printf() are unpredictable. The resulting output can vary from one compiler to another, and even from one version to another of the same compiler.

The solution would be to code,

```
printf("The escape character is \\.");
```

creates a single \ character

which would then print

```
The escape character is \.
```

\xdd...—*any character whose ASCII code is* xdd...

Most computers have characters that are either not printable, or not standard ASCII characters. For example, the character constants \n, \r, and \t represent characters that are not printable. By this we mean that printing these characters causes action to be performed rather than a character to be printed. For example, the \r in this example,

```
printf("This line ends in a carriage return.\r");
```

could also be coded like this,

```
printf("This line ends in a carriage return.\x0d");
```

both of which would display the statement,

```
This line ends in a carriage return.
```

The cursor (or print head) would be sent to the far left margin on the same line after the period was displayed or printed. Using the \r is in general a simpler, better choice.

Suppose we wish to display this character,

√‾‾   (the square root symbol)

which is one of the IBM-PC graphics characters. Rather than coding

```
printf("The √‾‾ of 16 is 4.");
```

we should instead write

```
printf("The \xFB of 16 is 4");
```

since using the square root symbol directly in the string is not as portable as using the hex escape sequence. Some compilers might object to the square root symbol because it is not a standard ASCII character.

Any character, including standard ASCII codes, may be coded using this escape sequence format. It is called the *hex escape sequence* and is very similar in format to a hex constant (explained in the next section).

The ANSI standard permits any number of hex digits after the \x, in contrast to the two digits that have been allowed for years. This change accommodates computers with 12-bit characters, and also other languages that have so many characters that it takes more than one byte to represent each one (some languages contain thousands of characters). However, most computers have 8-bit characters and two hex digits are enough to create the 256 possible characters that 8 bits can form. The number of hex digits a compiler allows depends on the compiler version being used.

3.1.2   *Integer (Decimal, Hex, and Octal) Constants*

An *integer constant* creates a numeric value. The integer constant cannot have a decimal point or exponent, but it may include other characters which indicate a number base (radix) other than 10.

   Decimal constants (base 10) begin with a nonzero digit. *Octal constants* (base 8) on the other hand begin with a zero and contain only the digits 0 through 7. A *hexadecimal constant* (base 16) begins with 0x or 0X and can contain both digits and the letters a (or A) through f (or F).

   Constant numbers that are coded directly in programs are commonly called *magic numbers*. They are numbers that can cause interpretation problems to others reading the code. For example,

```
index = 0;
while(index < 0x20)
    {
    printf("%c", '\x20');
    index = index + 1;
    }
```

associates the hexadecimal number 0x20 with two entirely different meanings. It is not precisely clear from the code what the programmer intended. However, if we code the program differently to yield,

```
#define SPACE '\x20'      /* this is a space, a blank character */
#define COUNT 0x20        /* this is decimal 32 */

index = 0;
while(index < COUNT)
    {
    printf("%c", SPACE);
    index = index + 1;
    }
```

the context of 0x20 is quite evident.

Antibugging Note 3.1   Always give names to integer constants

   Never code integer constants directly in a program. Give the constants names by using a #define directive. This is good documentation practice, but it is also important if the constant is to be used more than once.

   The choice of decimal, hexadecimal, or octal notation is largely a matter of choice when describing an integer. Many programmers, particularly system programmers, prefer hexadecimal or octal. A business applications programmer, on the other hand, might choose decimal. For example,

```
#define MAX_INT 0xffff
```

might describe the maximum integer size, while

```
#define MAX_DOLLARS 65535
```

might describe the upper numeric limit of a very limited accounting package. In the same manner a *bit mask* which would be used to add or remove bits from a data item, would probably be defined in hex notation, since that more closely represents the underlying bit pattern. The choice of notation should conform to the context in which the integer is used.

3.1.3   *Floating Point Constants*

Floating point numbers (also known as real numbers) can be used as constants. They look like this:

```
12.345
1E5
.555
```

The E which indicates that an exponent follows can be uppercase or lower-case. Either the whole number or fraction part of the number must be present, so a floating point constant of the form

```
e4
```

would not be valid since the whole number part of the constant is missing.

There are no data types in the C language that allow fixed-length numbers, like .555. This type of data can be managed by writing custom routines or buying a library of routines that support data in this format.

3.1.4   *String Constants, Including Concatenation and Merging*

Strings are not a fundamental type of data in C. This means that the word *string* is not reserved and that there is no such thing as this:

```
string my_string ...
```

All strings in C are merely sequences of characters which have a binary zero, or NULL character, at the end. The length of any string is determined by how many characters appear before the NULL character is found.

A *string constant*, or *string literal*, is coded directly into a program and surrounded by double quotes. As with character constants, a string literal cannot contain an actual line feed character, but all the escape sequences that can be used with character constants can also be used with strings. And although it is not coded directly into the program, the string terminator of binary zero is added automatically to the end of the string literal.

Long strings are awkward in C. They can be created by coding a backslash as the very last character on the line. The string literal then continues on the next line beginning with the first column or character of the line. For example, this creates a long string literal:

very last character of the first line

```
    printf("This is a very long string which will contin\
ue on the next line");
```

very first character of the second line

Using this technique requires that there be no space or other character after the backslash. When this `printf()` function executes it will display the following:

```
This is a very long string which will continue on the next line
```

Fortunately the ANSI C standard committee provided a much cleaner alternative. They decided that adjacent string literals would be concatenated automatically. Our example immediately above can now be written like this:

```
printf("This is a very long string which will "
       "continue on the next line");
```

These two strings could have appeared on the same line (which partially defeats the purpose of having two strings in the first place) or they can be placed on separate lines as we've shown above. Just don't put anything between the literals except characters like spaces, tabs, the end of a line, and so on. Clearly this technique is easier to read than the backslash technique shown first. All compilers that support the ANSI standard should concatenate adjacent string literals. Remember, the backslash technique can always be used if concatenation is not supported.

On some compilers, if the exact same character string constant is coded more than once in a program, each and every one of the strings is stored separately. On those compilers no check is performed to see if a particular string matches any that have already appeared. Obviously this can add significant length to a program if there are numerous copies of the same string literal. The popular solution to this problem is to use a string variable rather than a string literal.

The ANSI standard, however, allows vendors to merge duplicate strings if they wish, so that only one physical string is stored in the program. This feature is typically invoked through a switch or option setting of the compiler, so consult the documentation. Remember, only newer compiler versions will support this feature.

Further discussion of this, along with a program to test whether strings are merged, is provided in Chapter 10.

We also recommend that the #define directive be used when creating strings that will be used more than once in a program. This is a good habit whether duplicate string literals are merged or not. Here is one example of how to use the #define in this manner:

```
#define STRING "This is line"

printf("%s %d\n", STRING, 1);
printf("%s %d\n", STRING, 2);
```

This code would produce the output:

```
This is line 1
This is line 2
```

3.2 Variables

A C program manipulates pieces of data called *variables* (also called *items*, *objects*, or *identifiers*). The variables, along with constants, are combined and acted upon by *operators*. It is appropriate to think of the constants and variables as nouns and the operators as verbs. We then combine the variables (nouns) and operators (verbs) into *expressions* (phrases) and ultimately *statements* (sentences).

3.2.1 *Names*

Let's quickly review the characteristics of a *name* in C:

1. To conform to the ANSI standard at most 31 characters may be used to distinguish one name from another.

2. Names should begin with a letter (not a number or underscore) and can contain only letters, numbers, and the underscore character.

3. It is traditional to use lowercase letters for variable names, reserving uppercase letters for use with the #define preprocessor directive.

4. Case is important, so the name hours is not the same as either Hours or HOURS.

auto	break	case	char	const
continue	default	do	double	else
enum	extern	float	for	goto
if	int	long	register	return
short	signed	sizeof	static	struct
switch	typedef	union	unsigned	void
volatile	while			

Table 3.2   ANSI Keywords

Certain words cannot be used as names. These words, called *keywords*, are used in various capacities in the language and cannot be used for anything else. These words must be entered in lowercase, and the list of ANSI standard keywords appears in Table 3.2. Some implementations may also reserve other words in addition to those in Table 3.2. A sample of these extra words is shown in Table 3.3.

asm	cdecl	far	fortran	huge	interrupt
near	pascal				

Table 3.3   Additional Keywords

3.2.2   *Types*

Type describes the characteristics we associate with the name of a data item. A good analogy is the way we use the word in talking about people: "What type of individual is that person?" In programming we say "What type of data does that variable name represent?" C has only a few basic types of variables (note that these are the same as the types of constants):

1. characters

2. integers

3. floating point numbers

4. enumerated types (enumerations and void)

All other types are derived from these. The derived types are:

1. arrays
2. structures
3. unions
4. functions
5. pointers

C is a *weakly typed* language, which means that although each variable must be given a type when it is defined, the variable can be used as if it contained data of an entirely different type. In other words, although we have stored an integer in a particular variable, we can use that variable name as if it contained a character (or most other types of data). While this approach is flexible, it is not always safe. It is easy to use data incorrectly, and that will probably generate incorrect results. Other languages are more strongly typed. When programming in these languages it is more difficult to use a piece of data in a manner different from the type with which it was defined.

Let's put all this in perspective by looking at Figure 3.1, which shows the types of variables and their associations.

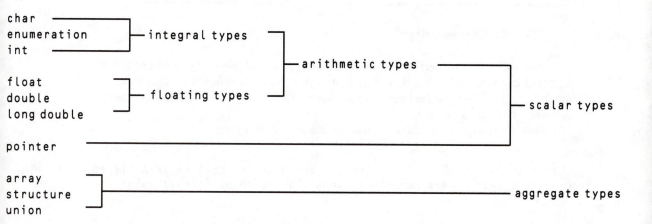

Figure 3.1 Relationship of Data Types

3.2.2.1 *Character Variables*

A *character* is defined as being big enough to hold any member of the machine's character set that can be specified as a single-character constant without using an octal or hexadecimal escape sequence. Characters are assumed to be *signed*, so the type specifier of signed char is usually replaced by char. There also exists an unsigned char which is the same size as char and signed char, but is interpreted as not being signed. Signed chars have their sign preserved when used in arithmetic expressions, while unsigned chars can hold a larger positive number since the sign bit is used to represent value rather than sign. Concern about signed and unsigned is important if characters will be used in arithmetic expressions.

The size of a character data item and the range of values it can contain are described in Table 3.4. The data in this and similar tables comes from the ANSI standard rather than from the documentation of any particular compiler. There may be some very slight differences between the data we've presented here and what a particular compiler will allow. A common difference is that many compilers will allow a signed char type to assume the value of minus 128 rather than just minus 127. The differences will not be substantial, so don't write programs that depend on them. In this and subsequent tables the names under the Type column are the actual type names that are used when programming.

Type	Range of Values	Storage Needed
char signed char	-127 to 127	1 byte
unsigned char	0 to 255	1 byte

Table 3.4 Character Types

Arithmetic can be performed on data stored in a variable of type char, but if that is explicitly intended then it is more appropriate to store that data in an integer variable. See the next section for more information about the association between char and integer.

Here are some examples of character variable definitions:

```
char a_space = '\x20'; /* the char a_space which contains an ASCII space */
char some_char;  /* a character, some_char, with no initial value */
```

3.2.2.2   Integer Variables

Integers are different from characters because the size of an integer is defined in the ANSI standard as being *implementation dependent*. This means that if a program is compiled on a machine where an integer is normally defined as a 16-bit number, then the integer will be 16 bits long. If the program is later compiled on a machine that normally uses 32 bits for integers, then the integer will be 32 bits long. Consequently, nothing should be assumed about the size of an integer when writing C programs.

Some forms of integers, however, do have a definite size. They are shown in Table 3.5. Remember that even if the storage needed for two different types of integers happens to be the same, they are still different types. This means that they may cause programs to behave differently depending on which type is used. The numbers in the Range of Values column come from the ANSI standard. The corresponding entries in the Storage Needed column are the number of bytes needed to store any value in the given range.

Type	Range of Values	Storage Needed
int signed signed int unsigned unsigned int	implementation dependent	implementation dependent (usually 2 or 4 bytes)
short signed short signed short int	$-32,767$ to 32,767	2 bytes
unsigned short unsigned short int	0 to 65,535	2 bytes
long signed long signed long int	$-2,147,483,647$ to 2,147,483,647	4 bytes
unsigned long unsigned long int	to 4,294,967,295	4 bytes

Table 3.5   Integer Types

Quick Note 3.1   Integers are different sizes

Integers have different sizes on different machines. Writing portable code means not assuming anything about how the data will be stored inside the machine. Just because two variables occupy the same amount of storage space does not mean that they are the same type.

Here are some examples of integer variables:

```
signed int signed_int = 0xffff;    /* the integer 0xffff, which would */
                                   /* be signed to yield -1 */
```

```
unsigned int signed_int = 0xffff;   /* an integer, treated */
                                    /* as unsigned, initialized with */
                                    /* absolute value of 65535 */

int sons, daughters, dogs;          /* three integers with values */
                                    /* undefined */

long int big = 80000;               /* an integer that has twice as */
                                    /* many bits as a short integer and */
                                    /* an initial value of 80000 */
```

Note also that char and int are not usually the same size (i.e., the same number of binary bits). As an example, consider the following variable definitions (an ASCII space is numerically equal to a decimal 32, or a hexadecimal 20):

```
char space = ' ';

int ascii_val_of_space = 32;   /* the ASCII value of a ' ' character */
```

Here we have no assurance that the size of space, in binary bits, is the same as the size of ascii_val_of_space. The variable space will contain 8 bits but ascii_val_of_space could be 8, 16, 32, or any number of bits depending on the natural integer size of the machine that compiled our program. The question of data size in bits is a fundamental consideration in producing truly portable programs.

As a further example, consider the following identical loops:

```
int index;

index = 1;                          /* first loop with a while statement */
while(index > 0) {
    index = index + 1;
}

for(index = 1; index > 0;) {   /* second loop with a for statement */
    index = index + 1;
}
```

These loops would produce 65,535 iterations on a 16-bit machine, and produce 4,294,967,295 iterations on a 32-bit machine! If our program logic depended on the number of actual iterations, we could be in big trouble.

3.2.2.3   *String Variables*

String variables are like string constants (literals) in that they both consist of characters. In fact, the official name for a string is *null terminated character array*. String variables are one of the most powerful aspects of the C language and can be used to give a name to a string literal. Remember that not all compilers support the merging of duplicate string literals. This means that if the same literal string is used many times on an older compiler version, many copies of the same string will be created in the executable program. Creating a string variable is the traditional way to avoid this situation, a better way than using the #define directive. While #define also gives names to strings, multiple string literals still exist in the program. Both the giving of names and the reduction in storage space are accomplished by using a string variable.

A string variable has no intrinsic size; rather, the size at any given time is determined by wherever the binary zero (NULL character) is found in relation to where the string begins. Even though the size is not fixed, enough storage must still be reserved to hold the string when it is defined. The amount of reserved storage should include room for the NULL character which must appear at the end of the string. Since the size of the string is the number of characters from the beginning of the string until the first NULL character is found (the NULL isn't counted in the size), if the NULL isn't where it should be then the string could end up being quite long!

The NULL character can be moved at any time, but if you attempt to make the string longer by merely moving the NULL character further away from the beginning of the string, data residing immediately after where the string is located will be destroyed. There is no problem in making the string shorter. If the NULL character appears in the first position of the string, the string has zero length.

A string variable definition looks like this:

```
char my_string[18] = "this is my string";
```

The string variable name is my_string. The 18 that appears in the square brackets reserves 18 *contiguous* (right next to each other) character locations in memory. There are only 17 characters between the double quotes because one character must be reserved for the terminating NULL (which is added automatically as part of the initialization process because string literals are assumed to have a terminating NULL).

By writing the following in contrast to the similar line immediately above:

```
char my_string[] = "this is my string";
```

we gain the advantage of never mismatching the number of characters to be reserved (18 from the first definition) and the actual size of the string literal. The number of characters reserved here is implicitly determined by the compiler from the size of the string literal. This is certainly one of the safest ways to define string variables. It avoids taking the chance of accidentally coding the following:

```
char my_string[17] = "this is my string";
```

which would not leave room for the terminating NULL character, and therefore would leave the program open to serious problems later.

Strings can be made shorter by merely moving the NULL character closer toward the beginning of the string, like this, for instance:

```
my_string[5]  =  '\0';
```

The string will now be five characters long. Positions 0 through 4 will contain data while position 5 contains the NULL. We have used *array subscripting* here (even though we haven't explained arrays yet) in order to illustrate that the NULL can be moved intentionally by the program. Where the NULL character is at any given time may have nothing at all to do with where it started out originally.

A string can be made longer by copying it to some other memory area large enough to hold the longer string. No operators work directly on strings. Rather, all string manipulation occurs through string functions such as strlen(), strcpy(), etc.

Quick Note 3.2   Strings must be be long enough for the NULL

Strings must be long enough so that there will be room for the terminating NULL character, otherwise the end of the string could be anywhere. The C language performs absolutely no bounds checking on strings.

To further illustrate just what a string contains, let's look at another example:

```
char message1[] = 'M','e','s','s','a','g','e';  /* array of characters */
```

and,

```
char message2[] = "Message";        /* character string */
```

These variables are identical in memory except that message2 contains a binary zero as the last byte. Here's how we might picture these arrays:

message1 looks like this:

M	e	s	s	a	g	e

while message2 looks like this:

M	e	s	s	a	g	e	\0

The first variable definition, message1, cannot and should not be used in situations where a string is needed. Any situation requiring a string will depend on the ASCII NULL character being present. Therefore, we should be careful to code a string as a string, not to confuse a string with a simple array of characters with no terminating `NULL`. Remember that the only difference between a character array and a true string is the terminal `NULL` character.

3.2.2.4   *Floating Point Variables*

Three *floating point* types have been defined in the new standard: `float`, `double`, and `long double`. The ANSI C committee did not specify explicit definitions about the values and storage needed for each of these types. They required only that each type be able to hold, at a minimum, any value in the range $1E-37$ to $1E+37$ (base 10). Typically, however, the type `double` uses twice as many bytes of storage as the type `float`, and `long double` uses twice as many bytes as `double`. Most compilers have always had the types of `float` and `double`, but the type `long double` was added to C as part of the ANSI standard.

Here are some examples of floating point variables:

```
float temp = 98.6;           /* a float with an initial value */
double pct_activity;         /* a double without an initial value */
```

Not all compilers will or can support `long double`. It was included because some computers have three distinct sizes for floating point numbers and can provide applications with more precision than was available with the type `double`. The type `long double` can be used on any computer, even those that have only two types of floating point numbers. If the computer does not have a specific data type of `long double` then the data item will have the same size and storage capacity as `double`.

Be sure to examine the review program `tempconv.c` at the end of this chapter. It uses floating point variables and type casts between types, and discusses the problem of function arguments of type `float` being widened to `double` when passed to a function. The widening of floats to doubles when passing values to functions is a characteristic of older compilers.

In order to print floating point constants and variables, a different `printf()` conversion character, `%f`, is used. Here are some examples of how to print floating point values:

```
printf("The temperature is %f\n", temp);
printf("Normal body temperature is %f", 98.6);
```

In Table 3.6 the values in both the Range of Values and the Storage Needed column are for some ANSI standard compilers on a variety of machines.

Type	Range of Values	Storage Needed
float	±3.4E-38 to ±3.4E+38	4 bytes
double	±1.7E-306 to ±1.7E+306	8 bytes
long double	often the same as double	

Table 3.6 Float Types

3.2.2.5   *Enumeration Variables*

Enumerations give names to constants in a more structured manner than with a #define. When an enumeration variable is defined it is associated with a set of named integer constants called the *enumeration set*. The variable can contain any one of the constants at any time, and the constants can be referred to by name. For example, this definition:

```
enum stoplight_colors {red,
                       yellow,
                       green = 10
                       } first_and_main;
```

creates the enum type of stoplight_colors, the enum constants of red, yellow and green, and the enum variable of first_and_main. All the constants and variables are type int, and each constant is automatically provided a default initial value unless another value is specified. In the above example the constant name red has the value 0 by default since it is the first in the list and was not specifically overridden. The value of yellow is 1 since it occurs immediately after a constant with the value of 0. The constant green was specifically initialized to the value 10, and if another constant were included in the list after green the new constant would have the value of 11. More than one name in the list can have the same value.

Having created stoplight_colors we can later define another variable, second_and_boston, by coding this:

```
enum  stoplight_colors  second_and_boston;
```

after which we can also say:

```
first_and_main = red;
```

and

```
second_and_boston = green;
```

which will place the value 0 into the variable first_and_main, and the value 10 into the variable second_and_boston.

A common mistake is thinking that stoplight_colors is a variable. It is a "type" of data which can be used later to create additional enum variables, like second_and_boston.

Since the name first_and_main is an enumeration variable of type stoplight_colors, first_and_main can be used on the left of an assignment operator and can receive a value. This occurred when the enum constant red was explicitly assigned to it. The names red, yellow and green are names of constants; they are not variables and their values cannot be changed.

Tests can be performed on the variables, in conjunction with the constants. Figure 3.2 shows a complete program that uses the above definitions:

```
/*
** enum.c - Enumeration Variables and Constants
*/

#include <stdio.h>

main()
{
    enum stoplight_colors {red,
                           yellow,
                           green = 10
                          } first_and_main;
    enum stoplight_colors second_and_boston;

    first_and_main = red;
    second_and_boston = green;

    printf("the value of first_and_main is %d\n", first_and_main);

    if (second_and_boston == green) {
        printf("the value of second_and_boston is %d\n", second_and_boston);
    }
```

(program continued on next page...)

```
   if (first_and_main == second_and_boston) {
      printf("first_and_main equals second_and_boston\n");
   }
   else {
      printf("first_and_main does not equal second_and_boston\n");
   }
}
```

Figure 3.2 Enumeration Variables and Constants—enum.c

The output of this program is:

```
the value of first_and_main is 0
the value of second_and_boston is 10
first_and_main does not equal second_and_boston
```

3.2.2.6   *Type Casts*

Often it is necessary to temporarily change the type of a variable so that it can be used in a different manner. This is known as *casting* or performing a *type cast*. The purpose of the type cast is to change the way a variable is viewed so that it can be used differently in the surrounding code.

The type cast is written by enclosing a valid type name in parentheses in front of the variable name, like this:

```
int input_value;
...
(float) input_value
```

Here we have cast an integer, input_value, into a float type. This cast in no way permanently changes the variable input_value, either in type or value. The cast is performed on a temporary copy of input_value and is in effect only while the copy is used. The next time input_value is referenced it will be viewed as its original type (unless it is type cast again).

There are some very important reasons for using type casts. For example, suppose we want to use a function that expects a floating point argument, like the sqrt() function supplied with most compilers. Since sqrt() has already been written, we have to conform to its specifications. Suppose also that we want to take the square root of an int value, which is not the type double that sqrt() expects. While we could create yet another variable of type double and assign our integer into the new variable, we can also just write this:

```
double sqrt(double);    /* sqrt expects and returns doubles */
...
double square_root;
int    input_value;
...
square_root = sqrt((double) input_value);
```

The variable `input_value` is not permanently affected by the type cast. If `input_value` is needed again as a double, it will have to be cast again.

We concede that many type casts can be eliminated by merely creating different variables where each has a particular type but the same value as other variables. This is a poor solution, however, since it introduces extraneous data items into programs and requires that all the various variables that are equal in value but not type be kept "in sync". Certainly the use of a type cast is much simpler and cleaner.

Antibugging Note 3.2   Excessive use of type casts

Excessive use of a type cast indicates that the wrong data type has been selected for a variable. Type casts should be used to handle exception conditions, not as a matter of course.

3.2.2.7   `const` *and* `volatile`

`const` and `volatile` are two new C language keywords. They were added by the ANSI standard to help identify which variables will never (`const`) or can unexpectedly (`volatile`) change.

For example, this definition

```
const int multiplier = 10;
```

specifies that the variable `multiplier` will never be changed by the program. Any line of code which attempts to change the value of the variable `multiplier` will cause a compile error message. Therefore, this statement

```
multiplier = 20;
```

would prevent the program from compiling.

The only time the value of a `const` variable can be set is when the variable is initialized. Specifying a variable as `const` allows the compiler to perform more extensive optimization techniques than would otherwise be possible, such as to remove `const` variables from inside loops and other repetitive expressions. Further, a data item which is found in ROM (Read Only Memory) would be declared with the `const` modifier because it will never have its value changed by the program. The `const` keyword allows C to provide better support for specialized hardware than is possible with other languages.

The `volatile` keyword signifies that a variable can unexpectedly change because of events outside the control of the program. For instance, this definition indicates that the variable `timer` can have its value changed without the 'knowledge' of the program:

```
volatile int timer;
```

A definition like this is needed, for example, if `timer` is updated by hardware which maintains the current clock time. The program which contains the variable `timer` could be interrupted by the time keeping hardware and the variable `timer` changed.

These two keywords can be used with any other data types (e.g. char, float, etc.) and can also be used with each other. This definition:

```
const volatile constant_timer;
```

specifies that the program does not intend to change the value in the variable `constant_timer`. However, the compiler is also instructed, because of the `volatile` keyword, to make no assumptions about the variable's value from one moment to the next. Therefore two things happen. First, an error message will be issued by the compiler for any line of code which attempts to change the value of `constant_timer`. Second, the compiler will not remove `constant_timer` from inside loops since an 'external' process can also be updating the variable while the program is executing.

3.2.3   *Declarations vs Definitions*

Students are often confused by the difference between a declaration and a definition of a variable. Basically, a *declaration* determines the name and attributes of a variable, while a *definition* is a declaration that also reserves storage. This means that there can be only one definition of an item, but many declarations.

A declaration of a variable is needed if the variable's definition is not available to the portion of a program where the variable is used. This can occur if the definition is in another program module which will not be present until all the pieces of the program are linked together. In this situation a declaration is needed when this source file is compiled so that the attributes of the variable can be established. Declarations are also used to establish the return type of functions that have not yet been "seen" by the compiler (i.e. they appear "further down" in the program). For example, in this simple program we have marked both a definition and a declaration:

```
main()
{
    int index;      /*  <================ the definition of 'index' */

    index = 15;     /*  assigning a value to 'index' */
    func1(index);   /*  invoking 'func1' passing 'index' as an argument */

        return;     /*  return from main, probably to the operating system */
}

/*--------------------------------------------------
func1()  a function requiring an integer argument
---------------------------------------------------*/
func1(count)
int count;          /*  <================ a formal parameter declaration */
{
    .
    .
    .
    return;         /*  return to the caller, i.e. main() */
}
```

In this example, index is defined in main(), where its storage is reserved. Meanwhile, in func1() the formal parameter, count, is declared to have type int; no storage is allocated. This information is needed by the compiler to implement the function properly.

Quick Note 3.3   The words declaration and definition are confusing

A declaration specifies the name and attributes of a variable. A definition is a declaration which also reserved storage. Many people use the terms interchangeably. Do not be confused if the words are not used in the proper context.

3.3   Self-Check

These statements are True or False. The answers are given at the end.

1. All escape sequences must be formed by using a backslash followed by a hexadecimal code, as in \x4f.

2. \13 represents the decimal value 13.

3. Strings are a fundamental data type in C.

4. The NULL character is not required as the last character of a character array.

5. If the literal "THIS STRING" is used many times in an ANSI standard program, each occurrence may or may not refer to the same physical string in storage.

6. The variable name this-is-a-name is valid.

7. C is considered to be a weakly typed language.

8. A character occupies a byte of storage.

9. The physical size of an integer depends on the computer being used.

10. The string definition my_string[5] = "mystr" will always generate a compiler error message.

11. It is not possible to temporarily change the type of a variable so that it can be used as a different type in a calculation.

12. A definition is a declaration that also reserves storage.

13. You can put a double quote mark inside a literal string by merely placing two double quote marks back to back, as in many other languages.

14. A newline character represents a carriage return-line feed sequence in every implementation of the C language.

15. A hex integer needs the leading zero so that the value will be considered to be numeric.

16. A compiler that conforms to the ANSI C standard must allow for at least 31 characters to uniquely represent a name.

17. The only fundamental data types in C are characters, integers, floats and enumerations.

18. Strings are a safe data type in C because the compiler performs much validity checking behind the scenes when the string is used.

19. There are three types of floating point variables, and all three can be used with an ANSI standard compiler even if the instruction set of the machine being used only has one or two of the types.

20. The terms declaration and definition mean such different things that they are usually used correctly by people describing the C language.

21. The const keyword specifies that a variable can not be changed, but the keyword does not take effect until the program executes.

22. The volatile keyword indicates to the compiler that a variable can have its contents changed unexpectedly.

Answers

1. F   2. F   3. F   4. T   5. T   6. F   7. T   8. T   9. T   10. F   11. F   12. T
13. F   14. F   15. T   16. T   17. T   18. F   19. T   20. F   21. F   22. T

3.4   Review Programs—ASCII and Temperature Conversions

In this chapter, we have been primarily concerned with data types and conversions. We will present two programs, `ascii.c` and `tempconv.c`, which print tables of data using various data types. You should be careful to note how the data types are defined (or declared) and how they are used in the context of each program.

☐ *Design Specifications*—`ascii.c`

Write a program that prints an ASCII code table for all ASCII values that fall between 32 (a space ' ') and 126 (a tilde ~). The table should be formatted in double columns conforming to the following example:

ASCII CHARACTER CODE TABLE

Char	Ascii Code	Char	Ascii Code
	32	!	33
"	34	#	35
$	36	%	37
	.		
	.		
	.		

☐ *Program Design*—`ascii.c`

This sounds like a fairly straightforward program. Writing the pseudocode gives us,

```
begin main
    <print the table title>
    <initialize start character>
    while (<there are more characters to print>)
        <print character/ASCII code and character+1/ASCII code+1>
    endwhile
end main
```

Of course, the pseudocode is quite general and the actual code will not be as simple. We feel that the program should be easy to code, therefore we proceed to the design implementation phase.

☐ *Design Implementation—*`ascii.c`

It appears from studying our pseudocode that we will need several variables and/or constants.

Variable/Constant	Type	Comments
table title	string	the title of our printed table
initial character	char	character to seed table generation
table heading	string	heading for entries in the table
loop counter	int	counter for table generation loop
minimum ASCII value	int	---
maximum ASCII value	int	---

Although the identification of variables and constants needed before actually beginning to code the program is not always necessary, it's not a bad practice and could save headaches on large and complex programs.

After completing the above outline, we write the actual code:

```
/*------------------------------------------------------------------
 ascii.c
 Program to generate an ASCII code table
-----------------------------------------------------------------*/
#include <stdio.h>

#define MIN_ASCII      32
#define MAX_ASCII      126
#define C              ' '
#define TABLE_HEADING   "\tAscii\t\t\Ascii\nChar\tCode\tChar\tCode\n\n"

char ascii_table_title[] = "ASCII CHARACTER CODE TABLE";
int index = 0;

main()
{
/*
print the table title centered using table heading for calculations
*/
    printf("%s\n\n", ascii_table_title);                 /* print title */
    printf("%s\n", TABLE_HEADING);                 /* print column heading */
    while (index <= MAX_ASCII - MIN_ASCII + 1)     /* loop through all values */
      {
/*
```

```
print a line on the table
*/
    printf("%c\t%d\t%c\t%d\n",
          C + index, C + index, C + index + 1, C + index + 1);
    index = index + 2;                              /* skip to next values */
    }
  return;
}
```

□ *Program Output*—ascii.c

ASCII CHARACTER CODE TABLE

Char	Ascii Code	Char	Ascii Code
	32	!	33
"	34	#	35
$	36	%	37
&	38	'	39
(	40	)	41
*	42	+	43
,	44	–	45
.	46	/	47
0	48	1	49
2	50	3	51
4	52	5	53
6	54	7	55
8	56	9	57
:	58	;	59
<	60	=	61
>	62	?	63
@	64	A	65
B	66	C	67
D	68	E	69
F	70	G	71
H	72	I	73
J	74	K	75
L	76	M	77
N	78	O	79
P	80	Q	81
R	82	S	83
T	84	U	85
V	86	W	87

(table continued on next page...)

X	88	Y	89
Z	90	[	91
\	92	]	93
^	94	_	95
`	96	a	97
b	98	c	99
d	100	e	101
f	102	g	103
h	104	i	105
j	106	k	107
l	108	m	109
n	110	o	111
p	112	q	113
r	114	s	115
t	116	u	117
v	118	w	119
x	120	y	121
z	122	{	123
¦	124	}	125
~	126		127

There is one important point we wish to note about this program. The constant C has been used in arithmetic expressions. This illustrates an important aspect of the C language character type: Characters are converted to type 'int' in arithmetic expressions. The value obtained is the character code value the compiler uses (usually ASCII or EBCDIC). Also note that to print the ASCII value of the character, we simply coded %d in the printf() control string instead of %c.

Points to Study—ascii.c

1. How the defined constant C and the variable index are used in arithmetic expressions.

2. Use of the escape sequences to produce the desired output.

3. Use of #define constants.

4. The usage of,

```
#define TABLE_HEADING "\tAscii\t\t\Ascii\nChar\tCode\tChar\tCode\n\n"
```

compared to,

```
char ascii_table_title[] = "ASCII CHARACTER CODE TABLE";
```

which are both treated as string constants. It appears that they are viewed as equivalent types by the compiler. How are they different?

□ *Design Specifications*—t e m p c o n v . c

Write a program that generates a Fahrenheit to Celsius temperature conversion table. The equation to be used to calculate the conversion is,

degrees C = (degrees F - 32) X 5/9

   where,

C: Celsius
F: Fahrenheit

   The program should allow the user to enter the range of the conversion table. For example, the user might specify that the table be printed from 32 degrees F to 212 degrees F, in which case the table might look like this:

```
Fahrenheit -> Celsius Conversion Table
---------------------------------------

°F                  °C
---------           ---------
32.000000           0.000000
33.000000           0.600000
            .
            .
            .
212.000000          100.000000
```

□ *Program Design*—t e m p c o n v . c

The value 33 degrees F in degrees C is actually .55555…This means that we will have to use floating point arithmetic and include provisions for rounding off the values for the table output. We also recognize that we will need some sort of loop construct, as in a s c i i . c, and we will need some limited input routines to get the user's wishes for the table value range.

Keeping these requirements in mind, we write the pseudocode:

```
begin main
    <get minimum value from user>
    <get maximum value from user>
    <print the table title>
    <print the column headings>
    i = minimum value
    while (i <= maximum value)
            c = celsius(i)
            c = round(c)
            print(<value of i and c>)
        i = i + 1
    endwhile
end main

begin celsius(i)
    <convert i to celsius, return result>
end celsius

begin round(c)
    <round c to nearest tenth, return result>
end round
```

Note that we will have to code two functions, celsius() and round(), in addition to the main logic. Since we don't perceive that to be a significant problem, we proceed to write the mainline code.

☐ *Design Implementation—*tempconv.c

```
/*-----------------------------------------------------------
tempconv.c
Program to print a Fahrenheit to Celsius conversion table
-----------------------------------------------------------*/
#include <stdio.h>

/*
 function prototype declarations - older style
*/
double celsius(double);
double round(double);
```

```
main()
{
   float   max_val, current_val;            /* variables local to main() */
/*
 get necessary data from the user
*/
   printf("Enter minimum temperature for table (degrees F): ");
   scanf("%f", &current_val);
   printf("\n");
   printf("Enter maximum temperature for table (degrees F): ");
   scanf("%f", &max_val);
   printf("\n\n");
/*
 now, print the table
*/
   printf("Fahrenheit -> Celsius Conversion Table\n");
   printf("-------------------------------------\n\n");
   printf("Fahrenheit\tCelsius\n\n");
/*
 loop from the base value to the upper limit in one-degree increments
*/
   while (current_val <= max_val) {
      printf("%f\t%f\n", current_val, round(celsius((double) current_val)));
      current_val = current_val + 1;   /* up one degree */
   }
   return;
}

/*-----------------------------------------------------------------
 celsius(f)
   convert a Fahrenheit temperature reading to Celsius

    parm          type            desc
---------------|---------------|-------------------------------------
    f             double          Fahrenheit temperature value

   ret value      type            desc
---------------|---------------|-------------------------------------
 <celsius>        double          equivalent temperature in Celsius

-------------------------------------------------------------------*/
double celsius(f)
double f;
{
   return((f - 32) * 5 / 9);                /* return Celsius value per */
}                                           /* a standard equation */
```

(program continued on next page...)

```
/*------------------------------------------------------------
round(n)
   round a double-precision floating point number to the nearest tenth

     parm         type           desc
--------------¦--------------¦--------------------------------------
     n           double         a double-precision floating point number
                                to round

   ret value      type           desc
--------------¦--------------¦--------------------------------------
     n           double         double-precision floating point number
                                rounded to nearest tenth
----------------------------------------------------------------*/
double round(n)
double n;
{
/*
 see text for explanation
*/
    if ((n * 10) - (int)(n * 10) >= 0.5) {
        n = ((int)((n + .1) * 10) * 1.0) / 10;
    }
    else {
        n = (((int)(n * 10)) * 1.0) / 10;
    }
    return(n);
}
```

As usual, we would code dummy functions for round() and celsius() to test the main line code, then write these functions one at a time, testing after the completion of each. For the sake of brevity we have left these dummy functions out, but, for example, in the case of the function round() you might simply code,

```
return(n);
```

as the body of the dummy version.

Now let's take a look at the output, then discuss some important aspects of this program.

☐ *Program Output*—tempconv.c

```
Enter minimum temperature for table (degrees F): 0
Enter maximum temperature for table (degrees F): 16
```

```
Fahrenheit -> Celsius Conversion Table
---------------------------------------

Fahrenheit        Celsius

0.000000          -17.700000
1.000000          -17.200000
2.000000          -16.600000
3.000000          -16.100000
4.000000          -15.500000
5.000000          -15.000000
6.000000          -14.400000
7.000000          -13.800000
8.000000          -13.300000
9.000000          -12.700000
10.000000         -12.200000
11.000000         -11.600000
12.000000         -11.100000
13.000000         -10.500000
14.000000         -10.000000
15.000000         -9.400000
16.000000         -8.800000
```

There are several important aspects of this program that we need to examine closely. First, note how an (int) type cast is used in the function round(). Here we are using (int) to force truncation of the decimal portion of (n * 10); the quantity (int)(n * 10) then becomes, as an intermediate result, an integer value. Since the other part of the expression (n * 10) is a floating point type, the entire expression (n * 10) - (int)(n * 10) is coerced to a floating point value. This allows us to write the expression,

(n * 10) - (int)(n * 10) >= 0.5

Only one major problem remains—the results of an expression like,

(14.5 * 10) - (int)(14.5 * 10)

when n is equal to 14.5, may not be exactly equal to 0.5. In fact, the result may be 0.499999, 0.499998, and so forth, due to round-off error. We will not discuss all the nuances of this type of error; suffice it to say that we must compensate for it. Because of round-off error, you may note in our table that some of the conversions are not quite correct. For example, solving our equation, C = (F−32) * 5 / 9, when F = 4, yields

C = (4−32) * 5 / 9 = −15.555556

which is not equal to 15.5 rounded to the first decimal place.

One solution might be to compare to a value sufficiently close to 0.5 in the if expression, a value such as 0.49999, recognizing that any round-off error introduced would occur in the last decimal place. Other solutions to this problem exist, but we will not cover them here.

The second aspect we need to examine is the expression,

```
((int)((n + .1) * 10) * 1.0) / 10
```

This expression contains a mixture of floating point and integer types. It might prove helpful to look at a diagram illustrating how this expression is evaluated:

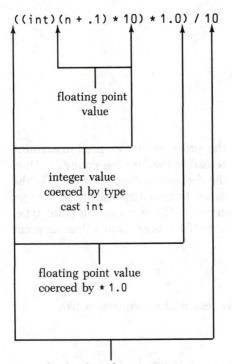

```
((int)(n + .1) * 10) * 1.0) / 10
```

floating point
value

integer value
coerced by type
cast int

floating point value
coerced by * 1.0

final value of expression is
floating point since last intermediate
value was a floating point value

As an example of the sequence of events taking place, let's trace through the conversions by solving each intermediary expression, letting n = 14.56:

Intermediary Expression	Resulting Expression	Value	Type
n + .1	14.56 + .1	14.66	double
((n + .1) * 10)	14.66 * 10	146.6	double
(int)((n + .1) * 10)	(int)146.6	146	int
(int)((n + .1) * 10) * 1.0	146 * 1.0	146.0	double
((int)((n + .1) * 10) * 1.0) / 10	146.0 / 10	14.6	double

The final point to note is that most of the floating point values in the program are defined with type `double` rather than `float`. This was done intentionally to reduce warning messages from the compilers used to compile and test this program. Some compilers always promote `float` arguments to `double` when passing `float` values to a function. The compilers we used did this, even though we explicitly defined the arguments as `float`. When we changed the program to use `double` arguments and return values rather than `float` the warning messages went away. This introduced another problem, however, which was that our `scanf()` accepted arguments of type `float`, while `printf()` handled `doubles`. The solution to this mix of types was that a type cast of `double` was added to the arguments passed to `celsius()`, causing all arguments and return values to agree in type.

Antibugging Note 3.3   Take warning and error messages seriously

Always request the highest and most stringent level of error and warning messages available by the compiler. These messages are indicators that something is not quite correct with the code. Continue to refine the code until all the messages have been eliminated.

Points to Study—`tempconv.c`

1. Type conversions using type casts.

2. Use of floating point and integer types.

3. Use of the `if/else` construct in `round()`.

3.5   Exercises

1. What would be the resultant output of the following `printf()` function calls?

Function call	Output

a. `printf("%s\n%s\n", "abc", "def");`
b. `printf("0x00, 0x00");`
c. `printf("\"This is a quote\"");`
d. `printf("The root path is \\");`
e. `printf("\"\"\'\\");`
f. `printf("(%f,%f,%f)", 1.0, 3.5, 0.75);`

   2. Evaluate the following expressions involving type casts. Give the final value and the type, where i = 1.75 and j = 3.

Expression	Value	Type
`(int)i`		
`(float)j * 10`		
`(int)(i * j) * 1.0`		
`(float)((int)((i * 10) + 0.1))`		

* 3. Write a loan amortization program with the following specifications:

   a. allow the user to enter the following variables
      an initial loan amount
      an interest rate
      a payback period in years
   b. the program should print a complete table, by month, until the loan has been paid back.

   Use the following compound interest formula in your program,

$$p = l * ((r / 12) / (1 - (1 + r / 12)^{(-n * 12)}))$$

where,

p: monthly payment amount
l: initial loan amount
r: annual interest rate (expressed as a decimal)
n: number of years for the loan

4. Write a program that acts as a simple calculator with the functions +, -, *, /. A sample session might look like this:

```
First operand  = 10.0
Operator       - *
Second operand = 5.5
Result of 10.000000 * 5.500000 is 55.000000
```

Devise some means to allow the user to exit the session.

5. What will the array contain after the following code fragment executes?

```
char s[] = "abcd";
int i = 0;

while (s[i] != '\0')
  {
  s[i] = s[i] + 'z' - 'z';
  i = i + 1;
  }
```

* 6. Write a program to output all possible prime numbers from 1 to 1000 using the Sieve of Erastothenes algorithm given below, assuming that the counting numbers, 1,2,3,...,1000 are stored in an array.
   1. Zero the first element, 1.
   2. Counting from the first array element, find the first nonzero entry that is not a prime found previously—number found is a prime number.
   3. Zero all elements in the array that are multiples of last prime found.
   4. Repeat steps 2. and 3. until last nonzero array element is a prime.
   5. Nonzero entries left in the array are all prime numbers.

7. Write `printf()` statements to produce the program output examples given below:
   A. MS-DOS requires path names to
      be in the form `'\path\filename'`.
   B. The tab character in C is coded as `'\t'`.
   C. "Oh my!" she stated. "I just love C strings!"
   D. He replied, "Yes, they're great. But when I need to print a string that is extremely long or extraordinarily wordy, I just don't know what to do!"

* indicates advanced exercises

3.6   Pretest

□ *Multiple Choice*

Circle one correct answer for each of the following:

1. Which variable definition does not represent a fundamental data type in C?
   a. `int an_integer = 3;`
   b. `char a_string[] = "A string";`
   c. `char a_char = 'c';`
   d. `float a_float = 1.356;`

2. Which variable definition is written incorrectly?
   a. `int xyz = 345;`
   b. `char c = 'z';`
   c. `char s[] = 'Message';`
   d. `float big_number = 1.75e35;`

3. What would be the output of the following code fragment?

```
float f = 1.375
printf("%d", (int)f);
```

   a. 1
   b. 2
   c. 0
   d. can't be determined

4. A type cast is used to
   a. define a variable type not provided in the C language
   b. force an expression to assume a different data type
   c. declare formal parameter variable types within functions
   d. force an expression to be evaluated even if written incorrectly

5. What would be the output of the following code fragment? (Assume ASCII encoding.)

```
printf("\x31\x32 %%");
```

   a. 3132 %
   b. 12 %
   c. %
   d. 0x310x32 %

6. Which variable definition below is written incorrectly?

```
a. char digits[] = "1234567890";
b. char continue[] = "Press any key to continue...";
c. char some_letters[] = "abcdefghijklmnop";
d. char string[] = "This is a string.";
```

7. What is wrong with the following variable definition?

```
signed int minus_one = 65535;
```

    a. An integer can't be that large.
    b. It's not portable.
    c. An integer cannot be signed.
    d. We should have used a `float` type.

8. The code fragment,

```
int i = 0;
while (--i)
   printf("%d", i);
```

would print the variable i how many times?

    a. 65535
    b. indefinitely
    c. can't tell, depends on bitsize of integer
    d. 0

9. What's wrong with the following code fragment?

```
char msg[] = 'H','i',' ','T','h','e','r','e','\0';
printf("%s", msg);
```

    a. Can't define a string like that.
    b. String length is too long for most compilers.
    c. The identifier `msg` is a reserved word.
    d. Nothing is wrong.

10. How do you suppose the compiler would treat the following code fragment?

```
int i = 65535;
printf("%d", (char)i);
```

    a. It would generate a syntax error.
    b. It would print the resultant character code, discarding high bits of i.
    c. It would just ignore the `(char)` type cast and print 65535.
    d. None of the above.

4

Operators and Expressions

I n Chapter 3 we discussed constants and variables. Those items make up the operands within expressions. In this chapter we will cover operators, which when combined with constants and variables allow us to create complete C expressions.

After studying this chapter, you will be able to do the following:

1. Identify C language operators.

2. Explain precedence and associativity.

3. Create correct C expressions and explain their meaning.

4. Discuss potential problems with different operators and expressions which can cause difficulty in programming.

4.1   Precedence and Associativity

When multiplication and addition operators are mixed in an algebraic expression without parentheses the multiplication is done first and the addition second. Thus, this assignment expression:

```
x = 2 + 4 * 6
```

yields 26 (from 2 + (4 * 6)) rather than 36 (from (2 + 4) * 6). When used together like this these two operators behave in C just as they do in algebra. However, in C there are more operators than * and +, and sometimes the expressions resulting from their combinations are not evaluated as you might expect.

Precedence determines how parentheses should be placed around parts of an expression. Parentheses are placed first around the operator with highest precedence, and then around operands that are related to operators with lower precedence. This has the effect of causing one operator to be evaluated before another. In the above example * has a higher precedence than +.

If two operators have the same precedence, *associativity* determines the order in which they are evaluated. Associativity is defined for each set of operators that have the same precedence. The associativity is either left to right or right to left, depending on the operator, meaning that this assignment expression:

```
x = a * b * c
```

becomes

```
x = (a * b) * c
```

rather than

```
x = a * (b * c)
```

since the associativity for the * operator is left to right.

Except for precedence and associativity there are no general rules about how an expression in C is evaluated. Each operator has rules concerning its interaction with the surrounding expression. In other words, expressions are not always evaluated right to left or left to right. For instance, this expression:

```
(a + b) * (c - d)
```

may or may not result in (a + b) being evaluated before (c - d). Since only one operator (*) is involved, the compiler is free to choose the order of evaluation of the two parenthesized expressions.

Table 4.1 defines the precedence of all operators. Operators occupying the same horizontal row have the same precedence. Lower number rows have higher precedence. Therefore, row 1 has the highest precedence, and the table is organized in order of decreasing precedence.

Precedence	Symbol	Name	Associativity	Class
1	() [] -> . ++ --	subexpression and function call * array subscript structure pointer structure member increment (postfix) decrement (postfix)	left to right	primary expressions and postfix operators

(table continued on next page...)

Precedence	Symbol	Name	Associativity	Class
2	! ~ ++ -- - + (type) * & sizeof	logical negation one's complement increment (prefix) decrement (prefix) unary negation unary plus * type cast pointer indirection address of size of	right to left	unary
3	* / %	multiplication division modulus (remainder)	left to right	multiplicative
4	+ -	addition subtraction	left to right	additive
5	<< >>	bitwise left shift bitwise right shift	left to right	bitwise shift
6	< <= > >=	less than less than or equal greater than greater than or equal	left to right	relational
7	== !=	equal test not equal test	left to right	equality
8	&	bitwise AND	left to right	bitwise
9	^	bitwise exclusive OR		
10	¦	bitwise inclusive OR		
11	&&	logical AND *	left to right	logical
12	¦¦	logical inclusive OR *		
13	?:	conditional test *	right to left	conditional

Precedence	Symbol	Name	Associativity	Class
14	= += -= *= /= %= <<= >>= &= ^= ¦=	plain assignment add subtract multiply divide remainder bit left shift bit right shift bit AND bit exclusive OR bit inclusive OR	right to left	assignment
15	,	comma *	left to right	sequence

* This operator generates a sequence point

Table 4.1 Order of Precedence

Parentheses are not operators in the classical sense but rather designate a subexpression, i.e., an expression inside an expression. Parentheses are also used to surround function arguments.

4.2 Operators

In this section we will discuss all operators defined in the C language. Some of these operators will already be familiar to you, but others are used in ways very different from both algebra and other computer languages.

We'll discuss the operators by loosely collecting them into groups. At the end of the chapter we will summarize how we combine operators into an *expression*, which is a combination of variables, constants and operators that together accomplish some meaningful work.

4.2.1   *Arithmetic Operators*

Arithmetic Operators	
+	add
-	subtract/unary minus
*	multiply
/	divide
%	remainder/modulus

Table 4.2   Arithmetic Operators

The arithmetic operators in C are listed in Table 4.2. An understanding of the basic arithmetic operators is fundamental to learning any computer language, and C is no exception. The +, - and * operators are used in the conventional sense, but take care when using the / operator. When / is used with integers it results in integer division, and the division of two integers is another integer. This means that the result is truncated if necessary. For example, 10 / 3 is 3, and the remainder of 1 is lost.

The % or modulus (remainder) operator is not often used in conventional programming. If we write 10 % 3 we get 1 (the remainder of 10 divided by 3), 11 % 3 is 2, and so on. This operator is frequently used in date calculations, especially those that involve determining the day of the week. It is also used in computations that "cycle", calculating an answer that is scaled to a certain range. It only makes sense to use the modulus operator on integers; it is not appropriate to use it with floating point numbers.

The precedence of C arithmetic operators conforms to standard algebraic rules with multiplication *, division /, and modulus % having equal precedence over addition + and subtraction -. All of these operators associate left to right. This means that if parentheses are not present the order of evaluation of arithmetic operators is left to right, after the rules of precedence are applied. For example, the expression,

i + j - k

would be evaluated as if written,

(i + j) - k

because + and - are of equal precedence and have left to right associativity. However, the expression,

i + j * l - k

is evaluated as,

```
(i + (j * l)) - k
```

since the * operator takes precedence, after which the expression is evaluated left to right because the two remaining operators, + and -, associate left to right.

Parentheses can be used to help specify the order of evaluation, like this:

```
(i + j) * (l - k)
```

which evaluates as follows,

1. Add i to j.

2. Subtract k from l.

3. Multiply the result obtained in step 1 by the result obtained in step 2.

It is a good idea to use parentheses in expressions whether they are needed or not. This is especially true for complicated cases. Additional parentheses in no way affect the execution speed of a program. On the contrary, parentheses help depict the programmer's intent in complicated expressions, and this leads to more readable code. For example, the expression,

```
i % j + k % l - m + n % o / p
```

might be written by a programmer who was intimately aware of the rules of precedence and associativity. However, when the expression is coded as

```
((i % j) + (k % l)) - m + ((n % o) / p)
```

there is no doubt what the programmer had in mind.

4.2.2   Assignment Operators

After we define *assignment operator* we can begin writing more complete expressions. The assignment operators are shown in Table 4.3.

```
                 Assignment Operators
    =        simple assignment
    +=       addition assignment (compound)
    -=       subtraction assignment (compound)
    *=       multiplication assignment (compound)
    /=       division assignment (compound)
    %=       remainder assignment (compound)
```

Table 4.3   Assignment Operators

The single equal sign is the simple assignment operator and is also used just like in algebra. It means:

1. Select what appears on the right of the equal sign.

2. Convert the type of what was selected to the type of the variable that appears on the left side of the equal sign.

3. Place the converted value in the left variable.

For instance,

```
float my_float;              /* define a float variable */
my_float = 5;
```

causes an integer 5 to be changed in type to a float and then placed into the variable my_float. It is very important that there be no confusion that the = operator often has a dual use in other computer languages. In those languages the single equal sign serves as both an assignment and equality test operator. In C, however, the single equal has one use: that of assignment (see the next section for the equality test operator).

Multiple assignments are allowed in C and are done like this:

```
x = y = z = 0
```

Here we have set all three variables, x, y, z all to 0. If we add parentheses we would see:

```
x = (y = (z = 0))
```

C provides assignment operators that are a combination of two others. These combinations are called *compound assignments*. This:

```
x = x + y;
```

can also be coded as

```
x += y;
```

No discussion of the assignment operator would be complete without mentioning a concept that might be obvious at first, but that plays a basic part in the definition of the language. This concept is that of *lvalue*. The term comes from the expression

```
E1 = E2
```

where E1 is the lvalue or left side value because it appears on the left side of the expression. While E2 can then be considered an rvalue, the term rvalue is not used in the C language. E1, and thus by definition all lvalues, must refer to a data item whose value can be changed. The expression

```
5 = x
```

is obviously incorrect because the value of 5 cannot be changed: 5 is a constant, and constants cannot be lvalues.

Variable names are always lvalues. Even in algebra variable names can appear on the left side of an assignment. For example,

```
x = 5
```

is correct since x can indeed be set to the value of the right side of the assignment, which in this case is a constant 5.

Certain operators can be used with a variable name while still leaving the name eligible to be an lvalue. For instance,

```
x[3] = 5
```

means to set the fourth element of the array named x to 5. The operator [] can be used with an array name and still yield an lvalue. Other operators cannot be used in this way, as in this example of an incorrect statement:

```
(x + 4) = 5
```

Expressions, like (x + 4), cannot be lvalues because they do not refer to memory locations.

Consider the following separate assignment expressions where we use these variables:

```
int x = 10, y = 2, z = 3;
```

Expression	Result	Equivalent To
x += y	x = 12	x = x + y
y -= z	y = -1	y = y - z
x %= z	x = 1	x = x % z
y /= z	y = 0	y = y / z
	(Integer arithmetic!)	
y *= z	y = 6	y = y * z

Now, some more complicated examples:

x += y - z	x = 9	x = x + (y - z)
y *= x / y	y = 10	y = y * (x / y)
x %= x / (y + z)	x = 0	x = x % (x / (y + z))

Note that in the last examples, the right side of the compound assignment is evaluated first because of the higher precedence of the arithmetic operators.

Although it may appear at first glance that the only advantage to using an expression like x += 5 is as a convenient shorthand for the equivalent expression, x = x + 5, this is not the case in more complicated expressions. For example, the expression,

```
a[b[i + j] / m - ( x * y * z)] = a[b[i + j] / m - (x * y * z)] + 5
```

is obviously quite complicated and an error in typing the expression a[b[i + j] / m - (x * y * z)] on both sides of the assignment could easily occur. Such complex expressions are not uncommon in C, and the advantage in writing this expression as

```
a[b[i + j] / m - (x * y * z)] += 5
```

should be evident.

4.2.3   Relational Operators

Relational operators give us the ability to make decisions in a program. We use them to test the value of variables and expressions and execute different portions of our program according to the outcome of the test.

The relational operators are similar to the logical operators which we will discuss next. Both types of operators can be used in if statements, and both relational and logical expressions can be represented by numeric values. However, the two types are evaluated differently. The relational operators are listed in Table 4.4.

```
        Relational Operators
==    equal
!=    not equal
<     less than
>     greater than
<=    less than or equal
>=    greater than or equal
!     not
```

Table 4.4 Relational Operators

One mistake made frequently by beginning C programmers is using the single equal operator to test for equality. The single equal sign does not test for equality; rather, it indicates assignment. It differentiates between the left and right sides of an assignment expression. The double equal operator is used to test for equality. This expression,

```
if (x = 5)
```

might look fine, but it is actually incorrect if we are trying to determine if x is equal to 5. In fact, this test will always be logically true, never false. The error is that we have assigned the integer 5 to the variable x rather than trying to test whether x is equal to 5. The correct way to code the expression if we want to do the test is to write:

```
if (x == 5)
```

If it is difficult to get used to the double equal sign when testing for equality, consider adding this line to the top of each program:

```
#define  EQ   ==            /* use EQ now in the test for equality */
```

which would allow the above test to be written as:

```
if (x EQ 5)
```

This technique may help reduce both the number of logic errors and also frustration and wasted time. Later, a conscious effort can be made to use the == operator.

It is very important to understand that a relational operator is not required when making a test. For example, both of the following are correct, and equivalent:

```
if (x != 0)
```

or

```
if (x)
```

The first asks "Is x not equal to zero?" and the second, "Is x currently true?"

A true condition can be expressed numerically as 1, and a false condition can be indicated by zero. The result of this test can be assigned to a variable so that the variable would then contain the value of either 0 or 1. The reverse is also true: we can test a numeric value to determine whether it is true or false. The rules are slightly different, though, because any nonzero value is considered true, while zero again is false. Therefore, in the example above the test would be considered true if x had a nonzero value. Negative numbers are also nonzero and therefore are true when they are tested. Table 4.5 summarizes this situation:

Logical Assignment and Testing	
Assignment	TRUE => 1 FALSE => 0
Testing through an if statement	!0 is TRUE 0 is FALSE

Table 4.5 Logical Assignment and Testing

The ! or not operator reverses the logical value of the item against which it is applied, as in this example:

```
if (!x)
```

If x has a nonzero value, normally it would be considered to be true. However, the expression !x would yield a false result with a nonzero value of x.

Relational expressions can range from simple ones like those above to more complex expressions like:

```
if (x -= 5 <= y - 7)
```

In all cases, however, the result is a simple logical true or false condition. Note that although other operators are also present the entire expression is still relational in nature, meaning that a true or false result will be computed.

Consider the following examples where we use these variables:

`int i = 10, j = 2, k = 3, x;`

Expression	Interpretation	Logical Result	Actual Value of Expression
i < j	Is i less than j?	False	0
j <= i	Is j less than or equal to i?	True	1
j + k < i / j	Is j+k (5) less than i/j (5)?	False	0
j == 10	Is j (2) equal to 10?	False	0
j = 10	Assign the number 10 to j.	True	10
	Observe difference in these expressions!		
x = (j == 2)	Assign to x the result of testing whether j (2) is equal to 2 (x will become 1).	True	1
i / j == 5 == j + k	a. Is i/j (5) equal to 5?	True	1
	b. Is 1 (the result of i/j) equal to j+k (5)?	False	0

Final state of this expression

The last example appears quite strange but is, in fact, a legitimate C expression. Note that since the arithmetic operators have a higher precedence than the relational operators, i / j and j + k are both evaluated first. Next the test i / j == 5 results in a logical true (a) which is compared to the number 5 for equality. Of course this is an unequal comparison, causing a false (0) result that makes the entire expression equal to 0. Obviously, care must be exercised in coding such expressions to avoid unexpected results.

If the last expression were changed to read,

`!(i / j == 5) == j + k`

the result would still be false (0) since !(i / j == 5) evaluates to false (0) which, of course, is not equal to j + k (5). If, however, we coded,

`!(i / j == 5 == j + k)`

the expression would evaluate to true since the expression is false (0) and the inverse of this (!) is true (1).

Quick Note 4.1   Numerical values of logical conditions

If the result of a relational or logical test is assigned to a variable, true becomes a 1, while false becomes a zero. When a variable is tested by itself (without an operator) any nonzero value logically tests to true while a zero tests as false.

4.2.4   *Logical Operators*

Logical operators are used to create combinations of tests by connecting individual decisions with an "and" or "inclusive or" connection. For instance, we may eat if we have money and if the store is open or if someone brings us groceries. The *and* and *inclusive or* operators in C are shown in Table 4.6.

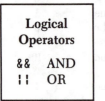

Table 4.6   Logical Operators

Both logical operators take up two character positions, just like many of the previous operators (==, <=, etc.). To join two tests and ask whether both tests are true the and operator, &&, is used like this:

x == 5 && y == 6

Here we have asked whether x is equal to 5 at the same time that y is equal to 6.

If either of the tests can be true, the or operator, ||, is used. The test would then be written

x == 5 || y == 6

An interesting (but often confusing) aspect of how C handles logical expressions is that they are evaluated left to right. Further, the evaluation stops when it becomes apparent that there is no point in continuing. For instance, if we assume that x has a value of 5, then when our example above actually executes the y would not even be examined since x has a logically true value. Since the x is true, the value of y is unimportant. Normally we would not care whether the compiler generated code that caused the y to be examined, but if we create a complex expression such as

x || (y = z + 4)

then the value of y is only set to z + 4 if x is zero (false). If x is zero (false) then the portion of the expression to the right of the || symbol must be examined to see if the entire expression can somehow be true. On the other hand if x is true (not zero) then there is no need to process the right side of the expression and the value of y is never changed.

Following are examples of how the logical connectives can be used in expressions where we use these variables:

```
int i = 10, j = 2, k = 3;
```

Expression	Interpretation	Logical Result	Actual Value of Expression
i !! j	Is i nonzero OR is j nonzero? (Evaluation actually stops at i)	True	1
i - 10 !! j	Is i-10 nonzero OR is j nonzero? (Evaluation continues to j)	True	1
i != 5 !! i != 4	Is i not equal to 5 OR is i not equal to 4?	True (always!)	1
i != 5 && i != 4	Is i not equal to 5 AND is i not equal to 4? (Evaluation checks both i's)	True	1

The last two examples illustrate a pitfall that unwary programmers can easily slip into if they do not take care. The expression i != 5 !! i != 4 will always be true since i can never be equal to both 5 and 4 at the same time! What the programmer probably intended was the fourth expression, i != 5 && i != 4, and probably intended to ask whether i is not equal to one of two values, not both at the same time.

A useful technique to determine whether a particular logical expression will work correctly is to break down the expression into its component parts and assign logical states to each. For example, we can build a truth table for the third expression above and would see that this expression is an exercise in futility:

Value of i	i != 5	i != 4	OR	
4	1	0	1	
5	0	1	1	
!5 and !4	1	1	1	
Can't be true that				
i == 4	0	0	0	<== This condi-
and i == 5				tion can
at the same time				never exist!

Quick Note 4.2   Skipping parts of logical expressions

Parts of a logical expression may not be evaluated if examination of the portion to the left is sufficient to determine whether the expression is true or false. This means that certain operations which may be coded as part of the logical expression may never be performed.

4.2.5   *Bitwise Operators*

As would be expected from a language designed to replace assembly language programming, C has a full set of operators to manipulate bits. While these operators are primarily used for systems work, we would be deficient if we did not explain them and provide examples of their use. The operators are shown in Table 4.7.

Bitwise Operators

&	bitwise AND
¦	bitwise inclusive OR
^	bitwise exclusive OR
<<	bitwise left shift
>>	bitwise right shift
~	bitwise 1's complement
&=	bitwise AND assignment (compound)
¦=	bitwise OR assignment (compound)
^=	bitwise exclusive OR assignment (compound)

Table 4.7   Bitwise Operators

Bitwise operators take their meaning straight from Boolean logic. The & (AND) and ¦ (OR) are identical to the logical counterparts && and ¦¦, which we just described. These operators however compare items bit for bit rather than taking the logical value of one entire item and comparing it to the logical value of another entire item. The ^ (exclusive OR) is the symbol for allowing only one bit of the pair to be a 1 in order for the bit of the result to also be 1. The truth table of these operators is shown in Table 4.8.

AND		
one bit	other bit	result of AND
0	0	0
0	1	0
1	0	0
1	1	1

Inclusive OR		
one bit	other bit	result of OR
0	0	0
0	1	1
1	0	1
1	1	1

Exclusive OR		
one bit	other bit	result of Exclusive OR
0	0	0
0	1	1
1	0	1
1	1	0

Table 4.8 Logical Truth Tables

The shift operators move the bits left or right within the data item. The left shift always places zeroes in the bits on the right out of which data is moved. The right shift fills with zeroes only if the data item is unsigned. If the data item is signed, the choice of whether the sign bit is propagated or whether a zero is filled depends on each compiler.

The *1's complement* operator merely reverses the bits in the data item without considering whether the item is signed, unsigned, or anything else. This differs from negating the data item in that negation (on most computers) is a *2's complement* operation, which reverses the bits and then adds one. For example, the value of 1 is represented by the bits:

00000001

The 2's complement would reverse the bits, which would first leave:

11111110

and then one would be added to make:

11111111

The bitwise operators are useful in situations where assembly language would normally apply. For example, integer division and multiplication by a power of 2 can be expressed by using the >> and << operators, respectively. If we let the variable i equal 16 then its bit pattern would be:

```
       ┌── 2 to the 4th power (4th bit) is 16
       ↓
00010000
      ↑
       └── 0th bit
```

To shift it right 3 bits would be the same as dividing by 2 three times, and to accomplish that we would write:

```
      ┌── right shift operator
      ↓
i >> 3      /* shift i right 3 bits, yielding 00000010 */
    ↑
     └─────── number of bits to shift
```

which would result in the value 2. Shifting the original number (16) left 2 bits is the same as multiplying by 2 twice, and to do that we would write:

```
      ┌──left shift operator
      ↓
i << 2      /* shift i left 2 bits, yielding 01000000 */
   ↑
    └── number of bits to shift
```

which would result in the value 64. Shift operations are often much faster than their multiply and divide counterparts. They can play an important part in helping to speed up programs where speed is more important than other things (like program clarity and maintainability).

The following expressions illustrate some of the bitwise assignment operators. Assume that

```
int i = 8; (00001000 binary)
```

and remember that 2 is 00000010 binary and 10 is 00001010 binary.

Expression	Interpretation	Final Value of i
i != 2	OR i with 2 and place the result in i	10
i ^= 10	XOR i with 10 and place the result in i	2
i &= 8	AND i with 8 and place the result in i	8

The next examples illustrate both bit testing on a variable and also some assignments. Assume that

```
int i = 39; (00100111 binary)
int j =  3; (00000011 binary)
```

and remember that 1 is 00000001 binary.

Expression	Interpretation	Final Value of i
i & 1	Is bit 0 (the first bit position) set?	39 (True) Expression Value 1 (True)
i & 8	Is bit 3 (2 to the 3rd) set?	39 (True) Expression Value 0 (False)
i &= 0	Clear all bits in i.	0
i ^= i	XOR all bits in i. This effectively zeros i.	0
i = (j << 3)	j is shifted left 3 bits (same as multiplying by 2 three times) yielding 24, which is assigned to i.	24 (j is 24 also)

This final example will illustrate a practical use for the ^ (bitwise exclusive or) operator. Assume that there exists the function working_func() which is passed an ASCII digit and returns either a zero or non zero value. We are not interested in the exact value of the result, only whether it is or is not zero.

Suppose that we wish to develop test_func() to replace working_func(), and as part of the development we need to test the two functions to insure that both return the same result if given the same input data. We might write this:

```
for (digit = 0; digit <= 127; digit = digit + 1) {
   if ((working_func(digit) != 0) ^ (test_func(digit) != 0)) {
     printf("error message");
   }
}
```

The if statement will only be true when the two expressions (working_func(digit) != 0) and (test_func(digit) != 0) have different values. Table 4.9 shows the four possible combinations of return values from the two functions:

working_func()	test_func()	working_func() !=0	test_func() !=0	exclusive OR (^)
0	0	False	False	False
!0	0	True	False	True
0	!0	False	True	True
!0	!0	True	True	False

Table 4.9   Exclusive OR Truth Table

In summary, the exclusive OR operator can be used when comparing variables or expressions that can only be 0 or 1. It can identify the conditions where the items being compared do or do not agree.

4.2.6   *Increment and Decrement Operators*

Two unusual operators can both simplify and greatly complicate C programming. These operators either add or subtract one from the data item to which they are applied. The operators are listed in Table 4.10.

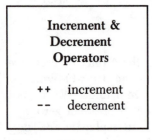

Increment & Decrement Operators

```
++    increment
--    decrement
```

Table 4.10   Increment and Decrement Operators

The *increment operator* can be written like this:

```
x++
```

It does exactly the same thing as either of these expressions:

```
x = x + 1       or       x += 1
```

The *decrement operator* works the same way, simply subtracting one from the data item to which it is applied.

These operators can be placed in front of or behind a variable. When placed in front of the name (*prefix form*) the action is applied to the variable before it is used in the surrounding expression. When placed after the name (*postfix form*) the action occurs after the variable is used in the expression.

Quick Note 4.3 Increment and Decrement Operators

The increment (++) and decrement (--) operators can cause some interesting and unexpected side effects in programs. Use them very carefully, and make sure that their full effect is understood under all conditions.

In an effort to clarify how these operators work, let's look at some examples that use these variables:

```
int i = 10, j = 2;
```

Expression	Interpretation	Value of Expression	After Expression Evaluation	
			i	j
++i	Add 1 to i	11	11	—
i++	Add 1 to i	10	11	—
(++i) - j	Add 1 to i, subtract j from the result	9	11	2
(i++) - j	Subtract j from i, then add 1 to i	8	11	2

The final values of i and j are the same in both of the last two examples while the value of the expression containing the two variables is different.

Sometimes it is difficult to anticipate how expressions that have increment and decrement operators will be interpreted. For instance, if we have these variables and the following expression:

```
int a = 0, x = -1, y = 1, z = 0;
a = x++ || y++ && z++ + 2;
```

how will the expression be evaluated, and what will be the resulting value of each variable? Here is how the statement looks after some of the parentheses are applied:

```
a = (x++) || ((y++) && ((z++) + 2))
```

The parentheses are applied based on the precedence of the operators, but that doesn't change the fact that we still have a logical expression. Since it is logical we do not evaluate the nested parentheses from inner to outer, but rather left to right. Here is a detailed analysis of the evaluation:

1. The variable x is evaluated first. Depending on its value the rest of the expression may or may not be evaluated. In this case x enters the expression having the value −1, which is not zero and therefore true.

2. Since x is true there is no need to examine any of the rest of the expression. Everything to the right side of the assignment operator is considered to be true.

3. Since the right side of the assignment is true, a is assigned the value of 1.

4. Of all the postincrement operators, only the one for x is actually performed. In this case all the other postincrement operators are ignored and not executed.

5. The constant value 2 never enters into the discussion because we never get far enough in the expression to consider it. As long as x is true, the constant 2 could be replaced by any value in the world and the result would be the same.

After the expression is completely executed the resulting values for each variable are:

```
a == 1, x == 0, y == 1, and z == 0
```

A very important aspect of the postfix increment and decrement operators is seen here. Just because they have a high precedence does not mean that they are actually performed first. Precedence controls how the parentheses are applied to the expression but it does not override the basic nature of the operator. Postfix increment and decrement are applied to a variable after that variable has been used in the expression, even though they have a high precedence.

There is another way to explain the behavior of the postfix increment and decrement. If we write the expression

```
(i++) - j
```

then we can think of (i++) as going ahead and incrementing i but **returning** to the expression the "old" (before being incremented) value of i. It is this "old" value from which we subtract j. This is a perfectly valid view and may help resolve the difficulties sometimes associated with understanding postincrement and postdecrement.

For one final example, this code fragment:

```
int i = j = 0;

if ((i++) - j) {
    ++j;
}
printf("i = %d\n", i);
printf("j = %d\n", j);
```

would produce this output:

```
i = 1
j = 0
```

The condition `(i++) - j` is false (has a numeric value of 0) because `i` is not incremented until after it is used in the expression. Therefore, the `if` statement is not true and `j` is never incremented. The variable `i` is incremented, however, and becomes 1.

4.2.7   *Conditional Operator*

The *conditional operator*, `?:`, provides a quick way to write a test condition. Associated actions are performed depending on whether the test is true or false. It is also called the *ternary operator* because it requires three operands. In the example

```
a ? (b += 1) : (c *= 4)
```

`a` is tested, and if `a` is true (not zero), then the expression `(b += 1)` is performed. If `a` is false (zero), then the expression `(c *= 4)` is performed. Only one of the two expressions, `(b += 1)` or `(c *= 4)`, is performed, but not both. This operator, then, is an extension of the relational and logical tests. The above test can also be coded like this:

```
if (a) {
    b += 1;
}
else {
    c *= 4;
}
```

Here are some more examples using these variables:

```
int i = 10, j = 2, k = 3;
```

Expression	Interpretation	Last Expression Performed	Value of Entire Conditional
i ? i = j : i = k	If i is nonzero, then assign i the value of j, else assign i the value of k.	i = 2	2
i - 2 * (j+k) : j : k	If i minus 2 times (j+k) is nonzero (it isn't), then the value of the conditional is j (2), else it is k (3).	k	3
i=(i < j) ? k=i : j=i	Evaluate 'i < j' (results in False (0)). Assign this value to i. If i is nonzero (it isn't), then assign the value of i to k, else assign the value of i to j.	j = i (0)	0

The last example above clearly illustrates the fact that the ?: operator is a sequence point (which we'll explain in the next section). The expression i=(i < j) is fully evaluated before either k=i or j=i is performed. This changes the value of i before i is used on the right side of the assignment expression. Since the value of i becomes zero, j also becomes zero. Therefore the value of the entire conditional expression is also zero, since that is the value of the last assignment performed.

It is important to realize that:

1. The conditional is composed of component expressions, each of which has a value.

2. The entire conditional has a resulting value, which can be used just like any other value.

These features extend the use of the conditional beyond simple control flow logic. For example, in the expression,

```
y = (x - 1 ? y - x : x + y)
```

y is assigned the value of y - x, if x - 1 is nonzero, else it is assigned the value of x + y.

Or, going one step further, this:

```
if (y = (x - 1 ? y - x : x + y)) {
    z = 1;
}
```

is functionally equivalent to this:

```
if (x - 1) {
    y = y - x;
}
else {
    y = x + y;
}
if (y) {
    z = 1;
}
```

4.2.8 *Sequence Points*

The comma, a *sequence point*, is used to insure that parts of an expression are performed in a left to right sequence. It allows multiple expressions to be used where normally only one would be allowed. It is frequently used in the for statement because in parts of the for multiple actions may be needed although the syntax only allows one statement.

Sequence points force all operations that appear to the left (of the sequence point) to be fully completed before proceeding to the right of that same point. This helps eliminate side effects, which are changes incidental to the particular evaluation being performed.

For instance, in the two expressions

```
x = y + 1, y = 2
```

the comma after the 1 insures that y will not be changed to a 2 before that same y has 1 added to it and the result placed in x. This particular expression requires the comma since without it we have a constant and a variable next to each other without an intervening operator, which would be an error.

Other operators are also considered sequence points. They are:

```
&&
```

```
||
```

```
?:
```

When any of these operators are encountered all activity associated with any operator to the left is completed before this new operator begins executing. The semicolon (which ends a statement) and the comma (which ends an expression) also perform this service, insuring that we have ways to control the order of when things happen in the program.

A point of caution: The commas that separate the actual arguments in a function invocation are not sequence points, but punctuation symbols. As punctuation symbols they do not guarantee that the arguments are either evaluated or passed to the function in any particular order. We'll provide an example of this later in the chapter.

4.2.9   sizeof *Operator*

The sizeof operator returns the physical size, in bytes, of the data item to which it is applied. It can be used with any type of data item except bit fields. The general form of the operator is:

```
sizeof(data_item)
```

Although it may look like a function, it is just an operator. It is replaced by a constant value when the program is compiled. When sizeof is used on a character field the result returned is 1 (if a character is stored in one byte). When it is used on an integer the result returned is the size in bytes of that integer. When it is used on an array the result is the number of bytes physically in the array (not the number of characters which appear before a NULL; sizeof has nothing to do with string length, measured by the strlen() function).

A frequent use for sizeof is to determine the physical size of a variable when the size of the variable's data type can vary from machine to machine. We have already discussed how an integer can be either 2 bytes (16 bits) or 4 bytes (32 bits) depending on the machine being used. If an additional amount of memory to hold 10 integers will be requested from the operating system, then some way is needed to determine whether 20 bytes (10 x 2 bytes/integer) or 40 bytes (10 x 4 bytes/integer) are needed.

For example, this code fragment,

```
int i[10];        /* an array of 10 integers */

printf("There are 20 bytes in the array i.");
```

would be correct on all machines that reserve 2 bytes for each integer, and false on other machines. To produce a true statement regardless of the machine on which the program is compiled and executed, we could have coded,

```
int i[10];

printf("There are %d bytes in the array i.", (int) sizeof(i));
```

With this technique sizeof will return the correct number of bytes in the array i regardless of the machine we use. For example, on a machine where integers are stored in 2 bytes the output would be:

```
There are 20 bytes in the array i.
```

On a machine that uses 4 bytes to store an integer the output would be:

```
There are 40 bytes in the array i.
```

This concept becomes essential when the program must be portable and independent of any particular hardware. In our example, the distinction could become critical if we need to write the array to a disk file. If we assume that the array contains 20 bytes (2 bytes per integer, a 16-bit machine), and we write only 20 bytes, the entire array would be written. If we compile the same program on a machine where 40 bytes are needed for the array (4 bytes per integer, a 32-bit machine) only half of the array would be written to disk.

Why did we perform an `int` type cast on the result of the `sizeof` operator? In the ANSI standard the `sizeof` operator does not return an `int`, but rather a data type (`size_t`) which is large enough to hold the value `sizeof` returns. This was added to C by the ANSI standard because on modern computers an `int` is not big enough to represent the size of all data items. In our example, casting the return value to an `int` allows it to match the `%d` conversion character of the `printf()` function. Without the `int`, if `sizeof` returns a value larger than an integer then the `printf()` function would not work properly. Neither would any other code that assumed `sizeof` returned an integer. For all programs and examples in this book, however, we assume that `sizeof` returns a value of type `int`.

4.3   Expressions and Statements

We have discussed the basic components used in expressions: constants, variables, and operators. It is now time to bring all that information together and illustrate the properties of expressions and how statements are formed.

An *expression* is a combination of operators and *operands* (things upon which operators act) which results in a value being computed. One or more expressions together make up a *statement*. This is straightforward enough, but various hitches can be encountered with certain expressions. We will try to cover most of them that might cause trouble.

4.3.1   *Form and Value*

The following are all valid C expressions because they contain both operators and operands:

```
x + 4            /* add 4 to x without permanently changing x */
x++              /* increment x */
x = y            /* place the value of y into x */
x = y + 1        /* add 1 to y and put the result in x; y is unchanged */
x = (y == z)     /* test if y equals z and put the logical result in x */
                 /* x will become 0 or 1 depending on outcome of test */
x + 4 * z        /* multiply 4 times z and then add x */
                 /* both x and z remain unchanged */
```

Parentheses can be used to group parts of an expression together to form another expression, sometimes called a *subexpression*. They are useful for designating an order of evaluation different from that which would occur without the parentheses, and for clarifying the order of evaluation even if the default order is being utilized. With one notable exception which we will discuss in a moment, the parentheses indicate that the portion of the expression inside the parentheses is to be evaluated first. The subexpression must be completely resolved first so that its value can be used in the resolution of the *primary*, or *outer expression*. Parentheses are not operators in the sense that other symbols like + and - are operators. Rather, they designate a hierarchy of expressions that must be analyzed from the inside out.

Expressions can be more complicated, as in this example:

```
x = (y = 4, z = 2)
```

What is the value that x receives? The answer illustrates a fundamental property of C expressions.

Quick Note 4.4   Value of a series of expressions

The value of a series of expressions is the value of the last (rightmost) one that is performed.

First y is given the value of 4, and then z is given the value of 2. The comma that separates the two expressions guarantees that the assignment of 4 to y will be completely evaluated with no residual (side) effects when the assignment of 2 into z begins. Since the last expression to be performed is z = 2, then 2 is the value of the entire parenthetical expression and also the value that x receives. To test this condition we might write this printf() statement:

```
printf("%d\n", (y = 4, z = 2));
```

Expressions that include an assignment operator are called *assignment expressions*. They have two sides, left and right, which are separated by the assignment operator. These expressions have two primary properties:

1. The left side (or only side in the case of x++) is an lvalue and refers to a data item that can be changed.

2. The right side of the expression, if present, computes a value that is placed into the left side.

For example, a simple assignment expression is:

```
x = 2                /* place the value of 2 into x */
```

This next expression, however, is of a slightly different form:

```
x + (y = 4)
```

Here we really have two expressions, one primary expression, x + (y = 4), and one subexpression, y = 4. The subexpression is the assignment expression. The primary expression is merely a plain expression consisting of an operator and two operands, with one of the operands being another expression.

To further emphasize the above two properties consider this expression:

```
(x + 2) = (y + 4)
```

The left side of the assignment is not an lvalue, but rather an expression. Expressions don't physically exist in the sense that data items both exist and can have their values changed. Therefore, an expression cannot be placed on the left side of an assignment operator, just as a constant cannot be placed there either.

Quick Note 4.5   Value of an assignment expression

The value of any assignment expression is the value of the right side cast (changed) into the type of the left side.

A *statement* is merely one or more expressions followed by a semicolon. While the semicolon is the basic way of indicating that a statement is present, we will see in the next chapter that braces can also denote statements. Statements are executed in sequence, and the semicolon acts as a sequence point in the same way as the comma. By adding a semicolon to expressions we make them into statements, like these:

```
x++;
x = y;
x = y + 1;
x = (y == z);
```

Expressions in C can take on complex forms, as we have already seen in some of our previous examples, and care must be taken to assure that:

1. The left side of the expression is capable of being modified, i.e., it is an lvalue.

2. The right side evaluates to a constant value such as integer, character, or float.

One of the major reasons the C language has been accused of being cryptic is because C expressions and statements can become very complex. It is important to note that C programs do not have to be cryptic, although the potential certainly exists. A few rules help produce readable code:

1. Use parentheses liberally in expressions, even when not required, to reveal fully the intent of the expression.

2. Do not combine unrelated expressions in the same statement. A statement in C, as in English, should express a complete thought, not two unrelated ideas. For example, with the comma operator it is possible to code several expressions on one physical line of code. Resist the temptation to do so.

Below are a few more examples of C expressions and statements to complete our discussion:

Expression/Statement	Interpretation
`q = (j == (x + w + z));`	Evaluate x + w + z; if j is equal to the result, set q = 1, else q = 0.
`z += -x++;`	Same as z += −(x++); which is the same as z = z + −(x++); The ++ has the highest precedence, so the first parentheses are applied around it and x.
`z += (-x)++;`	A syntax error because the ++ operator must be applied to a variable, not an expression. (−x) is an expression.
`--y++;`	A syntax error because the postdecrement has the highest precedence, making the expression the same as −−(y++). As in the previous example, here we've tried to apply a decrement operator to an expression.

4.3.2 Conversions

Most languages have rules describing how unlike data items are made alike before the operator between them is applied. C is no different. If we mix character, integer, and float types together in the same expression the compiler generates code to convert the types which can be converted without any loss of value. Generally this means that characters are converted to integers which are converted to floats. Therefore, if the types of data in an expression do not allow the expression to perform the computation correctly, use a type cast. For example, on a machine with 16-bit integers the following code doesn't work, as might be expected:

```
float float_item;
int   int_x = 30000;

float_item = int_x * int_x;
```

The reason this does not work is because there are only integers on the right side of the assignment, so the arithmetic is done with integers (which are not large enough to hold 30000 * 30000), even though the left side of the assignment is a floating point number and therefore has a format large enough to hold the result of the multiplication. The quickest and easiest solution to the problem is to temporarily change the type of one of the items on the right of the assignment, like this:

```
float_item = (float) int_x * int_x;
```

This changes the value of one of the occurrences of int_x into a float type only for the duration of the computation. It does not affect the storage int_x occupies. Now the expression is viewed as if it were a float type times an integer. C performs the computation in float format so that no loss of precision occurs.

Let's look at some examples of type conversions, showing the right and wrong ways to write different expressions. We'll use these variables:

```
char  c = 'A';
int   i = 1;
long  long1, long2 = 750000;
float f1,    f2    = 15.75;
```

Wrong Way	Correct Way	Comments
i = c + c	i = (int)(c + c)	First expression is okay, but the second reveals the intent of the programmer.
f1 = f2 + long2	okay	long2 is converted to type float since f2 is type float already.
f1 = long2 * long2	f1 = (float)long2 * long2	Information would be lost in first expression, since long2 * long2 is not converted to float until after the operation is performed.
c = c + f2	c = (char)(c + f2)	Result of c + f2 is type float and c is char; therefore we must cast result to type char.

As can be seen from these examples, it is important to recognize that:

1. The left side of the expression must be large enough to hold the object generated on the right side; if not, a type cast is in order.

2. If the left side is large enough to hold the result, take care to assure that information is not lost as a result of the way in which the right side is evaluated. If information may be lost, again a type cast may be needed.

3. Using a type cast where it is not needed is often a good idea to reveal explicitly what the programmer has in mind.

4.4 Antibugging Suggestions

Some areas often cause difficulties for C programmers. They are bypassed operators, expression rearrangement, and unspecified values for variables. These unexpected happenings are collectively called *side effects*. They will cause tremendous headaches and problems unless they are purged from programs, preferably before testing begins. Learn to recognize these types of coding mistakes while writing your programs. It will save a great deal of time later.

4.4.1 *Bypassed Operators*

When we discussed logical operators we stressed that since the evaluation of a logical expression was left to right, certain parts of the expression might never be examined. This would occur in the following example if x were a nonzero value:

```
x || y++
```

Here y is never incremented because the nonzero value of x makes the expression true, therefore y++ is never evaluated. In a similar way, in

```
x || (c = getchar())
```

the getchar() function may or may not be performed, depending on the value of x. This means that the program logic must allow for two conditions: both when the character is and when it isn't read. Resolving this uncertainty requires either the introduction of a flag or that x be tested again. You can see that expressions like these can cause real problems.

The operators to be cautious about are any assignment (either simple or compound) combined with increment and decrement. Increment and decrement are a form of assignment since

```
y++
```

is the same as

```
y = y + 1
```

Antibugging Note 4.1   Side effects inside logical expressions

Be careful when using any assignment, increment, or decrement operator, or when invoking a function inside a logical expression. Make sure that values on the left of a logical operator do not depend on the result of something happening to the right of the same operator, since the right side may never be performed.

4.4.2   *Reordered Expressions*

One aspect of the C language that disturbs many people is that the compiler can reorder expressions containing more than one occurrence of the same commutative or associative operator (*, +, &, ^ or ¦). As long as the types of the operands or the expected results are not changed the compiler is free to regroup the operands arbitrarily even though parentheses are specified. The parentheses might be ignored.

This feature of the language follows the rules of basic algebra, which says that

```
x + (y + z)
```

can be regrouped as

```
(x + y) + z    or even    (x + z) + y
```

and the resulting value of the expression will be the same in all cases.

This does not happen with just any expression. For instance, this:

```
x * (y + z)
```

will not be regrouped as:

```
(x * y) + z
```

nor as:

```
(x * z) + y
```

because the expected result would be different in either case. Since we did not use more than one occurrence of the same commutative or associative operator the expression was not eligible for regrouping anyway.

One reason that the C language allows this regrouping is because parentheses are often used to surround operators and operands even when there is no requirement that the expression be evaluated in any particular order. A high emphasis has always been placed on optimizing (i.e., making either as fast or as small as possible) the machine code from C programs. By allowing this reordering to take place we insure that this macro:

```
#define THRICE(x)   (3*(x))
```

can be expanded in these ways:

Macro Invocation	Expansion
THRICE(a+b)	(3*(a+b))
THRICE(c*3)	(9*c)

The second example illustrates the regrouping. If we did not allow the compiler to reorder the operands, we would be left with an expression having this form (which would not be the most efficient):

```
(3 * (c * 3))
```

Some expressions may benefit, however, from having the order of evaluation specified. This occurs if an intermediate operand in the calculation can overflow or if the amount of error being accumulated needs to be controlled. The ANSI standard now specifies that parentheses *will be respected, even if* the resulting expression is *not* the most efficient. The unary + operator is no longer allowed.

This new feature is *only* available on those compilers which have been revised to support the very latest version of the ANSI C standard.

Antibugging Note 4.2   Parentheses don't guarantee anything

In *older* compilers, if more than one occurrence of the same commutative or associative operator is used in one expression, parentheses don't necessarily guarantee the sequence in which the expression will be evaluated. Use multiple smaller expressions with explicit assignments to temporary variables. Newer compiler releases should support respecting parentheses.

4.4.3   *Using the Same Lvalue More Than Once*

One final side effect which can cause a great deal of confusion is when the same variable is used more than once in an expression and as part of one of the uses it changes value, i.e., it appears on the left of an assignment. For instance, this statement:

```
printf("the character %c is numerically equal to %d", my_int, my_int++);
```

might appear harmless enough. It looks as if we are going to print out both the character and numerical values of the integer `my_int`. However, we are assuming that the arguments to the `printf` function will be evaluated left to right so that the postincrement of `my_int` (the rightmost argument) will occur last, after `my_int` has been used in both places in the function call. We might need to do this if this statement appears in a loop to print a table of numbers and the corresponding ASCII character. What can happen (and did happen to one of the authors once) is that the arguments were evaluated right to left (there is no required order to how argument lists are evaluated), causing a moment of confusion as to why the space character did not show as being numerically equivalent to 32! After the last argument, `my_int++`, was used in the list (and evaluated first), `my_int` was incremented. Then when the next to last argument, `my_int` was used it had a value one greater than anticipated. This can be an insidious problem because the error might appear to be random and sporadic. It depends entirely on how the different compilers and compiler versions evaluate the offending expression.

Antibugging Note 4.3   Items used twice in the same expression

Don't use an item twice in an expression if in that same expression the item ever appears on the left of an assignment, or if the item has its value changed as part of a function call performed by the expression. Make sure that values on the left of the assignment operator do not depend on the result of something happening to the right of the same operator.

Remember that the increment and decrement operators are just shorthand for writing an assignment expression. They are some of the most frequent "offenders" of the above rule.

As a further example let's look at another situation:

```
int i = 0;
my_func(++i, i, ++i);
```

We do not know what value any of these function arguments will contain. Remember that the commas used here do not provide any guarantee of the order of argument evaluation. They are merely punctuation symbols which serve to separate one argument from another. For example, if we assume left-to-right evaluation of the arguments, we would have:

Argument	Value
++i	1
i	1
++i	2

However, if the compiler uses right-to-left evaluation then we get:

Argument	Value
++i	2
i	1
++i	1

But if it first evaluates the second argument then we are left with:

Argument	Value
++i	1
i	0
++i	2

or maybe this:

Argument	Value
++i	2
i	0
++i	1

We've shown that `my_func()` could receive at least four different sets of values from arguments that are written the same way. Obviously this can cause some tremendous debugging problems if not caught in advance.

4.5   Self-Check

These statements are True or False. The answers are given at the end.

1. `i + j * l - k` is evaluated as `(i + (j * l)) - k`.

2. The `^` sign means to do exponentiation, as in `x^y` meaning x to the y power.

3. `x = y = y = 0` tests whether all three variables are equal to zero and returns a true or false result accordingly.

4. x -= 5 is the same as writing x = x - 5.

5. 1 tests to logical true, 0 to logical false, and all other values are undefined.

6. Logical operators evaluate left to right only if there is no higher precedence operator in the expression.

7. Exclusive OR means that only one bit can be on for the result to be one, while inclusive OR means that either one or both bits can be on for the same result.

8. ++x; accomplishes the same result as x++;.

9. ++ and -- are two operators that can generate side effects in expressions.

10. The conditional (?:) is the only operator that requires three operands.

11. Since an array is not a fundamental data type you cannot apply the sizeof operator against an array name.

12. An lvalue is an item that is eligible to be used on the left side of an assignment in an expression.

13. 10 % 3 yields a result of 3.

14. If x has been set equal to the number 4, then if(x = 5) will yield a result of false.

15. if(x =< 4) is a valid expression in C.

16. Logical expressions evaluate right to left, and the left side may not be examined if the right side satisfies the condition.

17. The parentheses guarantee that C will always evaluate the portion of the expression inside the parentheses first.

18. Associativity is a property of operators which is always considered in addition to precedence when evaluating expressions.

19. A side effect occurs when the same data item is used twice in an expression and changes value during at least one of the uses.

Answers

1. T   2. F   3. F   4. T   5. F   6. F   7. T   8. T   9. T   10. T
11. F   12. T   13. F   14. F   15. F   16. F   17. F   18. F   19. T

4.6 Review Program—Drawing a Barchart

In this example program, we will review a potpourri of concepts covered in the chapter. In addition, we will introduce integer arrays. We have already been exposed to character arrays via the definition of strings in the C language. Anyone

who has ever programmed in a language that does not support arrays will appreciate the difficulties that arise in coding all but the most simplistic programs.

☐ *Design Specifications*

We wish to write a program that will produce a simple bar chart, using a fixed
number of values to plot and standard ASCII characters only for the output. In
addition to these general specifications, the program will have the following
features:

1. y-axis labels, represented as absolute numeric values

2. x-axis labels, represented as 0 for bar 1, 1 for bar 2, etc.

3. automatic adjustment for the graph y-axis range

After some introspection, we decide that this problem requires several variables and constants for its implementation, so, to aid our understanding, we sketch
a simple diagram, labeling the variables and constants needed.

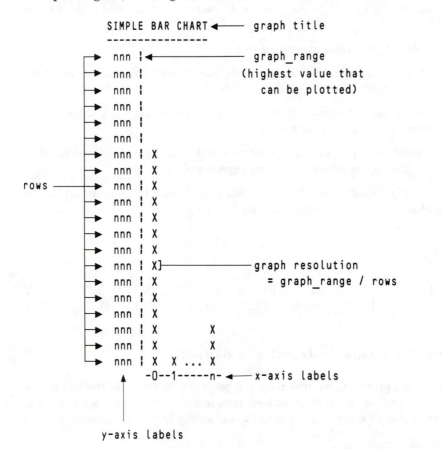

```
where,
```

```
n   : number of bars
nnn : n   1 * graph_resolution, 2 * graph_resolution, ...,
              rows * graph_resolution}
```

☐ *Program Design*

We will print the graph using printf() by displaying each row one at a time scanning from top to bottom. This immediately suggests a loop of some sort. A loop will require the use of an array to hold the values to plot. In our pseudocode, we will represent arrays using the same syntax that the C language uses, ignoring the actual data type. Let's proceed to write the pseudocode, after which we will discuss integer arrays and other pertinent aspects.

bar__value[] = {bar__value 1, bar__value 2,..., bar__value n}

```
begin main()
   <calculate rows>
   graph__range = suitable__range__function(bar__value)
   graph__res = graph__range / rows
   print (<graph title>)
   while (graph__range >= graph__res)
      print (<nnn>)
      n = <number of elements in array>
      while (n != 0)
         n = n−1
         if (bar__value[n] >= graph__range)
            print (" X ")
         else
            print (" ")
         endif
      endwhile
      graph__range = graph__range−graph__res
   endwhile
   n = <number of elements in array>
   while(n)
      print ("<piece of the x-axis + label>")
      n = n−1
   endwhile
end main

begin suitable__range__function(bar__value)
   <determine range for graph by a suitable algorithm,
      as yet, unknown>
   return(graph__range)
end suitable__range__function
```

First we consider the mainline code, and see that there are a few variables that will have to be determined at runtime, namely:

Type	Variable
int	graph_range
int	graph_res
int	nbr_bars (was n in the pseudocode)

In addition, constants identified are:

Type	Constant
int	rows
char[]	<graph title>
int[]	bar_value[] = {bar_value 1, bar_value 2, ... , bar_value nbr_bars}

Note that all of these constants could actually be treated as variables, yielding a more flexible program, but for our purposes we will consider them constants.

By carefully considering our generalized bar graph diagram, we deduce the following equations:

$$\text{rows} = \text{display rows} - \text{`overhead value'}$$
$$\text{(allow room for title, x-axis)}$$
$$\text{graph\_res} = \text{graph\_range} / \text{rows}$$
$$\text{nbr\_bars} = \text{number of elements in the array}$$
$$\text{graph\_title} = \text{``<a suitable string>''}$$
$$\text{bar\_value[]} = \{<\text{a set of integer values, containing}$$
$$\text{nbr\_bars values}>\}$$

The only one left is graph_range for which we must write a function, using some as yet unknown algorithm. We proceed to write the code.

☐ *Design Implementation*

```
/*------------------------------------------------------------------
barchart.c
simple bar chart program
----------------------------------------------------------------*/
#include <stdio.h>

#define DISPLAY_COLUMNS 80       /* 80 column display */
#define DISPLAY_ROWS 25          /* 25 row display */
#define HEAD_ROOM 5              /* allowance for title, etc. */
```

```
/*
values to plot
  (this is a global variable so that an older compiler will accept the
   initialization when the array is defined, otherwise it would be local
   to main())
*/
   unsigned int bar_value[] = {100, 250, 57, 375, 25, 468};

main()
{
   int nbr_bars, rows;
   int graph_range, graph_resolution;

   rows = DISPLAY_ROWS - HEAD_ROOM;          /* rows for chart itself */
/*
calculate a maximum y range for the chart and how big each bar 'pixel' is
*/
   graph_resolution = (graph_range =
                   or_em_up(bar_value,
                           sizeof(bar_value) / sizeof(int)
                           )
                   ) / rows + 1;

   printf("SIMPLE BAR CHART\n");             /* print graph title */
   printf("----------------\n\n");

/*
plot bar pixels until we run out
*/
   while (graph_range >= graph_resolution) {
     nbr_bars = sizeof(bar_value) / sizeof(int);  /* # of bars to plot */
     printf("%4d !", graph_range);               /* print y-axis labels */
/*
print a horizontal line of the bar graph
*/
     while (nbr_bars--) {                         /* loop til no more bars */
       if (bar_value[nbr_bars] >= graph_range) {  /* if it's within range */
         printf(" X ");                           /* print a piece of the bar */
       }
       else {
         printf("   ");                           /* else plot a blank pixel */
       }
     }
     printf("\n");
     graph_range -= graph_resolution;             /* adjust range down */
   }
```

(program continued on next page...)

```
/*
now, print the x axis and labels
*/
    printf("      ");                            /* over for y labels */
    nbr_bars = sizeof(bar_value) / sizeof(int);    /* # of bar labels */

    while (nbr_bars) {                           /* loop til no more bars */
        printf("-%1d-", sizeof(bar_value) / sizeof(int) - nbr_bars );
        --nbr_bars;
    }

    return;
}

/*-------------------------------------------------------------------
 or_em_up(bar, count)
 Produce a range for the bar chart by OR'ing all values to plot
 ---------------------------------------------------------------*/
or_em_up(bar, count)
int bar[], count;
{
    int max = 0;

    while (count-- > 0) {                 /* loop until no more bars */
        max != bar[count];                /* OR all bits into max */
    }
    return(max);
}
```

Most of the code is fairly straightforward except for the function or_em_ up(), which returns the graph range. The algorithm we have selected goes as follows:

1. Set the initial value of graph range to 0.

2. Inclusive OR graph range with each element of the array, replacing graph range with the result after each element is processed.

This simple scheme will insure that the graph range (the variable max in the function or_em_up()) will be greater than the largest value in the array, but not too large. Using this algorithm, we are assured that max will be no larger than,

$$(2^{hibit}) - 1$$

where hibit is the highest bit value of any of the values to be plotted. For example, if the largest array element is 17 (10001 binary) then the largest value that max can be is 31 (11111 binary), thanks to inclusive OR. Using this algorithm is much faster than searching the array for the largest element, then multiplying that element by some factor.

The main code of our program is a nested `while()` loop, with the outer loop controlled by decreasing values of `graph_range` and the inner loop controlled by `nbr_bars`, the number of bars. Note in the program how we determined the number of bars to plot. Instead of hardcoding the value 6 in the program, we use the `sizeof` operator to determine the number of elements in the array `bar_value` in a portable and flexible manner.

Now let's look at the output produced by our program.

☐ *Program Output*

```
SIMPLE BAR CHART
-----------------

511 ¦
485 ¦
459 ¦ X
433 ¦ X
407 ¦ X
381 ¦ X
355 ¦ X        X
329 ¦ X        X
303 ¦ X        X
277 ¦ X        X
251 ¦ X        X
225 ¦ X        X        X
199 ¦ X        X        X
173 ¦ X        X        X
147 ¦ X        X        X
121 ¦ X        X        X
 95 ¦ X        X        X    X
 69 ¦ X        X        X    X
 43 ¦ X        X    X    X    X
     -0--1--2--3--4--5-
```

Points to Study

1. Use of the `sizeof` operator.

2. Use of inclusive OR in the function `or_em_up()`; note how the `¦=` assignment operator was used.

3. Use of the post/predecrement operator, depending on the context.

4. Use of the `-=` assignment operator in the expression,

```
graph_range -= graph_res;          /* adjust range down */
```

5. Use of the relational operator, `>=`.

6. How array subscripting was coded.

7. Function arguments, formal parameters, and invocation for the function `or_em_up()`.

8. The expression,

```
graph_res = (graph_range =
             or_em_up(bar_value,sizeof(bar_value)/sizeof(int)))/rows;
```

and how it is equivalent to,

```
graph_range = or_em_up(bar_value,sizeof(bar_value)/sizeof(int)));
graph_res = graph_range / rows;
```

9. Why the bars are displayed in an order reversed from the manner that they are stored in the array.

10. Why the bar value 25 does not show up on the graph.

11. Consider if the function `or_em_up()` could be used on floating point numbers as well as integers; if so, what restrictions would apply.

4.7   Exercises

In exercises 1-5, use,

```
i = 10, j = 2, and k = 3
```

where i, j and k are all integers.

1. Evaluate the following expressions that use the arithmetic operators:

Expression	Result
i - j * k	
i - i/j	
k % i + j	
i % 2 * k	
i + j * k - i / j	

2. Evaluate the following logical expressions:

Expression	Result
i - 2 * (j + k) ‖ i	
i - 2 * (j + k) && i	
j = i ‖ k	
j = i ‖ k ‖ j	
j - k ‖ j && k	

3. Evaluate the following assignment expressions:

Expression	Result
i += j	
i %= k	
i ^= j + k	
i *= j / k	
i /= j	

4. Evaluate the following examples using the unary increment and decrement operators:

Expression	Result
++i	
j++	
i++ + ++j	
j-- + k--	
i++ / j--	

5. Describe the output of the following program:

```
main()
{
    printf("The value of function, 'func1()' is %d.\n", func1(i,j,k));
    return;
}

func1(i,j,k)
int i,j,k;
{
    if (i < j * k++) {
        k = 1;
    }
    if (k == 1 && j == 2 !! i != 1) {
        return(1);
    }
    else {
        return(0);
    }
}
```

* 6. Write a code fragment that would conform to the following algorithm,
    a. if expression el is true then c.
    b. if expression e2 OR e3 is true then a.
    c. while a. then b.

7. Write a program that performs the following tasks:

    1. Prompts the user for two integer values.
    2. Prints a table of all bitwise operations performed on the two numbers.
       An example run would look like this,

```
Enter number (1): 10
Enter number (2): 2
```

Operation	Result
10 ! 2	10
10 & 2	2
10 ^ 2	8
10 << 2	40
10 >> 2	2
2 << 10	2048
2 >> 10	0

8. Identify what is wrong with the following expressions:

Expression	Description of Error
i ^^ j	
i =+ j	
++i = j + k--	
(y ¦¦ z) = t - u	

9. Modify the example program `barchart.c` to include the following features:
   a. dynamic input of the bar values, as entered by the user
   b. logic in the code to space the bars evenly along the x-axis
   c. dynamic input of the x-axis labels (limited number of characters allowed)
  **d. bar values should be floating point values, not integer
  **e. a statistics section, giving the mean and standard deviation for the bar value

  * advanced exercises
  ** advanced enhancements

4.8   Pretest

☐ *Multiple Choice*

Circle one correct answer only.

1. What would be the result of the following expression,

i ¦ j ^ k ¦ i ¦¦ j

  given that,

i = 14, j = 38, k = 207

    a. 356
    b. 0
    c. 1
    d. 129

2. In C the pseudocode,

if (e1 OR e2)
    e3 AND e4
else
    e3 OR e5
endif

assuming that OR and AND are logical connectives, would be,
a. e1 ? e3 & e4 : e3 ¦ e5
b. e1 ¦ e2 ? e3 && e4 : e3 ¦¦ e5
c. e1 ¦¦ e2 ? e3 && e4 : e3 ¦¦ e5
d. e1 * e2 ? e3 + e4 : e3 * e5

3. What is wrong with the following code fragment?

```
float f_array[20];

printf("The # of elements in 'f_array' is %d", sizeof(f_array) / 4);
```

a. f_array only has 20 elements, not 4.
b. It may cause portability problems.
c. sizeof(f_array) / 4 cannot be printed using %d.
d. An array of floating point values has no definite size in C.

4. When we say the operators ¦, &, and ^ are bitwise, binary operators we mean that:
a. They are two of a kind.
b. They are really binary numbers.
c. They can be used as logical connectives, but only on binary numbers.
d. They operate on two numbers, one bit at a time.

5. The expression,

```
i = (k = x * y) + (q ? r : s)
```

is equivalent to,
a. i = x * y + r
   k = s
b. q ? r : s
   k = x * y
   i = k + q
c. k = x * y
   i = k + (q ? r : s)
d. none of the above

6. The expression,

```
++i+++j---k
```

would be interpreted by the compiler to mean,
a. `(++i++) + (j--) - k`
b. `(++i) + (++j) - (--k)`
c. `+(+i) + +(+j) - -(-k)`
d. `(++i) + + (+j-) - (-k)`

7. What is the resulting type of the expression,

```
(int)q = (int)k - l + (char)m
```

given that,

```
k: float
l: float
m: int
```

a. `char`
b. `float`
c. `int`
d. `long int`

8. The expression,

```
j % i && q - l * m ^ n
```

would be evaluated by the compiler as if written,
a. `(j % i) && ((q - (l * m)) ^ n)`
b. `j % ((i && q) - (l * m) ^ n)`
c. `((j % i) && q) - ((l * m) ^ n)`
d. none of the above

9. What would be the output of the statement,

```
printf("%d,%d,%d", i, ++i, ++i);
```

given that i = 1?

a. 1,2,3
b. 3,2,1
c. can't be determined
d. 1,1,1

Looping and Control Flow

S o far we have seen a working overview of C and also studied in detail the definition of various data items. You should be writing some simple C programs
now, although you may have recognized that the if and while statements alone
do not allow you to write very sophisticated programs. This chapter will address
that problem because here we will cover the entire subject of control flow.

After studying this chapter, you will be able to do the following:

1. Explain the basic concepts of block structured programming in C.

2. Create a block of code in C and explain the format and syntax.

3. Correctly identify all looping and control flow statements.

4. Discuss different techniques used in coding loops and changing the flow of
   control in a program.

5. Show various ways to terminate a loop.

5.1   Basic Structured Constructs

There are three basic structured programming constructs in any language:

1. Sequence

2. Decision (if-then-else)

3. Repetition (do-while, do-until, etc.)

Sequence is the "one right after the other" execution of computer instructions.
Decision is the "this one or that one or. . ." arrangement where the control flow of
a program divides into two or more possible directions. The *case* or *multiple-branch
construct* is part of this group. Finally, *repetition* is the "over and over" execution
of a group or block of instructions until some particular condition occurs. All
executable computer instructions (we're excluding definitions) can be categorized

into one of these three groups. Programs that use these constructs are considered to be *structured programs*.

5.2 Block Structure in C

A *block of code* in C is identified by its surrounding braces. Blocks can appear almost anywhere in a program. They must appear after certain statements, while after others they are optional. They can be placed right in the middle of a sequence of statements. Blocks contain one or more statements. They are sometimes called *compound statements* because a block allows many statements to be used in places where the syntax would otherwise allow only one.

5.2.1 *Use of Braces*

Braces in C are used to identify blocks. For example, when we discussed the `if` and `while` statements we illustrated the lesson with examples like these:

```
char c;
if(should_we_read_and_write)
   {
   scanf("%c", &c);        /* first statement in the block */
   printf("%c", c);        /* second statement in the block */
   }
printf("statement following the if");
```

Here the two statements following the `if` and the tested expression are viewed as if they were only one statement. This is because the syntax of the `if` allows only one statement for each side of the decision (i.e., true leg vs. false leg), as with this example:

```
char c;
int  d;
if(should_we_read_a_char)
   scanf("%c", &c);        /* statement done if expression is true */
else
   scanf("%d", &d);        /* statement done if expression is false */
printf("statement done after the if is completed");
```

We intentionally left the braces out of this example to illustrate how C would interpret an `if` statement without braces. With braces we can cause many statements to appear as if they were only one. Braces also help provide a measure of reliability to the coding, and make future program maintenance easier.

Blocks can be placed anywhere a single statement can be placed. The statements inside a block are executed sequentially (as if there were no block present). Also, blocks can be nested as deeply as the compiler will allow. It is important to note that there is no semicolon used after the closing brace that delimits the block of code.

Let's look at another example program in Figure 5.1.

```
/*
**   smplblk.c  Illustrates what happens without blocks (without braces)
**              This program intentionally has no braces to illustrate
**              what can happen when they are not used.
*/

#include <stdio.h>

main()
{
    int i = 2;
    int j;

    while (i > 0)            /* the while claims only the next statement */
        printf("We are now just inside the while() loop.\n");
        j = 3;                              /* we never get this far */
        while (j > 0)
            printf("The value of j is %d.\n", j);
            --j;            /* this statement isn't part of the while() */
        printf("The value of i is %d.\n", i);
        --i;
    printf("The end.\n");
}
```

Figure 5.1 The Need for Blocks—smplblk.c

If we ignore the comments, we might expect this output:

```
We are now just inside the while() loop.
The value of j is 3.
The value of j is 2.
The value of j is 1.
The value of i is 2.
We are now just inside the while() loop.
The value of j is 3.
The value of j is 2.
The value of j is 1.
The value of i is 1.
The end.
```

However, what we get is:

```
We are now just inside the while() loop.
```
   .
   .
   .

repeated indefinitely.

The reason lies in the manner in which the compiler associates statements within the the program. The `while` statement claims as its body the first statement that follows, regardless of indentation. Therefore, we never get to the `j = 3;` assignment. Without the `printf()` statement which immediately follows the `while` and makes up its body we run the risk of starting an *infinite loop*.

In order to produce the desired output, we must use compound statements by incorporating braces into our program in strategic locations, as shown in Figure 5.2.

```
/*
**  smplbrac.c   Illustrates what happens when braces are added
*/

#include <stdio.h>

main()
{
    int i = 2;
    int j;

    while (i > 0)
    {
        printf("We are now just inside the while() loop.\n");
        j = 3;
        while (j > 0)
        {
            printf("The value of j is %d.\n", j);
            --j;
        }
        printf("The value of i is %d.\n", i);
        --i;
    }
    printf("The end.\n");
}
```

Figure 5.2   The Need for Braces—`smplbrac.c`

We encourage the liberal use of braces in programs, even when they are not really needed. We would suggest writing this:

```
if (i == 3)
   {                              /* these braces are a good idea */
   printf("The value of i is %d.\n", i);
   }
```

instead of this:

```
if (i == 3)
   printf("The value of i is %d.\n", i);
```

The use of extraneous braces does not affect program execution speed, but it can be an invaluable aid in producing easily understood code. Braces also make subsequent program maintenance much easier and more reliable. Statements can be added to the block without worrying about indentation.

Quick Note 5.1   A block of code is a statement

A block of code surrounded by braces is syntactically equivalent to one statement. A semicolon is not coded after the closing brace when writing a block of code.

Antibugging Note 5.1   Make liberal use of braces

Many potential errors are avoided when braces are used with every control construct. Since they do not affect execution speed, make liberal use of them.

5.2.2   *Block Scope*

Our examples above may seem to have little application to the real world until we consider other situations. Suppose we want to use a particular variable name because it is meaningful to the immediate thing we are doing. Suppose also that the variable name was used earlier in the program as a global variable and that it already has something in it that must be preserved. Or suppose that for one minor calculation we need a temporary variable which will never be used anywhere else in the entire program.

The solution is to do something we mentioned earlier: define data immediately after the opening brace of a block. Data defined this way has the storage class of `auto`. It's called `auto` because it's automatically created when the control flow of the program enters the block, and in turn is automatically deleted when the control flow leaves the same block. This means that the piece of data does not exist outside the block, and any references to it outside the block will result in an error message when the program is compiled. In effect, the message will say that the piece of data does not exist. Its existence depends on where the program flow of control is at any given moment. The scope or range of statements within which this variable can be referenced is the block itself, hence the term *block scope*, which is the scope of that particular variable. The variable is also spoken of as being a local data item in the block, the term local being used in contrast to a global data item which can be referenced anywhere from its point of definition forward.

This piece of data can be referenced within other blocks if they are nested inside the block where the data is defined. This means that visibility can be passed downward or "into" blocks nested inside the outer block, but it is not possible to pass visibility outward to blocks that nest around the block within which the data is defined.

Another property of automatic variables is that they have no guaranteed initial value if one is not specified when the variable is defined. Do not assume that automatic numeric variables contain zero or that character data contains blanks.

Let's take another look at the scope and visibility of variables by examining the complete C program in Figure 5.3.

```
/*
**   scopevis.c   Illustrates the scope and visibility of variables
*/

char c = 'a';                       /* c defined at external level */

main ()
{                                   /* Block 1 */
    printf("\nBlock 1\n");
    printf("-------\n");
    printf("c = %c\n", c);
    {                               /* Block 2 */
        char c = 'b';               /* another c in block 2 */
        printf("\nBlock 2\n");
        printf("-------\n");
        printf("c = %c\n", c);
        {                           /* Block 3 */
            char c = 'c';           /* yet another c in block 3 */
            printf("\nBlock 3\n");
            printf("-------\n");
            printf("c = %c\n", c);
```

(program continued on next page...)

```
        }                               /* end block 3 */
        printf("\nBlock 2\n");
        printf("-------\n");
        printf("c = %c\n", c);          /* surprise! block 2 c */
    }                                   /* end block 2 */
    printf("\nBlock 1\n");
    printf("-------\n");
    printf("c = %c\n", c);              /* and now external c */
    return;                             /* is back */
}                                       /* end block 1 */
```

Figure 5.3   Scope and Visibility—scopevis.c

The output produced by this simple program looks like this:

```
Block 1
-------
c = a

Block 2
-------
c = b

Block 3
-------
c = c

Block 2
-------
c = b

Block 1
-------
c = a
```

We have defined three separate variables, each named c, at different nesting levels. There are several important points to note about these variables and their use:

1. Each variable c exists (or is visible) only within the logical block in which it was defined.

2. Although the c that is defined at the external level (i.e., outside main()) is redefined twice within deeper nested blocks, it retains its value at the outer level while the inner blocks are being performed. This is an important concept since it frees the programmer from worrying about naming conflicts, or about whether a variable's value will be destroyed unexpectedly.

3. Blocks 2 and 3 have access to any variables defined outside them which are not redefined inside the block by using the same name again.

Removing the word `char` from both blocks 2 and 3 would produce the output:

```
Block 1
-------
c = a

Block 2
-------
c = b

Block 3
-------
c = c

Block 2
-------
c = c

Block 1
-------
c = c
```

Note how the output is different for the second times that blocks 2 and 1 display something.

The variable c is global, and blocks 2 and 3 are free to change this global variable. As a final point, realize that the concepts of scope and visibility apply to any distinct logical block of code, including functions. Names of global variables can be reused within functions without fear that the name will conflict with a previously used name. However, variables outside a block cannot be referenced if the same name has been used to define a variable inside the block.

Quick Note 5.2 Visibility and use of automatic variables

Automatic variables are visible within the block where they are defined, and also within any nested inner blocks that are coded. An automatic variable is needed if a global variable already exists, has the same name, and we don't want to alter the value contained in the global variable. Automatic variable names can be reused without conflict or confusion.

5.2.3   *Static Data inside Blocks*

Since automatic variables are created again each time the control flow enters the block where they are defined, it would not seem possible to create a variable that retains its value from one entry of the block to another entry of the same block. This problem is solved by the static storage class *keyword*. This code fragment,

```
{
static int an_int_which_retains_its_value;
a statement which is inside the block;
}
```

creates an integer variable an_int_which_retains_its_value, which will retain its value from one execution of the block to the next. This is needed for variables used as counters, accumulators, totals, and so forth. A frequent use of the static keyword is in conjunction with automatic data defined inside a function, because often data is sent to a function for evaluation and the function maintains a count or total in an automatic variable. We'll discuss static further when we cover functions, but the program in Figure 5.4 will illustrate through nested blocks the idea of a counter retaining its value even though the flow of control has left the block where the counter is defined.

```
/*
** counter.c  A Static Counter
*/

#include <stdio.h>      /* standard I/O functions */
#include <ctype.h>      /* character & conversion functions */

main()
{
    int selection = 0;     /* receiving field for the input character */
    printf("Type in numbers and upper/lowercase letters\n");
    while(selection = getchar())
```

```
{
    {                           /* start a new block inside the while */
    static int number;      /* counter for 0 through 9 */
    static int lower;       /* counter for a through z */
    static int upper;       /* counter for A through Z */
    static int hex;         /* counter for valid hex digit */

    if(selection == '\n') /* a newline stops the program */
      {
          printf("\n%d numbers were entered\n", number);
          printf("%d lowercase letters were entered\n", lower);
          printf("%d uppercase letters were entered\n", upper);
          printf("%d hex digits were entered\n", hex);
          break;            /* note how break was used */
      }
    if(isdigit(selection)) {
      number++;             /* bump counter if a number */
    }
    if(islower(selection)) {
      lower++;              /* bump counter if lowercase */
    }
    if(isupper(selection)) {
      upper++;              /* bump counter if uppercase */
    }
    if(isxdigit(selection)) {
      hex++;                /* bump counter if hex digit */
    }
    }
    {
    /* the only purpose of this block is to insure that on */
    /* certain machines the above counters are wiped */
    /* out if they are not defined with the static keyword */
    int a = 0, b = 0, c = 0, d = 0;
    }
  }
}
```

Figure 5.4 A Static Counter—counter.c

This program uses nested blocks with integers defined inside one of the blocks to illustrate the need for the static keyword. The four counters are created inside a block which itself is inside the while statement. The counters are visible and available for use only when the program flow is inside that same block where the counters are defined. This is why the instances of the printf() function were placed inside that same block. To place the printf() function calls outside the while requires that the counters `number`, `lower`, `upper`, and `hex` somehow be communicated to the outside of the block so that they can be displayed.

When `counter.c` was executed and

```
123asdfASDFG
```

was entered from the keyboard, this correct output was printed:

```
3 numbers were entered
4 lowercase letters were entered
5 uppercase letters were entered
9 hex digits were entered
```

However, when the `static` keywords were removed from the program and it was compiled and executed again, also with the same keyboard input, then this incorrect output was displayed:

```
458 numbers were entered
1260 lowercase letters were entered
0 uppercase letters were entered
0 hex digits were entered
```

The particular numbers in the second set of values (displayed from the version without the `static` keyword) are meaningless. They could vary based on the compiler or machine used, or possibly other factors. While their specific values are unimportant, that they contain garbage indicates that the counters are not retained from one iteration of the block to the next.

Note that as each character is received with the `getchar()` function the flow of control does have to leave the first block inside the `while` (i.e., the block where the counters are defined). Not only does the flow exit the block but it enters a second block. The purpose of the second block is to destroy any automatic variables from the first block which are not `static`. (How it does this is, unfortunately, beyond the scope of this book to explain, although it is an interesting lesson on how stack based machines operate.) If the second block is left out of the program, it is not always possible to illustrate how automatic variables without the `static` keyword are guaranteed to retain their value when the block is exited and then entered again. Without the second block it is possible to create a program where variables without the `static` keyword appear to retain their values when the program exits and then reenters the block. What is really happening, though, is that the storage space where the variables are created is not being reused by other variables, and hence the variables appear to retain their values.

Antibugging Note 5.2   Missing 'static' keywords cause illusive program bugs

If the `static` keyword is left off a variable defined inside a block, the program may still appear to be retaining the variable's value even though the block is exited and reentered. This effect is exhibited only because no other variable has used the memory where the first variable was stored. Different conditions of execution or subsequent program maintenance may change that situation, causing a program bug to surface unexpectedly. Double-check that the `static` keyword is on all automatic variables whose values are expected to be retained from one use of the block to the next.

5.3   Structured Constructs in C

Five C constructs utilize block structure and support structured programming techniques:

```
1. if()
     {
     }
   else
     {
     }

2. while()
     {
     }

3. for(;;)
     {
     }

4. do
     {
     } while();

5. switch()
     {
     case:
     default:
     }
```

5.3.1   if *and* else

We introduced the if and else statements earlier so that they could be used when writing simple programs. In this section we will concentrate on what happens when logical expressions are used as part of the if statement test expression, and on how to nest multiple if statements properly.

Previously we have illustrated that a value can be tested to see if it is true or false. If the value is not zero (remember this includes negative values) then it is true. If the value is zero then it is false. For example,

```
if(5)
```

is always true since 5 is not zero.

```
if(x = 6)
```

is also always true since the value of an expression is the value of the last assignment performed inside the expression (assigning 6 to x in this case). Finally, this form,

```
if(x || y || z)
```

determines whether any of the three variables are not zero.

Note that we frequently use braces on if, while, and for statements even if there is only one statement following the keyword. This is a good habit to develop because the following situation can develop:

```
if(expression_to_be_tested)
    original_stmt_done_if_true;
    statement_you_just_added;
```

Here indentation misleads us because the code alignment implies that we successfully did what we intended to do, which was add another statement to the true leg of the if statement. What really happened, though, is that we merely added statement_you_just_added; in line with the if. This new statement is always executed regardless of the outcome of expression_to_be_tested. If braces had been used in the original example, like this,

```
if(expression_to_be_tested)
    {
    original_stmt_done_if_true;
    }
```

then it's very unlikely that the new statement would be placed incorrectly. This is also true with the while and for statements.

When nesting multiple if statements it is very important not to be misled by indentation. What matters is not how the statements are aligned but whether the various if and else statements are properly matched. Consider the following example:

```
if(first_test_expression)
    if(second_test_expression)
        true_leg_of_second_test;
else
    false_from_first_test;        /* or so we think! */
```

We have just misled ourselves by aligning the else after the first if, making it appear as if that else did indeed match the first if. Actually the compiler will match the else to the second if because the second if statement is the one closest to the else. The correct way to code this entire test is:

```
if(first_test_expression)
    {
    if(second_test_expression)
        {
        true_leg_of_second_test;
        }
    }
else
    {
    false_from_first_test;
    }
```

Here we used the braces to create a compound statement between the first if and the matching else. The compound statement creates a complete true leg for the first if and "shields" the second if from having the only else statement matched to it. The compiler will not match the else to the second if "across" the closing brace. To do so would leave the braces unmatched, and would also leave a block that began outside an if statement and then ended inside the statement. Not only is it incorrect but it's illogical and looks funny. This is another good reason always to use braces when coding if statements even if there is only one statement on either the true or false leg.

The null statement, which we will cover shortly, would also correct this situation but without adding the benefits that come from using braces.

We used braces extensively in this example. These braces somewhat lengthen the source code; not using the braces would probably make the code much shorter.

Quick Note 5.3   An `else` matches the nearest `if`

An `else` matches the closest `if` statement regardless of what the indentation may imply. Use braces or null statements to help avoid problems.

5.3.2   `while` *and* `for`

We've discussed the `while` and `for` statements already, so let's just quickly review their basic formats:

```
while(test_expression)
    {
    done_while_test_is_true;
    }

for(initial_expression; test_expression; increment_expression)
    {
    done_while_test_is_true;
    }
```

The braces are not required for either statement, but if they are absent then the first single statement that appears after the parentheses is the entire body of the `while`. They both always claim the first statement that appears after the parentheses as the body of the statement regardless of indentation or programmer intent.

The `for` statement has more required operators than the `while` because of the added initial and increment expressions. The `initial_expression` is ALWAYS performed before the `test_expression` is examined, and it is only done once. The `increment_expression` is done at the end of the body of the `for` and before the `test_expression` is examined the second and subsequent times.

Any desired test expressions can be used in either statement since, as with the `if`, the result of the test is reduced to a numeric value. Zero results are considered false, while nonzero results are true.

Remember that any `while` statement can be converted easily to a `for`, and vice versa. In both the `while` and `for` the body of the statement might never be performed. If the `test_expression` is false to begin with then the statement is immediately terminated and, in the case of the `for` statement, only the initial expression executes. If this occurs on the `while` statement then absolutely nothing happens. In both cases, if the `test_expression` is performed, then any pre- or postincrement or decrement operators or function calls included in the `test_expression` will be done according to the rules of evaluating expressions. This is always true of any `test_expression`, whether part of an `if`, `while`, `for`, `do` or `switch`.

The `for` statement also has an interesting format which is useful in certain situations. If all the expressions inside the parentheses are left out (the semicolons must remain because the compiler expects to find two of them), we have created what is traditionally termed the *forever loop*, like this:

```
for(;;)
    {
    }
```

We will discuss shortly the techniques for ending this type of loop.

Finally, both `while` and `for` can be nested. An example using `for` is,

```
for (i = 0; i < 2; ++i)
    for (j = 0; j < 2; ++j)
        for (k = 0; k < 2; ++k)
            printf("%d %d %d\n", i, j, k);
```

which would show all combinations of three 0's and 1's:

```
0 0 0
0 0 1
0 1 0
0 1 1
1 0 0
1 0 1
1 1 0
1 1 1
```

This example is interesting because it illustrates a potentially confusing use of the `for` statement (remember that `while` works the same way). Braces were left off purposely to demonstrate that `for` claims as its body the first statement occurring after the parentheses. In this case the first statement after the parentheses of the first `for` is yet another `for`. The body appearing after the second `for` is associated with the second `for`, not the first. This is similar to the way the `else` matches to the closest `if`, even if the indentation would indicate otherwise.

Note that the implied nesting order can be best represented by inserting braces at appropriate locations, like this:

```
for (i = 0; i < 2; ++i)
    {
    for (j = 0; j < 2; ++j)
        {
        for (k = 0; k < 2; ++k)
            {
            printf("%d %d %d\n", i, j, k);
            }
        }
    }
```

Quick Note 5.4   The body of if, while and for is always present

The if, while, and for statements always claim the next statement as their body, regardless of indentation or programmer intent. This is similar to the else statement matching the closest if.

5.3.3   do

The do statement is used much less frequently than the if, while, or for. It is a variation on the while statement and some people call it the do-while, which is fine because the while keyword must be included as part of the statement.

The do guarantees that the body of the construct is performed at least once regardless of the outcome of the expression test. Also like the while statement the body of the loop is executed as long as the expression tests true. It has this form:

```
do
    {
    done once and while expression is true
    }
        while(expression_to_be_tested);
```

Notice that the while is coded at the end of the block. This helps provide visual confirmation of what really is happening, that the test is done at the end of the block, not the beginning. Because the last character of the statement is not a closing brace but a right parenthesis, we need a semicolon to end the statement. It would also be an error to leave off the while statement and merely code the body of the do. In fact, leaving off the while() would really be no different than merely coding the matching braces by themselves.

The do-while construct is useful when we wish to ensure that the body of the loop is executed at least once before the test expression is evaluated. Consider the example of a user menu interface in Figure 5.5:

```
/*
** do-while.c   Illustrates the do-while construct
*/

#include <ctype.h>           /* has prototype of toupper() function */
#include <stdio.h>
```

```
main()
{
   char choice;
   do {                        /* always do the menu at least once */
      printf("1 - Choice #1\n");
      printf("2 - Choice #2\n");
      printf("X - Exit Program\n");
      printf("\n");
      printf("\nEnter your choice: \n");
      choice = getchar();              /* get an input character */
      choice = toupper(choice);        /* handles lowercase input */
                                       /* this is a nested if-then-else */
   if (choice == '\n') {               /* handles no input condition */
        printf("no input was entered\n\n\n");
      }
      else {
         if (choice == '1') {
            printf("do_choice1()\n\n\n");
         }
         else {
            if (choice == '2') {
               printf("do_choice2()\n\n\n");
            }
            else {
               if (choice != 'X') {
                  printf("Invalid choice. Please reenter.\n\n\n");
               }
            }
         }
         getchar();  /* flush linefeed character that follows input */
      }
   } while (choice != 'X');         /* terminate the program */
}
```

Figure 5.5   Illustration of `do-while`—`do-while.c`

The program `do-while.c` would produce the output,

```
1 - Choice #1
2 - Choice #2
X - Exit Program

Enter your choice:
```

In this example, we present the user with a simple menu interface to determine what path the program will take. The functions `do_choice1()` and `do_choice2()` (which are emulated through `printf()` statements) implement the user's selection, with a choice of X causing the `do-while` loop to terminate. Notice that had we coded this logic using a `while` construct, it would have been necessary to initialize the variable `choice` to some predetermined value before entering the loop body so that the test expression could be properly evaluated before displaying the menu.

This program also illustrates a very helpful program development technique, that of *drivers* and *stubs*. Here we can code and test the driver code without getting sidetracked developing the stubs, which are the `do_choice()` functions.

5.3.4   break *and* continue

We will introduce the `break` and `continue` statements here because the `switch` statement, which we will discuss next, is seldom coded without a `break`. `Break` and `continue` are also frequently used with the `for`, `while` and `do` statements to cleanly terminate the execution of one or all iterations of a loop. The forever loop mentioned above is terminated by using a `break` statement somewhere in the body of the `for` statement.

The format of both `break` and `continue` is:

```
break;
continue;
```

They are usually coded by themselves, and the semicolon is required only to make them into complete statements. While code can appear after a `break` or `continue` statement there is no point in doing so since they act as a type of jump statement.

We can diagram the action of the `break` statement this way:

```
for(init; test; increment)
   {
   various statements;

   if(test_exp)
     break; ──────────────────────┐
   }                               │
                                   │
next statement after the for; ◄────┘
```

The `break` completely terminates the smallest enclosing `for`, `while`, `do`, or `switch` statement. A `break` statement encountered in the middle of a `while` loop terminates the loop immediately. All the activity the `while` statement had accomplished prior to encountering the `break` is left finished and nothing is "undone." In the case of a `for` loop the program control does not go to the iteration statement within the parentheses, and the test expression is not checked again. In each case the program control flow immediately goes to the statement right after the closing brace of the `for`, `while`, or `do` statement body.

The `continue` statement is similar to the `break`. Rather than terminating a `for`, `while`, or `do` completely, however, the `continue` statement terminates the current iteration only. This means that with the `for` statement the iteration portion now receives control. In the case of the `while` statement we merely start over, again making the test before entering the block of code that makes up the body of the statement. We can diagram this action this way:

```
for(init; test; increment)
   {
   various statements;
   if(test_exp)
      continue;
   }
```

```
next statement after the for;
```

It is important to emphasize that if a `while` statement appears inside the body of another `while` statement, the `break` cannot be used to terminate the outermost while. Issuing the `break` will only terminate the innermost `while`, putting the control flow again in the outermost loop.

As a further example, in the following code fragment,

```
for (i=0; i < 10; ++i) {
   printf("The value of i is %d\n", i);
   if (this_condition) {          /* if condition is true, */
      break;                      /* exit loop right now */
   }
}
```

the `break` statement is executed if the value of `this_condition` is something other than zero. We could have coded,

```
i = 0;
do
   {
   printf("The value of i is %d\n", i);
   }
while(++i < 10 && !this_condition);
```

which would produce the same result without the `break` statement.

Everything we say about `break` applies to `continue` except that `continue` causes a skip to the next loop iteration, as in,

```
for (i = 0; i < 10; ++i) {
   if (this_condition) {
      continue;
   }
   printf("The value of i is %d\n");
}
```

which would prevent the printf() function from being executed if this_ condition was true.

Be careful when using break and continue. A good rule of thumb is that these statements should only be used (except in conjunction with the switch statement) when not using them would result in cloudy code.

Quick Note 5.5   Differences between break and continue

The break statement completely terminates the smallest enclosing for, while, do or switch. The continue statement ends this iteration of the smallest enclosing for, while or do. Neither can be used to terminate any outer loop of a nested for, while or do statement.

5.3.5   switch

The switch statement can sometimes eliminate the need for extensive nested branches. It does, however, have one primary deficiency and at least one hidden trap. The general format of the switch is this:

```
switch (integer_result_test_exp)
    {
    case:     done_this_case;
              break;
    case:
    case:     done_for_two_cases;
              break;
    default: done_if_no_cases;
              break;
    }
```

The integer_result_test_exp is an expression that evaluates to type int. This is the major deficiency of the switch statement. For instance, expressions containing floats can be used, but the final data type must be integer. It may help to think of the switch statement as a jump table in assembler or the ON N GOTO in BASIC.

Once the test expression is examined a decision is made by the switch statement. If the result of the test expression matches the value associated with any case statement, a jump takes place to the first executable statement after that case. Multiple case statements can be put back to back, like this:

```
    case():
    case():  done_for_two_cases;
```

where `done_for_two_cases;` then becomes the starting point for both `case` statements.

If the test expression value does not match any `case` statement then the jump takes place to the first statement that appears after `default`. If `default` is not present (it's not required), then nothing inside the `switch` body is accomplished and the next statement following the `switch` gets control.

The hidden trap is that once the jump from the `switch` to the `case` takes place, all the `case` statements in the entire `switch` statement can be ignored because they are no longer considered. When control is transferred to the statement after the `case` we begin execution of all `case` statements from that point through the end of the `switch` statement. This execution continues until a `break` statement is encountered. This is why the `break` statement is so important to the `switch`. Without it there is no way to partition off the various `case` statements. Without the break a cascading effect occurs where the first `case` includes the execution of all subsequent `case` statements, the second `case` all those that appeared afterward, and so on.

The rule that only the `break` statement or closing brace can terminate a switch applies to the `default` statement too. It is not required that a `default` be placed at the end of the switch, but it is found there most of the time. If `default` is placed before or between any other cases and a `break` statement is not included in the `default` then any transfer of control to the default will "fall through" to the next `case` appearing immediately below.

Antibugging Note 5.3   Using a 'break' statement after the last case

Be sure to place a `break` statement after the last `case` or `default` coded in the body of the switch. Even though the closing brace will end the `case` if another `case` is added after this last one, there is a risk of falling through into the new code. Adding a `break` also makes the code easier to maintain later.

To illustrate a typical use for the `switch` construct, let's revisit our simple menu interface, which was written with a `do-while` and a series of `if-else` constructs. Rewritten using a `switch` it yields the program in Figure 5.6.

```
/*
** switch.c  Illustrates the if-then-else construct
**           rewritten as a switch
*/

#include <ctype.h>    /* has prototype of toupper() function */
#include <stdio.h>
```

(program continued on next page...)

```
main()
{
    char choice;

    do
        {
        printf("1 - Choice #1\n");
        printf("2 - Choice #2\n");
        printf("X - Exit Program\n");
        printf("\n");
        printf("\nEnter your choice: \n");
        choice = getchar();
        choice = toupper(choice);      /* handle lowercase input */
        switch(choice)                 /* this switch replaces the */
            {                          /* if-then-else construct used */
            case '\n':                 /* before */
                printf("no input was entered\n\n\n");
                break;
            case '1':
                printf("do_choice1()\n\n\n");
                getchar();             /* flush linefeed character */
                break;                 /* the break statements insure that */
            case '2':                  /* we don't fall through */
                printf("do_choice2()\n\n\n");
                getchar();             /* flush linefeed character */
                break;
            case 'X':
                break;
            default:
                printf("Invalid choice. Reenter.\n\n\n");
                getchar();             /* flush linefeed character */
                break;
            }
        } while(choice != 'X');
}
```

Figure 5.6 Illustration of the switch statement—switch.c

In this program we have replaced the series of if conditions with a switch construct. Note the use of break as the terminal statement in each case. This is necessary to prevent subsequent execution of case statements after the one that matches the tested expression. Unlike similar constructs in other languages, each subsequent case after the one that matches is not tested. After a jump is performed to the one case that matches the test expression all the other cases are ignored. For example, look at the code fragment in Figure 5.7.

```
/*
** break.c   Illustrates the need for the break statement
*/

#include <stdio.h>

main()
{
    int index = 2;

    switch (index)                  /* the variable 'index' is tested */
       {
       case 1:                      /* if 'index' is 1 we come here */
          printf("w");
       case 2:                      /* if 'index' is 2 we come here */
          printf("xx");             /* we also fall through to all these */
       case 3:                      /*    statements if 'index' is 1 */
          printf("yyy");
       case 4:
          printf("zzzz");
       }
}
```

Figure 5.7 Illustrates Why the `break` Statement is Needed—`breaker.c`

The program `breaker.c` would produce the output,

xxyyyzzzz

because of the absence of the `break` statements. Although this may seem to be a hindrance when coding, it actually allows maximum flexibility. In C the `break` statements can be included or left out at the choice of the programmer.

Note that the special keyword `default` is only used with the `switch` construct to allow code to be executed in the event that each `case` fails. In our menu interface module, we used `default` to handle an invalid menu selection.

5.3.6 *Importance of Braces*

We should reemphasize the importance of using braces even if they are not required. Braces are optional for `if`, `while` and `for` statements. They are also optional for `do` and `switch`, although it is not possible to create a very complex statement without them. This is because the braces create a compound statement in which to put many other statements. Without the braces only one statement can follow the keyword. This is usually very restrictive.

Antibugging Note 5.4   Braces emphasized again

Braces are a great debugging aid because they avoid problems in the first place. Both authors will readily testify that they have unnecessarily lost too much time while programming because of errors which additional braces could have avoided.

5.4   Other Statements

5.4.1   `goto`

The `goto` statement allows a jump to somewhere in the same function. It cannot be used to bypass the normal function invocation and return mechanism. The `goto` statement looks like this:

```
    one_statement;
    goto a_label;
    a_dead_piece_of_code;
a_label:
    went_to_here;
```

The identifier `a_label:` marks a labeled statement within the same function. The `goto` merely transfers control to the label. This can potentially leave a dead piece of code if there is no other labeled statement immediately after the `goto`.

We discourage the use of the `goto` statement (see section 8.1.4), but some books on the C language cite a justified use for it in order to exit from a deeply nested block, for instance when a disaster situation has occurred. For example, suppose that deep within a nested block we attempt to open a file and the attempt is unsuccessful, as in,

```
while (condition_1)
    {
    while (condition_2)
        {
        for (i = 0; i < 3; ++i)
            {
            if (fp = fopen("a_file","r"))
                {
                do_if_successful();
```

```
            }
        else
            goto big_problems;          /* big problems. exit now */
        }
      }
   }
   .
   .
   .
big_problems:
   .                             /* disaster cleanup, never return from here */
   .
   .
```

Note that although such use of the goto statement may seem necessary, it isn't. For example, we could have used a function to handle the error condition like this,

```
int bad_error = FALSE;

while (condition_1 && !bad_error)
    {
    while (condition_2 && !bad_error)
        {
        for (i = 0; i < 3 && !bad_error; ++i)
            {
            if (fp = fopen("a_file","r"))
                {
                do_if_successful();
                }
            else
                {
                bad_error = TRUE;
                clean_it_up();
                }
            }
        }
    }
    .
    .
    .
clean_it_up()
    .                             /* disaster cleanup function */
    .                             /* we never return from here */
    .
```

We don't accept the argument that simply because of overhead a program should issue a `goto` statement rather than invoking a function. Only about 10% of a program's execution time is involved in function invocation and return. Therefore, 90% of the time the program is performing other activities, any of which could probably be speeded up. If a program is so time critical that every possible microsecond of execution time must be purged from the code, then it is a candidate for advanced optimization techniques, not merely a wholesale replacement of functions with `goto` statements. Use an execution profiler or similar product to identify the real source of the program's sluggish behavior.

5.4.2   `null` *Statement*

A `null` statement occurs when the semicolon is coded by itself without any keywords, operators, or anything else occurring before it. It is used when the syntax requires that a statement be coded, but where there is no action to be performed.

A common place for the null statement to appear is after the `while` and `for` statements when there is no block of code needed for the statement body. It also occurs inside the forever loop we discussed above. Sometimes this occurs intentionally, but sometimes programmers include an extra semicolon. By doing so they unintentionally create the null statement and with it incorrect program logic.

For instance, the following situation may look correct at first glance:

```
if(expression_to_be_tested);
    {
    this_statement_is_always_done;
    }
```

Closer inspection, however, reveals the semicolon after the right parenthesis. The semicolon will not generate a syntax error, but the indentation hints that it probably should not be present. What the semicolon does is terminate the body of the `if` statement. In effect, there is no body because the null statement, which is a valid statement in and of itself, constitutes the body. No syntax error occurs from the braces because they become a block of code written in line with the other statements. The block of code is always executed, making the `if` statement always appear to be true. In situations like this a programmer can spend significant time investigating why the `expression_to_be_tested` is never false when the root problem really has nothing to do with the test.

The problem might be clearer if we change the indentation, like this:

```
if(expression_to_be_tested);
{
this_statement_is_always_done;
}
```

Proper indentation is a tremendous help and should be used liberally, but when coupled with incorrect syntax it can be very misleading. In some cases indentation can distract a programmer from correctly identifying problems in the logic of a program.

If there had been an else condition in the above example a syntax error would have occurred because there would have been an else statement without a matching if. The compiler would have issued a message but, as above, if the programmer doesn't see the semicolon then it still "looks" correct. Look at the following:

```
if(expression_to_be_tested);
    {
    this_statement_is_always_done;
    }
else
    {
    now_we_get_an_error;
    }
```

Remember that the examples above can also apply to the while and for statements. The body of these statements can also be a null statement, effectively restricting the action performed to the expression(s) inside the parentheses. For instance, the for statement has the initialization, test, and increment expressions which can still perform action even if the body of the for is null.

We have emphasized the problems with null statements incorrectly affecting program logic, but there are valid uses for having a null body. For example, it can be used as an alternative to braces when using a nested if construct, like this:

```
if(first_test_expression)
    if(second_test_expression)
        true_leg_of_second_test;
    else                                /* completes the second if */
        ;
else
    false_from_first_test;
```

Here the else and solitary semicolon (a null statement) match the second if statement. This insures that the second else and associated false_from_first_test; statement are actually associated with the first if. Remember, appearances can be deceiving!

Now let's consider this code fragment:

```
clear_keyboard_buffer()         /* a function to clear the */
{                               /*   keyboard buffer */
    while(getchar() != EOF)     /* getchar() gets one character */
        ;
    return;
}
```

Here we have coded a function that repeatedly calls getchar() until no more characters are available, effectively clearing out the keyboard buffer. The null statement provides a body for the while loop while getchar() returns (one character at a time) all the characters from the buffer. Since we are only concerned with clearing out the buffer, we simply ignore all the characters unless we see an EOF (end of file) character.

Quick Note 5.6   Indentation doesn't tell the whole story

Indentation can be misleading because the compiler doesn't care how the program looks. Don't trust indentation when examining program logic.

5.5   Self-Check

These statements are True or False. The answers are given at the end.

1. The three basic structured programming constructs are sequence, decision and recursion.

2. Braces delimit a block in C.

3. A semicolon is needed after a closing brace that surrounds a block of code.

4. A compound statement is only a block of code with braces that acts like just one statement.

5. The term block scope describes limiting the visibility of data items defined in a block to only that or lower-level blocks.

6. Variables defined after an opening brace belong to the automatic storage class.

7. Automatic variables retain their value after the block is exited and then reentered.

8. An else must be coded with an if to enable the compiler to tell where the true leg of the if statement ends.

9. The statement for(;5;) is an easy way to make a loop execute only 5 times.

10. The C compiler respects indentation so that you can use it to help indicate nesting levels.

11. The while and for statements are virtually identical so that either can be used in place of the other with slight modifications to the code.

12. The if, while, and for statements always claim the next statement for their body.

13. A forever loop can never be terminated except by ending the program, which is why they call it the forever loop.

14. Nested `while` statements require braces to work correctly.

15. The `while` statement evaluates the test expression at the end of the body.

16. The `do` statement is used infrequently because it executes the body of the `do` at least once.

17. The break statement will terminate only the smallest enclosing `for`, `while`, `do`, or `switch` statement.

18. The `continue` statement allows the `for`, `while`, or do statement to continue execution, beginning with the next iteration.

19. The `switch` statement has limited use because the test expression must reduce to an integer.

20. Once the `case` labels in a `switch` have been used to identify the starting execution point in the body of the `switch`, they are not used again to alter the control flow of program execution.

21. The null statement counts as a complete statement and can be substituted for the body of an `if`, `while`, `for`, or any other set of braces.

Answers

1. F   2. T   3. F   4. T   5. T   6. T   7. F   8. F   9. F   10. F   11. T
12. T   13. F   14. F   15. F   16. T   17. T   18. T   19. T   20. T   21. T

5.6   Review Program—Compute the Area of Various Shapes

In order to review some of the concepts presented in this and previous chapters, we present a C program that uses several control constructs, functions, and various data types.

☐ *Design Specifications*

We wish to write a menu-driven program that allows a user to select various geometric objects, enter required data for each object selection, then output the area of the chosen object. This is a relatively simple task to program, but utilizes various features of the language.

☐ *Program Design*

Pseudocode for the program might look like this:

```
begin main()
    do
        <clear the screen>
        <print the menu>
        <wait for key press—get user's choice>
        <clear the screen>
        switch (<user's choice>)
            case <object 1>
                <display object 1>
                <get data>
                <calculate area>
                <print result>
                break
            case <object 2>
                <display object 2>
                <get data>
                <calculate area>
                <print result>
                break

                    .
                    .
                    .

            case <object n>
                <display object n>
                <get data>
                <calculate area>
                <print result>
                break
            case <exit program>
                break
            default <invalid choice>
                <print error message>
                break
```

```
        endswitch
        if (<exit>)
            continue
        else
            <print wait message>
            <wait for key press>
        endif
    while(<user hasn't chosen to exit>)
    enddo
end main
```

Looking at our pseudocode we decide on the following points:

1. Functions will be written for each object to <calculate area>.

2. We need a function to read a key pressed by the user.

3. We need a function to clear the display.

4. Control constructs needed are evident. We will need:
   a. `do-while`
   b. `switch`
   c. `if-else`

One of the beauties of writing pseudocode is that logic errors can be spotted early in development, long before a single line of code is written. For example, we can readily note that,

```
if (<exit>)
    continue
else
    <print wait message>
    <wait for key press>
endif
```

can be changed to,

```
if ( NOT <exit>)
    <print wait message>
    <wait for key press>
endif
```

eliminating the need for the `continue` statement. For the sake of illustration, however, we will leave it in the program.

Now that we're confident that the program logic is correct, we write the code.

☐ **Design Implementation**

```
/*------------------------------------------------------------
 area.c
 This program allows the user to calculate the area of several
 geometric objects via a simple menu interface.
 ----------------------------------------------------------*/
#include <stdio.h>

#define LINES 25

float rect(), tria(), trap();
                        /* the rectangle and triangle both are developed */
                        /* with long strings using line continuation */
char rectangle[] = "\n\n\
    ---------- \n\
^ |          |\n\
h |          |\n\
v |          |\n\
    ---------- \n\
  <--   l   --> \n\n";

char triangle[] = "\n\n\
  ^ |\\         \n\
  | | \\        \n\
  | |  \\       \n\
  a |   \\      \n\
  |  |    \\    \n\
  | |     \\   \n\
  v |      \\  \n\
     ------- \n\
     <--b--> \n\n";
                        /* the trapezoid is developed with the new ANSI */
                        /* C capability of concatenating literal strings */
char trapezoid[] = "\n\n"
"      <- b1 ->     \n"
"      --------     \n"
"     /    ^   \\    \n"
"    /     h    \\   \n"
"   /      v     \\  \n"
"   -------------- \n"
"   <---  b2  ----> \n\n";
```

```
main()
{
    char selection;
    do {
        cls();                              /* clear the screen */
        printf("Area Calculation Program\n");
        printf("------------------------\n");
        printf("<R>ectangle\n");
        printf("<T>riangle\n");
        printf("Trape<Z>oid\n");
        printf("e<X>it program\n");
        printf("\n\n");
        printf("Select object: ");
        scanf(" %1c", &selection);
        cls();
        switch (selection = toupper(selection))   /* make selection uppercase */
            {
            case 'R':                       /* selected rectangle */
                {
                float l, h;

                printf("%s\n\n", rectangle);
                printf("l ? ");
                scanf("%f", &l);
                printf("h ? ");
                scanf("%f", &h);
                printf("Area is %f\n\n", rect(l,h));
                break;
                }
            case 'T':                       /* selected triangle */
                {
                float a, b;

                printf("%s", triangle);
                printf("Side a ? ");
                scanf("%f", &a);
                printf("Side b ? ");
                scanf("%f", &b);
                printf("Area is %f\n\n", tria(a,b));
                break;
                }
```

(program continued on next page...)

```
        case 'Z':                        /* selected trapezoid */
            {
            float b1, b2, h;

            printf("%s", trapezoid);
            printf("Side b1 ? ");
            scanf("%f", &b1);
            printf("Side b2 ? ");
            scanf("%f", &b2);
            printf("h ? ");
            scanf("%f", &h);
            printf("Area is %f\n\n", trap(b1,b2,h));
            break;
            }
        case 'X':                        /* exit program */
            break;
        default:                         /* bad choice */
            {
            printf("\nInvalid menu choice. Reenter your selection.\n\n");
            }
        }
    if (selection == 'X') {
        continue;
    }
    else {
        printf("\n\nEnter X to exit, any other letter to continue...\n");
        scanf(" %1c", &selection);
        selection = toupper(selection);
    }
  } while (selection != 'X');
    return;
}

/*-----------------------------------------------------------------
 calculate area of rectangle
 ---------------------------------------------------------------*/
float rect(l,h)
float l, h;
{
    return(l * h);
}

/*-----------------------------------------------------------------
 calculate area of right triangle
 ---------------------------------------------------------------*/
float tria(side1,side2)
float side1,side2;
{
    return(rect(side1,side2) / 2);
}
```

```
/*-------------------------------------------------------------
  calculate area of trapezoid
------------------------------------------------------------*/
float trap(top,bottom,height)
float top,bottom,height;
{
   return(((top + bottom) / 2) * height);
}


/*-------------------------------------------------------------
  clear the screen
  (print LINES newlines)
------------------------------------------------------------*/
cls()
{
   int i;

   for (i = 0; i < LINES; ++i) {
      printf("\n");
   }
   return;
}
```

When actually writing programs using top-down principles, we would insert calls to functions, such as `rect()`, `tria()`, and `trap()` in the main function, and write dummy functions. For example, `rect()` might be coded initially as,

```
/*-------------------------------------------------------------
  calculate area of rectangle
------------------------------------------------------------*/
float rect()
{
   return();
}
```

This technique would allow us to test the menu interface first, without having to worry about the details of the various function calls. Later, after thoroughly testing the menu interface, we would code each of the functions necessary to complete the program. As we have mentioned earlier, top-down design allows the programmer to concentrate on one task at a time in a hierarchical fashion.

Now let's look at a sample session running our program.

□ *Program Output*

```
┌─────────────────┐
│ screen cleared  │
└─────────────────┘
```

```
Area Calculation Program
------------------------
<R>ectangle
<T>riangle
Trape<Z>oid
e<X>it program


Select object: z
```

```
┌─────────────────┐
│ screen cleared  │
└─────────────────┘
```

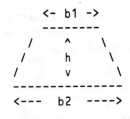

```
        <- b1 ->
        --------
      /     ^     \
     /      h      \
    /       v       \
    -----------------
    <---   b2   ---->
Side b1 ? 12
Side b2 ? 18
h ? 11
Area is   165.000000
```

```
Hit any key to continue...
```

```
┌─────────────────────┐
│ screen cleared      │
└─────────────────────┘
```

```
Area Calculation Program
------------------------
<R>ectangle
<T>riangle
Trape<Z>oid
e<X>it program
```

```
Select object: q
```

```
┌─────────────────────┐
│ screen cleared      │
└─────────────────────┘
```

```
Invalid menu choice. Reenter your selection.
```

```
Hit any key to continue...
```

```
┌─────────────────────┐
│ screen cleared      │
└─────────────────────┘
```

```
Area Calculation Program
------------------------
<R>ectangle
<T>riangle
Trape<Z>oid
e<X>it program

Select object: t
```

(program continued on next page...)

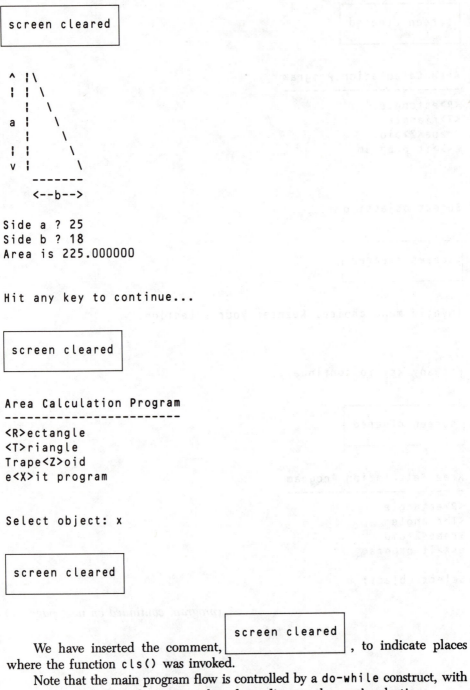

```
┌─────────────────────┐
│  screen cleared     │
└─────────────────────┘


  ^  |\
  |  | \
     |  \
  a  |   \
     |    \
  |  |     \
  v  |      \
     --------
     <--b-->

Side a ? 25
Side b ? 18
Area is 225.000000


Hit any key to continue...


┌─────────────────────┐
│  screen cleared     │
└─────────────────────┘


Area Calculation Program
------------------------
<R>ectangle
<T>riangle
Trape<Z>oid
e<X>it program


Select object: x


┌─────────────────────┐
│  screen cleared     │
└─────────────────────┘
```

┌─────────────────────┐
│ screen cleared   │
└─────────────────────┘

We have inserted the comment,   , to indicate places
where the function `cls()` was invoked.

Note that the main program flow is controlled by a `do-while` construct, with
a `switch` controlling the action taken depending on the user's selection.

Points to Study

1. Use of the \ character for string continuation.

2. Use of the \ character to print the \ character.

3. Use of the return statement in each of the functions. Note that in tria(), we actually invoke another function, rect(), within the return statement.

4. Note that in one function invocation, rect(l,h);, the variable names used when the function is invoked are the same name as the formal parameters in the function definition. This causes no problems because of the scope rules we have discussed.

5. Study the nesting order of each of the flow control constructs used, observing where braces were placed.

5.7   Exercises

1. Convert the following for code fragments to equivalent logic using the while construct:

a.
```
int j;
for (j = 0; j > -12; --j)
    {
    printf("The value of j is %d\n.", j);
    }
```
b.
```
int j;
char c;
char s[20];
c = getchar();
for (c, j = 0; c != '\r'&& j < 20; c = getchar(), ++j)
    {
    s[j] = c;
    }
```
c.
```
int i, j, k;
for (i = 0; i < 10; ++i)
    {
    for (j = 0; j < 10; ++j)
        {
        for (k = 0; k < 10; ++k)
            {
            printf("The value of i * j * k is %d when \n", i * j * k);
            printf("\t i = %d, j = %d, k = %d\n\n", i, j, k);
            }
        }
    }
```

```
d. int i, j;
   for (i = 0, j = 10; j > i; ++i, --j)
       ;
```

2. Convert the following `while` code fragments to equivalent logic using the `for` construct:

```
a. int i = 0;
   while (i < 10)
       ++i;
b. char c;

   while (more_files())
       {
       while ((c = fgetc(fp)) != EOF)
           {
           print_it(c);
           }
       fp = next_file();
       }
c. while (we_are_not_alone())
       {
       say_hi();
       while (they_want_to_talk())
           {
           talk_some_more();
           }
       if (they_are_leaving())
           say_goodbye();
       }
```

* 3. Write a program to calculate all the possible ways to make change for a dollar bill, including all combinations of pennies, nickels, dimes, quarters, and half dollars. Your program output should include each combination found and the total number of combinations. A sample output could look like this:

Halves	Quarters	Dimes	Nickels	Pennies
0	0	0	0	100
0	0	0	1	95
0	0	0	2	90
0	0	0	3	85
		.		
		.		
		.		
1	2	0	0	0
2	0	0	0	0

There are a total of ?? combinations of ways to change a dollar.

(?? of course we're not going to tell you!)

4. What would be the output of the following program? (We have left out indentation purposely.)

```
char s[] = "abcdefghijklmnopqrstuvwxyz";

main()
{
int i, j;
for (i = 0; i < sizeof(s); ++i)
{
printf("i = %d\n", i);
if (i % 2)
for (j = i; j; --j)
printf("%c", s[i]);
printf("\n");
}
return;
}
```

5. Describe the output of the following code fragments:
   a.
```
   int i, j;
   i = 3;
   do
       {
       for (j = 0; j < i; ++j)
           {
           printf("i = %d, j = %d\n", i, j);
           if (i * j >= 6)
               break;
           }
       }
   while (--i > 0);
```
   b.
```
   signed int q, r;
   for (r = -1; r <= 1; ++r)
       {
       for (q = -1; q <= 1; ++q)
           {
           if (!(q || r))
               continue;
           printf("%d,%d\n", q, r);
           }
       }
```

```
   c.  int x, y;

       for (x = 10;; --x)
          {
          for (y = 10;; --y)
             {
             printf("%d,%d\n", x, y);
             if (!y)
                break;
             }
          if (!x)
             break;
          }
   d.  char h1[] = "msaei w avs";
       char h2[] = "esg ntohle";
       int i = 0;
       int j = 0

       while (h1[i])
          {
          printf("%c", h1[i]);
          ++i;
          if (!h2[j])
             continue;
          else
             {
             printf("%c", h2[j]);
             ++j;
             }
          }
```

6. Now, code each of the examples in Exercise 5 without the use of `break` or `continue`.

7. Give the output produced by the following function calls to a function, `rep_char()`, coded as follows:

```
rep_char(c,n)
char c;
int n;
{
    switch(c)
       {
       case ' ':
          {
          while (n--)
             printf(" ");
          break;
          }
```

```
case '-':
    {
    while (n--)
        printf("-");
    break;
    }
case '/':
    {
    while (n--)
        printf("/");
    break;
    }
case '?':
    {
    while (n--)
        printf("?");
    break;
    }
    }
return;
}
```

a. rep_char('-',5);
b. rep_char('?',3);
c. rep_char(' ',7);

Write a simpler version of rep_char() using only a while loop.

8. Write a program to encode or decode a message entered by the user according to the following simple encryption algorithm:

Original Character	Substitution Character
a (A)	z (Z)
b (B)	y (Y)
c (C)	x (X)
.	.
.	.
.	.
z(Z)	a (A)
digits/punctuation	no change

Your program should include a simple menu, and error trapping where appropriate. A sample session might look like this:

```
Encryption Menu
---------------
<E>ncode a message
<D>ecode a message
e<X>it program

Enter your choice: e

Enter message to encode:
This is a message to encode, testing 1,2,3.

Encoded message:
GSRH RH Z NVHHZTV GL VMXLWV, GVHGRMT 1,2,3.



Encryption Menu
---------------
<E>ncode a message
<D>ecode a message
e<X>it program

Enter your choice: f

Enter E, D or X only!

Encryption Menu
---------------
<E>ncode a message
<D>ecode a message
e<X>it program

Enter your choice: x
```

9. Identify syntax errors in the following code fragments,
   a. `int m,n;`

```
        for (m = 0, m < 10; ++m)
          n += m;
          printf("%d", n);
          }
```

   b. `char c, s[80];`
       `int i = 0;`

```
        while ((c = getchar()) != '\r' && i < 80);
          {
          s[i++] = c;
          };
```

```
c.  int z = 0, y = 10, w = 8;

    do {
        y = y * z / w;
        }
    while (++z < 20)
```

*advanced exercise

5.8   Pretest

☐ *Multiple Choice*

Circle one correct answer for each for the following:

1. What would the following loop do:

```
while(5)
    ;
```

    a. Cause a compiler syntax error.
    b. Loop forever.
    c. Really need a `break` statement.
    d. Work better coded as a `for()` loop.

2. The `break` statement is used to,
    a. Exit early from a loop or `switch()` construct.
    b. Exit early from a function call.
    c. Invoke operating system calls.
    d. Cause a temporary halt in program execution.

3. The following loop,

```
for (i = 0; i < 5; ++i)
   printf("%d", i);
```

would be equivalent to,

a. ```
    i = 0;
    do {
        printf("%d", i);
    } while (++i);
    ```

b.  ```
    while (i = 0)
        {
        printf("%d", i);
        ++i;
        }
    ```

c. ```
    i = 0;
    while (i < 5)
        {
        printf("%d", i);
        ++i;
        }
    ```

d.  ```
    i = 0;
    while (i++ < 5)
        {
        printf("%d", i);
        }
    ```

4. What would be the output produced by the following code fragment:

```
char c = 'b';
switch (c)
    {
    case 'a':
        printf("%c", 'a');
    case 'b':
        printf("%c", 'b');
    case 'c':
        printf("%c", 'c');
    default:
        printf("%c", 'z');
    }
```
   a. b
   b. abcz
   c. bc
   d. bcz

5. An indeterminate loop is one in which:
   a. The variable values cannot be predetermined.
   b. The number of loop iterations is not known in advance.
   c. The number of loop iterations is known in advance.
   d. The scope cannot be determined.

6. What would be the output produced by the following code fragment:

```
int i;

i = 1;
printf("%d", i);
{
    int i = 2;
    printf("%d", i);
}
printf("%d", i);
```
   a. 120
   b. 122
   c. 121
   d. undefined because of last printf() statement

7. The visibility of a global variable means that it is:
   a. local to external functions
   b. capable of being modified by any block
   c. of local scope
   d. not capable of being modified except by main()

8. The concept top-down program design means:
   a. Writing code sequentially from top to bottom.
   b. Adhering strictly to the four stages of general program design.
   c. Design first, debug second, documentation last.
   d. Designing a program from the abstract level to the specific, in incremental steps.

9. A for() loop is best used when,
   a. A determinant looping construct is indicated.
   b. Two or more nesting levels are required.
   c. The variable i is needed.
   d. There are logical tests to be performed.

10. A compound statement in C is one in which:
   a. Sequential statements are executed.
   b. A block of code contains expressions and function calls.
   c. Braces enclose one or more statements.
   d. No expressions exist in the statement.

6

Functions

I n this chapter we will explain the concept of functions. Functions are the way subroutines are created in the C language, and most programs of significant size contain at least one function other than main(). The use of functions enhances program modularity, and facilitates writing well-structured, easily maintained code.

After studying this chapter, you will be able to do the following:

1. Define and invoke a function.

2. Declare in advance the return type of a function and the type of each argument to be passed to the function.

3. Define the terms actual arguments and formal parameters.

4. Explain the difference between call by value and call by reference.

5. Write a simple recursive function.

6.1 The Concept of Functions

A *function* in the C language is like a FUNCTION or subprogram in compiled BASIC, a function or subroutine in FORTRAN, and a function or procedure in Pascal. C functions, however, are very flexible. They can be invoked while inside expressions and statements, and from almost any other place in a program. Not only can they perform work but they can also return one value, which replaces the function name wherever the name is used in the invoking program. Functions allow us to break programs into smaller pieces, and smaller program parts are always easier to write and maintain than larger ones.

The execution of a function is hidden from the caller, i.e., the part of the program that called the function is not aware of how the function operates. Normally a function is not able to modify (or destroy!) data belonging to the part of the program that called it. Also, when a function is defined the decision is made whether any data items will be passed to the function. These data items are either copies of other data items or else the addresses in the computer where the items are located. When the function is finished it can, if defined to do so, pass back one (and only one) value which is represented by the name of the function. This return value can either be a piece of data itself, or it can be the location where a piece of data is stored.

Antibugging Note 6.1   Make liberal use of functions

Make liberal use of functions and break large functions into smaller ones. Only after the program works correctly in all circumstances should you examine the overhead of function invocation.

6.2   Function Definitions

The definition of a function consists of writing the name of the function, a parameter list, and the body of the function. This process creates the function. The function can then be called from any part of the program. Although a function can be written entirely on one line (remember that C programs are free-form and lines are not required) we will write them in a readable format using multiple lines. Figure 6.1 shows an example of a function.

```
                        Line:
int my_func(a, b)       /* 1:  return type, name, and parameter list */
int a;                  /* 2:  definition of parameters begins here */
float b;                /* 3:  the order of these illustrates a point */
{                       /* 4:  begin the function body */
    printf("my_func was sent the values %d and %f", a, b);    /* 5:  body */
    return(1);          /* 6:  the function name will have a value of 1 now */
}                       /* 7:  end the function body and the function */
```

Figure 6.1   Typical Function Definition

Line 1 contains the function return type, function name, and parameter list. The parameter list of the function in Figure 6.1 is not empty. The first word, int, is the return type. If the return type is left out, int is assumed. We suggest for clarity that the return type always be supplied even if it is int. The function my_func() can return one piece of data which has the type of integer.

The function name appears next, separated from the return type by one or more spaces. Functions are named in the same way as variables, so the same rules about how long they can be and what characters they can contain apply here.

The left parenthesis identifies the beginning of the parameter list, and since it is a symbol (rather than a letter or number) it can be placed immediately after the function name. A space can be left between the function name and left parenthesis if desired. Inside the parentheses are the names of the parameters, which represent the data passed to the function. The order of the names inside the parentheses must agree with the order of the data items they match in every argument list where the function is invoked. We'll say more about that below.

Finally, it is very important to note that there is no semicolon after the closing right parenthesis on line 1. Including one will cause all sorts of errors.

Line 2 begins the process of identifying or declaring the types of the parameters. For clarity it is a good idea to declare parameters in the same order as they appear in the parameter list, although this is not required. Regardless of the order, every parameter must be declared. Unlike the situation with the function return type, the type of int is not assumed if left off a parameter declaration. In our example function my_func() the variable b is a float and a is an int. Note that a semicolon should follow the variable name just like a variable declared anywhere else. More than one variable can be declared on each line if all variables have the same type.

The left brace (also called *opening brace*) on line 4 identifies the beginning of the function body. It is usually placed on a line by itself, and sometimes it is indented three spaces. It could have been placed at the end of the previous line, but we think that isn't very readable.

The body of a function contains code just like the code that might be placed in the main() function. There are absolutely no restrictions on the type of statements that can appear inside a function (except that a function cannot be defined while inside another function). There are some rules, however, on what pieces of data can be accessed while the flow of program control is in the function. We'll discuss more about this in the section on local variables.

The function body, and hence the definition of the entire function, ends when a right brace (also called *closing brace*) like the one on line 7 is encountered. It is not required that the opening and closing braces be aligned, although that certainly helps readability. Note that there is no semicolon after the closing brace. Semicolons only appear after closing braces when data is being defined, not when we are writing code. A function is a body or block of code, so the semicolon is not used.

Here are some examples of very simple functions. These will illustrate how a function definition is written if certain parts are left out:

```
A. my_func2()    /* the return type is int (assumed) */
   {             /* there are no parameters for this function */
     printf("my_func2 was sent no values\n");
   }             /* with no return statement the return value is undefined */
B. float my_func3(x)    /* the return type is float with one parameter */
   int x;              /* the parameter 'x' is expected to be an integer */
   {                   /* there was 1 parameter for this function */
     printf("my_func3 was sent 1 value\n");
     return(2.5);      /* we return a constant value */
   }
```

The ANSI C standard introduced a different style of writing function declarations and definitions. The style we showed above will be called the "classic" style in this book, and the style which was added by the ANSI standard will be described as the "modern" style. The basic difference is that the modern style includes the type of the identifier inside the parameter list rather than declaring the parameter types on subsequent lines. For instance, the above parameter list and opening brace would be written in the new modern style like this when defining the function:

```
int my_func(int a, float b)
{
```

If two adjacent parameters have the same data type, the type specifier must be repeated. For instance, if the function `my_func` had two integer parameters rather than an `int` and a `float` its definition would begin this way:

```
int my_func(int a, int b)        /* right */
{
```

rather than like this:

```
int my_func(int a, b)            /* wrong */
{
```

The modern style is more clear than the classic style because the parameter types are located right next to the parameter names. The form of the new style also makes it easier to create the function prototypes (which will be covered next). However, not all compilers support this new style yet, and the classic style should be used if portable code is needed.

6.3   Function Declarations (Prototypes)

When we use the word definition in conjunction with data variables we mean that storage for the variable is being reserved as part of the definition process. The same concept applies to functions. Above we saw that the definition of a function actually created a body of code which we could then call or invoke. Some aspects of a function are declared rather than defined however. These declarations do not create the function or parts of it, but rather describe the function as a whole or certain parts contained inside.

6.3.1   *Actual Arguments and Formal Parameters*

We should clarify the difference between two terms which we will be using frequently from now on through the end of the book. The first term is *actual arguments*. This refers to the data items actually passed to a function. The second term is *formal parameters*, which refers to the names used inside the parentheses when defining a function. There is a correlation between actual arguments and formal parameters, but the two things are not the same. Consider the following function:

```
int my_func4(a, b)
int a;
float b;
{
    printf("my_func4 was sent the values of %d and %f\n", a, b);
}
```

Here a and b are the formal parameters of function my_func4(). They do not exist in the same sense that a variable being defined has storage reserved for it. Rather, their names refer to the data items that will be passed to the function. The contents of a and b will assume the new values, which are passed each time the function is called. To call this function we might write:

```
main()
{
    int my_result;              /* define an integer without a value */
    int x = 5;                  /* define x with an initial value */
    float y = 7.0;              /* define y with an initial value */
    my_result = my_func4(x, y); /* pass x and y, return my_result */
}
```

The formal parameter a assumes the value of 5 from the variable x, while the formal parameter b assumes the value of 7.0 from the variable y. Note that the values of x and y are copied and sent to my_func4(). The function does not have access to the actual variables x and y (i.e., the original data items from which the copies were made) and hence cannot change them. Any changes made to a and b in the function affect only the copies of the variables x and y, not the original x and y.

Quick Note 6.1   Actual Arguments and Formal Parameters

Actual arguments are used when invoking a function, while formal parameters are used when defining a function.

6.3.2   *Declaring the Function Return Type*

We've mentioned that if the function return type is not included in the definition of a function, the int type is assumed. Obviously if the return type is not included and a type of data other than int is expected to be returned, then at minimum the return value will be incorrect. Worse yet, the type returned might appear to be close, but not right on target, making debugging very difficult or even tricking the programmer into thinking that all is well. For example, this code fragment appears (on the surface) to return the value with a type of float:

```
my_func5(a)             /* the return type is int by default */
float a;
{
   return(2.0 * a);   /* we only think we're returning a float */
}
```

The problem here is that while the function parameters, function body, and return statement are all coded correctly, the function return type has been left out, causing a default return type of integer to be assumed. This means that although we multiply the parameter a by 2.0, thereby creating another float value, the new float value is then converted to integer to be returned as the value which the function name represents. Using 2 rather than 2.0 would yield the same wrong result since the integer 2 would be promoted to the data type of float before the multiplication takes place. For instance, if the parameter a contained the value of 3.25, then 2.0 times 3.25 or 6.5 would be the value of the return statement expression. However, the conversion to integer causes 6.0 to be returned because the return value is truncated (not rounded).

The first line of the function should have been written like this:

```
float my_func5(a)       /* the return type is now set to float */
```

which would have allowed the return statement to retain the float type.

However, just because we include the return type when we define the function does not mean that the return type will be known when we call the function. The C language does not require that functions be defined ahead of any point in a program where they are called. The convention is to code the main() function first followed by all the functions called from inside main(). If the function my_func5() is to be invoked while in main(), then we need to tell main() to expect a float value to be returned from my_func5() rather than an integer value. We do this by declaring the function my_func5() before the point in main() where my_func5() is called. The declaration looks like this:

```
float my_func5();
```

Note what is different about this declaration. First, there is no parameter name inside the parentheses. The purpose of this statement is to declare the function return type, so no parameter names are needed. Second, there is a semicolon after the right parenthesis. The presence of the semicolon terminates the declaration and specifies that this is a declaration, not a function definition. The whole arrangement would then look like this:

```
float my_func5();             /* the function declaration */

a_float_variable = my_func5(another_float_variable); /* calling my_func */
```

When declaring a function that will not be returning a value, even an integer, use the `void` keyword. This function declaration:

```
void func_returns_nothing();
```

says that the function `func_returns_nothing()` will not be returning a value. It says to be on the watch for how the function is used and check that the function name is not used as if it represented a return value. The `void` keyword has been added by the ANSI standard to indicate this situation, but not all compilers support it yet. When using a compiler that supports the `void` keyword, be sure to use it to declare the return type for all functions that do not return a value through the `return` statement.

Some compilers may require that functions which return a value must make an assignment of that return value. Often, however, the return value is ignored when using some of the standard library functions. A good example is `printf()`. Many C programmers probably do not even realize that `printf()` returns the number of characters output by the function. This return value is seldom used, but indispensable when needed. Strict type checking by a compiler would require that this be written:

```
(void) printf(...)
```

if the return value from `printf()` should be ignored.

The technique of declaring the return type of a function in advance has been available for many years. Some people refer to this declaration as a *function prototype*, i.e., a model of the function itself. This book will follow the convention established by the ANSI standard. We will use the term function prototype to describe the process of declaring both the return and argument types of a function. We'll describe the process of declaring the argument types in the next section.

Quick Note 6.2   Function Return Types

If the return type of a function is not declared before the function is invoked, then a return type of integer is assumed. This can cause significant problems if integer is not the type of data that is really being returned.

6.3.3   *Declaring the Function Parameter Types*

No assumption is made about the data types of the parameters of a function. The type of each parameter must be declared when the function is defined or else the compiler generates an error. Further, just because the data types are declared when the function is defined does not mean that the correct data types will be used when the function is called. A feature called *argument type checking* has been included as part of the recent ANSI C standard so that one of the most common errors in

C programming can be eliminated—that being the mismatch of data types between actual arguments (used when a function is called) and formal parameters (used when a function is defined). This feature, argument type checking, is an extension of checking the function return type.

Consider this example from the last section:

```
my_func5(a)
float a;               /* we are expecting a float value to be sent */
{
    return(2 * a);
}
```

If we call this function with an integer data item, like this:

```
int    send_to_my_func;      /* oops - we are not sending a float */
float get_from_my_func;

get_from_my_func = my_func5(send_to_my_func);
```

then we are going to have some strange results. We will be placing an integer into the area where data is stored while on its way to a function (the stack in most computers). However, the function is expecting a float value to be in this area and it will obtain a float value regardless of what was actually placed there. Obviously it will obtain the wrong value, and the result of getting this wrong value is unpredictable. The effects can range from a wrong answer to the program crashing or the whole machine locking up.

The way to avoid this problem is to declare the function argument types at the same time that the return type is declared. To continue with the example from above where both a float return type and a float argument type are used, we would write the function declaration like this:

```
float my_func5(float);
```

The only difference between this declaration and the one above where only the function return type is declared is the presence of a type specifier inside the parentheses. This tells us that the function is expecting one argument of type float. If we place this declaration statement at the beginning of the program, our code will be checked both when we call the function and also when we define it. This insures that we always expect a float return type and that we always pass one float argument. This form of declaration is a complete function prototype because it includes both the return and argument type. If a prototype has already been encountered earlier in the program, then when either a call to the function or the function definition is encountered they are checked to make sure that both the return type and the argument type(s) match the prototype. If the return type does not match and cannot be made to match through a data conversion (such as integer to float), or if there are the wrong number or type of arguments, an error message appears. The actual intensity of the checking and the particular message received will depend on the compiler.

For example, another declaration might be:

```
char my_func6(int, char, float);
```

which indicates that our function expects to receive three arguments of type `int`, `char` and `float` (in that order) and will return a value of type `char`. If we try to call the function this way:

```
my_char = my_func6(1, 'a', 2.0, 'X');
```

we will get an error because there are more than three arguments.

It's possible to define a function that can receive a variable number of arguments. The standard library function `printf()` is just such a function. Its prototype looks something like this:

```
int printf(char *, ...);      /* the printf function prototype */
```

Here we see `printf()` declared as a function that returns an integer and that has only one required argument, a pointer to a data item of type character (we'll study pointers in the next few chapters). The three dots, an ellipsis, which appear just before the right parenthesis indicate that more arguments can follow but the exact number is not specified. We know this to be the case because when we described the `printf()` function we mentioned that the only required argument was the control string (represented by the character pointer argument), but that other arguments could also be used.

The next examples of `printf()` are all valid and can be checked against the same prototype:

```
printf("A message with only the control string");
printf("A message with one additional argument, %c", 'x');
printf("A message with two additional arguments, %c and %d", 'x', 5);
```

To create a function that receives no data when it is called, the `void` keyword is used in the same way that it is used when declaring the return type. For example, the declaration:

```
void clear_screen(void);
```

says that the `clear_screen()` function (which presumably clears the screen) neither accepts any arguments nor returns any value. Remember that `void` is a feature of the new ANSI standard and only recent compilers and compiler upgrades will include that keyword.

The standard library functions (e.g., `getchar()`, `printf()`, etc.) have prototypes provided in the header files that come with the compiler. Using these prototypes in a program will help check each invocation of the standard functions. The prototypes will at minimum guarantee that the correct function return type is being expected. Prototypes provided with better compilers will also check that the correct function argument types have been passed.

Some compilers may require that one or more switches be set or constants be defined for the prototypes to be placed into effect. At the very least the appropriate header files must be included in each program. These headers should be placed at the top of the file so that they appear before any of the standard library functions. Check the Appendix D for a list of the standard library functions and the header files needed for each.

As we mentioned above, the modern style of declaring the parameter type(s) for my_func4() could be used by including in the parameter list an actual parameter name. This would allow the function declaration and function definition statements to be identical, making it easier to write and double-check the program.

Many programmers use more than one compiler, and it is possible that two different compilers would each support a different style of prototypes (because of different compiler versions, lack of conformity to the ANSI standard, etc.). One way of dealing with such situations is to write different prototypes and surround them with preprocessor directives like this:

```
#ifdef MODERN_STYLE
    int my_func(char a, int b, float c);
#else
    #ifdef CLASSIC_STYLE
        int my_func(char, int, float);
    #else
        int my_func();  /* use this if only return type can be declared */
    #endif
#endif
```

All that is required to include the modern style prototype in the program is to place this preprocessor directive somewhere before the above code fragment:

```
#define MODERN_STYLE
```

Likewise the directive

```
#define CLASSIC_STYLE
```

will cause the classic style prototype to be compiled. The absence of either of the #define directives will cause the early style prototype to be included. This early style defines only the function return type and provides no help at all in checking the argument types. In this book we will use both the classic and modern styles in our code fragments and program examples.

What happens if a function does not have a prototype? Sam Harbinson, of Tartan Labs, suggested the solution which the ANSI standard committee adopted. His idea was that the compiler would construct a prototype based on the form of the function invocation. If a function has no prototype and is invoked once with one set of argument types, and then again with another set of types, an error should result. P. J. Plauger labeled this proposal the Miranda Rule because it reminded him of the famous court decision regarding what arresting officers must tell suspects. Here is how it applies to C:

You have the right to remain silent
about your arguments.

You have the right to a function prototype.

If you cannot afford a function prototype,
one will be appointed for you
by the translator (compiler).

Figure 6.2   Miranda Rule of C

This suggestion provided a way for ANSI standard conforming compilers to process both types of programs; those with and without prototypes.

Antibugging Note 6.2   Function Argument Types

Be fanatical about declaring both the function return type and the function argument types at the top of each program. This will eliminate one of the most common errors made by C programmers—disagreement between function argument and parameter lists. Use the header files supplied by the vendor to gain access to the standard library function prototypes.

6.4   Function Invocation

We've shown a number of examples of how functions are called or invoked. It should be clear that a function is called by writing the function name and following the name with a left or open parenthesis. Spaces can appear between the function name and the parenthesis, the same rule we used when defining a function. If arguments are passed to the function, they will be coded inside the parentheses. There may or may not be a semicolon after the right parenthesis, depending on the expression in which the function invocation is found.

For example, the following are all valid function calls:

```
A. getchar();              /* we get a character and do nothing with it */
```

B. `char input_char;`
   `input_char = getchar();   /* we get a character and put it somewhere */`

C. `char input_char;`
   `input_char = getchar() + 1;`
   `            /* add one to the character value before saving */`
   `            /* note the semicolon appears after the '1' */`

These should all be self-explanatory except possibly example C. Since the `getchar()` function returns a numeric value representing the character (e.g. A is 65 decimal, 41 hex, a is 97 decimal, 61 hex, etc.), we can perform arithmetic on that value before storing it in a variable. If we had read the character A, which equates numerically to a decimal 65, then by adding one we would have created a B.

What distinguishes a function declaration from a very simple invocation? Looking at these examples,

`int my_func();  /* the declaration */`

`my_func();      /* a simple invocation with an ignored return value */`

we see that the presence of a type specifier before the function name and the absence of anything after the closing parenthesis identify the first line as a declaration. Writing this,

`int my_func() + 3;`

will also guarantee an error. Prototypes cannot perform any other work except to define the "skeleton" of the function.

Another word of caution. Some compilers don't detect if parentheses are left out when a function name is written. For example, while this should be coded:

`getchar();   /* get and discard a character */`

but this is written instead:

`getchar;     /* generates a pointer only, not an invocation */`

there might not be any error message, but the results would be incorrect. Better compilers will recognize this as an error.

Finally, remember that earlier we showed that this function invocation:

`my_func(++i, i, ++i);`

produces a number of possible combinations of values to be passed to `my_func()`. When used to separate function arguments the comma is a punctuator, not a sequence operator. The comma does not guarantee that the arguments of a function invocation will be evaluated in any particular order.

The same is true if we use arguments that are return values from a function, like this:

```
myfunc(x(), y(), z());
```

In this example there is absolutely no guarantee of the order in which x(), y(), and z() will be invoked. Do not let the results of one function affect the results of another if both are used as arguments in the same function invocation.

6.4.1   *Call by Value vs. Call by Reference*

If the following statements are coded:

```
int my_func_return;                       /* the return variable */
int my_func_arg = 10;                     /* the argument variable */
my_func_return = my_func(my_func_arg);    /* send the argument value */
```

many computer languages would pass to my_func() the address of the variable my_func_arg. This would allow my_func() to change the contents of my_func_arg. We would have to trust my_func() not to destroy my_func_arg or to leave it unusable. This type of situation is described as *call by reference*, meaning that when the function is invoked the argument values passed to the function allow the function to reference the original data directly.

Rather than giving the function access to my_func_arg a safer technique is to give my_func() a copy of my_func_arg. This is similar to giving someone a photocopy of a document rather than the actual document itself. It is this technique that the C language uses, and the description for it is *call by value*. When an argument is used in an argument list the value of the argument (i.e., a copy of the item rather than its address) is placed where the data being sent to the function is stored (the stack in many computers). The function can then access this data (a copy of the original item) and the rest of the program can be assured that the data items named in the argument list remain safe.

C does provide the ability to pass to a function the address of a data item (i.e., it is possible to create a call by reference condition). This is necessary because sometimes a function must have access to the original data items themselves, not just copies. For example, if a function needs to exchange the value of two data items then it must be able to access both items. The return value of the function returns only one value, enabling only one of the values to be changed by that mechanism (without some sort of encoding scheme). To pass to my_func() the address of my_func_arg rather than the value of my_func_arg this would be coded:

```
my_func_return = my_func(&my_func_arg);   /* send the argument address */
```

When we discussed scanf() we mentioned that the & symbol means to take the address of the item which appears next. By coding &my_func_arg the function my_func() will receive the address of my_func_arg rather than a copy of its value. Now we must trust my_func() not to corrupt or destroy my_func_arg. In later chapters we will discuss how to declare the parameters of my_func() so that it can receive the address of an argument rather than the value. It is not important to cover all the details of that process right now, but this diagram may help illustrate the situation:

```
2000     <- location of my_func_arg in the computer

 42      <- contents of my_func_arg
```

Assume that the data item my_func_arg is located at address 2000 in the computer and that it contains the value 42. If we use call by reference, the value 2000 will be sent to the function. This will provide the function with the location of my_func_arg in the computer. The function can then update my_func_arg directly. If we use call by value, the value 42 will be sent to the function. This will not provide the function with the address of my_func_arg but will give the function a copy of my_func_arg instead.

Some types of data (pointer variables, array names, function names, etc.) are an address of something by their very nature. When any of these items is passed by value to a function the passed value is by definition an address, which gives the function access to the data to which the pointer points. This does not contradict the basic call by value nature of C because in fact a copy of the pointer is passed rather than the address of the pointer. It is then possible to alter the data to which the pointer points.

It is sometimes necessary to pass the addresses of data items to a function rather than the values of the items. A good example is illustrated by the program in Figure 6.3.

```
/*
** exchange.c - An Example of Call by Reference
*/

#include <stdio.h>              /* has function prototypes */

void exchange(int *, int *);    /* function prototype */

int array[] = {10,55,3,75,45,23,1};  /* size is automatically set */
                                      /* some compilers still do not */
                                      /* allow initialization of arrays */
                                      /* during definition unless the */
                                      /* array is global */
```

(program continued on next page...)

```
main()
{
    printf("[0] = %d, [3] = %d\n", array[0], array[3]);

    exchange(&array[0], &array[3]);       /* exchange 10 and 75 */

    printf("[0] = %d, [3] = %d\n", array[0], array[3]);
}

void exchange(element_ptr1, element_ptr2)
int *element_ptr1, *element_ptr2;                   /* be sure to read the */
{                                                   /* explanation below */
    int temp;
    temp = *element_ptr1;
    *element_ptr1  = *element_ptr2;
    *element_ptr2  = temp;
    return;
}
```

Figure 6.3   An Example of Call by Reference—exchange.c

Before the call to exchange() the array looks like this (notice that an integer array has no trailing NULL value to mark the end):

| 10 | 55 | 3 | 75 | 45 | 23 | 1 | <- array elements
|----|----|---|----|----|----|---|
| [0] | [1] | [2] | [3] | [4] | [5] | [6] | <- array subscripts

while after the call it looks like this:

75	55	3	10	45	23	1
[0]	[1]	[2]	[3]	[4]	[5]	[6]

It is not our intention to emphasize pointers in this chapter. We simply mention in passing that the symbol & means use the data item that appears next as a pointer to tell where to get a piece of data. Our intention in the function exchange() is to swap the array elements referenced by element_ptr1 and element_ptr2. By passing the address of each element, we use the addresses to reference the original copies of the data items themselves. Those original items can then be exchanged.

If a copy of each element (rather than the address of each element) was sent to the function, the elements could not be exchanged. A copy would be passed if the function invocation were coded like this (of course the function must be rewritten too):

```
exchange(array[0], array[3]);
```

If the values of the array elements are passed, the function would not have access to the original pieces of data. That lack of access would prevent the function from accomplishing the exchange. The integers would be passed by value rather than by reference, and the main portion of the program would be shielded from any damage exchange() might inadvertently cause.

This particular program also could have been written to pass subscript values rather than addresses. This alternate technique would also allow the exchange to take place. Passing subscripts rather than pointers (addresses) would require that that the function exchange() have access to the array itself. It would have to reference the array by name rather than referencing the elements through pointers. The exchange could be accomplished just as easily, but the array would have to be visible within the function. This technique does not work on all variables, only arrays. If there were a need to exchange (by passing to a function) separately defined integers which were not array elements then this problem of exchanging data items would be even more difficult. The examples using array elements were intentionally chosen so that different exchange methods could be illustrated.

The program in Figure 6.4 illustrates this point, i.e., it accomplishes the exchange by passing subscripts to the function rather than array element addresses. Note that the function has been changed slightly to receive integers rather than the addresses of integers.

```
/*
** exchgsub.c - One Alternative to Call by Reference
*/

#include <stdio.h>              /* has function prototypes */

void exchange(int, int);        /* function prototype */

int array[] = {10,55,3,75,45,23,1};  /* size is automatically set */
```

(program continued on next page...)

```
main()
{
    printf("[0] = %d, [3] = %d\n", array[0], array[3]);

    exchange(0, 3);                    /* exchange 10 and 75 */

    printf("[0] = %d, [3] = %d\n", array[0], array[3]);
}

void exchange(sub1, sub2)
int sub1, sub2;
{
    int temp;
    temp = array[sub1];
    array[sub1] = array[sub2];
    array[sub2] = temp;
    return;
}
```

Figure 6.4 One Alternative to Call by Reference—exchgsub.c

6.4.2 *Effect of Function Return Type*

We've mentioned that not declaring the function return type causes a return type of integer to be assumed for the function. Even if the return() statement contains an expression of type float the final value of the expression is converted to an integer. Consider the example program in Figure 6.5.

```
/*
** intsub.c - A Function with Integer Return Type
*/

#include <stdio.h>                /* has the library function prototypes */

main()
{
    printf("\"%d\"\n", sub());  /* print the result from calling sub() */
}
```

```
sub()                           /* a return type of int assumed */
{
    float x = 2.5;
    return (x);                 /* the 2.5 is converted to an integer */
}
```

Figure 6.5 A Function with Integer Return Type—`intsub.c`

In this example "2" is printed. Although we tried to return 2.5, it is converted to an integer and properly printed by the `printf()` statement. If we try to correct the situation by changing the `printf()` statement to this:

```
printf("\"%f\"\n", sub());
```

we just mess up the situation further because now the `printf()` statement has a problem. The control string has a conversion character of float, but the one argument (the function call to `sub()`) is of type integer (the type of the function definition). The `printf()` function will be looking for a float, but only an integer will be present, yielding unpredictable results. Note also that this shows another example of where function invocation can occur, i.e., to generate the argument for another function.

You might think that adding a type cast of float to the `sub()` argument would help, like this:

```
printf("\"%f\"\n", (float) sub());
```

This doesn't do much except make the `printf()` statement control string and subsequent argument agree. It doesn't solve the fundamental problem, which is that the function `sub()` still returns an integer.

The only way to solve the problem completely is to add the word `float` in front of the name of the function `sub()` when it is defined. This will cause the float type from the return statement to be retained and will prevent the return statement from converting the return value to an integer (causing truncation). Then we must also declare that the function is not returning an integer so that when the function is used it is understood that the return type is float. We do this by coding a function declaration (prototype) at the beginning of the program before calling the function. The final program (which works correctly) is shown in Figure 6.6.

```
/*
** floatsub.c - A Function with Float Return Type
*/

#include <stdio.h>               /* has function prototypes */
float sub(void);                 /* function declaration of sub() */

main()
{
    printf("\"%f\"\n", sub());   /* print sub's result */
}

float sub()
{
    float x = 2.5;
    return (x);                  /* 2.5 remains a float */
}
```

Figure 6.6   A Function with Float Return Type—`floatsub.c`

The return and argument types of `printf()` are checked by including `stdio.h` in our program. This is because the `stdio.h` header contains the function prototype for `printf()`. The function declaration of `sub()` insures that any use of `sub()` is interpreted as returning a float value, with no arguments allowed in the argument list. This line is really the key to the proper solution since the use of `sub()` in the `printf()` statement and the definition of `sub()` both will be checked to see that they agree with this declaration. The program then prints the final answer of "2.500000".

6.5   Local, Automatic, and Static Variables

We've mentioned that variables can be defined (have storage reserved) immediately after the opening brace of any block. This was illustrated by explaining the concept of blocks. The opening brace of a block includes the opening brace of a function since a function is nothing more than a block of code. Any variables defined in a block have the automatic storage class and block scope.

The storage class of automatic means that a variable has a *local lifetime*. The variable is created when the control flow of the program enters the function and is deleted when the control flow leaves the function. If the variable is not explicitly given an initial value when it is defined, its value remains undefined until something is assigned to it.

The block scope of the variables means that they can only be seen or referenced by statements that are also inside the same function. The variables cannot be used in statements outside the function because it is only after the control flow enters the function that the variables are created. This scope within which the variable can be referenced is also called the variable's *visibility area*.

If the name of a local variable of a function is the same as was used for the name of a global variable then all access (by name) is lost to the global variable while the flow of program control is inside the function. No keyword can override this lost access and bypass the local variable. Also, a good compiler will flag as an error an attempt to use the same name for a local variable as was used for a formal parameter to the function. Not all compilers flag this as an error, although it does not make sense to do this since the local variable name would have preference and would prevent access to the parameter. What good is a parameter that cannot be referenced?

Local variables for each function are stored together (on the stack on stack-based machines), and the amount of space available to them determines how big the variables can be and how many of them can exist. For instance, this code fragment:

```
main()
{                       /* no executable statements before */
                        /*   the opening brace of a function */
    int int_array[2000];   /* an array of 2000 integers */
...                     /* rest of program */
```

might not work if the amount of space available for the local variables is not enough for the array of 2000 integers (we use an array for the illustration because coding 2000 separate integer variable names would be tedious). If the program does not work, it might be necessary to move the array definition outside of main, like this:

```
int int_array[2000];       /* an array of 2000 integers */
main()
{
...                        /* rest of program */
```

This does two things. First, it allows the program to work when it might not otherwise because now the array is a global data item and it is not stored with other local variables. Second, making the array global also changes its visibility so that it can be referenced from anywhere in the program. No longer is access to the array restricted to just the main() function. This may or may not be what is desired, and it is not a good idea to arbitrarily make all large data items global just because they take up significant amounts of local variable space. The area where local variables are stored is usually adjustable and can be made larger if necessary.

In summary, define all data in the manner that best fits the program. Later, determine whether there is a need to reserve more than the default amount of local variable space.

Some compilers allow the programmer to include in the compiled and executable program module a test for the overflow of this local variable space. On stack-based machines this overflow is called "running out of stack space". When the test is included a small amount of additional code is compiled into the program. The purpose of this code is to detect when local variable space (stack space) has been exceeded and whether damage has occurred such that it would cause problems when the program executes, possibly crashing the machine. Although there is a slight performance penalty associated with using this check, we recommend that the code to perform this test be included in the program during the program development process and possibly excluded after the program is thoroughly tested.

Antibugging Note 6.3   Always check for stack space overflow

Make sure that if code to check for stack space overflow is available, it is included in each program during all development and testing phases.

There can be no executable statements between the opening brace and any definition of a variable, nor can there be any executable statements between any two definitions. All the definitions must appear together in a group immediately after the opening brace and before any executable code. For instance, this is not allowed and will cause an error:

```
main()
{
    getchar();
    char ary[] = "This is a string";
    int lary    = strlen(ary);
    int an_int;
    ...
```

The appearance of getchar() prevents the definitions of ary, lary, and an_int from appearing immediately after the opening brace of the function. If the getchar() function is removed, the remaining code fragment should be valid:

```
main()
{
    char ary[] = "This is a string";
    int lary    = strlen(ary);
    int an_int;
    ...
```

The use of a function invocation (strlen()) in the initialization of the variable lary seems to constitute executable code, and thereby contradicts the statements made above. While the strlen() function does indeed execute, the code is perfectly legal and does not cause a problem for better compilers. However, an error will occur if the same three lines are moved outside main() and placed so as to make global variables. The problem centers around the use of strlen() in the initialization of lary. Data items which are global variables are reserved and initialized separately from local variables. Initialization techniques valid for local variables (this situation for instance) may not work for global variables. The next code fragment is incorrect and will cause an error if compiled:

```
        char ary[] = "This is a string";
        int  lary  = strlen(ary);
        int an_int;

        main()
        {
            ...
```

Figure 6.7 shows some further examples of invalid initializations:

```
/*
**   autoinit.c  Demonstrating Disallowed Initializations
*/

#include <stdio.h>

char a[5];

int x = sizeof(a);    /* sizeof, an operator, generates a constant value */
                      /* the next variable is initialized illegally */
int y = strlen(a);    /* strlen, a function, generates executable code */
                      /* which is not allowed outside a function */

main()
{
    int x = sizeof(a);    /* both of these initializations are allowed */
    int y = strlen(a);
}
```

Figure 6.7   Demonstrating Disallowed Initializations—`autoinit.c`

To complete this discussion of local variables we will revisit the program `counter.c` which was introduced when blocks were explained. In that program we counted the input characters and characterized them by numeric, uppercase, lowercase, and hex digit categories. The program in Figure 6.8 does exactly the same thing but uses separate functions rather than nested blocks. Using separate functions is the more traditional way of writing this type of program.

```
/*
** localvar.c - A Static Counter Using A Separate Function
*/

#include <stdio.h>          /* standard I/O functions */
#include <ctype.h>          /* character & conversion 'is' functions */

void do_count(int c);       /* function prototypes */
void trash_stack(void);

#define  NEWLINE  '\n'       /* character that terminates input */

main()
{
    int input_char;          /* local automatic variable */

    printf("Type in numbers and upper/lowercase letters\n");
    while(input_char = getchar()) {
        do_count(input_char);
        trash_stack();
        if (input_char == NEWLINE) {   /* newline terminates input */
            break;
        }
    }
}

void do_count(int input_char)
{
    static int number;      /* counter for 0 thru 9 */
    static int lower;       /* counter for a thru z */
    static int upper;       /* counter for A thru Z */
    static int hex;         /* counter for valid hex digit */

    if(input_char == NEWLINE) {
        printf("\n%d numbers were entered\n", number);
        printf("%d lowercase letters were entered\n", lower);
        printf("%d uppercase letters were entered\n", upper);
        printf("%d hex digits were entered\n", hex);
        return;
    }
    if(isdigit(input_char)) {
        number++;           /* bump counter if a number */
    }
    if(islower(input_char)) {
        lower++;            /* bump counter if lowercase */
    }
    if(isupper(input_char)) {
        upper++;            /* bump counter if uppercase */
    }
```

```
    if(isxdigit(input_char)) {
        hex++;                   /* bump counter if hex digit */
    }
}

void trash_stack(void)
{
    /* the only purpose of this function is to insure that on */
    /* certain machines the counters are wiped out */
    /* if they are not defined with the static keyword */
    int a = 0, b = 0, c = 0, d = 0;
}
```

Figure 6.8   A Static Counter Using A Separate Function—localvar.c

The nested blocks from counter.c have been moved to separate functions, and other program statements have been modified slightly to account for this change. Note that the integer input_char which is defined immediately after the opening brace of main() is local to main() and not available anywhere else in the program except when the control flow is inside main(). The function do_count() uses a variable input_char but it is the one declared as a formal parameter to the function, not the one defined inside main(). The four counters defined inside do_count() need the static keyword so that the values they contain will be retained from one invocation of the function to the next. Note also the use of the defined constant NEWLINE, a valuable technique here because the terminating character must be coded at least twice in the program. If the value of the terminating character must be changed, changing it once in the #define directive is preferable to changing it two times (or more in other programs) in the specific places it is used. Those places usually are scattered throughout the program. Finally, the function trash_stack() serves the same purpose here as does the second nested block in the program counter.c. If the static keyword is left out of the program, trash_stack() insures that the automatic variables used as counters are destroyed between invocations of do_count(). Without trash_stack() it is possible to have the counters appear to retain their value when in reality they are vulnerable to being changed.

6.6   Recursion and Iteration

The C language supports *recursive* function calls, which means that a function can call itself. If a function calls itself within itself, the recursion is *direct*. If the function calls another function which then calls the first function, the recursion is said to be *indirect*. Recursion is appropriately used on problems where the basic structure of the data and/or solution is recursive. Processing a tree/root structure (like the UNIX and MS/PC-DOS directory structure) is often handled through recursion. So are certain computations where the depth of nesting in a nested loop is not known in advance. A good example of this type of application is illustrated in exercise 5 at the end of this chapter. A recursive solution to a problem will not be any faster or use less computer memory than a nonrecursive solution, but it will be more compact and easier to understand (although it might not appear so at first).

One calculation which is a good illustration of recursion is the computation of a factorial. The factorial of an integer is calculated by multiplying the integer and all other integers between it and zero together, i.e., the factorial of 5 is 5 * 4 * 3 * 2 * 1 = 120. The factorial of 0 is 1 (by definition). The code in Figure 6.9 will calculate this factorial.

```
/*
** factoral.c - A Factoral Computation
*/

#include <stdio.h>                          /* has library prototypes */
int factorial(int);                         /* our function prototype */

main()
{
    int start;                              /* an automatic variable */
    printf("Enter starting number: ");      /* prompt for input */
    scanf("%d", &start);                    /* get integer input */
    printf("\"%d\"\n", factorial(start));   /* compute and print */
}

int factorial(start)
int start;
{
    if(start <= 1) {                        /* done if one or less */
        return(1);
    }
    return (start * factorial(start - 1));  /* do recursion */
}
```

Figure 6.9 A Factorial Computation—factoral.c

The key to understanding the factorial() function is to notice that it calls itself as part of the second return statement. If the value passed to the function is 1 or less then the function returns 1 and does not call itself. But if the value passed is greater than 1 then the function calls itself and passes the value one less than it received. By checking whether start is less than or equal to 1 rather than just checking whether it is equal provides a safer function which does not run unchecked if it is passed a negative value.

One problem characteristic of recursive functions is that they use up a great deal of stack space. The stack is where function arguments and return addresses are stored. It is a LIFO (last in, first out) list which, on most computers, is controlled by dedicated hardware registers. An analogy is a spring-loaded tube that accepts and holds tennis balls put into the tube from one end (the other end is sealed). In a recursion situation all the arguments and return addresses remain on the stack until the last recursive call is made (in our analogy it would be until the last tennis ball is placed in the tube). The stack must be large enough to hold all these arguments and values, and if an uncontrolled stack overflow occurs the results are usually unpredictable.

A recursive function can be changed into a function that does not use recursion by adding one or more counters to control the looping process. By using counters we have an iterative function rather than a recursive one. This is why a recursive function is often easier to understand than one which solves the same problem without using recursion. The presence of the counters and tests for terminating conditions adds complexity to the function. Many people have a difficult time when they initially encounter recursive programming. In order to write clear and understandable programs use recursion only when it is absolutely necessary. We will leave it as an exercise for you to change the factorial() function to one that uses iteration rather than recursion.

Antibugging Note 6.4   Appropriate use of recursion

Do not make wide use of recursion until you understand the method of controlling how much stack space is allocated to the program, and unless the data being processed has a recursive structure.

Since recursion often causes beginning (and veteran) programmers considerable difficulty, we will further illustrate the concept with a practical, yet simple, example—conversion of an integer value to its ASCII (printable) representation. For instance, suppose we wish to convert the integer 57135 to an ASCII representation for direct output to the display. The process involves repeatedly taking the modulus of the integer, like this:

Iteration	Operation	Result
1	57135 % 10	5
2	5713 % 10	3
3	571 % 10	1
4	57 % 10	7
5	5 % 10	5

Our problem is that the digits to be printed are available in the reverse order in which they are needed. Recursion solves the problem. We simply apply the following algorithm:

1. Save n.

2. If n / 10 is greater than 0 then make n = n / 10 and goto #1.

3. Else restore n and put ASCII n mod 10 on the display.

Translating the algorithm to C code yields a set of functions which could be added to any program and called from any place in that program. The routines might look like those shown in Figure 6.10.

```
/*
** itoa.c - A Recursive Example of the itoa() Function
*/

#include <stdio.h>                        /* has library prototypes */

void itoa(unsigned);                      /* our function prototype */
int  ascii(int);                          /* our function prototype */

main()
{
    itoa((unsigned) 524);                 /* convert this to ASCII */
    putchar('\n');                        /* go to next line */
    itoa((unsigned) 9876);                /* convert this to ASCII */
    putchar('\n');                        /* go to next line */
}

void itoa(n)          /* integer to ASCII conversion */
unsigned int n;       /* classic style parameter list */
{
    if (n/10 > 0) {
        itoa(n/10);
    }
    putchar(ascii(n%10));
    return;
}

ascii(n)              /* convert a decimal value */
int n;                /*    into an ASCII character */
{
    return(n + '0');
}
```

Figure 6.10   A Recursive Example of the itoa() **Function—**itoa.c

The recursive code makes more sense if each recursive call to itoa() is thought of as a call to a separate itoa() function of the same name. Note that recursion depends heavily on the concept of local variables. In our function the variable n is private to each invocation, which is why the function works at all! In Table 6.1, we'll trace through a call to itoa(57135) and see how recursive calls accomplish our goal.

Recursive Calls	Value of n	What happens next...
1	57135	call itoa(5713)
2	5713	call itoa(571)
3	571	call itoa(57)
4	57	call itoa(5)
return	5	print 5
return	57	print 7
return	571	print 1
return	5713	print 3
return	57135	print 5

Table 6.1 Using Recursive Calls

We can emulate the recursive version with an iterative version using a local stack as shown in Figure 6.11.

```
/*
**   itoaiter.c - An Iterative Example of the itoa() function
*/

#include <stdio.h>                       /* has library prototypes */

void itoa(unsigned);                     /* our function prototypes */
int  push(int);
int  pop(void);
int  ascii(int);

#define MAXSTACK 64                      /* we use MAXSTACK multiple */
                                         /*    places in the program */
int stack[MAXSTACK], i=0;                /* a local stack defined */
                                         /*    here in our program */

main()
{
    itoa((unsigned) 524);                /* convert this to ASCII */
    putchar('\n');                       /* go to next line */
    itoa((unsigned) 9876);               /* convert this to ASCII */
    putchar('\n');                       /* go to next line */
}
```

(program continued on next page...)

```
void itoa(n)                        /* this is an alternative */
unsigned int n;                     /*    to the itoa() we've */
{                                   /*    already seen */
   do {
      push(n);
   } while ((n /= 10) > 0);         /* we never call outselves */
                                    /* rather we take the digits */
   while ((n = pop()) != -1) {      /*    and put them on our */
      putchar(ascii(n%10));         /*    local stack and call */
   }
}                                   /*    ascii() multiple times */

int push(v)                         /* store the digits on the */
int v;                              /*    local stack */
{
   if (i == MAXSTACK) {             /* quit if array is filled */
      return(0);
   }
   else {
      stack[i++] = v;
   }
   return(1);
}

int pop()                           /* pop a digit from the */
{                                   /*    local stack if one is */
   if (i == 0) {                    /*    there */
      return(-1);
   }
   else {
      return(stack[--i]);
   }
}

ascii(n)                            /* convert a decimal value */
int n;                              /*    into an ASCII character */
{
   return(n + '0');
}
```

Figure 6.11 An Iterative Example of the itoa() **function—**itoaiter.c

Our nonrecursive version requires the use of a local stack to temporarily store the converted digits until the last one is processed. At this point, digits are "popped" from the stack in the correct order to be output. Note that the recursive version is much less complicated and more natural.

6.7 Self-Check

These statements are True or False. The answers are given at the end.

1. C, like some other languages, has various types of functions.

2. A function definition actually creates the function code.

3. The function return type is undefined if it is not specified when the function is defined.

4. A function is really nothing more than another form of a block of code.

5. The names of the items in the argument list used when you invoke a function must be the same as the names in the parameter list used when you both declare and define a function.

6. You can leave spaces between the function name and the left parenthesis when you invoke, declare, or define a function.

7. The presence of a semicolon after the right parenthesis means we have created a function declaration rather than a function definition.

8. A return statement is required to be present in a function.

9. You can define more data immediately after the opening brace of the function.

10. The void keyword can be used to specify that there is no return value for the function.

11. There are two styles of function parameter declarations: classic and modern. Many compilers don't support the modern style yet.

12. Function prototypes help eliminate one of the most common problems that occurs when coding C programs—the disagreement between function argument and parameter lists.

13. C is a call by value language.

14. Placing an & in front of an integer's name in an argument list will cause the address of the integer to be passed to the function rather than the integer's value.

15. Some types of data are by definition pointers to an object but when they appear in a function argument list the value they point to is substituted instead.

16. If necessary and syntactically legal a conversion is performed on a function return value when the function invocation appears as part of an expression.

17. Local variables cannot have the same name as global variables.

18. If a local variable has the same name as a global variable then the global prefix can be added to specify that you want to reference the global rather than the local item.

19. Local variables are usually stored on the stack.

20. If the available stack space is exceeded the program can crash, possibly locking up the machine.

21. A recursive function is one that calls itself, either directly or indirectly.

Answers

1. F   2. T   3. F   4. T   5. F   6. T   7. T   8. F   9. T   10. T   11. T
12. T   13. T   14. T   15. F   16. T   17. F   18. F   19. T   20. T   21. T

6.8   Review Program—Scheduling Manufacturing Production

Our emphasis in this review program will be functions, the subject of this chapter. We will define several functions that illustrate variations in argument passing, return types and function prototypes. We include a recursive function, since this technique is important to modern algorithmic languages.

☐ *Design Specifications*

The best place to begin is with a scenario:

Real Good Manufacturing Inc. has determined, through extensive analysis, that to operate economically it must follow certain constraints in the manufacture of its products. The company currently manufactures five products, A, B, C, D and E. Warehouse maximum quantities for each product are set as follows:

Warehouse Maximums

Product	Maximum Quantity
A	4,000
B	10,000
C	20,000
D	75,000
E	4,000
Total	113,000

The major objective of the manufacturing facility is to produce as much product as possible each month without overrunning maximum stock quantities for each item. Minimum economic production run sizes are set as follows:

Product	Minimum Lot Size
A	1,000
B	2,500
C	5,000
D	10,000
E	250

For example, Product B may only be produced if, for any given month, at least 2500 pieces are needed.

Our job, as production schedulers, is to produce a schedule each month giving quantities to produce for each product, A, B, C, D, and E. The only information we are given is the current warehouse quantities for each of the products, one day before the schedule is due. Since RGM Inc. is a growing company, our scheduling system must include provisions to incorporate additional products if the need arises (for example, adding Product F to our product line).

Summarizing our constraints in the form of simple mathematic equations might be a good place to start. The maximum production we can produce in any given month may not exceed

$$\sum_{i=A}^{E} wqi_{max} - wqi_{on\_hand}$$

where

wqi_{max} : maximum warehouse quantity for product i

wqi_{on_hand} : on hand warehouse quantity for product i

In other words, the maximum that may be produced is the sum of all the differences between the maximum we may stock and the current quantity on hand for each product. If there were no other constraints on our problem, each difference, $wqi_{max} - wqi_{on\_hand}$, would represent the quantity to produce for any given month. Unfortunately, we are not so lucky. The additional constraint

```
wqi - wqi        >=  pqi
   max  on_hand       min
```

must be met for each product i. If not, product i may not be produced during the given month.

□ *Program Design*

Our next step is to rough out pseudocode for our scheduling system. We decide that arrays will be used to store all static and variable data. Thus we code

PRODUCTS 5

on__hand[**PRODUCTS**]
warehouse__max[**PRODUCTS**]
production__min[**PRODUCTS**]
quantity__to__run[**PRODUCTS**]

to hold the data we will need.

Next we decide that the on_hand quantities will be entered dynamically at runtime, with all others coded as static or calculated values. Continuing, we write pseudocode for the main() routine:

integer warehouse__max[**PRODUCTS**]
integer production__min[**PRODUCTS**]

begin main()
   integer on__hand[**PRODUCTS**]
   integer quantity__to__run[**PRODUCTS**]

   integer i = 0
   while(i < **PRODUCTS**)
      input (onhand[i])
      i = i + 1
   endwhile
   compute__run__quantities(**PRODUCTS**, quantity__to__run, on__hand)
   print__report(quantity__to__run, on__hand, **PRODUCTS**)
end main

Finally we code the functions needed in main()

begin compute__run__quantities(n, run, stock)
integer n, run[], stock[]
   if (n > 0)
      n = n—1
      compute__run__quantities(n, run, stock)

```
        endif
        if (warehouse__max[n]—stock[n] >= production__min[n])
            run[n] = warehouse[n]—stock[n]
        else
            run[n] = 0
        endif
        return
    end compute__run__quantities

    begin print__report(run, on__hand, n)
    integer run[], on__hand[], n
        int i = 0
        print (<report heading>)
        while (i < n)
            print (on__hand[i], run[i])
        endwhile
        print (sum__quantities(run, PRODUCTS))
        return
    end print__report

    begin sum__quantities(products, n)
    integer products[], n
        if (n)
            return(products[—n] + sum__quantities(n))
        else
            return(products[n])
        endif
    end sum__quantities
```

There are several points to note before proceeding. Pay careful attention to our design of the functions `compute_run_quantities()` and `sum_quanti-ties()`. Both of these are written using recursive algorithms although they could be coded using strictly iterative techniques. We wish to illustrate that any iterative function can be coded recursively. We will leave it to you to convert them to iterative implementations.

☐ *Design Implementation*

```
/*-------------------------------------------------------------------
   schedule.c
   A simple scheduling system for Real Good Manufacturing Inc.
------------------------------------------------------------------*/
#include <stdio.h>

#define PRODUCTS (sizeof(product_name) / sizeof(char))   /* # of products */
```

(program continued on next page...)

```
/*
 function prototypes for local function definitions
*/
void compute_run_quantities(int, long[], long[]);
long sum_quantities(long[], int);
void print_report(long[], long[], int);

/* product names */
char product_name[] = {'A','B','C','D','E'};

/* maximum warehouse quantities for each product */
long warehouse_max[] = {4000,10000,20000,75000,4000};

/* minimum production runs for each product */
long production_min[] = {1000,2500,5000,10000,250};

main()
{
    long on_hand[PRODUCTS];              /* on-hand quantities */
    long quantity_to_run[PRODUCTS];      /* production runs, to be computed */
    int i;
/*
 print program title
*/
    printf("RGM Inc. Simple Scheduling System\n");
    printf("-------------------------------\n\n");
/*
 get current warehouse levels on each product from user
*/
    for (i = 0; i < PRODUCTS; ++i) {
        printf("Product %c quantity on hand", product_name[i]);
        scanf("%ld", &on_hand[i]);
    }
/*
 compute quantities to run
*/
    compute_run_quantities(PRODUCTS, quantity_to_run, on_hand);
/*
 and print report
*/
    print_report(quantity_to_run, on_hand, PRODUCTS);
    return;
}
```

```
/*-------------------------------------------------------------------
   void compute_run_quantities(int n, long run[], long stock[])
   Compute each of the quantities to run according to constraints
   and store in the array run[]. This is a recursive version of
   an iterative algorithm.
-------------------------------------------------------------------*/
void compute_run_quantities(n, run, stock)
int n;
long run[], stock[];
{
   if (n > 0) {
      compute_run_quantities(--n, run, stock);
   }
   if (warehouse_max[n] - stock[n] >= production_min[n]) {
      run[n] = warehouse_max[n] - stock[n];
   }
   else {
      run[n] = 0;
   }
   return;
}


/*-------------------------------------------------------------------
   long sum_quantities(products, n)
-------------------------------------------------------------------*/
long sum_quantities(products, n)
long products[];
int n;
{
   if (--n) {
      return(products[n] + sum_quantities(products, n));
   }
   else {
      return(products[n]);
   }
}
```

(program continued on next page...)

```
/*-------------------------------------------------------------------
   print_report(run, stock, n)
---------------------------------------------------------------------*/
void print_report(run, stock, n)
long run[], stock[];
int n;
{
   int i;

   printf("\n\n%20s %20s %20s\n", "Product", "Qty On Hand", "Qty to Run");
   printf("%20s %20s %20s\n\n",    "-------", "-----------", "----------");
   for (i = 0; i < n; ++i) {
      printf("%20c %20ld %20ld\n",product_name[i], stock[i], run[i]);
   }
   printf("\n\n");
   printf("%20s %20ld %20ld\n\n","Total", sum_quantities(stock, n), sum_quantities(run, n));
   return;
}
```

☐ *Program Output*

```
RGM Inc. Simple Scheduling System
---------------------------------

Product A quantity on hand? 3500
Product B quantity on hand? 4000
Product C quantity on hand? 12500
Product D quantity on hand? 35500
Product E quantity on hand? 3800
```

Product	Qty On Hand	Qty to Run
A	3500	0
B	4000	6000
C	12500	7500
D	35500	39500
E	3800	0
Total	59300	53000

Note how we have entered values for A and E to check that the program filters out production runs that are too small. In a real situation, such a program would be thoroughly tested using data from each extreme and numerous values in between. For the sake of brevity, we will not be so thorough.

Points to Study

1. Implementation of the recursive functions `compute_run_quantities()` and `sum_quantities()`. Observe that the recursive call in `sum_quantities()` is embedded within the `return` statement. Recursive calls to `sum_quantities()` cause each previous `return` to be pending until the termination condition `if (--n)` is met.

2. Use of the two methods of function prototyping, classic and modern. Remember that many compilers do not yet support the modern version.

3. Format conversions used in the `printf()` function calls. Note how we align the output using right-justification in conjunction with a width specification.

4. Use of `long` data types in the program to accommodate large integer numbers.

5. Declarations for the formal parameters in each function definition. Note how the function prototypes "protect" the caller.

6. The summation notation used in the algorithm design of our program. You should become familiar with its use as it is commonly encountered.

6.9 Exercises

1. Convert the function `factorial()` given in Section 6.6 to an iterative implementation. Which method do you suppose is faster? Explain.

2. Write iterative versions of the functions `compute_run_quantities()` and `sum_quantities()` given in the Review Program. Do you feel either of these functions should have been written recursively? Explain.

* 3. A stack structure can be described as a last-in, first-out (LIFO) data structure. Stacks are often thought of as low-level constructions, although they are commonly used in high-level algorithms. Several operations can be applied to stacks as follows:

OPERATION	RESULT
pop()	Retrieve a value from the stack.
push(value)	Place a value on the stack.
size(stack)	Determine how much stack space is available.
clear(stack)	Remove all values from the stack and discard.

Write functions to manipulate an integer stack. A suitable representation would be an integer array. Be sure to write a driver program to demonstrate that your stack functions work.

4. Write function prototypes for all functions coded in Chapters 3, 4, 5, 6 and 7 Review Programs.

* 5. Recursive algorithms are a natural choice when manipulating tree structures. The best introduction to a tree structure is with a diagram

```
                    (A)
                    /\
                   /  \
(F)------(B)  (C)-----(H)
          /\       \     !\
         /  \       \    ! \
       (D)  (E)    (G)  (I) (J)
```

The labels A, B, C, D, E, F, G, H, I, and J are known as *nodes* with A being the *root node*. Nodes F, D, E, G, I, and J are called *terminal nodes* since there are no other nodes below them in the hierarchy. Each connection between nodes is known as a *branch*. You will also encounter the terms *parent* and *child* in connection with tree structures. In our simple tree, A is the parent of B and C, with their children being F, D, and E, and G and H respectively. Tree structures are used frequently in many real-life problems including database systems, artificial intelligence applications (expert systems), games such as chess and checkers, and numerous others.

In this exercise we will look at a novel use for a tree structure: navigation of a simple maze. The goal of our program will be, given a start location within the maze, to find the exit point and print out the optimal solution. Before we start let's look a simple maze and transform it to a tree structure.

```
+--+--+--+--+--+
!06 05 04 03!15!
+  +--+--+  +  +
!07 08 09!02!14!
+  +--+  +  +  +
!11 12!10!01 13!
+--+--+  +  +--+
```

OUT   IN

We have labeled each position within the maze with numeric labels to aid the transformation to a tree structure. The transformation yields:

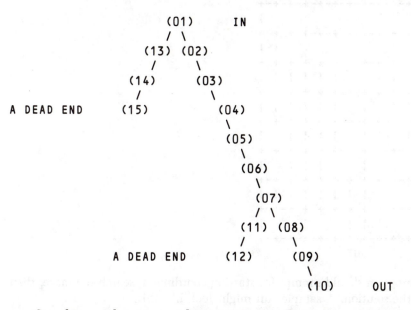

Searching such a maze reduces to viewing the maze as a tree structure and using an appropriate algorithm. Such an algorithm is the preorder search. The preorder search "travels" around a tree structure, always taking the left branch if possible, and "looks" at each node as it is encountered. In our situation, we are looking for the OUT node. So much for introductions. Given the maze below, write a program to implement the preorder algorithm (hint: it's recursive) to find the solution to the maze.

```
                COLUMN
ROW   0 1 2 3 4 5 6 7 8 9 0 1
      +-+-+-+-+-+-+-+-+-+-+-+-+
  0 ¦                         ¦
      ¦ +-+-+ +-+-+-+-+-+-+ + +
  1 ¦ ¦ ¦ ¦             ¦ ¦ ¦
      ¦ + + +-+ + + + + + + +
  2 ¦     ¦ ¦   ¦ ¦ ¦ ¦ ¦ ¦ ¦
      ¦ + + +-+-+ + + + +-+ +
  3 ¦ ¦ ¦ ¦   ¦   ¦ ¦ ¦ ¦ ¦ ¦
      ¦ + + +-+ +-+ + + + + +
  4 ¦ ¦ ¦   ¦ ¦   ¦ ¦ ¦ ¦ ¦ ¦
      ¦ + +-+-+ + +-+ +-+ + +
  5 ¦ ¦ ¦     ¦   ¦ ¦ ¦ ¦   ¦
      ¦ + +-+-+-+ + + + + +-+
  6 ¦ ¦         ¦ ¦ ¦ ¦ ¦ ¦ ¦
      ¦ +-+-+-+ + +-+ + + +-+ +
  7 ¦           ¦ ¦ ¦     ¦   ¦
      +-+-+-+-+-+ +-+-+-+-+-+
                OUT
```

Your program should prompt for starting coordinates, search the maze, then print the solution. A sample run might look like this:

THE AMAZING MAZE PROGRAM

```
                COLUMN
ROW   0 1 2 3 4 5 6 7 8 9 0 1
      +-+-+-+-+-+-+-+-+-+-+-+-+
  0 ¦                         ¦
      ¦ +-+-+ +-+-+-+-+-+-+ + +
  1 ¦ ¦ ¦ ¦             ¦ ¦ ¦
      ¦ + + + +-+ + + + + + +
  2 ¦       ¦ ¦   ¦ ¦ ¦ ¦ ¦ ¦ ¦
      ¦ + + + +-+-+ + + +-+ +
  3 ¦ ¦ ¦ ¦   ¦   ¦ ¦ ¦ ¦ ¦ ¦
      ¦ + + +-+ +-+ + + + + +
  4 ¦ ¦ ¦   ¦ ¦   ¦ ¦ ¦ ¦ ¦ ¦
      ¦ + +-+-+ + +-+ +-+ + +
  5 ¦ ¦ ¦     ¦   ¦ ¦ ¦ ¦   ¦
      ¦ + +-+-+-+ + + + + +-+
  6 ¦ ¦         ¦ ¦ ¦ ¦ ¦ ¦ ¦
      ¦ +-+-+-+ + +-+ + + +-+ +
  7 ¦           ¦ ¦ ¦     ¦   ¦
      +-+-+-+-+-+ +-+-+-+-+-+
                OUT
```

Enter starting row position: [7]
Enter starting column position: [3]

The solution to the maze is...

```
                COLUMN

ROW   0 1 2 3 4 5 6 7 8 9 0 1
     +-+-+-+-+-+-+-+-+-+-+-+-+
  0  |* * * *                |
     | +-+-+ +-+-+-+-+-+-+ + +
  1  |*| | |* * * *        | | |
     | + + + +-+ + + + + + + +
  2  |*     | |    |*| | | | | |
     | + + + +-+-+ + + + +-+ +
  3  |*| | |    |  *| | | | | |
     | + + +-+ +-+ + + + + + +
  4  |*| |    | |* *| | | | | |
     | + +-+-+ + +-+ +-+ + + +
  5  |*| |        |*  | | | |    |
     | + +-+-+-+ + + + + +-+
  6  |*|            |*| | | | | | |
     | +-+-+-+ + +-+ + + +-+ +
  7  |* * * S| |*|        |        |
     +-+-+-+-+-+ +-+-+-+-+-+-+
                OUT
```

6. Modify the Review Program to include the following features:

   a. Incorporate an average pieces per day calculation into the printed table by using a "lookup" into an array called `days_per_month[12]`. Write a function to perform the calculation with its associated function prototype.

   b. Incorporate cost data to manufacture each product with the subtotals and total printed in the table. Once again, write a function and prototype to perform the necessary calculations.

   c. Rewrite the `print_report()` function so that the printed output is centered on the display regardless of the width of the report. You might consider using `sprintf()` in conjunction with `printf()` to accomplish this.

7. String manipulation is fundamental to most modern high-level languages. Code string functions are described below:

Function	What it Does
strfilter(sl, s2, c)	Searches sl and replaces any occurrences of the characters contained in s2 with the character c.
strcompress(sl, s2)	Compresses sl by removing all occurrences of the characters contained in s2 from sl.
strreverse(sl)	Reverses all the characters in sl.
strinvert(sl)	Converts all uppercase letters in sl to lowercase and all lowercase letters to uppercase.

Example invocations for each function are given below:

```
strfilter("A string; with,, token;,.. separators.", ",;.", ' ');

Resultant string: "A string  with   token    separators "

strcompress("A string; with,, token;,.. separators.", ",;. ");

Resultant string: "Astringwithtokenseparators"

strreverse("abcdefg");

Resultant string: "gfedcba"

strinvert("AbcDeFghIJK");

Resultant string: "aBCdEfGHijk"
```

Write a header file called mystring.h that contains the function prototypes for the string functions given above. You should decide whether a return value is appropriate for any of the functions. Define the function accordingly and do not leave the return type undefined. If the return type is void, indicate this in the function definition and prototype.

8. Write functions to calculate the volume of the geometric objects given below with their associated equations:

OBJECT	VOLUME EQUATION
box	width X length X height
cone	(pi X radius^2 X height) / 3
sphere	4/3 X pi X radius^3
cylinder	height X pi X radius^2

where pi = 3.1416. Include a driver program to illustrate the operation of each function.

* advanced exercises

6.10 Pretest

☐ *Multiple Choice*

Circle one correct answer for each of the following:

1. When we say that a language uses call-by-value conventions in function invocations we mean that:
   a. The function itself reduces to a data type value just like an expression.
   b. The function is invoked as a pointer.
   c. Arguments are passed to the function as value copies rather than addresses.
   d. Automatic variables within the function are local variables.

2. A function definition in C may not:
   a. Be nested.
   b. Include the return type `double`.
   c. Include the formal parameter data types as in a function prototype.
   d. Occur before the `main()` function.

3. What is wrong with the following function?

```
int ipow(x, y)          /* calculate x^y and return result */
int x,y;
{
int result = 1;         /* initial value in case y is 0 */
while (y--)
    result *= x;        /* multiply x by itself y times */
return;
}
```

   a. Comments may not appear on the same line as the function definition.
   b. The formal parameters x and y should be of type `float` instead of `int`.
   c. The function will not return the correct result due to round-off error.
   d. The return type does not match the return type in the function definition itself.
   e. The function is useless since it does not return a value.

4. What would be the correct function prototype for the following function:

```
encrypt_string(string, lookup, number_of_characters)
char string[], lookup[];
int number_of_characters;
{
    ...
    return(1);
}
```

   a. `encrypt(char, char, int);`
   b. `int encrypt(char, char, int);`
   c. `encrypt(int, int, int);`
   d. `int encrypt(char[], char[], int);`

5. What is wrong with the following recursive function?

```
revstr(string)          /* print the characters of 'string' */
char string[];          /* in reverse order */
{
int i = 0;

while(string[i] != '\0')
   {
   revstr(string);
   ++i;
   }
printf("%c", string[i]);
return;
}
```

    a. A recursive function in C cannot receive an argument.
    b. There is no provision to terminate the recursion, which will lead to an infinite loop.
    c. The return statement should be placed first, thus allowing the recursion to terminate properly.
    d. The function should be implemented in an iterative manner, rather than recursively.

6. If a function returns type void this means that:
    a. The return type is equivalent to an integer type.
    b. The function is a dummy prototype.
    c. The function returns no value.
    d. The function does not take any arguments.

7. One problem with recursive functions is that:
    a. They have little value if an iterative solution can be found.
    b. They are difficult to implement.
    c. They can only call other recursive functions.
    d. They can be very stack intensive which can cause a stack overflow.

8. What is wrong with the following function?

```
float fstrlen(string)
{
    char string[];
    int i = 0;

    while(string[i++])
        ;
    return((float) i--);
}
```

a. The variable i should be type `float` instead of `int`.

b. The length of a string cannot be returned as a `float`.

c. The true length will not be returned since C is a call-by-value language.

d. A type cast cannot be applied to a postdecremented variable.

e. none of the above

9. What is wrong with the following code fragment?

```
do_a_lot("xyz", 45, "abc", 'x');
   ...
do_a_lot(string1, number, string2, a_char, another_char)
   char string2[], string1[];
   int number;
   char a_char, another_char;
   {
      ...
   return;
   }
```

a. The number 45 cannot be passed to the function as a constant.

b. The strings "xyz" and "abc" must be passed in the same order as defined in the formal parameter list.

c. The number of actual arguments does not match the number of formal parameters.

d. A function prototype for `do_a_lot()` must be declared.

10. When the ellipsis (...) is coded in a function prototype it means that:

a. The prototype is not finished yet.

b. The actual function can take a variable number of arguments.

c. The function can take any valid C data type as an argument.

d. none of the above

Standard Character Input and Output

Having covered the basic parts of a C program and how it is structured, it's now appropriate to discuss how data gets into and out of a program. Input and output will be studied in two phases. First we will discuss standard I/O mechanisms, which allow easy access to the keyboard, CRT screen, and printer. Then we will cover disk I/O and managing disk files in a later chapter.

After studying this chapter, you will be able to do the following:

1. Define and explain standard input and output.

2. Use the standard library functions `getchar()` and `putchar()`.

3. Discuss how `getchar()` differs from `getch()`.

4. Explain how to do formatted output using the `printf()` function.

5. Accomplish formatted input without using the `scanf()` function.

7.1   The Concept of Standard I/O

Some languages, like COBOL, are primarily record-oriented and use data that has a definite structure. Others, like BASIC, provide convenient interactive capabilities but process structured data with more difficulty. Specialized languages like FORTRAN process one type of data very well (numbers) but may be limited in other areas (e.g., text and character handling capabilities).

The input and output routines in the C language can process any type of data because they operate on individual characters rather than records (groups of characters). Only minimal formatted input capability is available through the standard compiler-supplied routines. The formatted output functions provided by the compiler vendor are more powerful, however, so this book will concentrate on building input routines while using the output routines already available.

C also provides each program a set of files, called *standard files*, which are already opened and ready for access. These are normal files in every sense except that they don't need to be opened or closed or to have anything else done to them except to read and write them.

With that introduction it is now necessary to discuss a number of seemingly unrelated topics. These next points, however, are crucial to the understanding of this section.

7.1.1 *Stream Files and* FILE *Data Items*

Files and devices in C are suppliers or receivers of individual characters, and the characters are associated with a *data stream* inside a C program. Data streams have more consistency and fewer idiosyncrasies than the various files and devices. Programs read and write, recognize the end of the file, and otherwise manage all streams the same way, regardless of what is physically supplying or receiving the characters.

Streams come in two types: text and binary. *Text streams* are files like C source programs. They are composed of records or lines. Each line consists of characters terminated by a newline (line feed) character. Lines don't have to contain any characters (except the newline), and the input/output functions can add, change, or delete characters if needed. For instance, the carriage return-line feed sequence indicates the end of a line in a text file. Therefore, when a text file is read with the C language the carriage return-line feed sequence is changed into just the newline (line feed) character. If the same program is compiled and run on another machine the translation might be different but the program will still see just the newline character.

Binary streams are exact representations of the external data file. No translation is performed on any characters. Examples of binary files are the executable programs created after C source code is compiled and linked.

A program makes the connection between a particular stream and its associated external file through the use of a data item of type FILE. This data item holds all information about the stream, such as whether buffering is used (and if so, the buffer location), whether to read, write, or update the file in place, whether the end of the file has been reached, and so on. Every stream has a FILE data item associated with it.

The individual FILE data items do not have explicit names. They are referenced through a pointer. The name of the pointer is used in functions that reference the file. For example, the definition:

```
FILE *fp1;
```

creates fp1 which is a pointer to a FILE data item. We can then initialize fp1 by assigning to it the return value of a function like fopen(). We can also send characters to fp1 by using it as the first argument for the fprintf() function.

7.1.2   *Standard* F I L E *Pointers and Redirection*

Years ago people like B. W. Kernighan and P. J. Plauger laid the groundwork for a philosophy of writing flexible and modular programs. They envisioned utilizing predefined files for a program's input and output. They also identified the mechanism for having two of these programs easily communicate with each other by defining a method for the predefined output file from one program to be connected to the predefined input file of another program. This removed from inside the program the responsibility for knowing the name and external characteristics of the physical file or device which was associated with a particular predefined file. The result was that it became very simple to combine these programs in ways which were not identified before they were written.

These predefined files were given names; collectively they were known as *standard files*. Although the initial work on this approach took place in the UNIX environment, MS/PC-DOS (beginning with release 2.00) adopted many of the concepts of standard files and the techniques for associating them together from outside the program. Standard files are assumed to be text files and have been given names and default associations to the physical world. The standard file names shown in Table 7.1 are really pointers to the F I L E data item associated with the standard file. Not all compilers have defined all these names.

Standard File Name	Description	Default MS/PC-DOS Physical Connection	Required by ANSI Standard
stdin	standard input	keyboard/console	yes
stdout	standard output	screen/display monitor	yes
stderr	standard error	screen/display monitor	yes
stdaux	standard auxiliary	first serial port	no
stdprn	standard print	first parallel port	no

Table 7.1   Standard File Names and Locations

The techniques of managing the association between a standard file name and its connection to a physical file or device are known as redirection and piping. *Redirection* is the method used to change the association of a standard file from its normal or default file or device to another file or device. *Piping* is the technique of directly connecting the standard output of one program to the standard input of another. The control and invocation of redirection and piping normally occur outside the program, which is exactly the intent since the program itself need not care where the data is really coming from or going to. All the program needs to do is receive data from standard input and send data to standard output. Where that data physically comes from or ends up is not the program's responsibility but rather that of the operating system, computer/terminal user, or parent process that invoked the program. If a file needs to be located, opened, created, closed, or anything else, the parent process will perform that function.

In both MS/PC-DOS and UNIX the symbol used by the terminal operator to change or redirect standard input is the less than sign, `<`. For instance, suppose there is a program named PGMNAME that reads data from standard input (which is by default the keyboard in MS/PC-DOS and UNIX) and does something with that data. Suppose also that the same program needs to read not what is entered through the keyboard but rather what has already been typed in and stored in a file whose name is `OLDWORDS.TXT`. This would be entered at the prompt:

```
PGMNAME < OLDWORDS.TXT
```

Suppose that `PGMNAME` normally places its results on the screen by sending its output to standard output. The output might need to be placed back into a file called `NEWWORDS.TXT`. Changing the association of standard output with a physical file or device is done with the greater than symbol, or `>`. Therefore, if this were entered:

```
PGMNAME < OLDWORDS.TXT > NEWWORDS.TXT
```

nothing will appear on the screen, but the file `NEWWORDS.TXT` will be written over (or created if necessary).

The way to connect the standard output from one program to the standard input of another program is by piping them together using the vertical bar symbol, `|`. Therefore, to connect the standard output of the program `FIRST` to the standard input of the program `SECOND` this would be entered:

```
FIRST | SECOND
```

The operating system handles all the details of physically getting the output from `FIRST` to the input of `SECOND`.

The program in Figure 7.1 is a simple illustration of how the `stdin` stream is copied to the `stdout` stream. By using redirection the program can receive input from any stream file and write output to any stream file. The program does not need to know in advance (i.e., when it was written) which files it ultimately would access. The standard character functions `getchar()` and `putchar()` used in this example were covered in an earlier chapter so their purpose should not be too obscure.

```
/*
** Copy standard input to standard output - getput.c
*/

#include <stdio.h>                        /* EOF is defined here */

main()
{
    int input_char;                        /* the character to read/write */
    while((input_char = getchar()) != EOF) { /* get characters until EOF */
        putchar(input_char);                      /* and send 'em out */
    }
    return;
}
```

Figure 7.1   A Simple File Copy—getput.c

For example, entering this command,

```
getput < infile.txt > outfile.txt
```

would cause the program getput to receive its input from infile.txt and write its output to outfile.txt. In essence we have written a program that functions as a copy command.

Quick Note 7.1   The value of redirection

If the input or output of a program must occasionally go to different places, consider using redirection in conjunction with standard input or output. Redirection also can be a big help in program development and testing.

7.1.3   *Buffering*

Buffering shields a program from the physical accesses associated with file I/O. The data read or written by a program may be moved from or to an area in memory where it is held until enough has been accumulated so that it is worth doing the physical file access. This is a common technique used to make file access more efficient.

C programs normally buffer the file stream associated with standard input, which usually is the keyboard. This means that if we call for one character from standard input and the input buffer is empty, the standard input routine will wait for the keyboard to supply a character. Once the keyboard is put in control, more than one character can be typed, and the keyboard does not return control to the program until the Enter key is pressed. When control returns to the program only one character at a time is made available to the input routine. Repeated calls to the input routine are necessary to obtain all the characters that were typed during that one time when control was relinquished to the keyboard.

The standard output stream is also normally buffered unless it is associated with a CRT. No buffering is used with a CRT so that each character can immediately be seen as it is sent to the video device. The standard error stream is normally unbuffered since we always want error information to appear and not lost in a buffer if the program crashes.

If a program written in a high-level language is doing sequential file access, it may be able to process a file as fast or faster than an assembly language program. The efficiency of reducing the number of physical file accesses completely overshadows any losses from high-level language overhead. Adding buffering to an assembly language program is not a trivial exercise, however, and high-level languages can provide significant advantages in this area.

Unbuffered input and output are normally allowed only on personal computers, i.e., computers whose input or output device can be directly connected to the program performing the data access. This sort of *dedicated device* arrangement (where an input/output device is not shared among programs and users) is not normally allowed on computers that must handle more than one user at a time. UNIX is a multiuser operating system, and consequently allows unbuffered input and output only under special circumstances. MS/PC-DOS however is not a multiuser operating system, and consequently can readily handle unbuffered input and output.

One place where buffering can cause frustration on the IBM-PC is when printer files (output to the :LPT1 device) are buffered. If both the program and the printer associated with the output stream are buffered, sometimes output does not appear on the printer as quickly as anticipated. If the printer does not print when it is expected to, check whether the program has sent either a carriage return or line feed (newline) to the printer. Most printers will not physically print anything until either the hardware buffer inside the printer has been filled or an activating character, like a carriage return or line feed, has been received. It might also be helpful to flush the program buffer associated with the printer (remember, this is not the buffer in the printer) by using the `fflush()` function. For example, if the `FILE` pointer `stdprn` references the printer, this is how to flush the print file buffer in the program:

```
fflush(stdprn);
```

7.1.4 *Standard Headers*

Each C compiler comes with a set of standard header files which are included in C programs by using the `#include` preprocessor directive. These header files have two primary uses.

First, they define commonly used items, some of which may be compiler-dependent. The ANSI standard specifies the particular name to be used for each of these items (e.g., `stdin`, `FILE`, `EOF`, etc.), but the exact form of the item may vary for each compiler, machine, and final operating environment. If these items were not specified in the header files they would need to be placed in each program, thereby making programs less portable and more difficult to maintain.

Second, the header files contain descriptions of the functions residing in the compiler's libraries. These descriptions, called *prototypes*, help to insure that the functions are being used correctly. They also specify whether any of the library functions return an item whose type is other than integer (integer being the default return type of a function). If one of these library functions that does not return an integer is used and the program expects it to be an integer, unpredictable results can occur.

The header file containing compiler-specific information about the standard character functions is `stdio.h`. It is included in a program by using this preprocessor directive:

```
#include <stdio.h>
```

Many of the standard I/O functions can be used without including this standard header file in the program. The function `printf()` is a good example of one that operates well without the header. However, if this next `printf()` function is coded in a program that does not include `<stdio.h>`,

```
printf(5, 6, 7);
```

the program certainly will not execute correctly even though it may compile.

7.1.5   *End of File*

There are only three conditions that can occur when a program obtains a character from standard input. These are:

1. A valid character will be received.

2. The end of the file will be reached.

3. An error will occur.

The last condition is encountered so infrequently that most programs have little or no code to handle error processing. The second condition, though, happens so frequently that C provides a convenient way to sense the end of the file. If the character received from a standard input function equals the defined constant `EOF`, then an end of file condition has been reached.

It is traditional that the value −1 represent end of file. Since standard input functions return an unsigned character value promoted to an integer, they cannot return a negative value regardless of the character being represented. The following code fragment will loop until the end of standard input (remember that `EOF` is defined in `<stdio.h>`):

```
while((input_char = getchar()) != EOF)
   {
   this body of code done until end of file is reached
   }
```

This code fragment obtains one character from standard input (via the getchar() function), assigns that character to the integer input_char, and then compares the same value to the defined constant EOF. As long as the value is not equal to EOF the body of the while loop is performed.

7.2 Standard Character Functions

There are certain character input and output functions defined in the ANSI standard and supplied by all C compilers. These functions access standard input and output and are considered to be high-level routines (as opposed to low-level routines which access the machine hardware more directly). I/O in C is implemented through vendor-supplied functions rather than keywords defined as part of the language. All functions which we discuss here should be present on any compiler that conforms to the ANSI standard.

7.2.1 getc() *and* putc()

The most basic of all I/O functions are those which receive and send one character. The getc() function receives one character from a specified file stream, like this:

```
int input_char;                /* int needed to recognize end of file */
input_char = getc(stdin);      /* get a character from standard input */
```

The received character is passed back to us as the return value of the getc() function itself, so input_char is not coded as one of the arguments. The FILE pointer to the desired stream is the only argument needed. It is not required that input_char be defined immediately before getc(); we did it to show that input_char is an integer.

The getc() function returns an unsigned character which has been converted to an integer. This use of an unsigned character preserved as an integer guarantees that the ASCII values above 127 are not represented as negative values. Negative values can then be used to represent unusual situations like errors and the end of the input file. For instance, end of file has traditionally been represented by -1, although the ANSI standard merely states that the defined constant EOF represent some negative value.

The putc() function sends one character to the file stream represented by the specified FILE pointer. To send the same character that we just read to standard output we could code this:

```
putc(input_char, stdout);
```

The decimal value in input_char would be 97 if it contained a lowercase ASCII a, and 65 if it contained an uppercase ASCII A. It would contain different values if run on a computer that used a character set other than ASCII (e.g., a lowercase a in EBCDIC is decimal 129).

Because an integer value is returned by getc(), the data item that receives the value from getc() must also be defined as an integer. While it may seem odd to be using an integer in a character function, the C language actually makes very little distinction between characters and integers. If a character is provided when an integer is needed, the character will be converted to an integer. If for some reason it is not possible for that conversion to be performed automatically, then the compiler will produce a warning that an actual character is needed.

We've been using the names stdin and stdout in these examples. Remember that they are defined in stdio.h, which is made available by placing this statement:

```
#include <stdio.h>
```

at the top of the program. Using stdio.h insures that all compiler-specific definitions of standard I/O related constants will be available for use.

The getc() function is normally buffered, which means that when a request for a character is made by the program, control is not returned to the program until a carriage return is entered into the standard input file stream. All the characters entered before the carriage return are held in a buffer and delivered to the program one at a time. The program will invoke getc() repeatedly until the buffer has been exhausted. After the carriage return has been sent to the program by getc(), the next request for a character results in more characters accumulating in the buffer until a carriage return is again entered. This means that the getc() function cannot be used for one-key input techniques that do not require pressing the carriage return.

A final point is that getc() and putc() are actually implemented as macros rather than as "true" functions. However, don't be surprised if they are described as functions, since they are supplied by the compiler vendor and look just like functions from the programmer's viewpoint. As macros, however, any of the arguments passed to them may be evaluated more than once. This means that expressions like

```
putc(++input_char, stdout);
```

should be avoided since input_char might be incremented more than once. This property of macros is described as using macro arguments that generate side effects. We will discuss more about side effects in later chapters.

7.2.2   `getchar()` *and* `putchar()`

The functions `getchar()` and `putchar()` are merely specific implementations of the `getc()` and `putc()` functions, respectively. They are always associated with standard input and standard output. The only way to use them on other file streams is to redirect either standard input or standard output from within the program.

The above examples could also be coded this way:

```
int input_char;
input_char = getchar();
```

and

```
putchar(input_char);
```

Like `getc()` and `putc()`, `getchar()` and `putchar()` are implemented as macros. Writing `putchar(++input_char)` is not a wise coding technique since side effects can cause the variable `input_char` to be evaluated more than once, resulting in something more than one being added to `input_char`.

`putchar()` indicates an error condition by returning `EOF` as the function's value. The way to test for the error condition (as distinguished from the end of file condition) is by coding something like this:

```
if(putchar(input_char) == EOF)
    {
    printf("Error occurred writing to standard output");
    ... abort logic ...
    }
```

The program in Figure 7.2 illustrates how `getchar()` and `putchar()` can be put to a very practical use. Using redirection, the program `detab.c` can remove the tab characters from any file and write an altered stream of characters to any other file. The algorithm used to remove the tabs and replace them with spaces is not terribly sophisticated, but the authors use the program to do two important and repetitive things:

1. Remove the tabs from program files before they are printed. (One of the two text editors used to prepare the programs in this book can be configured to insert tabs automatically into the program code, thereby saving disk space.) Traditional C programming calls for setting tabs to every three characters, while many printers default to eight spaces for each tab. Either the tabs must be replaced with spaces or else the printer must be set to recognize a tab every three rather than eight spaces. If you change the printer you may have to change it back before you do other printing, resulting in extra work.

2. Add a form feed (\f) character at the end of the output so that subsequent programs start printing on a new sheet of paper.

```
/*
**   detab.c - Expands tab characters to a fixed tab setting of every 3 spaces
**             Adds a form feed to the end of the file output file
**             Invocation:
**                                 detab < infile > outfile
*/

#include <stdio.h>

int  main ()
{
   int input_char;                          /* holds the input character */
   int nbr_chars_tween_tabs = 3; /* number characters between tabs (fixed) */
   int nbr_chars_to_tabs;  /* number characters till tab (variable counter) */

   nbr_chars_to_tabs = nbr_chars_tween_tabs;
   while ((input_char = getchar()) != EOF) {
      if (nbr_chars_to_tabs == 0) {         /* reset the variable tab counter */
         nbr_chars_to_tabs = nbr_chars_tween_tabs;
      }
      switch (input_char) {                 /* look at last char read */
         case '\n':
         case '\r':                                 /* end of line read */
               nbr_chars_to_tabs = nbr_chars_tween_tabs;
                                              /* reset tab counter */
               putchar(input_char);        /* put out end of line char */
               break;                       /* break is required here */
         case '\t':
               while (nbr_chars_to_tabs) {  /* if tab is encountered */
                  putchar(' ');             /* put out as many spaces as */
                  nbr_chars_to_tabs--;        /* variable tab counter */
               }
               break;                       /* break is required here too */
         default:
               putchar(input_char);         /* put out the character */
               nbr_chars_to_tabs--;     /* reduce distance to next tab */
               break;                    /* break encouraged to be put here */
      }
   }
   putchar ('\f');                          /* put out terminating form feed */
}
```

Figure 7.2   Tab Character Expansion—detab.c

As further illustration of this concept we have also included a program we used to "massage" the files that make up this book before we sent them to the manuscript editor. As this book was being written we included printer formatting information in the files to help indicate, for example, which words had to be highlighted. The manuscript editor did not need this highlighting, and it just slowed down the printing process if the printer control characters were left in when the manuscript editor's copy was printed. The program manuedit.c in Figure 7.3 strips out all form feed characters, along with certain printer escape sequences like escE, escF, escG, and escH (the letters esc stand for the escape character, a hex 1b). Note how the switch statements are nested and where the break statements are placed. After the escape character is encountered, another character is read, and if it is not an expected character, an error message appears. After the innermost switch is exited, the outermost switch is again entered because the break only terminates the smallest enclosing switch, not both switch statements. This requires that break statements appear in a number of places.

```
/*
**   manuedit.c - Removes Printer Formatting Information from a File
**                 manuedit < infile > outfile
*/

#include <stdio.h>

int  main ()
{
    int input_char;                         /* holds the input character */

    while ((input_char = getchar()) != EOF) {
        switch (input_char) {                   /* look at last char read */
            case '\f':                              /* form feed */
                        break;                  /* break is required here */
            case 0x1b:                          /* the escape character */
                        input_char = getchar();        /* get next character */
                        switch (input_char) {
                            case '3':                    /* variable line feed cmd */
                                putchar(0x1b); /* send escape character */
                                putchar(input_char);    /* put out char */
                                putchar(getchar());    /* put next char */
                                putchar(0x1b);        /* send escape char */
                                putchar('0');        /* cancel skip perf */
                                putchar(0x1b);     /* send the escape char */
                                putchar('N');         /* set skip perf */
                                putchar(0x02);      /* amount to 2 lines */
                                break;
```

(program continued on next page...)

```
                              case 'E':                    /* check all combinations */
                              case 'F':
                              case 'G':
                              case 'H':
                                      break;                         /* drop char */
                              default:
                                      fprintf(stderr, "Character %c followed an"
                                          " escape character and was not "
                                          "written to the output file\n",
                                          (char) input_char);
                                      break;
                      }
                      break;   /* break required here to execute properly */
              default:
                      putchar(input_char);          /* put out the character */
                      break;                /* break encouraged to be put here */
      }
  }
}
```

**Figure 7.3   Removes Printer Formatting Information
from a File—manuedit.c**

For example, entering this command,

```
detab < detab.c > prn
```

would cause (in MS/PC-DOS) the program detab to remove the tabs from its own source code (detab.c) and write the output directly to the printer. Remember that in UNIX the executable file created by the compiling and linking process is called a.out, and will have to be renamed if it is to be executed as the name detab.

If the detab program will be used to create another disk file which is subsequently printed with the MS/PC-DOS PRINT command, the final statement in the program in Figure 7.2,

```
putchar ('\f');
```

should be removed because the PRINT command adds a form feed after printing each file. This is how the MS/PC-DOS commands would then look:

```
detab < detab.c > detab.out
print detab.out
```

If the program is used in a UNIX environment, a disk file should always be created since UNIX, as a multiuser system, does not normally allow a program to access printers directly. Printers, like other shared devices, must have their printing managed for them by the operating system (UNIX). The following two commands would accomplish in UNIX the same thing as shown above for MS/PC-DOS:

```
detab < detab.c > detab.out
lp detab.out
```

Another illustration of the practical use of standard character I/O is found in the program in Figure 7.4. The authors also used this program to check the files that comprise this book. No line in any file should have more than a certain number of characters, and we preferred that tab characters not be included. This program reports the line number and length of the longest line and also reports if there are any tab characters in the file.

```
/*
**   linelgth.c - Finds the longest line in a file and reports the length
**                Also tells if there are any tab characters in the file
**                Program invocation:
**                              linelgth < filename
*/

#include <stdio.h>          /* for standard i/o definitions */

main()
{
   int  this_char;                       /* holds each char read */
   int  this_line_char_count = 0;    /* number chars on current line */
   int  this_line = 0;                   /* line number current line */
   int  max_line_char_count = 0;     /* size of longest line */
   int  longest_line = 0;                /* number of longest line */
   int  number_tabs = 0;                 /* number tab characters found */

   do {
      this_char = getchar();                         /* read a character */
      if (this_char == '\t') {                       /* see if it is a tab */
         number_tabs++;
      }               /* next is done at end of line and also end of file */
      if (this_char == '\n' || this_char == EOF) {
         this_line++;
         this_line_char_count++;
         if (this_char == '\n') {  /* if end of line, bump line counter */
            this_line_char_count++;    /* newlines count two characters */
         }
         if (this_line_char_count > max_line_char_count) {
            max_line_char_count = this_line_char_count;
            longest_line        = this_line;
         }
```

(program continued on next page...)

```
            this_line_char_count = 0;        /* reset chars in line counter */
        }
        else {
            this_line_char_count++;       /* increment chars in line counter */
        }
    } while (this_char != EOF);

    if (number_tabs) {       /* this message only seen if there are tabs */
        printf ("There are %d tab characters in the file\n", number_tabs);
    }
    printf("Line number %d is the longest with %d characters\n",
            longest_line, max_line_char_count);
}
```

Figure 7.4   File Line Length Analysis—linelgth.c

In both of these examples standard character I/O was combined with redirection to create stand alone utility programs. The programs were not tied to particular file names, thereby allowing the person using the program to choose the needed input and output files each time the program was used.

7.2.3   getch() *and* putch()

The functions getch() and putch() are not described in the ANSI C standard because they are low-level functions that interface closely with the hardware. On the IBM-PC these functions do not utilize buffering, which means that they immediately receive a character typed into the keyboard. They are subject to being redirected however, so they are not associated solely with the keyboard. On UNIX, these functions are usually redefined through the use of a #define directive to become getchar() and putchar().

The getch() function is used exactly like getchar(), and putch() like putchar(). Programs running on the IBM-PC use getch() to trap keystrokes ignored by getchar(), e.g. Home, End, PgUp, and so on. The program sees characters entered from the keyboard as soon as the key is pressed; a carriage return is not needed to send the character to the program. The getch() function can then be used to provide that one-key technique that is not available with getc() or getchar().

In Figure 7.5 we have a simple program which illustrates how getchar() differs from getch(). This program can also be used to determine whether a particular computer has buffered or unbuffered input.

```
/*
** Illustration of getchar() vs getch() - kbd.c
*/

#include <stdio.h>
#include <conio.h>

main()
{
   int input_char;                /* need someplace to put the characters */
   printf("beginning getchar loop\n");       /* tell that a loop starts */
                                             /* loop until EOF on stdin */
   while((input_char = getchar()) != EOF) {
     printf("getchar returned %d\n", input_char);
   }                                       /* print the decimal value */
                                           /*   of the character      */
   printf("beginning getch loop\n");       /* tell about another loop */
                                           /* loop until carriage rtn */
   while(input_char != '\r') {             /*   is seen */
     printf("getch returned %d\n", (input_char = getch()));
   }                                       /* note this form */
}
```

Figure 7.5 `getchar()` **and** `getch()` **Contrasted—**`kbd.c`

7.2.4   `getchar()` *and* `getch()` *Contrasted*

On the IBM-PC the `getc()` and `getchar()` functions are very different from the `getch()` function. The similarities and differences are summarized in Table 7.2:

getchar()	getch()
Echoes to the screen.	No echo.
Buffered—program does not regain control until a CR is entered.	Unbuffered—every keystroke is immediately returned to the program.
CR is translated to a decimal 10, which is a line feed.	CR is translated to a decimal 13, a true carriage return.
Function keys and other key combinations are translated, e.g. Ctrl-A => ^A, F7 => ^ə, and F6 => ^Z (end of file). Home, End, and others are not recognized.	Function and other extended keys operate like $INKEY in BASIC. The first value returned is a binary zero; the second value represents the character.
Will wait for keystroke if one is not present.	Will wait for keystroke if one is not present.

Table 7.2   Comparison of getchar() **and** getch()

The differences are magnified by the fact that the IBM-PC is able to easily determine when an individual key on the keyboard (standard input) has been pressed. Other types of hardware do not always allow programs to "trap" individual keystrokes (i.e., process input characters in an unbuffered manner). For instance, on various DEC machines using VAX C version 2.3, the getch() function is part of the "curses" routines, requiring that the file <curses.h> be included in the program by using a #include directive. In that environment getch() operates more like getchar(). First, the input echoes (the character appears when it is typed). Second, pressing a carriage return is required to send the input characters to the program. Third, the carriage return character itself is not seen by the program unless no other characters have been entered. If no other characters have been entered, the carriage return provides a NULL character (decimal value zero). Finally, function keys are not available and if they are pressed, they produce unreliable results.

7.2.5   fprintf() *and Accessing Printers*

The fprintf() function works just like printf(), but also provides the ability to direct the output to any other file stream. This function makes it very easy to send information to the printer. The format is:

```
fprintf(FILE stream pointer, control string, optional arguments);
```

For example, if stdprn has already been defined for the compiler in one of the vendor-supplied header files, then this statement:

```
fprintf(stdprn, "This printer message is going to standard print\n");
```

will send the string literal to the printer.

The first argument coded in the function is the standard name of the printer. We used stdprn, but any of the standard names that accept output can be used (it doesn't make any sense to send information to stdin). A FILE pointer that represents a disk file can also be used.

The second and subsequent arguments in fprintf() are identical to the first and subsequent arguments of printf(). The only addition fprintf() needs is the FILE stream pointer.

The \n is placed in the control string because standard print, in addition to the hardware of many printers, is buffered. The fprintf() function does not send characters to the printer until either a newline character is received (carriage return also works) or the program's buffer is full. Likewise, the printer does not actually begin printing until it either receives a newline or carriage return or its hardware buffer is full.

For printers directly attached to the computer (like many IBM-PC configurations), this function is an easy way to place the printer into any of the various modes, like compressed, 1/8 lines per inch, enhanced, and so forth.

We will illustrate this printer control concept by coding a function call that forces an Epson (or compatible) printer to enter compressed printing mode with continuous underlining.

```
#define COMPRESSED  "\x1b\x0f"          /* ESC 15 */
#define UNDERLINE   "\x1b-\x01"         /* ESC '-' 1 */

fprintf(stdprn, "%s%s", COMPRESSED, UNDERLINE);
```

Some compilers do not have stdprn already defined, in which case the name stdprn can be created if MS/PC-DOS is being used. This statement should be placed at the top of the program to make stdprn visible globally:

```
FILE *stdprn;            /* create a FILE pointer called stdprn */
```

Then use either this statement:

```
stdprn = fopen("LPT1", "wt");    /* open device LPT1 in write text mode */
```

or this one:

```
stdprn = fdopen(4, "wt");    /* use handle 4 and create a FILE pointer */
```

before any characters are sent to stdprn.

It is not as easy to send information directly to the printer in UNIX. A printer in UNIX is a shared device, and output is "spooled" or queued up for later printing. Some IBM-PC configurations also use shared printers. Although these printers should not be accessed directly, a file can be opened for output and a file pointer called stdprn created which references this new file. Send the output to stdprn as described above, then print and delete the file after the program ends. Initiating the print and deleting the file should be done outside the control of the C program, and will require the use of commands specific to the machine on which the operation occurs. The deleting especially requires manual intervention because obviously the file cannot be deleted until it has finished printing. Browse through Chapter 12 to see the details about how a disk file is opened and closed.

7.2.6   ungetc()

A seldom used (but indispensable when needed) function is ungetc(). Its name implies what it does, which is "un" get a character. It puts the character back on the input stream specified by the function so that a subsequent getc() will obtain the same character. A sample form of the function invocation is:

```
ungetc(c, stdin);
```

Here we place one character back into the standard input file stream, but any input stream can be referenced. The character we push back will be read by the next function to obtain a character from the specified file stream. Do not try to push more than one character back without doing a read or file position operation between pushes, since the operation will probably fail.

This function does not change any file or device external to the program. The character that is pushed back is held internally by the program until the next request for a character occurs.

A useful application of ungetc() is to push a character back on an input stream that has been retrieved by mistake so that it is available to other logic in the program. For example, suppose we have written a function called get_an_integer() which appears below main() in the program in Figure 7.6.

```
/*
** Illustration of ungetc() - getanint.c
*/

#include <ctype.h>
#include <stdio.h>
#include <stdlib.h>

int get_an_integer(void);        /* function prototype */
```

```
main()
{
   printf("Enter a series of characters\n");
   printf("get_an_integer() returned %d\n", get_an_integer());
      /* these next statements require that there be characters left */
      /* on standard input - they will wait until characters are present */
   printf("%c was left on stdin\n", (char) getchar());
   printf("%c was left on stdin\n", (char) getchar());
   printf("%c was left on stdin\n", (char) getchar());
}

int get_an_integer()
{
   char temp_buffer[5];                     /* buffer to hold digits */
   int index;                               /* buffer index */
   for (index = 0;
        (temp_buffer[index] = getchar()) &&
         isdigit(temp_buffer[index]) &&
         index < 4;
       ++index)
      ;                                     /* the for() ends here */
   if ((temp_buffer[index] != EOF) && (temp_buffer[index] != '\n')) {
      ungetc(temp_buffer[index], stdin);    /* if last character was valid */
   }                                        /* then put it back */
   temp_buffer[index] = '\0';               /* append null to buffer */
   return(atoi(temp_buffer));               /* return the numeric integer */
}
```

Figure 7.6 Illustration of ungetc()—getanint.c

Here we are retrieving characters from stdin until the character received is not a numeric digit, or until four characters that are all numeric digits have been received. Since the function receives the character before examining it, it must push the character back if the character will not be needed. Here are some sample executions of this program:

```
Enter a series of characters
1234567
get_an_integer() returned 1234
5 was left on stdin
6 was left on stdin
7 was left on stdin

Enter a series of characters
12abcd
get_an_integer() returned 12
a was left on stdin
b was left on stdin
c was left on stdin
```

(program continued on next page...)

```
Enter a series of characters
a12345
get_an_integer() returned 0
a was left on stdin
1 was left on stdin
2 was left on stdin
```

7.2.7   feof() *and* ferror()

The last two functions that we will discuss in this chapter provide the ability to check for end of file and error conditions on the input stream. They are:

```
feof(file stream);
ferror(file stream);
```

These return a nonzero value if their respective condition is present on the specified file stream. For instance, instead of comparing each character read to the defined constant EOF, we could place this code in our program:

```
if(feof(stdin))
    {
    ... end of file actions placed here ...
    }
```

This call to feof() would return a nonzero (logically true) value if end of file has been reached on standard input, and would return zero (logically false) if it has not been reached. A similar test could be performed to see if an error has occurred.

7.3   Formatted I/O

The C language provides the basic I/O routines to perform any type of keyboard, display, printer, or file manipulation. However, extensive output formatting features are not defined as an integral part of the language standard. This section will show ways to accomplish basic output formatting with the printf() function, and will fulfill our promise to provide a safe input mechanism to use in place of scanf().

7.3.1   *Formatted Output with* printf()

The printf() function has some additional features beyond those we discussed earlier. A particular compiler may or may not support all the techniques discussed in this section. We will show features added to the C language by the recent ANSI standard, and older versions of some compilers may not provide all these capabilities.

The basic format of the extended `printf()` conversion character is:

`%[flags][width][.precision]conversion character`

where the items inside square brackets are optional.

For example, this is a valid combination for a conversion character:

`%8d`

It requests that the minimum width of the field be 8 characters. If the number printed is less than 8 characters wide it will be right-justified in the field and space-filled on the left. If the number is larger than 8, no truncation occurs (significant digits are never truncated).

The extended conversion character:

`%-12.4f`

requests that we use a minimum of 12 character positions for the output, that the number be left-justified (the − sign), and that 4 decimal positions be displayed.

One of the most useful values that can appear in either or both of the width and precision fields is the * character. The * indicates that the final field value(s) will not be known until the program executes. This allows the field width to be determined dynamically, making the output more flexible. For example:

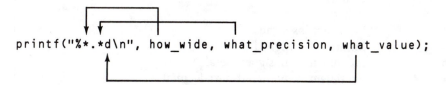

`printf("%*.*d\n", how_wide, what_precision, what_value);`

This line says that the resulting column of numbers will be as wide as the value held in the variable `how_wide`, as precise as that specified by the variable `what_precision`, and each row printed will contain the value from the variable `what_value`.

The use of the precision field overlaps somewhat with the use of the width specification. It signifies the following, depending on the data type being printed:

1. The minimum number of digits that should appear for an int value.

2. The number of digits to the right of the decimal point for a float type.

3. The number of characters to be written from a string.

If there is a conflict between the width and precision specifications, the precision value prevails. If a precision is given that exceeds the number of significant digits in the value being printed, zeroes are used to pad the output.

The precision value is now the suggested method for producing an output field that contains leading zeroes. Currently, including a leading zero on the width specifier will also produce that same result. However, using the width specifier for that purpose is contrary to the future direction of the language as stated by the ANSI standard committee.

Valid flag characters are explained in Table 7.3.

Flag	Result
-	left-justify the output within the field
+	always show a + or − character
blank	put out a blank space where the + would be, otherwise put out a − sign
#	an alternate form in which octal numbers have a leading zero appended to the front and hex numbers have 0x (or 0X)

Table 7.3   Flag Characters for `printf()`

There is a robust set of conversion characters, as shown in Table 7.4.

Character	Resulting Display or Action
%	the % character itself
c	character
s	string
d or i	int shown as signed
u	int shown unsigned
o	int shown as unsigned octal
x or X	int shown as unsigned hexadecimal
f	float, −ddd.ddd style
e or E	float, −d.ddde±ddd style
g or G	float, style f or e picked automatically by the function
p	pointer shown in readable form
n	argument is pointer to int into which is placed the number of characters already written to the output stream by this printf()

Table 7.4   Conversion Characters for `printf()`

One technique that we have not emphasized is the writing of printf() statements like this:

```
char ctrl_str[] = "He has %d sons\n";     /* this is the control string */
...
printf(ctrl_str, 2);  /* the control string appears in the normal place */
```

This approach allows the reuse of the same control string because the control string has a name, ctrl_str, which is used in the printf() statement rather than a string literal.

In order to illustrate various printf() conversion characters, the program in Figure 7.7 shows a matrix of combinations. Unfortunately, not all vendors implement the printf() conversion characters exactly the same. The code produced from some compilers does not produce a table whose lines align straight. One vendor, for instance, adds the leading zero for octal output and the leading 0x for hex output to the field width, making the field longer than the output width even if there is blank space in the output that could absorb the additional characters. While these problems could be worked around in a production program, they mean that the "pretty" output of the program could only be produced on some compilers.

```
/*
** Samples of printf() Extended Conversion Characters - printf.c
*/

#include <stdio.h>

main()
{
    int i = 234, j = 5678, k = 19;
    float e = 432.6, f = 3.7, g = 18.9;
    printf("%-6s!%-6s!%-6s!%-8s!%-10s!%-10s!%-10s!\n",
           "codes", "  6d", "  6o", "    8x", "  10.2e", "  10.2f", "  10.2g");
    printf("------------------------------"
           "------------------------------\n");
```

(program continued on next page...)

```
   printf("%-6s!%-+#06d!%-+#06o!%-+#08x!%-+#010.2e!%-+#010.2f!%-+#010.2g!\n",
        "%-+#0", i, j, k, e, f, g);
   printf("%-6s!%-+#6d!%-+#6o!%-+#8x!%-+#10.2e!%-+#10.2f!%-+#10.2g!\n",
        "%-+#", i, j, k, e, f, (g *= 2));
   printf("%-6s!%-+06d!%-+06o!%-+08x!%-+010.2e!%-+010.2f!%-+010.2g!\n",
        "%-+0", i, j, k, e, f, (g *= 2));
   printf("%-6s!%-+6d!%-+6o!%-+8x!%-+10.2e!%-+10.2f!%-+10.2g!\n",
        "%-+", i, j, k, e, f, (g *= 2));
   printf("%-6s!%-#06d!%-#06o!%-#08x!%-#010.2e!%-#010.2f!%-#010.2g!\n",
        "%-#0", i, j, k, e, f, (g *= 2));
   printf("%-6s!%-#6d!%-#6o!%-#8x!%-#10.2e!%-#10.2f!%-#10.2g!\n",
        "%-#", i, j, k, e, f, (g *= 2));
   printf("%-6s!%-06d!%-06o!%-08x!%-010.2e!%-010.2f!%-010.2g!\n",
        "%-0", i, j, k, e, f, (g *= 2));
   printf("%-6s!%-6d!%-6o!%-8x!%-10.2e!%-10.2f!%-10.2g!\n",
        "%-", i, j, k, e, f, (g *= 2));
   printf("%-6s!%+#06d!%+#06o!%+#08x!%+#010.2e!%+#010.2f!%+#010.2g!\n",
        "%+#0", i, j, k, e, f, (g *= 2));
   printf("%-6s!%+#6d!%+#6o!%+#8x!%+#10.2e!%+#10.2f!%+#10.2g!\n",
        "%+#", i, j, k, e, f, (g *= 2));
   printf("%-6s!%+06d!%+06o!%+08x!%+010.2e!%+010.2f!%+010.2g!\n",
        "%+0", i, j, k, e, f, (g *= 2));
   printf("%-6s!%+6d!%+6o!%+8x!%+10.2e!%+10.2f!%+10.2g!\n",
        "%+", i, j, k, e, f, (g *= 2));
   printf("%-6s!%#06d!%#06o!%#08x!%#010.2e!%#010.2f!%#010.2g!\n",
        "%#0", i, j, k, e, f, (g *= 2));
   printf("%-6s!%#6d!%#6o!%#8x!%#10.2e!%#10.2f!%#10.2g!\n",
        "%#", i, j, k, e, f, (g *= 2));
   printf("%-6s!%06d!%06o!%08x!%010.2e!%010.2f!%010.2g!\n",
        "%0", i, j, k, e, f, (g *= 2));
   printf("%-6s!%6d!%6o!%8x!%10.2e!%10.2f!%10.2g!\n",
        "%", i, j, k, e, f, (g *= 2));

   printf("\n%-6s!%-6s!%-6s!%-8s!\n",
        "codes", " 6.6d", " 6.6o", "  8.8x");
   printf("----------------------------\n");
   printf("%-6s!%-+#6.6d!%-+#6.6o!%-+#8.8x!\n", "%-+#", i, j, k);
   printf("%-6s!%-+6.6d!%-+6.6o!%-+8.8x!\n", "%-+", i, j, k);
   printf("%-6s!%-#6.6d!%-#6.6o!%-#8.8x!\n", "%-#", i, j, k);
   printf("%-6s!%-6.6d!%-6.6o!%-8.8x!\n", "%-", i, j, k);
   printf("%-6s!%+#6.6d!%+#6.6o!%+#8.8x!\n", "%+#", i, j, k);
   printf("%-6s!%+6.6d!%+6.6o!%+8.8x!\n", "%+", i, j, k);
   printf("%-6s!%#6.6d!%#6.6o!%#8.8x!\n", "%#", i, j, k);
   printf("%-6s!%*.*d!%6.6o!%8.8x! <- dynamic width\n", "%", 6, 6, i, j, k);
}
```

Figure 7.7   Samples of printf() **Extended
Conversion Characters—**printf.c

The output from the program in Figure 7.7 is shown in Figure 7.8. Note that there are two blocks of output. The second block provides leading zeroes by using the precision modifier rather than a leading zero on the width value. Also, the last line of the second block was created by using dynamic values on both the width and precision specifiers.

codes	6d	6o	8x	10.2e	10.2f	10.2g
%-+#0	+234	013056	0x13	+4.33e+002	+3.70	+18.9
%-+#	+234	013056	0x13	+4.33e+002	+3.70	+37.8
%-+0	+234	13056	13	+4.33e+002	+3.70	+75.6
%-+	+234	13056	13	+4.33e+002	+3.70	+151
%-#0	234	013056	0x13	4.33e+002	3.70	302.
%-#	234	013056	0x13	4.33e+002	3.70	605.
%-0	234	13056	13	4.33e+002	3.70	1.21e+003
%-	234	13056	13	4.33e+002	3.70	2.42e+003
%+#0	+00234	013056	0x000013	+4.33e+002	+000003.70	+4.84e+003
%+#	+234	013056	0x13	+4.33e+002	+3.70	+9.68e+003
%+0	+00234	013056	00000013	+4.33e+002	+000003.70	+1.94e+004
%+	+234	13056	13	+4.33e+002	+3.70	+3.87e+004
%#0	000234	013056	0x000013	04.33e+002	0000003.70	07.74e+004
%#	234	013056	0x13	4.33e+002	3.70	1.55e+005
%0	000234	013056	00000013	04.33e+002	0000003.70	003.1e+005
%	234	13056	13	4.33e+002	3.70	6.19e+005

codes	6.6d	6.6o	8.8x
%-+#	+00234	013056	0x000013
%-+	+00234	013056	00000013
%-#	000234	013056	0x000013
%-	000234	013056	00000013
%+#	+00234	013056	0x000013
%+	+00234	013056	00000013
%#	000234	013056	0x000013
%	000234	013056	00000013	<- dynamic width

Figure 7.8 Output of printf.c

Antibugging Note 7.1   Double check uses of printf()

Carefully check for agreement between printf() conversion characters and arguments. Absolutely no checking is done by the compiler. Further, the function prototype for printf() does not help to ensure agreement, since the prototype allows for a variable number of arguments.

7.3.2   *Formatted Input and Data Conversion Without* scanf()

The problems with scanf() are numerous. Begin right now to forget that scanf() even exists, and plan on using a more reliable method of getting information into programs. The technique that you should use is to read all input data character by character and then convert it to the needed data type. Although standard functions that get strings (gets() and fgets()) are already available, we will not use them. The gets() function is not considered safe because there is no control over how many characters are entered through the keyboard. All characters not read remain in the input buffer to be read next time gets() is invoked. The fgets() function solves that particular problem by allowing you to specify a maximum number of characters to be read. However, fgets() can be difficult to use because it leaves the newline character in the input data, often requiring that the newline be immediately removed before the string is used.

The function shown in the program in Figure 7.9, get_chars_safely(), solves all the abovementioned problems and difficulties. It reads the standard input file stream character by character and checks after each character whether it should continue. Characters are stored in the character array whose location is passed as the second argument of the function. After the input characters have been read they can be edited and converted to another data type, like integer, long, or float. Neither of the problems associated with gets() and fgets() are present in get_chars_safely() since the newline character is not stored in the string, and no characters are left on the input stream to be read by the next input function.

The function atoi(), used in the main() function in this program, converts ASCII data to integer. A string name is passed as the argument and atoi() returns the internal numeric value which the digits in the string represent. For instance, the string "123" becomes the number 123 in internal numeric format. The atoi() function performs almost no error checking (it quits converting when the first nonnumeric is found), so good validity checking must take place by examining the characters in the string before the conversion is requested. The function atol() converts a string to long numeric format (for numbers bigger than 32,767) and atof() converts a string to double. Note that the standard header file <stdlib.h> is included in the program because it is in <stdlib> that all ASCII to...(ato...) function prototypes are found.

In our sample program we have included a character array, chars_go_here, even though we have not yet studied arrays. Character arrays are used to store strings of characters. If we expect to write programs that receive more than one character of input, we need an array. The array chars_go_here contains 10 characters, which means that it is large enough to hold all the characters that can be converted to an integer, and some forms of floating point numbers. Other floating point numbers might require that chars_go_here be made larger. It is a good practice to have more character storage than the input format requires.

```
/*
** A Safe Character Input Technique - getcsafe.c
*/

#include <stdio.h>               /* printf() and getchar() declared here */
#include <stdlib.h>              /* ato...() prototypes are here */

int  get_chars_safely (int, char *);    /* function prototype */

main()
{
    char chars_go_here[10];     /* the array where the input will go */
    int  converted_int;
    long converted_long;
    double converted_double;

    printf("\nEnter a numeric string to be converted:\n");
    get_chars_safely(
                    (sizeof(chars_go_here) / sizeof(char)) - 1,
                    chars_go_here
                  );
    printf("\nThe input chars were \"%s\"\n", chars_go_here);
    converted_int = atoi(chars_go_here);
    printf("The converted integer is %d\n", converted_int);
    converted_long = atol(chars_go_here);
    printf("The converted long integer is %ld\n", converted_long);
    converted_double = atof(chars_go_here);
    printf("The converted double is %lf\n", converted_double);
}

/*
** get_chars_safely()
**    This function accepts characters from standard input until ONE of
**    three conditions is met:
**       1. As many characters as max_num_chars have been entered.
**       2. End of file on standard input has been reached.
**       3. A newline is received on standard input.
**    You must define where_chars_go at least as big as max_num_chars + 1.
**    \0 is placed in where_chars_go after the last character received.
**    The newline, if received, is not placed into the string.
**    The function returns the actual number of characters in the string
**       without counting the terminating null.
**    No characters are left on the input stream.
**    The defined constant EOF is located in <stdio.h>.
*/
```

(program continued on next page...)

```
int  get_chars_safely (max_num_chars, where_chars_go)
int  max_num_chars;
char where_chars_go[];
{
    int input_char, index = 0;          /* initialize the subscript to zero */
    while (index < max_num_chars &&
           (input_char = getchar()) != EOF &&
           input_char != '\n'
          ) {
       where_chars_go[index] = input_char;        /* put character in array */
       index++;
    }
    where_chars_go[index] = '\0';  /* the terminating null makes a string */
    while(input_char != EOF && input_char != '\n') {
       input_char = getchar();                      /* flush the input stream */
    }
    return (index);
}
```

Figure 7.9   A Safe Character Input Technique—getcsafe.c

To illustrate how this function would work, here are two sample runs:

```
Enter a numeric string to be converted:
123456789

The input chars were "123456789"
The converted integer is -13035
The converted long integer is 123456789
The converted double is 123456789.000000
```

and:

```
Enter a numeric string to be converted:
123.456789

The input chars were "123.45678"
The converted integer is 123
The converted long integer is 123
The converted double is 123.456780
```

Note that in the first run we entered a number larger than that which could be stored in a 16-bit integer, yet atoi() tried its best to do the conversion we requested. This should illustrate that the conversion routines perform virtually no validity checks on the data itself; all checking must be coded explicitly in the program by the programmer. Note also that in the second run we entered 10 characters, but only 9 were accepted and used. The array `chars_go_here` can only hold 9 significant digits since one position must contain the \0 character to terminate the string.

7.4   Self-Check

These statements are True or False. The answers are given at the end.

1. C input and output is oriented toward characters.

2. File streams come in only two types: text and character.

3. When you use a text file on the IBM-PC, the newline character (line feed) is changed upon output to a carriage return-line feed sequence.

4. The `FILE` pointer associated with a stream is optional and only sometimes needed by the program.

5. Standard files can be either text or binary.

6. By default, `stdout` and `stderr` send data to the same place, although only `stdout` can be redirected on the IBM-PC.

7. Standard input is redirected with the > sign, standard output with the < sign, and piping is accomplished with the ¦ character.

8. Buffering can enable a C program to process disk file data faster than an assembly language program.

9. Output streams that will contain diagnostic information should not be buffered because some of the information could be lost.

10. The only way to test for end of file in your program is to use the `feof()` function.

11. The standard character input function `getc()` will only read standard ASCII characters.

12. The function `putc()` requires two arguments, but `getc()` only requires one.

13. The header file `<stdio.h>` is required to be present in each program that uses any of the standard character functions.

14. Although not described in the new ANSI C standard the function `getch()` provides the ability to trap additional keystrokes that are ignored by the `getc()` function.

15. The function `fprintf()` provides a convenient way to send control codes to the printer.

16. Although the * character can be used as the width in a `printf()` conversion character sequence, it must be replaced by a constant value from the argument list when the program is compiled.

17. Neither `scanf()` nor `gets()` are considered truly safe input functions.

18. The function `atoi()` performs extensive edit checking of the string being converted and returns error information accordingly.

19. The function `atod()` converts a string to type `double`.

Answers

1. T   2. F   3. T   4. F   5. F   6. T   7. F   8. T   9. T   10. F
11. F   12. T   13. F   14. T   15. T   16. F   17. T   18. F   19. F

7.5   Review Program—Maskable Data Entry

Since the primary emphasis of this chapter has been console input and output techniques, we will illustrate some of the pertinent topics by developing a function to retrieve user inputs.

☐ Design Specifications

The first design consideration will be to define what is meant by a data entry field. A data entry field can be described as a data entry area presented to the user on the display in which he or she may enter requested data. The extent to which the user is allowed to edit the entry and the maximum number of characters he or she may enter are controlled by the edit mask string and the length attribute of the entry field respectively. Such a scheme controls the data that may be entered, and produces a predictable and safe means to retrieve the data that the controlling program requires. The maskable data entry field consists of the following:

1. A user prompt, consisting of a string.

2. An entry field, where the data is stored after being retrieved from the user input.

The first component is a simple string used to inform the operator what input is expected. It should be descriptive and leave no doubt what the user is required to enter. The second component, the entry field itself, possesses the following attributes:

2.1 a data type

2.2 an edit mask string

2.3 an entry field length

The attribute 2.1 is the data type required, i.e., integer, string, float, and so on. The second, 2.2, is an optional string which is displayed but not included as part of the user's input. For example, consider the following diagram of a data entry field used to retrieve the current date from the operator,

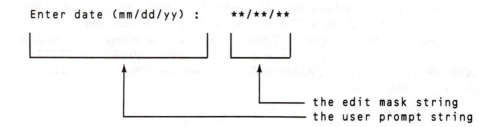

The operator would be allowed to enter the date within the edit mask string, while the cursor would simply skip to each region of the entry field over the edit mask characters.

The last component, 2.3, is the maximum number of characters the user may enter.

We must answer several questions before attempting to write the pseudocode for our function:

1. How will we allow the user to terminate entries to the data field?

2. How will we allow editing of the field before termination is reached?

3. Will different data types be directly mapped to the entry field, or will a simple string be returned, which can later be converted to the desired data type?

4. What special considerations are necessary when the user chooses to terminate entries immediately, before any characters are entered?

5. Should our function be written to be portable across all environments, or specifically for one environment?

Answering all the questions beforehand will give us clear directions before we embark on writing the pseudocode itself. We decide the following:

1. The Return key or EOF character will provide the only means to terminate entry to the data field.

2. The backspace key will be the only means allowed to delete previously entered characters in the data field.

3. The function will only return an ASCII string representation of the data entered. No implicit data type will be associated with the retrieved data. It will be the calling program's responsibility to convert the retrieved string to the proper data type desired.

4. If the user simply hits Return before entering any data into the field, a null length string will be the returned value.

5. The function will be portable across all environments supporting the ANSI standard C language.

The last design consideration will restrict the aesthetic appeal of our input routine but ensure portability. Compare our input routine implementation here with those illustrated in Appendix F and Appendix G. These appendices contain versions of our input function specific to the UNIX/CURSES and MS/PC-DOS/ANSI.SYS environments. Although they are more appealing, they are not completely portable.

□ *Program Design*

Now that we have clarified some of our design details, we proceed to write the pseudocode:

```
begin get_field_input(prompt, edit_mask, dest_buffer)
string prompt, edit_mask
character array dest_buffer

    character array temp_buffer

    print(prompt)
    print(edit_mask)
    print(<carriage-return/linefeed>)
    <position cursor directly under first valid character in edit_mask>
    <get user input to dest_buffer>
    <transfer characters from temp_buffer to dest_buffer stripping
        out mask characters>
    return(<length of dest_buffer>)
end get_field_input
```

You will notice that this is the first review program where we take a somewhat backward approach to our normal design procedures; i.e., we are not writing the main function pseudocode first, but rather a utility function. In this program, the `main()` function will be used to test our completed function, rather than acting as a stand-alone program. This technique is commonly used to construct libraries for program development. You will often see the `main()` function referred to as a "test jig" or a driver program.

Now we return to the task at hand. Examining our pseudocode, we determine that we will need several variables:

Variable	Type	Description
prompt	char[]	user prompt string
edit__mask	char[]	field edit mask string
dest__buffer	char[]	buffer which receives the user's inputs
i	int	index into the edit__mask[] array
j	int	index into the dest__buffer[] array 3

Now, let's code the function.

□ Design Implementation

```
/*-------------------------------------------------------------
 getinput.c
 The main() function is simply a driver to test the function
 get_field_input()
 -----------------------------------------------------------*/
#include <stdio.h>
#include <string.h>

#define IN_CHAR '*'

main()
{
   int in_buf_length;                  /* length of input retrieved */
   char in_buffer[80];                 /* buffer where input is placed */
/*
 get date from user and print what's returned with its length
*/
   in_buf_length = get_field_input("Enter date ", "**/**/**", in_buffer);
   printf("in_buffer = %s, in_buf_length = %d\n\n", in_buffer, in_buf_length);
/*
 get user's initials and print what's returned with its length
*/
   in_buf_length = get_field_input("Enter your initials (first,middle,last) ",
                        "*,*,*", in_buffer);
   printf("in_buffer = %s, in_buf_length = %d\n\n", in_buffer, in_buf_length);
/*
 get user's height in feet/inches and print what's returned with its length
*/
   in_buf_length = get_field_input("Enter height ", "*'**\"", in_buffer);
   printf("in_buffer = %s, in_buf_length = %d\n\n", in_buffer, in_buf_length);

   return;
}
```

(program continued on next page...)

```
/*------------------------------------------------------------------
   int get_field_input(prompt, edit_mask, dest_buffer)

   Generate a maskable entry field and store input as a string into
   the destination buffer. The edit mask is used as a template only
   and is not included in the returned input string.  This function is
   portable across all environments supporting the C language.

   The user input is terminated by pressing the <Return> (or <Enter>)
   key.  No validation checking is performed on the input.

   parm          type         description
   ...........................................................
   prompt        char[]       the user prompt
   edit_mask     char[]       the edit mask, a string consisting of
                              characters & input characters;
                              the input characters are defined in the
                              macro IN_CHAR
   dest_buffer   char[]       buffer where input retrieved is stored; will
                              contain the actual characters input not
                              including the edit_mask string; should be
                              dimensioned at least field_length + 1 to
                              accommodate null character appended to
                              characters retrieved

   return        type         description
   ...........................................................
   ---           int          the actual number of characters retrieved
                              which will be <= edit_mask
------------------------------------------------------------------*/
int get_field_input(prompt, edit_mask, dest_buffer)
char prompt[], edit_mask[], dest_buffer[];
{
    int spaces_over;                     /* used to position cursor for input */
    int field_length;                    /* # of spaces in edit_mask */
    char temp_buffer[80];                /* temporary buffer for user input */

    printf("%s", prompt);                /* print user prompt */
    printf("%s", edit_mask);             /* print edit mask string */
    printf("\n");                        /* move down to next display row */
```

```
/*
 calculate cursor positioning
*/
   spaces_over = strlen(prompt);        /* first half of spacing adjustment */
   {
   int i = 0;                           /* find first valid position in mask */
   while(edit_mask[i] != '\0' && edit_mask[i] != IN_CHAR)
      {
      ++i;
      }
   spaces_over += i;                    /* second half of spacing adjustment */
   }
/*
 space over to proper position on display under the edit mask
*/
   {
   int i = spaces_over;
   while(i--)
      {
      putchar(' ');
      }
   }
/*
 get the user input
*/
   get_chars_safely(strlen(edit_mask), temp_buffer);
   {
   int i = 0, j = 0;
/*
 move user input to destination buffer stripping out mask characters
*/
   while(edit_mask[i] != '\0' && temp_buffer[i] != '\0')
      {
      if(edit_mask[i] == IN_CHAR)
         {
         dest_buffer[j++] = temp_buffer[i];
         }
      ++i;
      }
   dest_buffer[j] = '\0';               /* tack on null terminator */
   }
   return(strlen(dest_buffer));         /* send back the input length */
}
```

(program continued on next page...)

```
/*--------------------------------------------------------------------
    get_chars_safely()
        This function accepts characters from standard input until ONE of
        three conditions is met:
            1. As many characters as max_num_chars have been entered.
            2. End of file on standard input has been reached.
            3. A newline is received on standard input.
        You must define where_chars_go at least as big as max_num_chars + 1.
        \0 is placed in where_chars_go after the last character received.
        The newline, if received, is not placed into the string.
        The function returns the actual number of characters in the string
            without counting the terminating null.
        No characters are left on the input stream.
        The defined constant EOF is located in <stdio.h>.
-------------------------------------------------------------------*/
int   get_chars_safely (max_num_chars, where_chars_go)
int   max_num_chars;
char where_chars_go[];
{
    int input_char, index = 0;          /* initialize the subscript to zero */
    while (index < max_num_chars &&
            (input_char = getchar()) != EOF &&
            input_char != '\n'
            ) {
        where_chars_go[index] = input_char;      /* put character in array */
        index++;
    }
    where_chars_go[index] = '\0';   /* the terminating null makes a string */
    while (input_char != EOF && input_char != '\n') {
        input_char = getchar();                    /* flush the input stream */
    }
    return (index);
}
```

Note that we have used a function, get_chars_safely(), coded earlier in this chapter to safely retrieve the user's input. The primary purpose of our new function, get_field_input(), is to provide the user with an edit mask to guide correct input.

☐ *Program Output*

```
Enter date **/**/**
         01/01/88
in_buffer = 010188, in_buf_length = 6
```

```
Enter your initials (first,middle,last) *,*,*
                                          R R S
in_buffer = RRS, in_buf_length = 3

Enter height *'**"
               5 11 1/2
in_buffer = 511, in_buf_length = 3
```

Note how we printed the values contained in `in_buffer` and `in_buf_length` to check the operation of our newly coded function. You should realize that although the function only returns an integer (the length of the actual input), it also sends input back to the caller (`main()`) via the character array `in_buffer[]`. We'll study exactly how this works when we discuss arrays and pointers in depth.

Points to Study

1. Use of the `getchar()` standard library function.

2. Use of the `putchar()` standard library function.

3. How the function positions the cursor without using machine and/or environment-specific functions.

7.6 Exercises

* 1. Modify the Review Program function `get_field_input()` to include the following features:
   a. End of line wrap in case the edit field mask must continue to the next display line.
   b. Picture definitions for the input field positions. For example, instead of using spaces for the valid positions within the entry field, you might modify the function to recognize the following:

Picture Character	Meaning
X	Alphanumeric characters only
9	Numeric characters only
space	Any alphanumeric character plus punctuation characters

As an example the edit mask,

```
[99/99/99]
```

would only allow the operator to enter numeric values in our sample date field. Incorporating such features in our function complicates the code but provides a simple form of data validation on the user's input.

c. Different colors for the prompt and edit mask.

2. Write a function that prints a string centered on the display. Also include a test jig main function to demonstrate that the function works properly.

3. Write a simple menu interface function that could be used in any applications program. The function should be designed to receive a single string argument that represents the menu selections to be displayed. A suitable format for the string would be to divide the string into substrings separated by a delimiter character. For example, a sample call to the function might look like,

```
users_choice = menu("1-Add record*2-Delete Record*3-Exit program");
```

which would produce the output,

```
        1-Add record
        2-Delete record
        3-Exit program

Enter your choice [_]
```

after which the function, menu() would return the user's choice as an integer representing the menu selection.

4. Write a simple mailing label program that prints return address labels allowing the user to enter the following:
   a. First name
   b. Last name
   c. Street address
   d. City
   e. State
   f. Zip code

You may use the Review Program function, get_field_input() to retrieve the necessary data from the user. You should also allow the user to specify the number of labels to be printed and the print format, either one column or two columns of labels. A sample session might look like this:

```
          GENERIC LABEL PRINTER
          ---------------------

First name  : [John                 ]
Last name   : [Doe                  ]
Address     : [Noname Street, Suite 1 ]
City/State  : [Anywhere        ]  [OK]
Zip Code    : [12345]

How many labels ? [10]

Make sure printer is ready. Hit <Return> to print labels..._
```

5. Write a generalized function to set the display color attributes using either the ANSI.SYS escape sequence (if using MS/PC-DOS) or CURSES (if using UNIX). Include provisions for a monochrome or color display adapter. Write an associated driver program to demonstrate that your function works properly. See Appendix F for information about ANSI.SYS and Appendix G for information about CURSES.

* 6. Write a command-driven printer driver program. The program will accept a string input from the user which represents printer commands, process the string and send the extracted printer commands to the stdprn stream file. For example, a sample session might look like this:

```
     Printer Driver Command List

     Command          Meaning
```

Command	Meaning
lf	line feed
ff	form feed
com	compressed print
exp	expanded width print
rst	printer reset
lm, n	set left margin to column n
rm, n	set right margin to column n
bm, n	set bottom margin to n rows

```
Enter command string: [ff,lm,4,rm,82,bm,6,clear,com            ]
```

(program continued on next page...)

```
Executing commands...

    form feed
    left margin 4
    right margin 82
    bottom margin 6
    UNRECOGNIZED COMMAND: "clear"
    compressed print

End command list.
```

You may vary the printer commands for your particular printer brand. Some research may be required to find out the control strings understood by your printer. Hint: Define the valid printer commands and associated descriptions in a single string. Use standard library string functions to process the commands.

7. Write a menu-driven but less powerful version of exercise 6 that allows the user to execute printer commands. An example session might look like this:

```
            Printer Driver Command List

        1: lf            - line feed
        2: ff            - form feed
        3: com           - compressed print
        4: exp           - expanded width print
        5: rst           - printer reset
        6: lm, n         - set left margin to column n
        7: rm, n         - set right margin to column n
        8: bm, n         - set bottom margin to n rows
        99: Exit program

    Enter command choice [6 ]
    What column setting? [10]
    Done.

    Enter command choice [2 ]
    Done.

    Enter command choice [3 ]
    Done.

    Enter command choice [99]
    Exiting program...
```

* advanced exercises

7.7 Pretest

☐ *Multiple Choice*

Circle one correct answer for each of the following:

1. The stream file stderr is:
   a. Not redirectable.
   b. Used to display error messages.
   c. Automatically opened by the operating systems.
   d. All of the above.
   e. a and b.
   f. a and c.

2. The standard library function fprintf():
   a. Can be used to output information to any stream file.
   b. Can be redirected for any stream file.
   c. Cannot take a variable number of arguments.
   d. Is normally implemented as a macro.

3. Stream files in UNIX are normally buffered because:
   a. The concept was discovered after UNIX was written.
   b. Most multiuser computer systems use buffering rather than allow direct access to physical devices.
   c. It is a faster I/O technique.
   d. It is difficult to implement buffering in assembly language.

4. The library macro getchar() is equivalent to:
   a. getch()
   b. getche()
   c. getc(stdin)
   d. putchar(getch())

5. When we say that a stream file is buffered we mean that:
   a. It has been stripped of carriage return and line feed characters.
   b. Characters read or written are delayed in a temporary storage area by the operating system or hardware.
   c. The file is padded with 0x1a to fill the last record of the file if necessary.
   d. It can only be accessed with macro implementations in the standard library.

6. What is wrong with the following code fragment?

```
char my_buffer[80];
int i;

for (i = 0; i <= sizeof(my_buffer) / sizeof(char); ++i)
   {
   my_buffer[i] = getchar();
   }
```

   a. The array my_buffer[] will be overrun by one character.
   b. The getchar() macro cannot be used inside for loops.
   c. Should have used getche() instead of getchar().
   d. The for loop would iterate indefinitely.

7. The standard library function scanf() is not considered a safe method to retrieve user inputs because
   a. It does not perform length checking on inputs.
   b. It can be redirected to a null device causing the machine to lock up.
   c. It is specific to the keyboard which fails frequently.
   d. End of file (EOF) checking cannot be performed.

8. When we say that stdout and stdin can be redirected we mean that
   a. They can be implemented as preprocessor macros.
   b. They can be attached to a different stream file.
   c. Buffering can be disabled for both functions.
   d. They are available no matter what operating system is used.

9. The standard library function feof() is:
   a. Used to detect the end of file condition for stdin and stdout.
   b. Used to detect the end of file condition for any stream file.
   c. Used to strip carriage-return/line feeds from a stream file.
   d. None of the above.

10. The standard library function ferror() is:
   a. Most useful when used to detect an end of file condition.
   b. Used to determine how many characters were retrieved on the last read to a stream file.
   c. Used to determine if an error occurred when accessing a stream file.
   d. All of the above.
   e. None of the above.

8

Scope, Storage Duration, and Storage Classes

S cope, storage duration and storage classes are concepts associated with newer computer languages. Many older languages (e.g. COBOL, BASIC) either do not have these characteristics or provide them in a limited fashion. By understanding these features, you will be able to utilize all the capabilities which the C language has to offer.

After studying this chapter, you will be able to do the following:

1. Define the concept of scope.

2. Explain each of the two types of storage duration.

3. Identify the scope and storage duration associated with a storage class.

4. Illustrate how scope can cause variables to be visible only in certain circumstances.

5. Show examples of how scope, storage duration and storage class can be beneficial when programming.

8.1   Scope

The *scope* of a data item is the part of the program where the item can be seen, and therefore used. Each variable and function has a scope. Certain keywords control how far that scope extends.

The association between scope and "seeing" an item comes from the idea that "if it can't be seen it then it isn't there". Hence, the word *visibility* is often used interchangeably with scope to describe exactly the same thing.

C has four types of scope:

1. File

2. Block

3. Function Prototype

4. Function

8.1.1   *File*

If a data item is declared or defined outside any function, it has *file scope*. This means that its visibility spans from the point where it is declared or defined through the end of the same source file. A data item with file scope is often referred to as being a global variable.

A C program can consist of one or more source files. These files can be compiled separately and combined by a linking process into one executable program. The entire set of source files is a complete C program, but file scope does not extend throughout all the various source files that make up the program. Rather, a data item with file scope can be seen in only the one source file in which the declaration or definition appears. It can also be seen in any lines of code which are brought into the one source file through the #include preprocessor directive if the directive appears after the definition or declaration of the data item.

A data item also might be defined on a line of code which appears in an included file named in a #include directive. If so, then the scope of that data item extends past the end of the included file and through to the bottom of the including file. It is also visible in all other included files that appear "below" this included file. Once a file named on a #include directive has been included in a compilation process by the preprocessor, there is no longer any distinction about separate files. The files continue to remain separate on disk, but are not considered separate by the compiler.

Pieces of data in one source file can be referenced from another file when the two are combined into one program. In such an instance there will be a definition of the item in one source file (where storage will be reserved and the item will physically reside) and a declaration of it in another (which will refer to the physical storage located in the other file). Each file will have a separate file scope for the same item, with each scope determined by the placement of the declaration or definition in that file. We'll explain this concept in this chapter when we discuss the extern storage class.

The program in Figure 8.1 will illustrate some of these points. Included in the program is a variable definition which occurs not only outside any function but also after main(). We do not recommend this approach as a good programming practice, however, because it can cause the reliability of the program to hinge on the correct placement of a variable definition or declaration within a source file.

Antibugging Note 8.1   Don't define data items between functions

Although the language permits it, don't define variables or use the #define or #include preprocessor directives between functions. Doing so introduces confusion about the scope of various global variables.

```
/*
** filscope.c    Illustrates file scope
*/

int x;                /* the integer x will be visible inside stdio.h */

#include <stdio.h>    /* the scope of anything found in stdio.h extends */
                      /*    into and through the end of the including file */
#include <ctype.h>    /* things found in stdio.h are also visible while */
                      /*    inside ctype.h */
main()
{
    int b;
    b = a;            /* a is undefined here, and this line will */
}                     /*    generate a compile error */

int a = 1;            /* a is defined from this point forward */

int subfunc()         /* this function is never used */
{
    return (a);       /* a is defined at this point */
}
```

Figure 8.1   An Example of File Scope—filscope.c

In the program filscope.c we find the variable x, which is defined above two #include directives. The visibility of x extends through the files stdio.h and ctype.h. If we had provided our own header files, and if they needed the variable x in order to have an error-free compile, then x would have to be defined above the #include directive.

This program, however, will not compile correctly because of the statement b = a which appears inside main(). The statement is there to illustrate that if the definition of a appears after its use, then an error results. That a is available for use in the function subfunc() is illustrated by how it can be used as the function return value without a compile error.

Quick Note 8.1   File Scope

File scope is limited to one source file and describes where in the file a particular data item is visible. It extends from the point of declaration or definition through the end of the same source file. It also extends into any lines of source code in included files if the `#include` directive occurs after the declaration or definition.

8.1.2   *Block*

Each time a local variable is created inside a function, i.e., a variable known only to that function and not visible outside the function, then *block scope* is being used. The span of block scope extends from the point where the data item is declared or defined to the closing brace that ends the block.

Two groups of items have block scope:

1. Data items that are defined immediately after the opening brace of any block.

2. Parameters that are declared in a function definition.

The first group includes both definitions inside a nested block within any function and also definitions immediately after the opening brace that begins the function body. Remember that functions are blocks of code also, and the braces that delimit a function serve the same purpose as those that delimit any other block of code. The second group includes the parameters in the function definition, but not those in the function declaration (function declaration scope will be discussed in the next section). Because these two groups have the same scope it is inappropriate to use the same name for a parameter of a function as for the definition of a variable immediately after the opening brace of the function body. This is really no different than writing the same variable name twice on two separate lines of the source file, one immediately after the other.

Some key things should be noted from the example program in Figure 8.2. First, the variable name b was used in both functions without any conflict. Two separate and distinct variables were created, each visible within its own block. Second, had we left the comments off the first line after the opening brace of `sub-func()`, a compile error would have resulted. The name a would have been used twice within the same scope, once as a parameter to the function and then a second time as a local variable within the same function. Third, the scope of the variable b is "passed down" from the level in the function where the definition appears into the inner block. Scope, or visibility, is passed down into inner blocks, but not up into outer blocks. This is further illustrated in the fourth point. The variable a is created in the inner block within `subfunc()`. No compile error results even though the same name was used for a parameter of `subfunc()` because the scope of variables defined within blocks is not passed up or out of the inner block.

```
/*
** block.c    Illustrates block scope
*/

#include <stdio.h>

int subfunc(int x);                      /* prototype for the function */

main()
{
   int b = 2;     /* b has block scope which extends only through main */
   printf("%d\n", subfunc(b));           /* here we print the value 6 */
}

int subfunc(int a)  /* a has block scope which extends through subfunc */
{
/* int a = 1;              a redeclaration error would occur right here */
   int b = 4;         /* this b is not the same one as defined in main */
   {                        /* inner block inside subfunc begins here */
      int a;          /* no redefinition error occurs here because */
      a = 3;          /*    the block level has changed            */
      b = a;          /* this b is the one defined 4 lines above */
   }
   return (b * a);
}
```

Figure 8.2 An Example of Block Scope—block.c

In examining this program, note that in the innermost block of subfunc()
the local variable b changes, but not the formal parameter a of the function. The
reason a doesn't change is because another variable a is defined inside this innermost block, eliminating access to the formal parameter. The parameter a retains
the value passed to the function, but b becomes the value given to it in the innermost block. Therefore, the value returned by the function is 6 rather than 9.

Quick Note 8.2   Block Scope

Block scope applies to both function parameters and items declared or
defined after the opening brace of a block. It extends until the matching
closing brace is encountered and is passed into any nested blocks are
defined.

8.1.3 *Function Prototype*

Function prototype scope is a recent addition to the language. It did not exist prior to the later drafts of the current standard because it was in those drafts that the new, modern style of function prototypes was added. The classic style of prototypes did not allow a variable name to be included, hence there was never any conflict between names used in the prototype (there weren't any) and others in the program.

The example program in Figure 8.3 illustrates that there is no problem using the name x both in a function prototype and also to name a global variable. The scope of the x used in the prototype extends from the point where x is used through the end of the prototype, so it would be incorrect to use the name x twice within the same prototype. After the correct example we show a second line (commented out so it won't stop the compile) to illustrate the incorrect alternative. Of course, y exhibits the same characteristics.

```
/*
** funproto.c    Illustrates function prototype scope
*/

#include <stdio.h>

    int protofunc(int x, int y);            /* prototype for the function */
/*  int protofunc(int x, int x); */     /* here x is redeclared, an error */

    int x = 4, y = 5;            /* no duplicate definition occurs here */

    main()
    {
        printf("%d\n", protofunc(x, y));        /* here we print the value 20 */
    }

    int protofunc(int a, int b)
    {
        return (a * b);
    }
```

Figure 8.3 An Example of Function Prototype Scope—`funproto.c`

Quick Note 8.3   Function Prototype Scope

Function prototype scope extends from the point where a name is used in the prototype through the end of the same prototype. The names used in a prototype do not conflict with other prototypes or any other variable names.

Antibugging Note 8.2   Matching function prototypes to definitions

While there is no obligation to use the same parameter names in the prototype as in the definition, doing so adds clarity to the program. Write either the prototype or the definition first, then immediately build the other.

8.1.4   *Function*

The `goto` statement (which we have intentionally avoided in this book) needs a label name as the target of the goto action. This label, which is identified as such by the colon following the name, is the only type of item in the C language that has *function scope*. This means that the label name must be unique within the function. The same label name can be used in any and all other functions without compile errors resulting from duplicate labels.

Using a `goto` breaks no laws, but any code containing a `goto` should be closely examined to see if there is a structured way to write the same code (thereby eliminating the goto). Usually that code can be modified with a minimal amount of effort to remove the `goto` statement, and the resulting program will actually be clearer and more easily maintained.

8.2   Storage Duration

While the unofficial term visibility describes scope, the (also unofficial) word lifetime characterizes storage duration. *Storage duration* describes how long the contents of a data item can remain unchanged while the program executes. Scope and storage duration are not directly related, although data items with a particular visibility are often associated with the same lifetime.

C has two types of storage duration:

1. static

2. automatic

This subject is further confused by the fact that the words `static` and `auto` are also keywords that specify storage class, and when used carry with them the attributes of the static and automatic storage durations, respectively. Therefore, it helps to qualify the use of each word as to whether duration or class is being discussed. This section will discuss both static and automatic duration, while the next will explain class.

8.2.1   *Static Duration*

Data items that have static storage duration are only created once each time a program executes. If the definition of the item includes any initialization also done once, as if it occurred at the very beginning of the program. In fact, the storage will be reserved and the initial values (if any) established when the program compiles rather than when it executes. This avoids including unnecessary code in the executable program. Having the compiler prepare the data means that it will already be formatted and initialized when the program is loaded from disk.

Global data items (those defined outside any function) always have the storage duration of static (without using the `static` keyword explicitly). A global item has its value set when the program begins, and when that value changes it remains changed until some executable statement changes it again. If no initialization code is supplied with the definition of a global item then the item has a value of binary zero (this is a standard rule and all compilers, both old and new, should do this). There is no way to recreate the initial value of any global item except to load and execute the program once more (or of course to explicitly assign its initial value again). The initial value that appeared as part of the definition is in the load module that resides on disk. It is not created by machine instructions, which execute at the beginning of the program. Consequently there is no keyword, function, or other mechanism in C to recapture those initial values automatically.

Quick Note 8.4   Static Storage Duration

Variables with static storage duration are given an initial value of zero, and their value is never automatically changed simply by the flow of control. If the value of the variable changes it is because of an explicit change made by statements in the program, not by an entry to or exit from a block.

8.2.2   *Automatic Duration*

Data items that have the storage duration of *automatic* are defined inside blocks, either blocks which are themselves functions or other blocks within functions. The items are created "from scratch" each time the block (function or otherwise) is entered, and they cease to exist when the flow of program execution leaves the block. These variables are placed on the stack (on machines that have a hardware-based stack), and manipulation of the registers that indicate the current size of the stack enable the storage associated with automatic variables to easily be reserved or set free. These variables have no default initial value to be counted on, in contrast to static variables, which have an initial value of zero.

Block scope and automatic storage duration are frequently seen together, although they are clearly two separate concepts. Without using storage class keywords like `static`, a variable defined immediately after the opening brace of a block has both these attributes. Since most local data has both these qualities it is sometimes difficult to distinguish between the effect of the two terms. There definitely is a difference, however, between scope and duration, as we'll see in the next section on storage classes.

Quick Note 8.5   Automatic Storage Duration

Variables with automatic storage duration have no default initial value, and their value changes simply by the flow of control. The variable exists upon entry into the block where it is defined, and it ceases to exist when it exits from the block.

8.3   Storage Classes

Scope and storage duration are easier to visualize than storage class. This may be because they have physical counterparts: lines of code or physical locations in storage. They also have a certain consistency because all four scope terms perform a similar service, i.e., they describe the visibility of an item. Likewise the two storage durations define how long a data item remains in existence and unchanged (except by the programmer).

A *storage class* can, in some cases, combine aspects of both scope and storage duration. In fact, two of the storage classes even have the same names as the two storage durations, while the other three have nothing obvious to do with any particular lifetime or visibility. Collectively the purpose of storage classes is to segregate data into groupings with common characteristics. But because the terminology isn't definitive, and because the effects of the storage class keywords often overlap, the whole subject sometimes seems confusing.

Every data item and function has a storage class, either because of how the item was defined or through the addition of a storage class keyword to the declaration or definition. An item can have only one storage class, though, whether explicitly provided or not. Some of the storage classes also have characteristics of other storage classes as part of their definition. This eliminates the need for using multiple keywords.

If a storage class is not explicitly supplied, then one is assumed. Data items defined inside a block of code are assumed to have the `auto` storage class, while data items defined outside all blocks (global data), along with all functions, are assumed to have the `extern` class. In addition, the global data items also have file scope and static storage duration, both discussed above.

The storage class keywords are:

1. static

2. register

3. extern

4. typedef

5. auto

Quick Note 8.6   Class keywords versus duration concepts

The `static` and `auto` storage class specifiers are language keywords, while static and automatic storage duration are simply concepts. Some data items, like global variables, already have the duration of static without needing the keyword.

8.3.1   `static` *(class) Keyword*

The `static` storage class is probably the most popular storage class. The effect it exhibits depends where and on what it is used.

The most common use of `static` is in conjunction with automatic variables inside a function. Normally automatic variables are created each time the function is invoked, and destroyed when the function terminates. This insures that we can have data that is "private" to the function, but it makes it difficult to retain any results from one function invocation to the next (without using global data items). Counters and accumulators, for example, need to retain their values and not be destroyed, created again, or reinitialized while the program executes. Using the `static` keyword with an automatic variable will cause it to have the same lifetime as a global variable, i.e., it will only be created and optionally initialized once at the beginning of the program. Each time the function in which this `static` variable is found is invoked the variable will contain the value it had the last time the function terminated. The scope of the automatic variable is not affected, however, and adding the `static` keyword does not mean that the data item can be used outside the function even though it has the lifetime of a global variable.

In older versions of some compilers (not compilers that are fully ANSI standard) `static` was also used to allow automatic aggregate data items (arrays, structures, and unions) to be initialized as part of their definitions. Without the static keyword the aggregate had to be defined and then explicitly initialized with assignment statements. This never did make sense and was always a significant point of confusion for beginning students. Fortunately the ANSI committee recognized the problem and eliminated this limitation. Now any aggregate can be initialized when it is defined, whether the aggregate appears as an automatic (after an opening brace) or a global variable. If the static keyword is also used when defining an automatic aggregate, then, just like a global variable, the automatic will retain its value from one function invocation to the next.

If a global variable or function name also has the static keyword, the visibility rather than the lifetime changes. The storage duration does not need to change since it is already global, but the visibility is now restricted to the source file where the definition is found. We'll discuss this concept more when we explain the extern keyword, and when we talk of separately compiled source files.

The example program in Figure 8.4 illustrates static automatic variables defined inside functions. Note how char_array is not initialized each time sub-func() is invoked, and also how the visibility of char_array has not changed since the array can't be seen from main(). Because code in main() can't see char_array, we have to return the address of char_array each time the function is invoked.

```c
/*
** static.c    Illustrates automatic variables with static storage class
*/

#include <stdio.h>
#define  ARRAY_SIZE  5

char *subfunc(int c);                       /* the subroutine prototype */

main()
{
    char *str;                              /* holds the return value */
    int input_char, index;

    printf("Enter more than %d characters, then RETURN\n", ARRAY_SIZE);
    while((input_char = getchar()) != '\n' && input_char != EOF) {
        str = subfunc(input_char);          /* always save return value */
    }
    printf("The last %d characters entered were\n", ARRAY_SIZE);
    for(index = 0; index < ARRAY_SIZE; index++) { /* now print the array */
        printf("char_array[%d] is %c\n", index, str[index]);
    }
}
```

(program continued on next page...)

```
char *subfunc(int passed_char)
{
    int index;
    static char char_array[ARRAY_SIZE] = "     ";       /* note the static */

    for(index = 0; index < ARRAY_SIZE - 1; index++) { /* move the values */
        char_array[index] = char_array[index + 1];
    }
    char_array[ARRAY_SIZE - 1] = passed_char;           /* save latest value */
    return(char_array);                              /* return array address */
}
```

Figure 8.4   An Example of the Static Storage Class—static.c

Basically this program simply has a loop in the main() function which retrieves characters and passes them on to a function called subfunc(). The function retains the last five characters entered, and each time the function is called it returns the address of the array char_array. Whenever the input stream "dries up" the address of char_array will be used to print the last five characters entered.

A sample execution of this program might look like this:

```
Enter more than 5 characters, then RETURN
abcdefghijkl
The last 5 characters entered were
char_array[0] is h
char_array[1] is i
char_array[2] is j
char_array[3] is k
char_array[4] is l
```

Quick Note 8.7   The Static Storage Class

The static keyword, when used with an automatic variable, gives the variable static duration (lifetime) while retaining the scope (visibility) of an automatic. When used with a global variable or a function it restricts the scope (visibility) to the same source file, but leaves the lifetime (duration) unaltered.

8.3.2   `register` *Keyword*

Specifying `register` on a data item asks the compiler to keep the data item in a hardware register if at all possible. This can speed up the access for the particular data item by a factor of as much as 10 or more, depending on the machine. The compiler is under no obligation to honor the request, since the program could easily request more registers than available.

The `register` storage class keyword designates that an item is also an automatic variable, meaning that it appears and disappears upon entry to and exit from a block. This makes sense because it wouldn't be at all wise, or even possible, to keep numerous variables tied up in registers for an extended period of time. Usually there are only a few registers available at any given moment for assignment to register variables.

Register variables are typically used for counters, accumulators, and other similar integer values which will be accessed frequently. This definition:

```
register int accum;
```

creates an integer called `accum` which would, if possible, be stored in a register. An important property to remember is that the & (address of) operator cannot be used with `register` variables.

8.3.3   `extern` *Keyword*

The `extern` storage class may be the most confusing of all the classes. Using it with a declaration identifies a data item as external and allows the referencing of data that is defined:

1. In another source file.

2. Later on in the same source file.

3. At a higher nesting level in the same source file.

When we described file scope above, we explained that a complete C program can consist of more than one source file. A typical implementation would be to place all the global data definitions and the `main()` function in one source file (we'll call it the primary source file), while placing one or more other functions in each of the other source files (we'll call them the secondary source files). The files are then compiled separately and linked together.

If global data definitions appear in any of the secondary source files, those definitions are combined with the global definitions from the primary file and all the definitions are stored together in the same place. If the same name is used for a global definition in any two or more of the files, a redefinition error will result when the entire program is finally linked.

How, then, is data defined in the primary source file referenced from the secondary files? Since the compilations occur separately, there must be some way to inform the secondary files about the characteristics of the needed data items without writing a data definition statement, which will generate the redefinition error.

The solution is to add the `extern` keyword to one or all of the global data definitions. Adding it to only one of the definitions means that the data item is defined (and storage reserved) in the source file where `extern` is not used, while statements in the file where `extern` was used will reference the storage reserved in the other file. When used in this way `extern` means that the data item exists "external to this source file". This illustrates that the `extern` keyword has many facets, since often it is used on items that are already external in nature.

All global data items in all source files that comprise the whole program are normally visible to all other source files. The `extern` keyword then allows a statement in one file to reference data defined in another file. An opposite effect is achieved by using the `static` keyword. When modified by `static` the global data item or function is no longer available for reference from another source file. The visibility is restricted to the one file where the definition occurs. The `static` keyword is often used to eliminate potential conflicts in data and function names. Multiple functions can appear in a source file, and possibly those functions should not be referenced from any other file. Including the `static` keyword as part of the data item or function definition will eliminate that possibility.

Actually, `extern` is very accommodating because we can also:

1. Use `extern` on data items when only one source file makes up the entire program. The one occurrence then becomes the definition and reserves the storage.

2. Use `extern` on all the definitions of a data item in all the source files. Only one storage location is ultimately reserved, and all statements in all files reference that one location.

The `extern` keyword also brings visibility to a data item when that item is defined in the same source file but after the point of reference. We don't recommend using it in this way, but it is important to understand this capability of `extern` in order to fully appreciate how it works.

It is also possible to use `extern` when defining a data item inside a block. This definition should reference the definition of the same item that occurred at a higher nesting level. This means that if x is defined as a global piece of data, and then in the same source file x is again defined inside a function with the `extern` keyword, the definition inside the function will not create another data item with automatic storage duration. The utility of this is questionable, however, since the definition inside the function is superfluous and unnecessary, and the same results are generated when it is left out entirely.

One further point of confusion arises when noting that the `extern` keyword must be used more frequently with data items than with functions. Global data items and function names both have `extern` as their default storage class, but there are some significant differences between them:

1. Function names have an assumed return type of int if one is not declared ahead of time. Data items have no such assumed type. If data items aren't declared or defined before they are referenced, an error occurs.

2. The final physical location of a function in a program is not determined until the program is linked, and all references to functions are not resolved until that time. Some data items, however, have their locations compiled directly into the program even before it is linked.

3. A function can also have a prototype, which can override the default return type of int. The prototype performs some of the same services as the extern keyword by altering that default return type. Data items don't have prototypes, but can only be declared ahead of type through the use of extern.

The first point shows how a function can be referenced before it appears in the source file, but the same cannot be done with a data item before it is declared or defined.

The example in Figure 8.5 illustrates how definitions inside functions may not cause a local variable to be created if the extern keyword is used (look at ext_ int). Also, variables that have not yet been defined can be used (see forward_ ref). And finally, the most typical use of extern is shown in how the file ext-func.c can see a definition occurring inside extmain.c. To use terminology we've already mentioned, extmain.c is the primary file, while extfunc.c is the secondary one.

To compile these two files, the command in UNIX would be:

```
cc extmain.c extfunc.c
```

which would compile the two modules separately but link them together. In MS/PC-DOS the commands needed vary based on the compiler used, but the concept is the same. Once the files have been compiled in either system, the name of the executable program is extmain in MS/PC-DOS, or a.out in UNIX.

```
/*
** extmain.c   Illustrates the extern keyword
*/

#include <stdio.h>

void extfunc(void);        /* the function prototype (like an extern) */
```

(program continued on next page...)

```
int ext_int = 11;                  /* this is referenced from inside main() */

main ()
{
    extern.int ext_int;            /* this does not create a local variable */
    extern.int forward_ref;                         /* nor does this */

    printf("%d\n", ext_int);        /* here we print the global variable */
    extfunc();                      /* as does the other file's function */
    printf("%d\n", forward_ref);            /* now we can see ahead */
}

int forward_ref = 20;                   /* this illustrates file scope */

/* end of extmain.c source file */


/*
** extfunc.c  Further illustrates the extern keyword
*/

#include <stdio.h>

extern int ext_int;        /* this references the other file's definition */
void extfunc(void)
{
    printf("%d\n", ext_int);
}
```

Figure 8.5   An Example of Using the Extern Storage Class—`extmain.c`

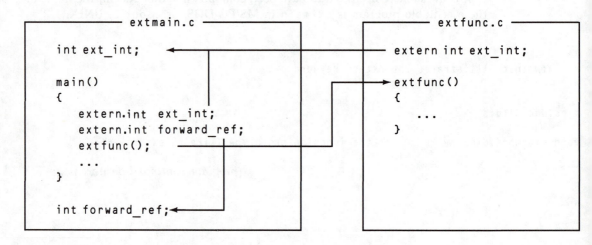

Figure 8.6   Relationship between `extmain.c` and `extfunc.c`

Figure 8.6 provides a diagram of the relationship between `extmain.c` and `extfunc.c`. Note that the function `extfunc` did not need the `extern` keyword, while the variable `ext_int` did. Function names, if not present in the same source file, are assumed to have the `extern` class and will not cause an error until the program is linked. If the requested function is still not present when the program is linked, a message like "unresolved external reference" will appear. This can also happen if the function name is misspelled.

Execution of this program will yield this result:

```
11
11
20
```

Quick Note 8.8   The `Extern` Storage Class

The `extern` keyword allows the use of data that is either in another source file or not yet defined in the same source file.

8.3.4   `typedef` *Keyword*

The `typedef` keyword will be introduced here and further discussed along with structures. While it is actually a storage class specifier, it exists primarily for the purpose of convenience and clarity. With it we can create "new" storage classes; that is, we can create synonyms for names and keywords that already exist. For instance, this statement:

```
typedef long int LIGHTYEARS;
```

creates the term `LIGHTYEARS` which can be used in place of the type `long int` each time a `long int` is needed.

Unlike the `#define` preprocessor directive, `typedef` is actually a C language keyword, and hence must obey all C syntax rules. Some people like `typedef` rather than `#define` for that very reason, because they feel it provides a small measure of additional validity checking by the compiler during the compile process.

Antibugging Note 8.3   `Typedef`s can add clarity to programs

The `typedef` keyword allows the creation of synonyms for data types and also other C keywords. Use it (or the `#define` directive) to improve the readability and clarity of programs.

8.3.5   `auto` *(class) Keyword*

The auto storage class actually does exist, but there is little use for the `auto` keyword itself. The keyword, although it is a class specifier, indicates automatic storage duration. That duration is already the default for data items defined inside a block, which is the very place where the `auto` keyword would be used anyway!

Data items defined outside all blocks cannot be specified as `auto` because auto only makes sense when used with things that can be destroyed and reallocated. Global data items have the normal properties of global lifetime and external visibility, so using the `auto` keyword with a global data item would generate an error. The place to use the `auto` keyword is with data being defined inside a block, which is redundant and unnecessary.

8.4   Self-Check

These statements are True or False. The answers are given at the end.

1. A data item with file scope can be seen from anywhere in the source file.

2. File scope means that an item can only be seen in the file where it is defined.

3. The file scope of an item extends into any `#include` file that is included after the item's definition or declaration.

4. Block scope applies only to nested blocks and not functions.

5. Block scope is passed down, but not out.

6. Block scope is a great advantage to programmers because it enhances modular programming.

7. Function prototype scope has been around since the C language was first invented in the early 1970s.

8. Function scope is just another name for block scope when the block scope is used within a function.

9. The word visibility is used to describe scope, while lifetime describes storage duration.

10. Static storage duration describes all variables whose initial value can never be changed.

11. Automatic storage duration is a property of local variables.

12. Storage classes segregate items into groups with common characteristics.

13. The static storage class can extend the lifetime of local variables.

14. Static can also restrict the visibility of global variables and functions.

15. Specifying the `register` storage class generates a compile error if there are not enough registers to satisfy all requests.

16. The `extern` keyword is needed to reference a piece of data defined in another source file.

17. `Extern` can also make visible a data item defined in the same source file but after the point of reference.

18. `Extern` is not used with function names because functions have prototypes and also a default return type.

19. The `typedef` keyword can create any desired storage class, even those not envisioned by the language designers.

20. The `auto` storage class keyword has little use because the storage class itself is the default class for data items defined after the opening brace of any block.

Answers

1. F   2. F   3. T   4. F   5. T   6. T   7. F   8. F   9. T   10. F
11. T   12. T   13. T   14. T   15. F   16. T   17. T   18. T   19. F   20. T

8.5 Exercises

* 1. C is often called a stack-oriented language. This means that C uses the hardware stack extensively to store variables of block scope, function arguments, and return addresses from function calls. The hardware stack is a special region of memory that is recognized for this express purpose. Do you suppose that C would be as fast and as easy a language to implement on a machine whose architecture did not include a hardware stack? Explain.

2. Write a function that illustrates a valid use for static variable usage within the function itself. Demonstrate your function with a simple test jig.

3. Give two examples of external variables that would need to be accessible to all programs. Demonstrate how these variables would be accessed.

* 4. A section of code (or an entire program) is said to be "reentrant" if it can be executed by more than one program at the same time. Essentially this means that one or more programs executing the code may be executing different sections of the code at any given instant. Obviously such reentrant code must be very robust and carefully constructed. Write a general set of guidelines that should be followed when writing reentrant code.

5. Explain the differences between code that is "included" in a source file at compile time as opposed to code that is "combined" with the same file at link time. You should consider both data and functions in your discussion.

6. A new company, Up and Down Inc., produces elevator scheduling and control systems for high-rise buildings. The first computerized system under development will control three elevators that have a range of first to tenth floors and, of course, each be capable of traveling up or down. Your job, as an expert on computerized control systems, is to develop the core program for the scheduling and control system. The scheduling algorithm, given a floor stop, destination after arriving, and direction, goes as follows:

1. If more than one elevator is not currently busy, pick one at random to go to the given floor stop.

2. If no elevator is currently available, find the closest elevator that will pass the given floor stop and place the floor stop in that elevator's queue.

3. If only one elevator is available, send that elevator to the given floor stop.

Your scheduling and control system should be driven by a test jig that feeds it random floor stops with an associated destination for each and updates a loop-controlled clock. Each loop through the test jig can be considered a clock tick or multiple of ticks as you deem necessary. Each elevator should be given a floor traversal speed in loop clock ticks. This will allow the driver to simulate an actual working system. Each elevator should have a floor-stop queue that tells the elevator the stops it must make.

* advanced exercises

8.6 Pretest

☐ *Multiple Choice*

Circle one correct answer to each of the following:

1. What would be the output of the following short program?

```
/* strange.c */

#include <stdio.h>

main()
{
    char j;
    for (j = 'a'; j < 'd'; ++j)
        {
        putchar(strange_func(j));
        }
}
```

```
strange_func(i)
char i;
{
    static char ret_value;
    if (i == 'a')
        {
        ret_value = i;
        }
    return(ret_value++);
}
```

    a. abc
    b. bcd
    c. bbb
    d. aaa

  2. Which change to the following code fragment most probably will result in a speed increase?

```
int i = 0;
char in_string[81];

while (++i)
    {
    get_user_response(in_string);
    }
```

    a. Use a pointer for in_string instead of the name of the array.
    b. Use a postdecrement operator instead of ++i.
    c. Define i with the register storage class.
    d. Initialize i separately instead of in the definition.

  3. What is the output of the following code fragment?

```
{
int i = 3;

printf("%d", i);
    {
    int i = 2;

    printf("%d", i);
    }
--i;
printf("%d", i);
}
```

    a. 321
    b. 322
    c. 323
    d. None of the above.

4. If a variable is defined outside of `main()`, which statement below is not true about that variable?
   a. The variable will retain its value even when passed to a function residing in another source file.
   b. The variable can retain its value, even after the program terminates, by using the keyword `static`.
   c. The variable cannot be defined using the `register` storage class.
   d. Another source file cannot access the variable unless it is declared **extern in** the calling defining **program.**

5. What is the proper interpretation of the following declaration?

```
register int fast_func();
```

   a. `fast_func()` is a function taking no arguments and returning an integer that should be a hardware register if possible.
   b. `fast_func()` is an external function that returns a register integer.
   c. `fast_func()` returns a hardware register which is an integer.
   d. None of the above.

6. The term *scope* when used in reference to a variable means
   a. The duration of the variable in a program.
   b. The number of times the variable is used in the same source file.
   c. Whether the variable is `external` or `static`.
   d. The extent to which the variable is visible to the code.

7. If a variable has block scope then
   a. It is only visible to `main()`.
   b. It is only visible to the block in which it is defined.
   c. It is only visible to the block in which it is defined and all functions in the same source file.
   d. None of the above.

8. What is wrong with the following code fragment?

```
int i;

for (i = 0; i < 10; ++i)
   {
   for (i = 0; i < 5; ++i)
      {
      do_funct(i);
      }
   do_other_funct(i);
   }
```

a. The compiler will become confused because i is used twice in different contexts.

b. do_funct() will receive an undefined value causing unpredictable results.

c. The inner block i needs an int i definition so that the code will work properly.

d. do_other_funct() will use the inner block i instead of the intended outer block i.

9. Which answer below correctly identifies all of the errors in the following code fragment?

```
static floor(float);
register float users_number;

main()
{
    printf("Enter your number: ");
    scanf("%f", &users_number);
    printf("Floor of %f is %f\n", users_number, floor(users_number));
}

floor(n)
float n;
{
    return(n);
}
```

a. —register variable defined outside of main()
   —use of static keyword with floor()

b. —return type of floor() (a floating point number) has not been declared

c. —register variable defined outside of main()
   —use of & with a register variable

d. —return(n); should read return((int) n);

10. The keyword static when used with a function name

a. Identifies the function as local to the source file in which it is defined.

b. Implies that the function retains its return value from call to call.

c. Implies that the function does not return a value.

d. Identifies the function's definition as residing in another source file.

9

Arrays

This chapter will describe how to define and use arrays. Many books do not differentiate between the subjects of arrays and pointers in the C language, but we will distinguish clearly between them. It is quite possible to make significant use of arrays in C without understanding anything about pointers. Also, there is a large amount of material to cover about arrays in general before we confuse the topic further by discussing pointers. Pointers, however, allow us to fully comprehend just how an array is processed, so we'll complete our explanation about arrays when we discuss pointers in Chapter 10.

After studying this chapter, you will be able to do the following:

1. Define and initialize an array.

2. Use array subscripts properly.

3. Pass an array as an argument to a function.

4. Explain how multidimensional arrays are defined and used.

5. Describe how various operators can be used with arrays.

9.1   Basic Properties of Arrays

An *array* is an indexed variable which contains many data items of the same type. The array has one name, and the individual elements of the array are referenced by associating a *subscript*, or *index*, with the array name. An array is not a basic type of data in C, but rather an aggregate type made up of any other type of data. It is possible to have an array of anything: characters, integers, floats, arrays, pointers, structures, and so forth. This chapter will describe arrays of characters and integers, and arrays of arrays. Arrays of pointers, structures, unions, and more will be covered in later chapters.

Arrays have four basic properties:

1. The individual data items in the array are called *elements*.

2. All elements must be of the same data type.

3. Elements are stored contiguously in the computer's memory, and the subscript (index) of the first element is zero.

4. The name of the array is a constant value representing the address of the first element in the array.

It is not possible to define an array of mixed data types. The elements must all be the same data type because it is assumed that the elements are all the same physical size. Without that assumption it would be very difficult to determine where any given element was stored.

It is possible to have arrays within arrays, i.e., multidimensional arrays. Additionally, if an array element is a structure (which we haven't covered yet), then other data types can exist in the array by existing inside the structure member. We'll show how this is done in Chapter 11.

Since the elements are all the same size, and that fact is used to help determine how to locate a given element, it follows that the elements are stored contiguously in the computer's memory. This means that there is no filler space between elements and that they are physically adjacent in the computer.

Finally, the name of an array represents a constant value which cannot change during the execution of the program. This may seem like a small thing, but some forms of expressions which might appear to be valid on the surface are not allowed in C. All C programmers eventually learn these subtleties, but it will help your understanding if you can explain why these differences exist.

9.1.1   *Defining an Array*

The following are examples of array definitions:

```
char array1[4];      /* an array of four characters */
int  array2[3];      /* an array of three integers  */
```

To define an array, write the data type, array name, and then a pair of matching square brackets enclosing a constant expression. The constant expression defines the size of the array. A variable name cannot be used inside the square brackets, i.e., it's not possible to avoid specifying the array size until the program actually runs. The expression must reduce to a constant value because the compiler must know exactly how much storage space to reserve for the array. If you need *dynamic arrays*, i.e., arrays whose size is not known until the program runs, or whose size changes while the program is running, use pointers and dynamic memory allocation.

Here is a simple picture of how the above arrays might be viewed. We will provide arbitrary values for each array element:

array 1 would look like:

a	b	z	f

while array2 would look like:

1	5	3

Each box of the set is one element of the array, and the set of boxes together make up the whole array.

Whenever square brackets occur in a variable definition you should read them as if they represented the words "array of." For example, the first definition above should be read starting at the array name and working out, right to left, which would yield "array1 is an array of four characters."

We encourage the use of defined constants to specify the size of the array, like this:

```
#define ARRAY1_SIZE 4
#define ARRAY2_SIZE 3

char array1[ARRAY1_SIZE];    /* an array of four characters */
int  array2[ARRAY2_SIZE];    /* an array of three integers  */
```

Using these defined constants helps guarantee that subsequent references to the array do not exceed the defined array size. For instance, we might write the beginning of a code fragment that loops through array1 like this:

```
main()
{
    int i;                        /* an automatic variable used as a subscript */
    for(i = 0;i < ARRAY1_SIZE; i++) {  /* array subscripts start at zero */
        ...
    }
```

Antibugging Note 9.1   Using defined constants to specify array size

Use defined constants to specify the size of arrays, both when defining the array and when referencing it later.

Earlier we mentioned that a string was a null terminated character array. This means that while all strings are character arrays, not all character arrays are necessarily strings. A character array can be transformed into a string by adding a null character (a binary zero, represented as \0) anywhere within the bounds of the array. For instance, to insure that `array1` is a valid string we can write this assignment statement:

```
array1[3] = '\0';   /* put a null in the last element of the array */
```

The first three elements of the array `array1` comprise the string body, with the fourth element being the terminating null. Using our box diagram from above `array1` would then look like this:

a	b	z	\0

Quick Note 9.1   Character Arrays Contrasted to Strings

All strings are character arrays, but not all character arrays are strings. There are many uses for an array that contains characters but does not have a terminating null value. An array of characters without the null should not be used as a string, but should be accessed through a subscript or pointer.

9.1.2   *Initializing an Array*

Arrays can be initialized in any of three ways:

1. By default when they are created. This only applies to global and static automatic arrays.

2. Explicitly when they are created by supplying constant initializing data.

3. During program execution by assigning or copying data into the array.

Only constant data can be used to initialize an array when it is created. If the array elements must receive their values from variables then the array must be initialized by writing explicit statements as part of the program code.

9.1.2.1   *Initializing an Array By Default When it is Created*

According to the ANSI standard, arrays that are either global (defined outside of main and any other function) or static automatic (static, but defined after any opening brace) will always be initialized to binary zero if no other initialization data is supplied. To check whether our compiler does this (it should!) we can write the simple program shown in Figure 9.1.

```
/*
**   init.c - Testing Default Data Initialization
*/

#include <stdio.h>               /* has the printf prototype */

int array1[5];                   /* a global array */
                                 /* whose subscripts are 0 through 4 */
main()
{
    static int array2[5];        /* a static and automatic array */
    printf("%d\n", array1[0]);   /* print the first element of array1 */
    printf("%d\n", array2[0]);   /* print the first element of array2 */
}
```

Figure 9.1   Testing Default Data Initialization—init.c

We should see two zeroes print out on the screen if these two types of arrays are initialized to zero by default. It's a pretty good bet that most compilers will do this, but this program also illustrates a very important point: that the first subscript for all arrays in C is zero. There is no way to make C think that the first subscript is 1, a feature that some languages allow. Remember that C was created as a systems programming language, with the original emphasis on power and flexibility. It is not a language that protects the programmer from him/herself.

Antibugging Note 9.2   Assuming initial values in automatic arrays

Make no assumptions about the initial value of elements in automatic arrays which are not static. Although the elements may happen to contain zeroes, the zeroes could just as easily not be there the next time the program executes

---

9.1.2.2   *Initializing an Array Explicitly When It Is Created*

When we define an array we can also supply initialization data. Compilers that have not been updated to conform to the ANSI C standard may allow initialization values for an array only if the array is global or has the static storage class. The new standard, however, states that initialization values can be supplied for any array defined anywhere in the program, global or otherwise. This eliminates the double standard that frequently confused beginning C programmers.

The two arrays above could then be defined and initialized in this way:

```
#define ARRAY1_SIZE 14
#define ARRAY2_SIZE 3

char array1[ARRAY1_SIZE] = "Your Name is:"; /* leave room for the null! */
```

or

```
char array1[ARRAY1_SIZE] = {'Y', 'o', 'u', 'r', ' ',
                            'N', 'a', 'm', 'e', ' ', 'i', 's', ':','\0'};
```

and

```
int  array2[ARRAY2_SIZE] = {10, 20, 30}; /* don't need a null here */
```

They would look like this:

array1

Y	o	u	r		N	a	m	e		i	s	:	\0

array2

10	20	30

The character array can be initialized when it is defined by placing a normal assignment expression after the right square bracket. The initialization data is placed inside double quotes, which will automatically cause the character array to have the terminating null character placed in the proper location providing that there is room in the array. If room is not left for the terminating null, it is dropped and the array cannot be considered a string. This means that a character array defined to contain five elements can only hold four characters other than the terminating null. Writing something like this:

```
char ary[4] = "this";    /* the null is dropped here */
```

which could be pictured this way:

guarantees that we will have problems if we intend to use ary as a string because we specified that ary would have four elements and we used all four to contain characters, leaving no room for the null. Also remember that double quotes enclose a string literal and only character arrays can contain strings, so the use of double quotes with any other type of array (e.g., int, float, etc.) will not create an array of the other data type, but will again create a string literal, eligible for assignment to a character array.

   We might provide more initializing characters than there are elements in the array. The better compilers will identify the situation as an error, and hopefully the program will not compile (although older compilers might not catch it!). This statement, then, is incorrect:

```
char ary[4] = "this is an error";   /* this should generate an error */
```

   We have also shown above that the array can be initialized by coding a series of characters inside a pair of braces. Doing so means assuming full responsibility for including any terminating null if the array will be used as a string. Typically this form of initialization is used when a string is not being created. It has the additional safeguard that supplying more characters than the array has defined elements generates a compile-time error. The same would be true for arrays of other data types, like this:

```
int x[3] = {11, 12, 13, 14, 15};  /* this shouldn't compile */
```

   The initialization of the integer array demonstrates that the matching braces are also used with other data types like integers, floats, and so forth. These forms look exactly like the form of placing the individual characters inside single quotes, except of course single quotes are not used.

   Finally, a common form of array initialization allows the array size to be determined from the size of the initializing data, like this:

```
char ary2[] = "The size of ary2 depends on how far I type...";
```

   We have not explicitly given ary2 a size, but the correct size is generated automatically depending on the length of the string literal used to initialize ary2. Room for the terminating null is also reserved, and ary2 ends up being an array no different from one whose size is explicitly stated. The following two arrays, then, have different sizes:

```
char k[]   = "mine"; /* this array has 5 elements, including the null */
                     /* the size is determined by the initializing data */
char k2[4] = "mine"; /* this array has 4 elements, no null is included */
                     /* because all 4 elements are taken by letters, */
                     /* leaving no room for the null */
```

The array k[] looks like this:

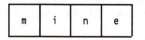

while k2[] looks like this:

m	i	n	e

Defining an array and letting the initializing data determine the array size is a good technique to use when creating a string literal with a name, and then using the name in a program in multiple places. The technique is primarily used with compilers that make all string literals distinct, even if the exact same characters are used in the literal. For example, these two statements:

```
printf("%s", "A string literal");
printf("%s", "A string literal");
```

are identical, but some compilers will generate two string literals even though the literals are identical. The ANSI C standard states that the literals do not have to be distinct, and some compilers will provide a switch or other technique to allow the choice of whether identical strings are made distinct or not.

The technique is also useful when the number of elements in the array changes frequently and the program is being compiled over and over to incorporate the changes. To create an integer array whose size is determined by the number of items included in the initializing block, we could write:

```
int x[] = {11, 12, 13, 14, 15};  /* this is fine */
```

which would look like this:

11	12	13	14	15

9.1.2.3   *Initializing an Array Through Program Logic after Definition*

If an array is not initialized when it is created, it can be initialized any time during the execution of the program by using different forms of an assignment statement or string function. For example, these arrays:

```
#define ARRAY1_SIZE 4
#define ARRAY2_SIZE 3

char array1[ARRAY1_SIZE];      /* an array of four characters */
int  array2[ARRAY2_SIZE];      /* an array of three integers  */
```

could be initialized at a later time by these different statements:

```
array1[0] = 'c';       /*/these next four would be used together */
array1[1] = 'a';       /* and assign values to the first four elements */
array1[2] = 't';       /* of the array */
array1[3] = '\0';

strcpy(array1, "cat");  /* this does what the four above do, but */
                        /* uses a function to copy a string */

array2[0] = 10;        /* arrays of data types other than characters must */
array2[1] = 20;        /* have their elements explicitly referenced, so */
array2[2] = 30;        /* you can't later say: array2 = {10, 20, 30}; */

    for(i = 0;i < ARRAY2_SIZE; i++) { /* we'll assume that i is defined */
        array2[i] = (i + 1) * 10;
}
```

In each case the resulting arrays would look like this:

array1	c	a	t	\0

array2	10	20	30

Notice the forms of initialization expressions we have and have not used here. First, we never used the name of the array by itself on the left of the assignment operator. For instance, we did not write this:

```
array1 = "cat";
```

which would guarantee a compile error. The error occurs because the name of an array is a constant value and can no more be used on the left of an assignment than can any other constant value. This means that an array name is not an lvalue. By way of comparison we already know that we cannot write something like this:

```
5 = x;
```

because a constant cannot be assigned a value. For this same reason an array cannot have something assigned directly to it because doing so would indicate an attempt to change the value of the array name (i.e., the address of the array and its resulting memory location), not the contents of the array identified by the name.

Second, we also did not use our technique of grouping values inside braces. This would require that we use the array name on the left of the assignment, like this:

```
array1 = {'c', 'a', 't', '\0'};
```

and we have already agreed that this would imply that we are trying to change the array name itself, not the contents of the storage identified by the name.

In summary, we need to use a series of assignment statements or a loop if we want to initialize array elements after the array has been defined. To initialize a string we can use the `strcpy()` function or we can explicitly assign a character value to each array element. For arrays with a data type other than character we cannot use the string functions but must use a program loop or assignment statements. We can also read data from an external source and place it into the array, but even that technique would take place within a loop.

Quick Note 9.2   The Value of an Array Name

An array name is a constant which is equal in value to the address of the first element of the array. As a constant it cannot be used on the left side of an assignment without an additional modifier, such as a subscript.

9.1.3   *Referencing an Array*

In the above examples we included various statements that utilized a subscript to reference an array element. For example, if we define this array:

```
#define ARRAY2_SIZE 3

int   array2[ARRAY2_SIZE];        /* an array of three integers */
```

then we have created these array elements:

```
array2[0], array2[1], array2[2]
```

which look like this:

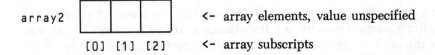

array2   <- array elements, value unspecified

    [0] [1] [2]   <- array subscripts

We have not created these elements:

```
array2[1], array2[2], array2[3]
```

as might be true in other languages. All arrays in C have zero as the subscript of their first element.

To walk through this array a loop can begin in this way:

```
for(i = 0;i < ARRAY2_SIZE; i++) {         /* assume that i is defined */
   ...
}
```

Observe that we did not check for "less than or equal" in the test to end the loop. Remember that if n is used to define the size of an array, then (n - 1) is the largest subscript that can be used with the array. The following statement would therefore be incorrect:

```
for(i = 0;i <= ARRAY2_SIZE; i++) {      /* references past the array end */
   ...
}
```

To correct this the < operator rather than <= should be used.

Any integer expression can be used to form the subscript inside the square brackets, like this for example:

```
int i = 4;
printf("%d", array2[i / 2]); /* final subscript value is 2 */
```

The above printf() statement would reference this element:⌐

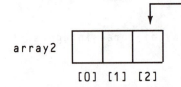

array2

    [0] [1] [2]

With arrays, other expressions, such as adding an integer value to an array name, can be used as in the example program in Figure 9.2.

```
/*
**   arrayref.c - Array Names Plus Integer Values
*/

#include <stdio.h>

              /* remember this is global and not local because some */
              /* compilers do not yet support the initialization of */
              /* arrays when they are defined */

char ary[10] = {'a', 'b', 'c', '\0', 'd', 'e', '\0', 'f', '\0', '\0'};

main()
{
    printf("%s \t: ary\n", ary);
    printf("%s \t: ary + 0\n", ary + 0);
    printf("%s \t: ary + 1\n", ary + 1);
    printf("%s \t: ary + 2\n", ary + 2);
    printf("%s \t: ary + 3\n", ary + 3);
    printf("%s \t: ary + 4\n", ary + 4);

    printf("%c \t: (ary + 0)[0]\n", (ary + 0)[0]);
    printf("%c \t: (ary + 0)[1]\n", (ary + 0)[1]);
    printf("%c \t: (ary + 0)[2]\n", (ary + 0)[2]);
    printf("%c \t: (ary + 0)[4]\n", (ary + 0)[4]);

    printf("%c \t: (ary + 1)[0]\n", (ary + 1)[0]);
    printf("%c \t: (ary + 1)[1]\n", (ary + 1)[1]);
    printf("%c \t: (ary + 1)[3]\n", (ary + 1)[3]);

    printf("%c \t: (ary - 1)[2]\n", (ary - 1)[2]);
    printf("%c \t: (ary - 1)[3]\n", (ary - 1)[3]);
}
```

Figure 9.2 Array Names Plus Integer Values—arrayref.c

This is the output of the program:

```
abc        : ary
abc        : ary + 0
bc         : ary + 1
c          : ary + 2
           : ary + 3
de         : ary + 4
```

(program continued on next page...)

```
a        :  (ary + 0)[0]
b        :  (ary + 0)[1]
c        :  (ary + 0)[2]
d        :  (ary + 0)[4]
b        :  (ary + 1)[0]
c        :  (ary + 1)[1]
d        :  (ary + 1)[3]
b        :  (ary - 1)[2]
c        :  (ary - 1)[3]
```

Expressions of the form ary + 1 are interesting because they illustrate a concept which is not fully explainable without discussing pointers. We have chosen to separate the coverage of arrays and pointers in order to emphasize that they are indeed two separate and distinct topics. Arrays can be used in a variety of ways without complicating matters by considering pointers. So rather than discuss the actual technical meaning of ary + 1, we'll merely state that it designates another array which begins one element past the beginning of ary. In the same way, ary + 2 is yet another array which begins two elements past the beginning of ary. Further, ary - 1 is an array which begins one element before ary. It is a program logic error to reference data before the array even though the language will compile and execute the expression (with unpredictable results).

Further, expressions like (ary + 1)[3] are also valid and denote "the fourth element of the array that begins one element past ary". An array name can be subscripted, as can an array name that has a constant value added or subtracted to or from it. Note that while ary + 3 indicates another array, (ary + 3)[1] indicates the contents of an array element, hence the need for the %c in the printf() control string rather than %s as used for ary + 3. The program output above shows that these three expressions are all equivalent:

(ary + 0)[1]

(ary + 1)[0]

(ary - 1)[2]

The expression ary + 3 deserves special note because it references a null string, which consists of nothing more than the null character itself, hence generating the fifth line of output, which is blank. This example also illustrates that more than one string within the same character array can be created by merely placing more than one string-terminating null character in the array. If multiple null characters exist in the same character array, then any use of a part of the array to form a string will obtain only the characters from that point up to the next null character encountered. In the same way, if there is no null character within the array then any use of the array as a string will include characters past the end of the array until a null character is encountered somewhere in memory.

Finally, a technique used when referencing an array is to dynamically determine the number of elements currently in the array by writing an expression like this:

```
num_items_in_array = sizeof(array) / sizeof(array[0])
```

If the total array size is known, and the length of an individual element of the array is also known, then one can be divided into the other to compute the number of items in the array. This is an especially useful technique when the size of the array is determined by the initializing data, like this:

```
int how_big_this_array[] = {200, 400, 600};
```

Antibugging Note 9.3   Using 'magic numbers' with arrays

Never hard-code "magic numbers" in a program in order to specify the size of an array. Use either defined constants or else the sizeof operator.

Given this array,

```
sizeof(how_big_this_array) / sizeof(how_big_this_array[0])
```

the computation should reduce to a constant value of 3.

Quick Note 9.3   Properly Referencing an Array

Creating an array of five elements means that the subscript values 0 through 4 will be used, not the values 1 through 5.

9.2   Array Names as Function Arguments

Do not confuse using an array name as an argument to a function with using the name of an array element. The difference can be subtle and misleading, but it is consistent with all the other properties of array elements and array names.

9.2.1   *The Array Name Itself as an Argument*

Wherever an array name is used it is replaced with a constant value representing the address of the first element in the array. If we write this statement:

```
strcpy(myarray, "this goes into myarray");  /* assume myarray exists */
```

we indicate that we want to pass two arguments to the strcpy() function. The first argument, myarray, is the address of the array, i.e., the address of the first element of the array. The name of an array is a constant value which contains the address in the computer where the array is stored. When an array is used as a function argument, the entire array is not passed to the function. What is passed is a copy of the address of where the array is stored. This means that strcpy() can alter the array, which indeed it does by copying the string literal into the memory locations occupied by the array (hopefully we have enough room!). In the same way the rightmost argument, the string literal, also has its address passed to strcpy(). The string itself is not physically sent to strcpy(), only its address. This is in keeping with the concept of call by value because we pass a copy of the value that the string literal represents, i.e., a copy of its address in the computer. The string literal will have been stored in the same place where other constant data is stored. Only the address of the literal will be used here.

The printf() function is an example of how the name of an array equates to the address of the array. We can write this statement:

```
printf("%s", myarray);   /* myarray is the string we created above */
```

Since the term myarray is the address of the first element of the array, then myarray can be used as if it represented the location of the entire array.

The function definition for strcpy() would start off something like this (we'll ignore the return type for the moment):

```
strcpy(char a[], char b[])       /* modern style function definition */
```

The formal parameters of the function must match the actual arguments that are used when the function is invoked. Both arguments in this case are character arrays (specifically they are strings, or null terminated character arrays), and we use the same form for the parameter declarations that we used when defining the arrays in the first place. If we were to write our own version of strcpy() and include it in a program it might look like the one in Figure 9.3.

```
/*
** strcpyf.c - Array Names Passed as Function Arguments
*/

#include <stdio.h>

void strcpy(char [], char []);  /* classic prototype */

char ary1[] = "the first string";
char ary2[] = "a second one which is longer";
```

```
main()
{
   printf("The string at ary1 starts as \"%s\"\n", ary1);
   printf("The string at ary2 starts as \"%s\"\n", ary2);

   strcpy(ary2, ary1);                        /* copy the strings */

   printf("The string at ary1 is now \"%s\"\n", ary1);
   printf("The string at ary2 is now \"%s\"\n", ary2);
}

void strcpy(array2, array1)
char array2[];
char array1[];
{
   int index = 0;

   while((array2[index] = array1[index]) != '\0') {
      index++;
   }
}
```

Figure 9.3   Array Names Passed as Function Arguments—strcpyf.c

In this example we have replaced the strcpy() function supplied with every compiler by including a function with the same name in our program. The important thing to notice about the function is how the array names are used in the invocation of strcpy(), how they are declared in strcpy(), and the logic of strcpy() itself. A while loop is used inside the strcpy() function to copy, character by character, the contents of the first string into the second string. The copy process terminates when the NULL character from the sending string is encountered, but only after the NULL itself is also copied. After the copy is finished the storage associated with each array looks like this:

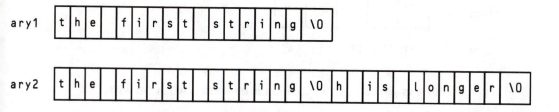

The copy leaves two NULL characters in ary2. When ary2 is used as a string, the first NULL terminates the string. Both printf() statements done after strcpy is invoked print the same characters, i.e., they both print "the first string" (but not the quotes). Here is the output from the program:

```
The string at ary1 starts as "the first string"
The string at ary2 starts as "a second one which is longer"
The string at ary1 is now "the first string"
The string at ary2 is now "the first string"
```

Quick Note 9.4   Array Names used as Function Arguments

Using an array name in a statement yields a constant whose value is the address of the first element of the array. When used as a function argument only the address of the array is passed to the function, not the contents of the array.

9.2.2   *Passing Individual Elements*

While referencing the name of an array yields the address of where the array is stored in the computer, referencing an array element yields the contents of that element. We can change the example directly above to this:

```
printf("%c", myarray[0]);    /* myarray is the string we created above */
```

We mentioned that the term myarray is the address of the first element of the array. This address can be subscripted, which creates an expression identical to some of those shown in section 9.1.3. The expression myarray[0] means to reference the memory location zero elements away from the start of the array. Likewise myarray[4] means to reference the location four elements away, or the fifth element (i.e., 0 is first, 1 is second, etc.). Remember that an array can be pictured in this way:

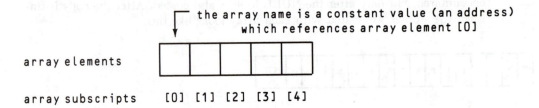

There is no difference in which memory location is referenced when we write

```
myarray + 3;
```

and when we write

```
myarray[3];
```

but there is a big difference in the type of data the expressions create. The expression myarray + 3 can be used just like an array name or a string (it is an address of a character), while the expression myarray[3] is of the type char. The difference is clearly seen in the printf() conversion characters which must be used with the two expressions. The conversion characters %s are used with the expression myarray + 3 because it acts like a string, while the characters %c are used with myarray[3] because it represents a character. It is not sufficient merely to have an expression that refers to the correct memory location. The expression also needs to be of the correct type. It is not appropriate to use myarray + 3 when myarray[3] should have been used instead. Here are the printf() statements just described:

```
printf("%s", (myarray + 3));    /* 'myarray + 3' acts like a string */
printf("%c", (myarray[3]);      /* 'myarray[3]' is a character */
```

In the same way

```
myarray + 3;
```

is not at all the same as

```
myarray[0] + 3;
```

We already explained the first form, but the second form says that the first element of myarray, myarray[0], is to have 3 added to it (on a temporary basis, of course, since there is no assignment operator). This expression works even if the array contains characters. Figure 9.4 shows an example program which subtracts one from each character of an array. Before reading the explanation of the program, attempt to spot the key differences between this example and the one in Figure 9.3.

```
/*
**   chgelmt.c - Array Elements Passed as Function Arguments
*/

#include <stdio.h>

char decelmt(char ary_elmt);    /* modern prototype */

char ary1[] = "IBM";
```

(program continued on next page...)

```
main()
{
    int index;

    printf("The string at ary1 starts as \"%s\"\n", ary1);
    for(index = 0; index < (sizeof(ary1) - 1); index++) {
        ary1[index] = decelmt(ary1[index]);
    }
    printf("The string at ary1 is now \"%s\"\n", ary1);
}

char decelmt(char ary_elmt)
{
    return(ary_elmt - 1);
}
```

Figure 9.4   Array Elements Passed as Function Arguments—chgelmt.c

The first thing to note is that instead of using the name of the array as a function argument an array element is used instead. This is confirmed by looking at both the prototype and also the function definition. Second, when an array element is used as a function argument a copy of the actual element itself is sent to the function. No address is involved, as occurs when the array name is used as the argument. Because no address is passed to the function, the function has no way to directly alter the storage occupied by the array. The only way the function can send back an altered array element is to return it as the function return value. The invoking code must then make the assignment of the function return value into the same array element that was passed to the function. Third, note that the terminating expression of the for statement is when index is no longer less than the sizeof the array minus one. The sizeof operator determines the size of ary1 to be 4, and one less would of course be 3. The value of index is then restricted to the range 0 through 2, which are the correct subscripts for an array of three characters.

The final effect of this program is to change the characters in the array from "IBM" to "HAL." This alteration assumes that the letter H occurs immediately before the letter I in the character set of the computer (which is true for ASCII based computers), that A comes right before B, and so forth.

9.3   String I/O Functions That Use Arrays

When we studied standard character input and output we deliberately avoided mentioning those functions that used a character array as a function argument. Specifically these functions are gets(), puts(), fgets(), fputs(), and sprintf(). These functions are similar to functions we have already studied. The easiest way to explain the functions is to show a program example (see Figure 9.5).

```
/*
**   stringio.c - String I/O Functions Program Example
*/

#include <stdio.h>

#define  ARRAY_SIZE  10

main()
{
    char input_array[ARRAY_SIZE];

    fputs("Enter the first string : ", stdout);
    gets(input_array);
    fputs("The first string is    : ", stdout);
    puts(input_array);
    fputs("Enter the second string: ", stdout);
    fgets(input_array, ARRAY_SIZE, stdin);
    fputs("The second string is   : ", stdout);
    fputs(input_array, stdout);
    sprintf(input_array, "I am %s", "me");
    fputs("sprintf() created      : ", stdout);
    fputs(input_array, stdout);
}
```

Figure 9.5   String I/O Functions Program Example—stringio.c

Here is the output from the first run of the program:

```
Enter the first string : one
The first string is    : one
Enter the second string: two
The second string is   : two
sprintf() created      : I am me
```

Since all the strings we entered were less than the size of input_array, the program works fine. However, when we enter a string which is longer than input_ array, something like this can occur when we run the program a second time:

```
Enter the first string : one
The first string is    : one
Enter the second string: abcdefghijk
The second string is   : abcdefghisprintf() created      : I am me
```

When this program runs we must be careful not to enter too many characters when we use gets() to control the input. The gets() function receives characters from standard input (stdin, the keyboard by default for most computers) and places them into the array whose name is passed to the function. When the Enter key is pressed to terminate the input, a newline character is transmitted.

When the gets() function receives this newline character it changes it into a null character, thereby insuring that the character array contains a string. No checking occurs to insure that the size of the array is big enough to hold all the characters entered. For this reason the gets() function is not considered to be a safe input function. This is one reason that we did not introduce it when we studied standard character input and output, and why we provided our own safe input function.

Notice that the puts() function echoes back to the terminal just what we entered with gets(). It also adds a newline character on the end of the string in the place where the null character appeared. The null character, remember, was automatically inserted into the string by the gets() function. This means that gets() and puts() are symmetrical because strings that are entered with gets() can be properly displayed with puts().

When we use the fgets() function we can guarantee a maximum number of input characters. This function stops reading the designated file stream when one fewer characters are read than the second argument designates. This means that since ARRAY_SIZE is a 10, only 9 characters will be read by fgets() from stdin. A null character is automatically placed into the string in the tenth position, and if a newline were entered from the keyboard it would be retained in the string (it would appear before the null). The fgets() function does not eliminate the newline character (like gets() did), but merely adds the null character at the end so that a valid string is stored. Like the gets() and puts() combination, fgets() and fputs() also work in conjunction with one another. fgets() does not eliminate the newline, nor does fputs() add one. Like gets(), fgets() cannot be considered safe.

To illustrate how important the newline character is to these functions look closely at the second run output above. Notice that the phrase "sprintf() created..." follows immediately after the characters abcdefghi which had just been entered. We actually entered two more characters than abcdefghi, but we only allowed fgets() to read nine. The others were left on the input buffer. Also dropped was the newline that terminated the input from the keyboard (it is left on the input stream because it occurs after the ninth character). Therefore, no newline character was stored in the string. Since fputs() does not add one back, the next fputs() output begins on the line where the previous output ended. We had been relying on the newline character read by fgets() and printed by fputs() to help control our display format. Obviously this was a mistake since without additional code we cannot insure that the newline is always present.

We also used a defined constant ARRAY_SIZE to insure that the size of the array is conveniently available for use in the fgets() function and anywhere else in the program where it might be needed.

Finally, notice the function sprintf(), whose name stands for "string printf()". It uses a control string with conversion characters in exactly the same way as does printf(). The additional feature is that sprintf() places the resulting formatted data in a string rather than immediately sending the result to standard output. This can be beneficial if the exact same output must be created twice (such as when the data must be sent to both the terminal and the printer). Table 9.1 lists the characteristics of the string I/O functions.

Function	Characteristics
gets()	newline becomes null
puts()	null becomes newline
fgets()	newline retained, null added
fputs()	null dropped, no newline added

Table 9.1   Characteristics of String I/O Functions

Antibugging Note 9.4   Plan Uses of String I/O Functions Carefully

Carefully plan in advance any uses of gets(), puts(), fgets(), and fputs(). The idiosyncrasies of these functions require that you give deliberate attention to their application.

9.4   Multidimensional Arrays

An array that contains one or more other arrays is *multidimensional*. All arrays in C actually have only one dimension, but an element of any dimension can contain other arrays of the same type, i.e., an array of characters cannot be created inside an array of integers.

A multidimensional array is defined by placing two sets of matching square brackets side by side, like this:

```
char mult_ary[3][4];
```

The resulting definition is read as "mult_ary is an array of three arrays, each having four characters." The brackets are replaced by the phrase "array(s) of" as the definition is read starting at the array name and moving from the inside out, right to left, leaving the char for last.

To illustrate these and other aspects of multidimensional arrays we've written the small program in Figure 9.6. Read the comments in the program carefully and study each line of output. The program illustrates some of the basic features about arrays of more than one dimension.

```
/*
** multidim.c - Multidimensional Array Program Example
**
** This program illustrates:
**    - how to define and initialize a multidimensional array
**    - what values the sizeof operator returns when applied to the array
**        as a whole and also the various parts
**    - what to expect when an array is passed to a function
**    - how to walk through the different dimensions of the array
**        and access the elements.
*/

#include <stdio.h>                    /* has the printf() prototype */

void sub_routine(char x[][3][4]);  /* sub_routine() prototype */

char w[3][4][5] = {                      /* a global multidimensional array */
             {                                   /* w[0] values here */
               {'a', 'b', 'c', 'd', 'e'},   /* w[0][0] values */
               {'f', 'g', 'h', 'i', 'j'},   /* w[0][1] values */
               {'k', 'l', 'm', 'n', 'o'},   /* w[0][2] values */
               {'p', 'q', 'r', 's', 't'},   /* w[0][3] values */
             },                              /* note the need for the comma */
             {                                   /* w[1] values here */
               {'1', '2', '3', '4', '5'}    /* w[1][0] values */
             },
          }; /* semicolon needed after brace when initializing data */

     /* the next array is initialized in an interesting fashion */
int z[4][3] = { {1}, {2}, {3}, {4} };

main()
{
    char x[2][3][4];                             /* local 3-dimensional array */
    printf("sizeof x        = %d\n", sizeof(x));    /* size of local array */
    printf("sizeof x[0]     = %d\n", sizeof(x[0]));    /* first dimension */
    printf("sizeof x[0][0]  = %d\n", sizeof(x[0][0])); /* second dimension */
    printf("sizeof x[0][0][0] = %d\n", sizeof(x[0][0][0]));   /* third dimen */

    sub_routine(x);      /* call sub_routine(), send address of local array x */

    printf("w[0][1][2] is %c\n", w[0][1][2]);  /* will print an 'h' */
    printf("w[1][0][2] is %c\n", w[1][0][2]):  /* will print a '3' */
```

```
    printf("print part of array w\n");
    {                                       /* show how w is organized */
       int i, j;                            /* can define variables after open { */
       for(i = 0;i < 4; i++) {              /* loop through second dimension */
          for(j = 0;j < 5; j++) {           /* loop through third dimension */
             printf("%c", w[0][i][j]);      /* print a through t */
          }
       }
    }

    printf("\nprint array z\n");
    {                                       /* show how z is organized */
       int i, j;                            /* can define variables after open { */
       for(i = 0;i < 4; i++) {              /* loop through first dimension */
          for(j = 0;j < 3; j++) {           /* loop through second dimension */
             printf("%d", z[i][j]);         /* print all the values */
          }
          putchar('\n');
       }
    }
}


void sub_routine(char y[][3][4])        /* modern style parameter declarations */
{                                           /* size of address of passed array */
    printf("sizeof y     = %d\n", sizeof(y));
                                            /* size of passed array 1st dimen */
    printf("sizeof y[0] = %d\n", sizeof(y[0]));
    printf("sizeof w     = %d\n", sizeof(w));  /* size of entire global array */
                                            /* size of global array 1st dimen */
    printf("sizeof w[0] = %d\n", sizeof(w[0]));
}
```

Figure 9.6 Multidimensional Array Program Example—`multidim.c`

The output of this program is as follows:

```
sizeof x          = 24
sizeof x[0]       = 12
sizeof x[0][0]    = 4
sizeof x[0][0][0] = 1
sizeof y     = 2
sizeof y[0] = 12
sizeof w     = 60
sizeof w[0] = 20
```

(program continued on next page...)

```
w[0][1][2] is h
w[1][0][2] is 3
print part of array w
abcdefghijklmnopqrst
print array z
100
200
300
400
```

We'll start our discussion of this program by noting how the array w has its initial values defined. Braces are used to group the characters together so that they have a form similar to the dimensions of the array. This helps us to visualize the form of the array. The braces are not required in this case since we are not leaving any gaps in the array with our initializing data. If we were only initializing a portion of any dimension then various sets of the inner braces would be required to designate which initializing values should apply to which part of the array. We can graphically illustrate what this array looks like by the diagram in Figure 9.7. Each small box containing numbers and letters represents an element of the array. The information inside the box signifies:

Any number of diagrams could be used to illustrate what a multi-dimensional array looks like, but we've chosen a staggered layer approach, with the large planes of the array moving away from the reader as they are viewed from bottom to top.

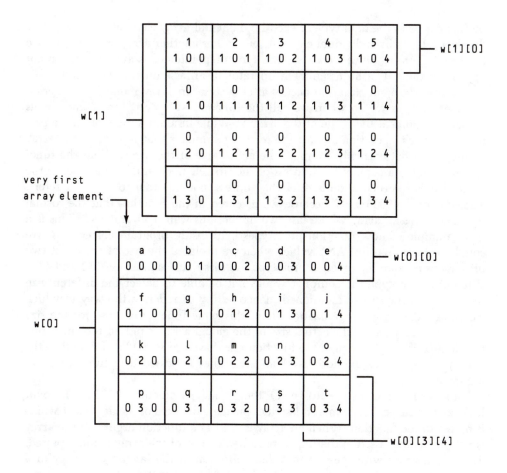

Figure 9.7 Drawing of a Multidimensional Array

The first four lines of the program output show the sizeof operator performed on the arrays of x, x[0], x[0][0], x[0][0][0]. The output illustrates how the total size of a multidimensional array is the product of all the dimensions times the size of the array data type, i.e., 2 * 3 * 4 * sizeof(char) or 24.

The array element x[0] is really an array itself which contains a two-dimensional array of [3][4]. This gives x[0] a size of 12. The size of x[0][0] is 4, which is the number of elements in the final dimension since each element has a size of one, as the sizeof (x[0][0][0]) shows. That x[0] really identifies a two-dimensional array with a total size of 12 illustrates the concept of *scaling*, which means that x[1] is 12 bytes away from x[0], not one byte as would be true for a one-dimensional array. We'll illustrate scaling further when we study pointers.

In order to fully understand multi-dimensional arrays it is very important to realize that x[0] is both an array name and a pointer constant. Because we did not use the subscript on the final or last dimension, the expression does not have the same type as the data type of each fundamental array element. Because x[0] does not refer to an individual element, but rather another array, it does not have the type of char. Since x[0] has the type of pointer constant, it also cannot appear on the left of an assignment operator in an assignment expression.

A very different situation occurs after we use an array name in a function argument list, as we do when we call the function sub_routine() and use as an actual argument the name of the array x. While inside the function, if we perform a sizeof operation against the formal parameter that represents the array name, we do not correctly compute the actual size of the array. What the function sees is only a copy of the address of the first element in the array; hence the value that is returned is the size of the address, not the item to which it refers. The sizeof (y[0]) is 12 because we declared in the function that the formal parameter was an array whose last two dimensions were [3] and [4]. This is a good example of how function prototypes help insure program correctness. We could not have used just ANY values when we declared the size of these last two dimensions because the function prototype specifies that we must use [3] and [4]. Without a prototype the compiler would not be able to detect the difference in the way the array was dimensioned, hence letting us redefine the way in which we viewed the array's organization. If in this same function we ask for the size of a global array name, the actual size of the global array is indeed returned, further illustrating that although the function may have access to global data directly, it only has access to the address of an array that is passed to a function as an argument.

In the function sub_routine() the formal parameter y[][3][4] might look rather strange, but in fact it describes precisely the type of the argument which is passed to the function. When an array is used as a function argument the array is not physically passed to the function; rather, a copy of the array name is passed. This is consistent with the call by value definition of the language: a copy of a value rather than the address of a value is passed to a function. Because an array name is a pointer constant, copying the value of the array name creates another pointer. The expression y[] indicates that this parameter is a pointer, and [3][4] indicates the size of the second and third dimensions of the array to which y[] points. This will become more clear when we discuss pointers.

Let's return to the main() function and examine the next two printf() statements, which illustrate how to reference specific elements in the array w. Many languages use a form of array referencing that looks like this: name[i, j, k]. It is important not to use this form when writing array subscripts because, for example, w[0][1][9, 2] references the character h. The presence of the 9 does not affect the subscript in the slightest. This is because the expression [9, 2] is interpreted as meaning "evaluate the 9 fully before passing the comma sequence point, then evaluate the 2." Since the last expression evaluated is the 2, the value of that expression becomes the value for the entire [9, 2] expression. This mistake probably will not cause a compile error because what was written is in keeping with how C allows multiple expressions to be separated by commas. The last expression becomes the value of the entire set of expressions.

The next block of code in main() contains two nested for() statements, which through their output illustrate that arrays are stored in *row major order*. This means that the rightmost (column) subscript of the array varies the fastest when we view the array in a linear fashion. We illustrate this by displaying some of the characters in the array w.

Finally we display all the elements from the array z in the form of a rectangle, similar to the way that many people visualize a two-dimensional array. It is interesting to compare this output to the nested braces used to initialize array z. Note that each inner set of braces corresponds to one row of the array. If not enough values are supplied inside the inner braces, then when the supplied values run out, zeroes are used since z is a global array. All global data items are initialized to zero when they are created (unless specified otherwise).

9.5 Self-Check

These statements are True or False. The answers are given at the end.

1. An array is an indexed variable.

2. Array elements do not have to be stored contiguously in memory.

3. The name of an array is a constant which represents the address of the first element of the array.

4. The expression char ary() = "a string"; will create an array and initialize it to contain a string.

5. Arrays are stored in row major order, which means that the rightmost subscript varies the fastest.

6. You can easily change the base for subscripting an array from 0 to 1.

7. Creating an array of 5 characters means that the largest subscript you can correctly use is 4.

8. An array can contain only one string at a time.

9. Arrays with the static modifier have their characters initialized to blanks when the program is compiled.

10. The expression char ary[4] = "this"; creates a string which can be used with string functions in your program.

11. All literals (string constants) must be stored separately and kept distinct by the compiler.

12. You can initialize an array after it is defined merely by writing array_name = "a string";.

13. Subscripts should be integers, or expressions type cast to an integer.

14. When you use an array name as a function argument the entire array is passed to the function.

15. The standard character string input functions like `gets()`, `fgets()`, etc. are not safe functions and cannot be used reliably for "bulletproof" data input.

16. The expression `ary[2,3]` references the second row, third column of a two-dimensional array.

17. The expression `char ary[2] = {'a', '\0'};` is perfectly valid and creates a string equivalent to "a."

18. If we define `char myarray[9];`, then the expression `myarray + 3` is a pointer to character, while `myarray[3]` is a character.

19. All character arrays are strings, but not all strings are character arrays.

20. You can make no assumptions about the initial value of character arrays that are defined as automatic rather than global variables.

Answers

1. T   2. F   3. T   4. F   5. T   6. F   7. T   8. F   9. F   10. F   11. F
12. F   13. T   14. F   15. T   16. F   17. T   18. T   19. F   20. T

9.6   Review Program—Dimensionally Independent Code

In this review program we will look at various methods used to manipulate arrays of arbitrary dimensions including one-dimensional, two-dimensional and three-dimensional definitions. In addition, we will develop a general-purpose function that 'maps' the coordinates of an array of an arbitrary number of dimensions (n-dimensional) to a simple, one-dimensional array. Such a transformation function will allow us to write dimensionally independent code. Often you will find that array data will be read/written from/to a mass storage device (such as a disk drive). It is advantageous to view the data as a linear array regardless of the logical organization of the data itself. In addition, functions that receive multidimensional arrays as arguments must be modified each time for different dimensions or array sizes. Our mapping function will allow us to write functions that offer flexibility in handling arrays of different dimensions and sizes.

☐ Design Specifications

Before designing our mapping function, let's investigate how an array of arbitrary dimension might be mapped to a linear (one-dimensional) array. Consider the following two-dimensional array definition:

```
char array_2d[3][3] = {'a','b','c',
                       'd','e','f',
                       'g','h','i'};
```

If we code:

```
printf("%c %c", array_2d[2][0], array_2d[1][2]);
```

we would see the output:

g f

It is helpful to view the array as a square matrix of characters, like this:

```
     0   1   2
   ┌─────────────── x
0  │  a   b   c
1  │  d   e   f
2  │  g   h   i
   │
   y
```

The y-axis coordinates represents the rows of the array and the x-axis the columns. This representation can be extended to three dimensions by adding a third axis, z, at right angles to the other two. For example, the array definition

```
char array_3d[2][2][2] = {'a','b',
                          'c','d',

                          'e','f',
                          'g','h'};
```

can be viewed as:

```
                        0 1
                       .---- x
              a b    0 /| 0
              c d    1 / | 1
                       z  y
        e f
        g h
```

As an example, suppose x = 1, y = 0, and z = 1. Then:

```
printf("%c", array_3d[z][y][x]);
```

would print the letter f on the display.

Note that both array definitions can be written by coding:

```
char array_2d_as_1d[] = {'a','b','c',
                         'd','e','f',
                         'g','h','i'};
```

for our two-dimensional array and:

```
char array_3d_as_1d[] = {'a','b',
                         'c','d',

                         'e','f',
                         'g','h'};
```

for our three-dimensional representation. It is important to realize that when a multi-dimensional array is viewed in this manner, the array subscripts are reversed from the normal (x, y, z) representation used in the Cartesian coordinate system. Notice in our example we referenced the array with:

```
printf("%c", array_3d[z][y][x]);
```

instead of:

```
printf("%c", array_3d[x][y][z]);
```

to print the point (x, y, z). The C language always places the most rapidly changing subscript LAST in the chain of subscripts.

It seems reasonable that we should be able to develop a formula to calculate a one-dimensional linear index given (1) the number of dimensions and (2) the length of each dimensional axis. For the sake of simplicity we will assume that the axes are of equal length.

We can observe that the linear index for a one-dimensional array, given a point x, is given by:

$$i = s^0 * x$$

where i is the linear index. Similarly for a point (x, y) in two-dimensional space the index becomes

$$i = (s^1 * y) + (s^0 * x)$$

and

$$i = (s^2 * z) + (s^1 * y) + (s^0 * x)$$

for a point (x, y, z) in three-dimensional space. It follows that for n-dimensional space the linear index is given by:

$$i = (s_d^{d-1} * c_d) + (s_{d-1}^{d-2} * c_{d-1}) + \ldots + (s_1^{d-d} * c_1)$$

where

> i : linear index into linear mapping
> s : length of each dimensional axis (must be equal!)
> d : number of dimensions
> c : coordinate value of point for axis n

Our formula will allow us to map the logical coordinates of an n-dimensional point to the physical, linear array itself.

Note that our equation implies that we will need a function to calculate x^y where x and y are integers. The standard library of most compilers includes such a function for floating point numbers, but we will write our own to operate on integers only.

□ *Program Design*

Writing pseudocode for our transformation function yields

```
    begin point_index(d, s, c)
    integer d, s                    the number of dimensions and size of axes
    character c[]                   array holding point coordinates

        integer i                   the linear index

        while (d > 0)               start at highest dimension and work down
            d = d-1
                      d
            i = i + (s * c[d])      sum for each point
        endwhile
        return(i)
    end point_index
```

Note that we must also write pseudocode for a function to calculate s^d:

```
begin ipow(x, y)                        calculate x^y and return result
integer x, y

   integer result

   while (y > 0)                        multiply x by itself y times
       y = y-1
       result = result * x
   endwhile
   return(result)
end ipow
```

We will now proceed to write our functions along with a simple main function driver that prints a one-dimensional array as two-dimensional and three-dimensional representations.

□ Design Implementation

```c
/*-----------------------------------------------------------------------
ndindex.c
Manipulation of a 1-dimensional array as 2-d and 3-d
------------------------------------------------------------------------*/
#include <stdio.h>

#define SIZE_3D 3               /* length of each axis, 3-d */
#define DIM_3D 3                /* number of dimensions, 3-d */

#define SIZE_2D 5               /* length of each axis, 2-d */
#define DIM_2D 2                /* number of dimensions, 2-d */

/*
 function prototypes
*/

int point_index(int, int, int[]);
int ipow(int, int);
```

```
/*
 1-dimensional array viewed logically as

    2-D
    ---
                    01234
    ABCDE      0 .------ x
    FGHIJ      1 |
    KLMNO      2 |
    PQRST      3 |
    UVWXY      4 |
                 y

and

    3-D
    ---
                    012
    ABC   JKL   STU   0 .--- x
    DEF   MNO   VWX   1 |\0
    GHI   PQR   YZ!   2 | \1
                      y  \2
                         z
*/

char arry_1d[] = "ABCDEFGHIJKLMNOPQRSTUVWXYZ!";

main()
{
    int x, y, z;
    int test_point[4];                  /* test point array */

/*
 do 2-d test routine
*/

printf("\n1-D Array Viewed as 2-D");
printf("\n----------------------\n");

/*
 loop through all x and y combinations
*/
```

(program continued on next page...)

```
   for (y = 0; y < SIZE_2D; ++y) {
      test_point[1] = y;              /* set current y value */
      for(x = 0; x < SIZE_2D; ++x) {
         test_point[0] = x;           /* set current x value */
                                      /* print the current point value */
         printf("%c ", arry_1d[point_index(DIM_2D, SIZE_2D, test_point)]);
      }
      printf("\n");
   }


/*
 do 3-d test routine
*/

printf("\n1-D Array Viewed as 3-D");
printf("\n----------------------\n");


/*
 loop through all x, y and z combinations
*/

   for (z = 0; z < SIZE_3D; ++z) {
      test_point[2] = z;              /* set current z value */
      for(y = 0; y < SIZE_3D; ++y) {
         test_point[1] = y;           /* set current y value */
         for (x = 0; x < SIZE_3D; ++x) {
            test_point[0] = x;        /* set current x value */
                                      /* print the current point value */
            printf("%c ", arry_1d[point_index(DIM_3D, SIZE_3D, test_point)]);
         }
      printf("\n");
      }
   printf("\n");
   }
}


/*--------------------------------------------------------------------------
 point_index()
 This function performs a mapping function from n-dimensional coordinates
 to a linear array that stores the actual point values contained within
 the n-dimensional address space. The array c[] contains the
 n-dimensional coordinates of the point, which are used to calculate the
 linear index. We use the following formula:
```

$$i = (s_d * c_d^{d-1}) + (s_{d-1} * c_{d-1}^{d-2}) + \ldots + (s_1 * c_1^{d-d})$$

```
where,

      i   : linear index into linear mapping (1-dimensional array)
      s   : length of dimensional axes (must be equal!)
      d   : number of dimensions
      c   : coordinate of point for axis n

-----------------------------------------------------------------------*/
int point_index(d, s, c)
int d, s, c[];
{
   int i = 0;
   while (d--) {                        /* start at highest dimension and */
      i += ipow(s, d) * c[d];           /* work down */
   }
   return(i);                           /* return linear array index */
}

/*-----------------------------------------------------------------------
 ipow()                          y
 This function calculates x   where x and y are integers.
-----------------------------------------------------------------------*/
int ipow(x, y)
int x, y;
{
   int result = 1;                      /* initial value in case y is 0 */
   while (y--) {
      result *= x;                      /* multiply x by itself y times */
   }
   return(result);
}
```

You should note that the function point_index() depends heavily on the fact that the axes are of equal length. We will leave it as an exercise to convert the function to handle dimension spaces with unequal axis lengths.

You may also have observed that it should be possible to write a general purpose print function for n-dimensional array representations of a physical linear array. This will also be left as an exercise.

□ *Program Output*

```
1-D Array Viewed as 2-D
-----------------------

A B C D E
F G H I J
K L M N O
P Q R S T
U V W X Y
```

(program continued on next page...)

```
1-D Array Viewed as 3-D
-----------------------
A B C
D E F
G H I

J K L
M N O
P Q R

S T U
V W X
Y Z !
```

Points to Study

Useful applications for our viewing transformation function will be presented in the Exercises. For now, review the following:

1. Loops used in `main()` to print the two-dimensional and three-dimensional representations.

2. Equation used to accomplish the linear mapping.

3. Definition of the one-dimensional array. How could this be redefined as a two-dimensional or three-dimensional array?

4. Order of the subscripts in multidimensional arrays. Remember to reverse subscripts from the normal Cartesian conventions.

9.7   Exercises

1. Write a function named `point_ok(d, s, c)` where

> d : number of dimensions in address space (e.g., 1,2,3, etc.)
> s : length of each axis
> c : integer array containing point coordinates

The purpose of `point_ok()` is to determine if a given point (whose coordinates are stored in `c[]`) lies within the address space defined by d and s. The function should return a logical TRUE if the the point is valid, otherwise a logical FALSE if invalid. Write a driver to test values for one, two, three, and four dimensions including valid and invalid points. Sample calls are given below.

```
#define SIZE_2D 3
#define DIM_2D 2

char c[2];...

c[0] = 1;
c[1] = 3;
if (point_ok(DIM_2D, SIZE_2D, c))
   printf(''Point within address space.\n'');
else
   printf(''Point outside of address space. Invalid.\n'');
   ...

c[0] = 0;
c[1] = 1;
if (point_ok(DIM_2D, SIZE_2D, c))
   printf(''Point within address space.\n'');
else
   printf(''Point outside of address space. Invalid.\n'');
   ...
```

□ *Program Output*

```
Point outside of address space.  Invalid.
Point within address space.
```

2. Define a three-dimensional array for the data set illustrated below:

```
                             0 1 2
                             +------ x
                 a b c     0 /¦0
                 d e f     1 / ¦1
                 g h i     z   ¦2
                 j k l         ¦3
                               y

        m n o
        p q r
        s t u
        v w x
```

Do not use a linear (one-dimensional) representation of the array. Write a function to print the array to the display.

3. The transpose of an n × n matrix is obtained by interchanging all rows and columns in the array. For example, given the 3 × 3 matrix

$$A = \begin{matrix} 1 & 2 & 3 \\ 4 & 5 & 6 \\ 7 & 8 & 9 \end{matrix}$$

B, the transpose of A, is given by

$$B = \begin{matrix} 1 & 4 & 7 \\ 2 & 5 & 8 \\ 3 & 6 & 9 \end{matrix}$$

Write a function to produce the transpose of a 4 × 4 matrix. As usual, write a test jig to demonstrate that your function works properly.

* 4. Write a size-independent version of the matrix-inversion function specified in exercise 3. Write a driver to demonstrate that your function works on any square matrix of arbitrary size.

5. Write a program to summarize the sample census data given below:

AGE			SEX		INCOME IN 1000s			
21-40	41-60	OVER 60	M	F	10-35	36-50	51-75	OVER 75
X				X			X	
	X			X		X		
	X		X			X		
X				X	X			
		X	X		X			
	X		X					X
X			X		X			
	X			X			X	
X			X		X			
X			X		X			
X			X			X		
		X		X		X		
	X		X					X
X			X				X	
X				X		X		
X			X			X		

Use a two-dimensional array to hold the census data.

9.8 Pretest

☐ *Multiple Choice*

Circle one correct answer for each of the following:

1. Consider the three-dimensional array below:

```
                    0 1 2
                    +------ x
             1  2  3   0 /:0
             4  5  6   1 / :1
                       z    y
        7   8   9
       10  11  12
```

A suitable definition for this array would be:
a. int a[][][] = {1, 2, 3, 4, 5, 6, 7, 8, 9, 10, 11, 12};
b. int a[3][2][2] = {1, 2, 3, 4, 5, 6, 7, 8, 9, 10, 11, 12};
c. int a[2][2][3] = {1, 2, 3, 4, 5, 6, 7, 8, 9, 10, 11, 12};
d. int a[2][3][2] = {1, 2, 3, 4, 5, 6, 7, 8, 9, 10, 11, 12};

2. In order for a function to access a locally defined array, the function must receive:
a. The name of the array.
b. Any element of the array.
c. The first element of the array.
d. The address of any element in the array.

3. Given the array definition:

```
char a[2][4][3] = {'a','b','c',
                   'd','e','f',
                   'g','h','i',
                   'j','k','l',
                   'm','n','o',
                   'p','q','r',
                   's','t','u',
                   'v','w','x'};
```

the statement:

```
printf("%c", a[1][3][2]);
```

would print the letter:

a. m

b. w

c. x

d. none of the above

4. Multi dimensioned arrays in C can have a maximum of:

a. Five dimensions.

b. 32,000 elements.

c. As many dimensions as your compiler allows.

d. Four duplicate definitions.

5. What is the actual number of elements in the following array:

```
char sample[] = "This is a test.";
```

a. 16.

b. Can be determined with `sizeof(sample)`.

c. Can be determined with `strlen(sample)`.

d. All of the above.

6. What is wrong with the array definition given below?

```
char test_array[][2][4] = {"ABCD",
                           "EFGH",

                           "IJKL",
                           "MNOP"};
```

a. The first array dimension must be quantified.

b. The array is not large enough to hold all the characters.

c. The dimensioned sizes are coded backwards.

d. Nothing is wrong with the array definition.

7. The total number of bytes in the array:

```
char big_array[10][3][45][9];
```

would be given by:

a. `sizeof(big_array) / sizeof(char)`.

b. `(10 + 3 + 45 + 9) X sizeof(char)`.

c. `sizeof(big_array)`.

d. All of the above.

e. None of the above.

8. What is wrong with the following array definition?

```
char mixed[] = {'a', 1.0, 'b', 2.0, 'c', 3.0, 'd', 4.0};
```

    a. An array dimension size must be given.

    b. The array should be defined as:

```
char mixed[] = {a, 1.0, b, 2.0, c, 3.0, d, 4.0};
```

    instead of the way it was written.

    c. Different data types cannot be mixed in an array in C.

    d. The type specifier should be `int` instead of `char`.

9. The standard library function `fgets()` is not considered a safe input function because:

    a. No length checking is done on the input string retrieved.

    b. The function cannot retrieve data other than of type `char`.

    c. The input can be redirected to an invalid device.

    d. The line feed character is not eliminated.

10. Given the following code fragment:

```
int x[2][3] = {10, 15, 25, 30, 35, 40};
    ...

swap_em(x[0][1], x[1][1]);
    ...

swap_em(i, j)
int i, j;
{
    int temp;

    temp = i;
    i = j;
    j = i;
    return;
}
```

    what would be the resultant array after the call to `swap_em()`?

    a. 10 15 25
       40 35 30

    b. 10 15 25
       30 35 40

    c. 10 40 25
       30 35 15

    d. 10 20 30
       25 35 40

Pointers

P ointers are an extremely important part of the C language. We have been using
them already; for example, the `printf()` function's first argument is a pointer
to a character string. Names like `stdin` and `stdout` are pointers to areas of
memory that contain file control information. In this chapter we will explain the
basic types and uses of pointers. Then, as we gain more C programming experience,
it will become clear that pointers provide a powerful tool to access data from any
structure or organization.

After studying this chapter, you will be able to do the following:

1. Explain the concept of pointers.

2. Define, initialize, and perform arithmetic on pointers to different types of data.

3. Show how to pass a pointer as a function argument and return a pointer from
   a function.

4. Explain the relationship between pointers and arrays.

5. Demonstrate the use of pointers to other pointers.

10.1 The Concept of Pointers

When we define a variable we are reserving storage in the computer's memory.
The definition of the variable states that the storage now has a name (the name
of the variable) and a format (the format of the type of the variable, e.g., `char`,
`int`, `float`, etc.). For example, this definition:

```
int x;          /* the definition of an integer */
```

states that some part of the computer's memory contains data that should "look"
like an integer. We can read and write to the storage area by using `x`, the name
of the variable. Remember that if we are defining an automatic rather than a global
variable, the storage is not initialized and we must put something into the variable before we use it.

We can draw this picture to represent the situation:

```
storage name     : x
storage location: 1000
storage type     : integer
storage contents: 40
```

```
┌───────────┐
│           │
│    40     │
│           │
└───────────┘
```

The choice of 1000 as the storage location for our example is completely arbitrary. We will use various memory locations for our examples about pointers in this book. The choice does not imply any similarity to actual storage locations on any computer.

In addition to creating the variable x we can also create a pointer to x. This *pointer* is a variable containing the address of where x is located, rather than containing x itself. We can call this variable any name we want, like px for example (for "pointer to x"). This picture would then represent the situation:

```
storage name     : px                storage name     : x
storage location: 567                storage location: 1000
storage type     : pointer to integer storage type     : integer
storage contents: 1000 (address of x) storage contents: 40
```

```
┌───────────┐                        ┌───────────┐
│           │                        │           │
│   1000    │───────────────────────▶│    40     │
│           │                        │           │
└───────────┘                        └───────────┘
```

Again, the storage locations used above are chosen for illustration purposes only. Likewise, the name px is arbitrary and could just as easily be any valid variable name.

This relationship between px and x can be described as "px points to x", or "the integer to which px points". We can also say that x can be referenced indirectly through px as opposed to directly referencing x by using its name. Since we are using only one pointer to access x, we have only one level of indirection involved when we access x through px. The term *indirection* is important to remember since some compiler error messages identify errors in the use of pointers with phrases like "invalid indirection". Each pointer accessed during the process of obtaining the data is said to be one level of indirection.

This example shows how a pointer contains the address (i.e., storage location) of the variable to which it "points". We can also create pointers to pointers, and further pointers to pointers to pointers to. . . . Almost any data arrangement or structure can be created or simulated by using pointers: hierarchical, network, linked list, and even relational. The only limitation is the ability to understand and correctly navigate the data structure created.

10.2 Defining and Initializing a Pointer

The definitions needed to create the above example are these:

```
int x   = 40;        /* the definition of an integer */
int *px = &x;        /* the definition of a pointer to the same integer */
```

The first line is no different from the syntax used to define any other integer. The second line is new, however. The part on the left of the assignment reads "px is a pointer to an integer." The * character is placed between the type specifier int and the variable name px. Whenever the * character is encountered in a variable definition it is replaced by the words "pointer to". The * character is also employed when x is accessed through the pointer, and this dual use of the * is often a source of confusion. All of the descriptions in this section apply only to the definition of pointers. In another section of this chapter we will thoroughly describe the use of pointers and how the * is used in conjunction with a pointer to actually access the data.

The & symbol is a request to create the address of where x is stored in the computer so that the pointer px can be initialized with this address. From our example this would place the value 1000 (the address, or location of x) into the storage location whose name is px. It is not correct to assign the result of the & operator to anything except a pointer.

Pointers are defined to point at only one type of data. Our example above creates px, a pointer to an integer. The variable px should not be used to point to any other type of data except integer. Better compilers will catch that misuse of a pointer (using a pointer to access the wrong type of data) and require a type cast to temporarily change the offending pointer into a pointer to the other type of data. Here is an illustration of the misuse we just described:

```
int x     = 40;        /* the definition of an integer */
float y   = 40.0;      /* the definition of a float */
int *px   = &y;        /* error - integer pointer pointing to a float */
                       /* hopefully the compiler will catch this error */
```

Even if the compiler being used allows this type of error checking to be disabled, we strongly recommend that all compiler error and warning checks be left enabled. This may seem harmless enough, but if x (an integer pointer) is used to access the memory location(s) occupied by y (a float variable) then actually neither an integer nor a float is being used. The internal machine format of an integer is very different from the internal machine format of a float, and trying to use as an integer the area where a float resides usually does not make sense. Later in the book we will see how it is possible to legally allow two items of different type to occupy the same storage location(s) (although not at the same time, of course!) by using a union.

Here are some other pointer definitions:

```
char c       = 'x';      /* the definition of a character */
char *pc     = &c;       /* a character pointer that points to c */

float f;                 /* the definition of a float */
float *pf    = &f;       /* a float pointer that points to f */
```

The definition of f immediately above shows that a variable does not need to contain an initial value before its address is assigned to a pointer. The contents of the variable and the calculation of the variable's address are two separate and distinct things.

10.3 Pointers and Arrays

In Chapter 9 we promised to illustrate the connection between array names and pointers. This is it! One of the more interesting aspects of pointers is that array names are really pointers in disguise. In the C language the name of an array is really a constant value, a pointer to the first element of the array. Each occurrence of array name in a program is replaced with a pointer constant to the first element of the array. For example, the following printf() statements produce identical results:

```
char *cstrptr   = "I am learning C\n";   /* create a pointer variable */
char  cstrary[] = "I am learning C\n";   /* create an array */

printf("I am learning C\n");             /* use the string literal */
printf(cstrary);                         /* use the character array */
printf(cstrptr);                         /* use the character pointer */
```

These statements illustrate that string literals, character pointers (variables, i.e., cstrptr) and character array names (constants, i.e., cstrary) can sometimes be used interchangeably if they all are initialized to the same value. The first argument to the printf() function must be a pointer to a string, and all three of these data types meet that requirement.

However, cstrptr creates a pointer (a separate data item) which is initialized to point to a literal string that is stored somewhere by the compiler, as this diagram illustrates:

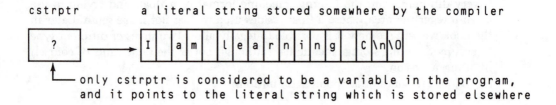

cstrptr   a literal string stored somewhere by the compiler

only cstrptr is considered to be a variable in the program,
and it points to the literal string which is stored elsewhere

In contrast, the array cstrary is available as a variable within the program, and no additional pointer is created to reference cstrary. Rather, the name cstrary refers to the array itself, which is initially populated by the letters in the literal string. There is no additional literal string stored elsewhere by the compiler. A character pointer and a character array are two different things.

the array string stored somewhere by the compiler

cstrary points to here

Some of the next statements are not correct. They illustrate how string literals, character pointers, and character array names are not the same type and cannot be used interchangeably in all cases:

```
"I am learning C\n" = "A new str value";      /* this won't fly */
cstrary = "A new string value";               /* neither will this */
cstrptr = "A new string value";               /* only this will work */
```

While we might know intuitively that the first of the three lines immediately above will not work, let's examine these statements more closely. Using a string literal in a program means that a pointer constant which represents the location in the computer where the string literal is located is really being used. The location of this literal cannot be changed. The statement "I am learning C\n" = "A new str value"; does not result in the string "A new str value" being copied on top of and thereby replacing the string "I am learning C\n." There are no operators that copy strings directly, and even if there were it would be dangerous to use them to change the contents of a string literal. Compilers may or may not merge identical string literals into the same storage location, and altering the content of the string may affect other uses of the same literal elsewhere in the program. Some compilers have an option allowing the control of whether or not duplicate string literals are merged. If that option is set so that duplicate string literals are indeed merged together, the program in Figure 10.1 will actually display the phrase "A new string" on the screen because the strcpy() function will have changed the contents of the first literal. There is only one physical copy in the final compiled program of the literal "I am learning C\n." This is because the two instances of this literal are identical and only one of them is stored. When that one copy changes, all references to the original string pick up the new changed string. Fortunately we chose (intentionally) to use a new string which is shorter than the original string. This eliminated any chance that we would destroy something outside the boundaries of the original string. Remember: strings in C do not have firm borders but end when the first NULL character is encountered. The program in Figure 10.1 is for illustration purposes only. Actually, it represents a poor programming practice.

```
/*
** mergestr.c - An Example of Merged Strings
*/

#include <stdio.h>

main()
{
    strcpy("I am learning C\n", "A new string");
    printf("I am learning C\n");
}
```

Figure 10.1 An Example of Merged Strings—mergestr.c

Antibugging Note 10.1 Changing literal strings

Be careful when using literal strings as function arguments. Incorrect use can cause the string itself to be changed, resulting in some very elusive program bugs.

Continuing with the incorrect examples above, the second line,

```
cstrary = "A new string value";         /* neither will this */
```

won't work either since cstrary is an array name, and hence a pointer constant. Constants cannot appear on the left of an assignment when pointers are involved any more than when integers are being used. This statement illustrates with integers what we just tried to do with pointers:

```
5 = x;   /* this shouldn't work, should it? */
```

For the same reason the statement cstrary = "A new string value" does not result in a string being copied into the existing array.

The third line, shown below, is the only one of the three statements which is legal:

```
cstrptr = "A new string value";              /* only this will work */
```

In this statement a pointer variable appears on the left side of the assignment and is being assigned the value of a pointer constant. We can always assign a constant into a variable as long as the constant and variable are of the same type. If they are not the same type then either an automatic conversion must take place, or else we must explicitly cast the right side of the assignment expression to the type of the left side.

An array name is actually a constant value representing the address of the first element of the array. If we have these two variables:

```
char x[5];
char *px;
```

we can either initialize px so that it points to x by saying:

```
px = &x[0];            /* set px equal to address of first element */
```

or we can simply say:

```
px = x;                /* set px equal to array name */
```

which does exactly the same thing. The relationship between arrays and pointers is very close. When a C program is being compiled array names are actually converted to a pointer constant whose value is the address of the first element of the array.

Quick Note 10.1   Array Names and Pointers

Array names and string literals are pointer constants, while a pointer to characters is a pointer variable. They can all be equal in value (i.e., they can point to the same thing) but they are not all equal in type (i.e., they cannot always be used interchangeably in expressions and statements).

10.4 Using a Pointer to Reference Data

We mentioned above that the * character serves a dual use in C. Not only does it designate that the variable we are defining or declaring is a pointer, but it is also used to *dereference* the pointer, i.e., to access the data being pointed to rather than the value in the pointer itself. If we have these two definitions:

```
int x      = 40;        /* the definition of an integer */
int *px    = &x;        /* an integer pointer that points to x */
```

then we can reference the value 40 either by using the variable name x (*direct reference*) or the expression *px (*indirect reference*). The * character when used as part of an executable statement, can be read "obtain what the pointer points to" or "contents of" rather than "pointer to" when we define a pointer. For example, both of these printf() statements will print the same thing:

```
printf("%d\n", x);       /* referencing x directly */
printf("%d\n", *px);     /* referencing x indirectly through px */
```

We can also update x in two different ways:

```
x   = 5;    /* update x directly */
*px = 5;    /* update x indirectly through the pointer px */
```

Both of these statements change the value of x. The format of the first statement is obvious, but the second might not be so clear. The second statement reads "place a 5 into the storage location to which px points." Since px is a pointer to an integer, then dereferencing the pointer or removing one level of indirection leaves us with a storage location has the type of integer, so the integer constant 5 is placed into x without conversion. If the 5 had been written 5.0, making it a float constant, then the normal C conversion rules would have applied before the value was placed as an integer into the storage location occupied by x.

Be very careful with pointers. It is possible to change almost any storage in the computer by using them. The operating system may prevent a program from changing some areas of storage, but certainly storage has already been allocated to the program and is available to be altered. In addition, some older compilers are very lax about letting pointers reference things like constants. The constant can be changed through the pointer where the compiler would certainly not let the constant be changed directly. The program in Figure 10.2 is an example of how a string literal (a constant) can be changed with a pointer.

```
/*
** chgconst.c - Changing Constants with Pointers
*/

#include <stdio.h>

char *cptr = "At first $100 was in my bank account";

main()
{
    printf("%s\n", cptr);
    strcpy(cptr, "Now $100,000 is in my bank account");
    printf("%s\n", cptr);
}
```

Figure 10.2   Changing Constants with Pointers—chgconst.c

The output of this program is:

```
At first $100 was in my bank account
Now $100,000 is in my bank account
```

Unfortunately (or fortunately) it is not quite as easy to change the actual balance in a bank account.

Antibugging Note 10.2   Changing data through a pointer

Pointers can be used to change any type of data, including data that should remain constant. Double-check and test very carefully programs that use pointers.

Pointers can also be subscripted the same way we subscript an array name. This is because the language defines the subscript operator, [ ], such that x[5] is really (*(x + 5)), i.e. a subscript is converted to a pointer anyway. The code fragment in Figure 10.3 illustrates how an array and a pointer to the memory locations occupied by the array are both subscripted identically.

```
/*
** ptrsub.c - Subscripting Array Names and Pointers
*/

#include <stdio.h>

char x[] = "abcd";

main()
{
    char *px = x;              /* this definition is key to this example */
    int sub;

    for(sub = 0; sub < strlen(x); sub++) {
        printf("%c  %c\n", x[sub], px[sub]);
    }
}
```

Figure 10.3   Subscripting Array Names and Pointers—ptrsub.c

The output produced is:

```
a    a
b    b
c    c
d    d
```

There are some interesting things to note this above example. First, x is defined as a plain character array whose size is dynamically determined by the size of the initializing string literal. Second, px is a pointer to character which is initialized to the value x represents. Since px is a variable of type pointer to character, and x is a constant of type pointer to character, then we can assign the value of x into px. Once that is done, x and px both reference the same memory locations. Third, both px and x can be subscripted, and with the same subscript they will both reference the same character in the array x. And fourth, using the expression:

```
*px[sub]
```

would not provide the same results as would:

```
x[sub]   or   px[sub]
```

since *px[sub] implies that we will first use a subscript in conjunction with the pointer px to reference a value from the array. Then the * means to use that referenced value itself as a pointer and to obtain the value which it (the element from the array) references. That is, *px[sub] means to dereference a pointer twice, which is inappropriate for this situation since we only have one level of pointer relationship established (pointer to character), not two levels (pointer to pointer to character).

Since an array name is a pointer constant, and a character pointer is a pointer variable, they can be used interchangeably as long as the array name is not used on the left side of an assignment. This also means that the increment and decrement operators (++,--) cannot be used with an array name because this is the same as adding and subtracting one from the identifier with which they are associated.

A final point to notice about the above code fragment is that the strlen() function was used as part of the process to determine when to terminate the loop. The body of the loop (the single printf() statement) is performed as long as the subscript is less than the string length. This is because the subscript must vary between 0 and one less than the string length (between 0 and 3 in this case). Although the string is four characters long we do not reference an element whose subscript is 4. Letting the subscript get out of bounds by using it when it contains a value of 4 or more may or may not cause the program to crash. The program does not care what value is placed into the subscript, and absolutely no run-time checking is done to insure that all referenced storage exists inside the defined bounds of the array.

One error which is sometimes made is retaining a pointer to automatic storage after a function terminates. The pointer can exist after the function ends if it is the return value from the function. The obvious problem, however, is that the storage to which the pointer refers is no longer there. The contents of the memory location(s) can easily have been altered. Automatic storage reserved in a function is given up when the function terminates, so keeping a pointer to that storage is inappropriate.

In the next example, the variable `temp_int` has its address returned as the return value of the function. The problem is that once the function `autofunc()` terminates, the variable `temp_int` no longer exists, and using a pointer that refers to the storage which did exist is incorrect.

```
/*
**   Illustrates how not to use automatic storage
*/

int * autofunc(void)       /* a function called by someone else */
{
    int temp_int = 10;     /* this auto variable exists only while here */
    return (&temp_int);    /* this pointer will cause problems */
}
```

Antibugging Note 10.3   Saving a pointer to automatic storage

It is wrong to save a pointer to automatic storage so that the pointer can be used after the block is exited. Since the storage referenced by the pointer no longer exists, using the pointer can cause disastrous results.

The solution to this problem is to include the `static` keyword on the definition of `temp_int`, like this:

```
static int temp_int = 10;
```

Now `temp_int` will not be destroyed when the function terminates, and returning a pointer to `temp_int` is valid since the pointer can be used legitimately after the flow of control has left the function. Don't forget that the use of `static` in this situation also means that `temp_int` is not reinitialized each time the function is invoked.

Quick Note 10.2   Subscripting Array Names and Pointers

Both array names and pointers can be subscripted and the resulting expressions can often be interchanged. Absolutely no checking occurs to insure that there has been no reference beyond the defined boundaries of the array.

10.5 Initializing Pointers and Pointer Arithmetic

Above we showed that the & operator could be used when defining a pointer to give the pointer an initial value. Similar syntax can be used to initialize the pointer in the code portion of the program. This statement:

```
pi = &i;          /* set an integer pointer to point to i */
```

places the address of the variable i into the pointer variable pi. The value of a pointer variable can be changed anytime during the execution of a program, just as the value of any other variable can be changed.

```
/*
** ptrarith.c - Pointer Arithmetic
*/

#include <stdio.h>

int iary[] = {10, 20, 30, 40, 50};     /* an array of integers */

main()
{
    int *iptr;                          /* a pointer to an integer */

    printf("Integers need %d bytes on this machine\n", sizeof(iary[0]));

    iptr = iary;                        /* initialize the pointer */
    printf("%d\n", *iptr);              /* print a few elements */
    iptr++;
    printf("%d\n", *iptr);
    iptr++;
    printf("%d\n", *iptr);
    printf("%d\n", *(iptr + 1));
    printf("%d\n", *(iptr + 2));

    iptr = iary;                        /* initialize the pointer again */
    printf("%2d   %2d\n", (iptr + 0)[0], (iary + 0)[0]);
    printf("%2d   %2d\n", (iptr + 0)[1], (iary + 0)[1]);
    printf("%2d   %2d\n", (iptr + 0)[2], (iary + 0)[2]);
    printf("%2d   %2d\n", (iptr + 0)[3], (iary + 0)[3]);

    printf("%2d   %2d\n", (iptr + 1)[0], (iary + 1)[0]);
    printf("%2d   %2d\n", (iptr + 1)[1], (iary + 1)[1]);
    printf("%2d   %2d\n", (iptr + 1)[2], (iary + 1)[2]);

    printf("%2d   %2d\n", (iptr - 1)[1], (iary - 1)[1]);
    printf("%2d   %2d\n", (iptr - 1)[2], (iary - 1)[2]);
    printf("%2d   %2d\n", (iptr - 1)[3], (iary - 1)[3]);
}
```

Figure 10.4   Pointer Arithmetic—ptrarith.c

Arithmetic can also be performed on a pointer while the program executes. For example, the code fragment in Figure 10.4 will print this output:

```
Integers need 2 bytes on this machine
10
20
30
40
50
10   10
20   20
30   30
40   40
20   20
30   30
40   40
10   10
20   20
30   30
```

Except for the first line, the above output will be the same regardless of the particular machine being used. Note the similarity of this program to `arrayref.c` from Chapter 9. This example also helps to further illustrate the connection between array names and pointers. Especially note that the double column of numbers shows that when referencing data (not changing it) there is absolutely no difference between using an array name and using a pointer to the first element of that same array. Further, the pointer and array name both can participate in arithmetic and be subscripted.

This program relies on the concept of *scaling*, which occurs when any arithmetic is done on any pointer. The output above came from a computer where each integer required two bytes of storage, i.e., the `sizeof` operator returned the value 2 when applied against an integer. Yet from this example we see that adding one to a pointer that points to an integer actually increments the pointer by whatever it takes to point to the next integer in memory. The C language insures that adding one (or anything) to a pointer will actually cause the pointer to be physically incremented by the size of the data item (or multiple thereof) to which the pointer refers. For instance, adding 5 to a pointer really adds to the pointer 5 times the size of the data item to which we point.

We can prove this by remembering we just stated that the language defines the array subscript operator, [], in such a way that x[2] is really (*(x + 2)). We already know that x[0] references the first array element, and that x[1] references the second. The only difference between these expressions is a difference of one (1) in the subscript value, and they can be converted to these expressions:

```
(*(x + 0))
```

and

```
(*(x + 1))
```

If x[1] identifies the array element that occupies memory next to x[0], and if those expressions are converted into the equivalent pointer expressions that add a constant into the pointer, then reversing the process and adding a constant into the pointer will cause the same process to happen "backwards". We speak of "backwards" in concept only, of course. The resulting pointer should point to a valid element even if that element is larger than one byte in size. All arithmetic used in conjunction with pointers is scaled to the size of the data item to which we point.

Only a few operators and operations are valid to use with pointers. They are:

1. pointer + integer

2. pointer − integer

3. pointer − pointer (pointers of like type)

4. pointer compared to same type of pointer

5. pointer compared to zero (the null value)

Adding or subtracting an integer to or from a pointer yields a new pointer which points to a storage location integer elements after or before the original pointer. There is no check to see if the pointer is outside the defined boundaries of the array.

Subtracting two pointers yields a constant value which is the number of array elements between the two pointers. This assumes that both pointers are of the same type and initially point into the same array. Subtracting pointers not of the same type or which initially point to different arrays will yield unpredictable results.

We can illustrate this process of subtracting pointers if we assume that:

if p1 points to a[4] then p1 is the same as (a + 4), and

if p2 points to a[0] then p2 is the same as (a + 0)

Therefore,

p1−p2 is the same as (a + 4)−(a + 0), or 4

illustrating that the difference between two pointers is indeed a constant.

Pointers of like type (i.e., which reference the same kind of data, like int, float, etc.) can also be compared to each other, and the resulting TRUE or FALSE can either be tested or assigned to an integer, just like the result of any logical expression. Comparing two pointers tests whether they are equal, not equal, or less than/greater than each other. One pointer is less than another pointer if the first pointer refers to an array element with a lower number subscript (remember that pointers and subscripts are virtually identical). This operation also assumes that the pointers reference the same array.

Finally, pointers can be compared to zero, the null value. In this case only the test for equal or not equal is valid since testing for negative pointers makes no sense. The null value in a pointer means that the pointer has no value, i.e., does not point anywhere. Null, or zero, is the only numeric value that can be directly assigned into a pointer without a type cast.

In each of these cases we are really speaking of expressions and not restricting ourselves to single integer values. For instance, it is proper to add an integer expression to a pointer. The same is true of subtracting or comparing pointers. Any expression that has pointer as its value can be subtracted from or compared to another pointer of like type. The key point is that the types of the expressions must all match.

Quick Note 10.3   Scaling of Pointer Arithmetic

Pointer arithmetic is scaled to the size of the data item pointed to, i.e., adding one to a pointer actually adds one times the size of the data item to which the pointer refers.

10.6   Pointers as Function Arguments

When a pointer is used as an argument to a function the value of the pointer, i.e., the address that it contains, is passed to the function. Figure 10.5 shows how we might write a program to pass a pointer to a function.

```
/*
** ptrpass.c - Passing a Pointer to a Function
*/

#include <stdio.h>

void sub_func(char *msg2);              /* the function prototype */

main()
{
    char *msg = "This is our message"; /* msg is a pointer variable */
    sub_func(msg);                      /* invoke the function */
}

void sub_func(char *msg2)               /* note how the declaration */
{                                       /*    is done */
    printf("%s\n", msg2);               /* note how the parameter is used */
    printf("The \'sizeof\' msg2 is %d\n", sizeof(msg2));
    printf("The \'strlen\' of msg2 is %d\n", strlen(msg2));
}
```

Figure 10.5   Passing a Pointer to a Function—ptrpass.c

The function `sub_func()` in the program `ptrpass.c` will print:

```
This is our message
The 'sizeof' msg2 is 2
The 'strlen' of msg2 is 19
```

One important thing to note here is how the function declaration is written. The pointer variable `msg` is defined inside `main()` with the data type of `char *`. In `sub_func()` the formal parameter `msg2` is also declared as a `char *`. Using a pointer variable as a function argument is the same as using an array name (a pointer constant), as we discussed in Chapter 9.

Another important thing to understand is the data types of `msg` and `msg2`. They are both pointer variables, not arrays. They both exist separately from each other, as the next diagram illustrates. When `sub_func()` is called, `msg` is used as the function argument. This creates a copy of `msg`; the copy is known within `sub_func()` as `msg2`. Both `msg` and `msg2` reference the same literal string.

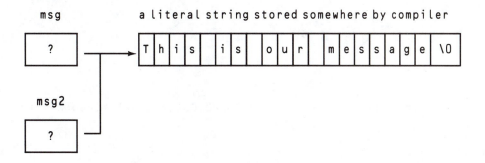

A common mistake is to use the & operator on a function argument that is already a pointer, like this:

```
sub_func(&msg);                 /* the & may well be incorrect */
```

What this actually creates is a pointer to a pointer, or two levels of indirection. This mistake can also be made if an array name is being passed to a function. Taking the address of an array name is certainly not the same as using just the array name itself. We'll further illustrate this concept of pointers to pointers later on in the chapter.

Using function prototypes will help insure that mistakes like the one shown above do not go unnoticed. Adding the address of the operator introduces an additional level of indirection to the function argument. This is not wrong in every case (i.e., if it's planned for), but in the above situation it is unnecessary. It may reflect an incomplete understanding about what a pointer represents and how a pointer is passed to a function. Some compilers have a specific flag to produce a warning when the & operator is used with an array name. Make sure that this flag is on if it is present.

If the `sizeof` operator is used with the formal parameter `msg2` within the function `sub_func()` we may not get the results we expect, as we demonstrate by the output of the program in Figure 10.5. We encountered this same situation when an array name was passed to a function in Chapter 9. The expression `sizeof(msg2)` computes the size of the pointer `msg2`, not the size of the array or string to which the pointer refers. The `strlen()` function, on the other hand, will return the current string length because `strlen()` actually goes to the string and examines it to see where the null value is stored. The `sizeof` operator looks at the defined size regardless of where the terminating null happens to be. What `sizeof` sees is a pointer, not the underlying data item to which the pointer refers.

In fact, `sub_func()` has no way to tell how the character pointer which is passed to the function was formed. The actual argument used in the function invocation could have been a character pointer (it was), or it could have been an array name. It actually could have been any valid C expression that reduced to a character pointer after the expression was evaluated. The resulting value is then passed to the function, which has no way of knowing how the value was formed in the first place.

10.7 More Examples of Pointer Usage

1.

```
/*
** farptr.c - Write Directly to IBM/PC Color (CGA) Video Memory
*/

main()
    {
    char far * p = (char far *) 0xb8000000;  /* color video address */
    *p       = 'a';       /* lowercase a in upper left corner */
    *(p + 1) = '\x9C';    /* a is blinking bright red on blue */
    *(p + 2) = 'b';       /* lowercase b next to the a */
    return;
    }
```

Explanation: This will write a lowercase a to the upper left corner of the CGA color monitor on an IBM/PC. A lowercase b will follow next. The a will be bright red on a blue background, and will blink. This code is NOT very portable and depends on the memory locations of the video display. It will NOT work on a monochrome adapter without changing the 8 in 0xb8000000 to a 0, and obviously no colors will be generated. The `far` keyword creates a pointer that allows access to the entire 1Mb memory space that the 808x chip architecture can address.

2.

```
/*
**   strcpy2.c - A Simple String Copy Function
*/

#include <stdio.h>

void strcpy(char *to, char *from);    /* function prototype */

char ary1[]  = "The first array";
char ary2[]  = "The second array";

main()
{
    printf("%s\n", ary1);            /* before image */
    printf("%s\n", ary2);

    strcpy(ary2, ary1);

    printf("%s\n", ary1);            /* after image */
    printf("%s\n", ary2);
}

void strcpy(char *to, char *from)    /* this is used rather than the */
{                                    /* standard library function */
    while((*to++ = *from++) != '\0') {
        ;
    }
}
```

Explanation: This is a simple string copy function. Two arguments are passed to the function, both character pointers. The while loop test condition compares the value of the expression (*to++ = *from++) to the null character. Characters are copied from the from string into the to string character by character until finally a null character is copied. When the null is finally copied the expression value will be null and the test condition will no longer be true, terminating the loop. The expression *to++ is evaluated as *(to++) because the ++ binds to the variable to before the * does. If it did not, we would have (*to)++, which would indicate that we were incrementing what to pointed to, not to itself. Note how all processing takes place in the test loop and nothing is left for the code body, which is why we used the null statement.

3.

```
/*
** ptrinc.c
*/

#include <stdio.h>
#include <string.h>

#define STRING "abcdefgh"

char ary[] = STRING;

main()
{
    char *aryptr;

    aryptr = ary;                /* make pointer point to array */
    printf("*aryptr++ is %c\n", *aryptr++);
    printf("The string at aryptr is now \"%s\"\n", aryptr);
    printf("The string at (aryptr - 1) is now \"%s\"\n", (aryptr - 1));

    aryptr = ary;
    strcpy(ary, STRING);
    printf("\n(*aryptr++)++ is %c\n", (*aryptr++)++);
    printf("The string at aryptr is now \"%s\"\n", aryptr);
    printf("The string at (aryptr - 1) is now \"%s\"\n", (aryptr - 1));
}
```

Explanation: The expression (*aryptr++)++ must be carefully evaluated using the rules of precedence. The parentheses form a subexpression which is the object of the outer ++ operator. This means that the outer ++ operator will increment whatever is referenced by the expression inside the parentheses. The expression *aryptr++ can also be written *(aryptr++), meaning that the object of the inner ++ operator is not *aryptr, just aryptr. This is seen in the first three lines of the program's output. The expression *aryptr++ produced those lines and shows that the inner ++ operator does not increment the data item pointed to by aryptr, but rather increments aryptr itself. However, it is done after aryptr is used in the expression, meaning that *aryptr++ references the same physical character as *aryptr. The first line of the program output, which displays the character a, shows this. The inner ++ operator is also applied to aryptr after the outer ++ is applied against the subexpression. The object of the outer ++ is the memory location referenced by aryptr before aryptr is incremented. Therefore, ary[0] is incremented, but aryptr (the pointer itself) also is incremented after ary[0], which leaves aryptr pointing at ary[1]. It is this incrementing of the pointer which causes the string to start displaying at ary[1]. We must display the string starting at (ary-1) to see the full effect of the expression.

How do we explain the fact that the outer `++` is effectively performed before the inner `++`? It is neither inside the `()` nor on the left (the postincrement operator associates left to right). One way to visualize the process is to think of the postincrement operator as returning the "old" predecremented value to the expression, while actually performing the increment. This concept may help eliminate the confusion about when the postincrement operator is actually performed.

The output of this program is:

```
*aryptr++ is a
The string at aryptr is now "bcdefgh"
The string at (aryptr - 1) is now "abcdefgh"

(*aryptr++)++ is a
The string at aryptr is now "bcdefgh"
The string at (aryptr - 1) is now "bbcdefgh"
```

10.8 Pointers to Pointers

Pointers can point to anything, including other pointers. Each level of pointer that must be used before the data item is finally accessed constitutes one level of indirection. Figure 10.6 shows what the diagram we used at the beginning of the chapter would look like if we added an additional pointer. This new pointer, `ppx`, will point to the existing pointer, `px`, and either `px` or `ppx` can be used to access `x`. As you study the figure take special note of the contents of each pointer.

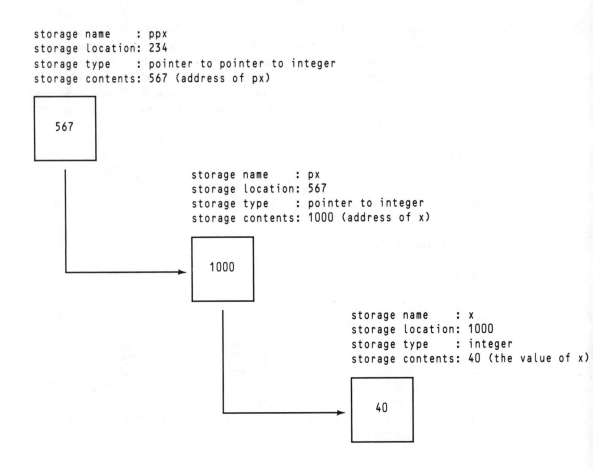

```
storage name    : ppx
storage location: 234
storage type    : pointer to pointer to integer
storage contents: 567 (address of px)
```

```
storage name    : px
storage location: 567
storage type    : pointer to integer
storage contents: 1000 (address of x)
```

```
storage name     : x
storage location: 1000
storage type     : integer
storage contents: 40 (the value of x)
```

Figure 10.6   Pointers to Pointers

10.8.1   *Simple Pointers to Pointers*

The definitions of the variables found in Figure 10.6 would be written like this:

```
int x       = 40;      /* the integer itself */
int *px     = &x;      /* a pointer to an integer with address of x */
int **ppx = &px;       /* pointer to pointer to integer, points at px */
```

The first pointer defined, px, is no different than any other pointer to integer. The second pointer, however, does not point to the variable itself, but rather to a pointer. Note how two asterisks appear before the variable ppx. The definition of `ppx` is read "`ppx` is a pointer to a pointer to an integer." It is initialized with the address of a pointer to an integer.

Besides using the variable name itself, we can use either pointer to access `x`. If we use the pointer `px`, the expression that yields the contents of `x` is:

```
*px
```

This expression can be used in place of `x` anywhere in the program, on either side of the assignment operator. The single `*` used in conjunction with the pointer means to use "the contents of that to which `px` points." In this case `px` points to an integer, so the resulting type of the expression is integer.

If we want to use the pointer `ppx` to access `x`, this expression:

```
**ppx
```

The dual `*` used in conjunction with this pointer means to use "the contents of that to which we point as a pointer to obtain something," and the resulting something would be the variable `x`. In short, each level of indirection (i.e., each pointer) must be "reduced" by the presence of an `*` in the expression in order for the actual variable to be referenced.

If only one `*` were applied to the pointer `ppx` then we would obtain "that to which `ppx` points," which is of course the pointer `px`. Therefore,

```
px is the same as *ppx
```

and this relationship is true of any pointer to pointer arrangement.

10.8.2   Ragged-Edge Arrays

A good illustration of pointers to pointers is to study how command line arguments are passed to a C program by the operating system. Suppose that we have a program named `compare` which can be invoked from the command line like this:

```
compare  -l  99  29  77
```

Remember that in UNIX the executable program produced by the compilation process is normally called `a.out` and must be renamed to create an executable file with the same name as the source file.

The purpose of the program `compare` is to compare a series of numbers entered on the command line to determine which is smallest or largest. The two characters immediately after the program name, `-l`, form a *command line switch* which indicates that the largest of the numbers is to be found. For this particular program the switch `-s` is also valid, and indicates that the smallest of the numbers is to be found. We will explain and develop this program in order to illustrate the concept of *ragged edge arrays*, which is a colloquial term for an array of pointers to character strings.

The prologue part of the program will examine all the characters entered from the command line and will build an array containing the information in usable form. This prologue code is supplied by the compiler, is contained in the executable file, and executes before the main() function receives control. The prologue can do many things, such as check the operating system version number, see if certain equipment is available, release unneeded memory, and so on. It also examines the command line used to invoke the program and places the contents of the command line into a ragged-edge array. The term ragged edge is used in contrast to the term square array because each "line" of the ragged edge array is only as long as it needs to be, not as long as the fixed length of one of the dimensions of the square (multidimensional) array.

The definition:

```
char ary[4][5]
```

creates a two-dimensional array consisting of four arrays each containing five characters. If instead we had written:

```
char *ptr_ary[4]
```

then we would have created an array of four pointers to character. The expression

```
ptr_ary[4]
```

is NOT an array itself, but rather an individual element of the array ptr_ary. This element has the type of pointer to character. In the first case ary[2] is a pointer constant, but in the second case ptr_ary[2] is a pointer variable, a critical distinction.

If this command line is used:

```
compare  -l  99  29
```

then Figure 10.7 illustrates the ragged-edge array that the prologue code would create.

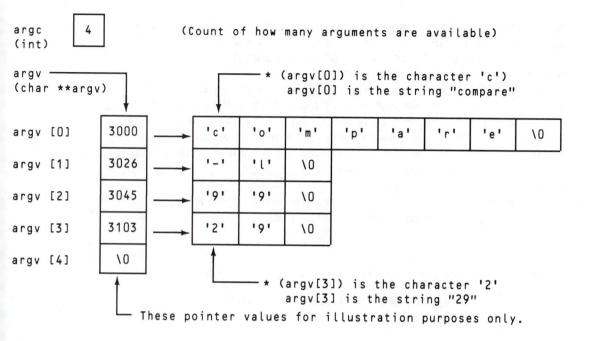

Figure 10.7   Command Line Arguments

The variable argc is an integer created by the prologue code. It contains the number of separate items, or arguments, which appeared on the command line. Spaces are used to separate arguments when the command line is entered, and double quotes can usually be used to enter embedded spaces into one item, like this: "this is one argument." The variable argc does not need to be defined, and although tradition says that the name argc is to be used for the variable, in fact any name desired can be chosen.

The variable argv is also created. It refers to an array of pointers to character strings. Although we used the word array just now we could also call argv a pointer to an array of pointers to character strings. The variable argv is not a constant. It is a variable whose value can be altered, a key point to remember when viewing how argv is used below. As with argc the use of the name argv is not required, but that's traditionally the choice.

The first element of the array, argv[0], is a pointer to a string of characters that contains the program name. In some older environments argv[0] points to a null string because the program name is not available. Subsequent elements in the array point successively to the separate command line arguments: the order of the array elements reflects the order in which the arguments were entered. The ANSI C standard requires that argv[argc] be a null pointer. This simplifies the process of "walking the array" since we can not only check argc to see how many array elements exist, but we can also be on the lookout for a null pointer that designates the end of the array. Older compilers, however, may not provide the null pointer in location argv[argc], so check the documentation provided with your compiler before counting on the presence of the \0.

In Figure 10.7 we intentionally used values which were not consecutive memory locations for the elements of argv (each of which is a character pointer) so that there is no suggestion that the strings are stored consecutively in memory. In fact, it is quite likely that the strings will not be stored consecutively in memory, and quite likely that they will be scattered throughout memory. Make no assumptions about where the strings are stored; assume only that they are pointed to by the elements of the array argv.

It will be helpful to see some code that can actually process this command line. The complete program is shown in Figure 10.8.

```
/*
** compare.c - Finds the smallest or largest number of all those
**             entered on the command line.  A switch can also be entered
**             to specify either smallest or largest.
*/

int main(int, char **);      /* classic prototype for main */

#include <stdio.h>           /* includes prototype for printf() */
#include <process.h>         /* includes prototype for exit() */

#define  LARGE  1
#define  SMALL  0

int main(argc, argv)         /* argc and argv, remember, are created for you */
int argc;                    /* argc is an integer */
char *argv[];                /* argv is an array of pointers to characters */
{
   char *str;
   int num_values;              /* number of values to examine */
   int small_large_flag = 0;    /* smallest = 0 (default), largest = 1*/
   int best_value = 32767;      /* holds the best value so far */

   if ( argc < 2 ) {
      printf ( "\nusage: compare [-sSlL] integer 1...[integer n]\n" );
      printf ( "  -s/S find the smallest number (default)\n" );
      printf ( "  -l/L find the largest number\n" );
      exit(0);
   }
```

```
while(--argc > 0 && (*++argv)[0] == '-') {  /* process the switches */
    for(str = argv[0] + 1; *str != '\0'; str++) { /* first point past - */
        switch(*str) {
            case 's':              /* find the smallest number */
            case 'S':
                    small_large_flag = SMALL;
                    best_value = 32767;
                    break;
            case 'l':              /* find the largest number */
            case 'L':
                    small_large_flag = LARGE;
                    best_value = 0;
                    break;
            default:
                    fprintf(stderr, "unknown arg %c\n", *str);
                    exit(1);
        }
    }
}

if(argc == 0) {
    fprintf(stderr, "Error - at least one number is required\n" );
    exit(1);
}

num_values = argc;

while(argc--) {
    int current_value;
    current_value = atoi(*(argv++));
    if (small_large_flag == LARGE && current_value > best_value) {
        best_value = current_value;
    }
    if (small_large_flag == SMALL && current_value < best_value) {
        best_value = current_value;
    }
}

printf("The %sest of %d value%s is %d\n",
                            (small_large_flag) ? "larg" : "small",
                            num_values,
                            (num_values - 1) ? "s" : "",
                            best_value);
}
```

Figure 10.8 Find the smallest or largest number—compare.c

The first thing to note is that the main() function now has formal parameters. The names argc and argv are optional arguments which can be passed to main() if their names are included in the parameter list. The parameter declarations follow the name of the function (remember that `main()` is a function just like all the others), and the variable `argv` is an array of pointers to characters.

The first `if` statement in `main()` tests to see if any arguments were present on the command line. If the value of `argc` is less than 2 then it means that only the program name, `compare`, is present and no switches or file names were supplied. This situation normally means that the user does not know how to use the program, so the program's response is to explain a little about itself before it terminates.

The test condition of the first `while` loop contains a logical expression that will be evaluated left to right, meaning that the predecrement of `argc` will be the first thing that happens. If after one is subtracted from `argc` it is still greater than zero, the right side of the logical expression will be examined. It is on this right side that some interesting expressions are found.

It might not be obvious what the expression `(*++argv)[0]` means. To analyze it, note that the `()` symbols separate `*++argv` from `[0]`. The parentheses are necessary since the `[]` symbol has a higher precedence than the `*` and would therefore "bind" to the variable name `argv` before the `*` would. This way the entire expression `*++argv` is resolved before the `[0]` is considered. We read `*++argv` as "increment `argv` and then obtain the contents of where `argv` now points." When the program begins `argv` points at the first element of the array. This first element is itself a pointer to the program name. However, we want to point at the first command line argument that was entered. The second array element points at the first command line argument, so by incrementing `argv` it will point at the second element. The `*` then says to obtain the contents of that to which we are pointing, which is a pointer to a character string. This finishes the evaluation of the expression inside the parentheses and provides a pointer to a character string. We then add the subscript, `[0]`, which subscripts the pointer, reducing the level of indirection by one, leaving us not with a pointer to character but the actual character itself, i.e., the first character of the string. We test this first character to see if it is equal to the `-`, which has historically been used as the character to indicate that a switch immediately follows on the command line. If the first character of the argument is a `-` then both sides of the logical expression are true, resulting in the execution of the body of the `while` loop.

Remember that `argv` has been incremented and now points to the second element (subscript `[1]`) of the pointer array, i.e., it points to the pointer that contains the address of the first command line argument after the program name. Since `argv` is a pointer to a pointer it can be subscripted, which means that `argv[0]` is then a pointer to a character. The expression `argv[0] + 1` is also a pointer to a character, the character being the one immediately following the `-` character. This expression is assigned into the automatic variable `str`, which is also defined as being a pointer to a character. This assignment makes up the initialization sequence for the `for` statement. Once the pointer `str` has been initialized, the expression `*str` can be used to obtain the character to which `str` points. The `for` loop continues until the character to which `str` points is a null, meaning the end of the string has been reached. Of course `str` must be incremented for each iteration of the loop so that it points to successive characters in the switch argument.

Each pass of the `for` loop uses the character pointed to by `str` as the value to drive the `switch` statement. The various `case` statements indicate which switch characters are recognized, and the `default` statement reports when an unrecognized character is discovered.

If after the switches are examined on the command line there is nothing left to process, an error message is produced before the program terminates with an exit code of decimal one.

The second `while` loop processes the values entered after the switches. The `atoi()` function converts each of the remaining arguments into an integer (no validity checking here), and the result is saved in the variable `current_value`. Then `current_value` is compared to `best_value` to see whether it meets the condition of being smallest or largest, whichever was requested through the command line switches.

Finally, the result of the program is printed using some interesting combinations of string literals and the conditional operator. Study this program carefully until you thoroughly understand all the statements that use `argc` and `argv`.

Table 10.1 lists various command lines which could be used to invoke this program, and gives the resulting output of each.

Command Line	Resulting Output
compare	usage: compare [`-sS1L`] integer 1...[`integer n`] `-s/S` find the smallest number (default) `-l/L` find the largest number
compare 99	The smallest of 1 value is 99
compare 99 55	The smallest of 2 values is 55
compare −s 99	The smallest of 1 value is 99
compare −s 99 55	The smallest of 2 values is 55
compare −l 99	The largest of 1 value is 99
compare −l 99 55	The largest of 2 values is 99

Table 10.1 Command Lines of `compare.c` and Their Output

10.9   Void Pointers

The ANSI standard has provided a new type of pointer called a `void` pointer. It is closely related to the `void` data type we've already discussed. Rather than being a pointer to nothing, similar to a `void` return type (which means that nothing is returned), a `void` pointer is a pointer to any type of data.

One of the primary purposes for `void` pointers is to generalize the return type of functions that previously returned a specific type of pointer (usually a pointer to `char`). These functions are now declared to return a pointer of type `void`.

Any type of data pointer can be cast into and back from a `void` pointer and the result will be identical to the original pointer. For instance, when the `malloc()` function (which returns a pointer to `void` on ANSI standard compilers) is used to obtain storage for a character array, its return value should be cast into the type of specific pointer we need, like this:

```
cptr = (char *) malloc(sizeof(cary));   /* get storage for a char array */
```

The `*` operator cannot be used with a `void` pointer because a `void` pointer is not defined as pointing to anything in particular. Rather it is a pointer to everything and anything. To use `*` with a pointer means that the data type to which the pointer refers is known, but there is no way to know the data type of the item referred to by a `void` pointer. To use the `*` operator with a void pointer, first convert the pointer to a specific data type and use the `*` operator with the new pointer.

10.10 Pointers to Functions

We have discussed how various items of data can be referenced by a pointer. Portions of code can also be accessed through a pointer to a function. Pointers to functions serve the same purpose as do pointers to data; that is, they allow the function to be referenced indirectly, just as a pointer to a data item allows the data item to be referenced indirectly.

Pointers to functions have a number of uses. For example, consider the `qsort()` function. `qsort()` needs to have a pointer to a function as one of the arguments so that the specified function can make a comparison between the array elements as they are being sorted. Because the comparison between any two elements can be a complex process, not something that a simple flag can control, `qsort()` needs a function to do the comparison. It is not possible to pass a function by value, i.e., pass the code itself. C does, however, support passing a pointer to the code, or a pointer to a function. Pointers to code must be pointers to a function.

Creating a function pointer is as simple as creating a pointer to an array. Usually the function pointer is passed to another function as an argument. To help avoid confusion as we discuss this concept, we will refer to the function whose pointer is being developed as the indirect function, and the function that is receiving the pointer as the invoked function. Whenever an array name is used as a function argument a copy of the value of the array name is passed to the function being called. In the same way when a function name is used as an argument to an invoked function the address of where the indirect function is located is passed to the invoked function. This address of the indirect function can then be used in the invoked function to actually call the indirect function. The review program at the end of the chapter will develop a sorting function. Examine it carefully to see a good example of how a pointer to a function works.

The next example in Figure 10.9 will illustrate the minimum amount of code needed to call a function indirectly. This is provided to help facilitate understanding of the review program. Be sure to study how the two functions in funptr.c are declared in advance, and make sure you understand every part of the code.

```
/*
** funptr.c - Function Pointers
*/

#include <stdio.h>

int func_a(int (*indirect_func)()); /* argument is a function pointer */
int func_b(void);                    /* func_b has no argument */

main()
{
                            /* note how func_b is passed as an argument */
   printf("%d was returned by func_b via func_a\n", func_a(func_b));
}

                  /* the argument of the function is a pointer to another */
                  /* which returns an integer */
int func_a(int (*indirect_func)())
{
     /* the expression (*indirect_func) becomes exactly the same thing */
     /* as if the name func_b were written instead */
   return((*indirect_func)());
}

int func_b()
{
   return(7);
}
```

Figure 10.9   Function Pointers—funptr.c

The key function in this example is func_a(), which receives the name of a function as an argument and then calls that function. The invocation of func_a() requires that the name of func_b() be used explicitly as the actual argument. The reference to the function func_b() generates an argument, which is the address where func_b() is located. The one parameter of the function func_a() is defined as (*indirect_func)(), which reads "indirect_func is a pointer to a function." The parentheses around *indirect_func are necessary because the other parentheses (which signify the function reference) have a higher precedence than the *. Without the parentheses the expression becomes *indirect_func(), or "function returning a pointer." Finally, func_a() calls func_b() through the expression (*indirect_func)(), which is found in the return statement. The returned value from func_b() is passed back through func_a() and printed by main().

10.11 const, volatile *and Pointers*

Previously we discussed the keywords const and volatile, and described how they can be used with variables. It is also possible to create a const pointer, a pointer to a const variable, a volatile pointer, and a pointer to a volatile variable. Consider this definition:

```
const int c = 3;
int const * cptr = &c;
```

Here cptr is a pointer to a const, not a const that also happens to be a pointer. The const keyword modifies the item that is to the immediate right, in this case the *, not the variable name cptr. Had we instead coded this:

```
int d = 4;
int * const dptr = &d;
```

then the const keyword would have modified dptr, not the *, and would have created a const pointer to an integer. The pointer itself, not the item pointed to, would be const.

If a pointer points at a const variable then the variable cannot be modified through the pointer. The pointer however, not being const, can itself be modified. It can be changed to point at a variable that is not const. This could cause problems if, for instance, a pointer to a const was changed to point to a volatile variable.

If a pointer itself is defined as being a const pointer then it (the pointer) can never be modified but the memory to which it refers can be changed.

The volatile keyword can be substituted into the above discussion everywhere that the const keyword appears. The syntax rules for using volatile are the same as for const, even to the extent that this definition is valid:

```
const volatile int confusion = 0;
const volatile int * const volatile confusion_ptr = &confusion;
```

Here we have created a pointer, confusion_ptr, that points to an integer variable confusion. confusion has the properties of both const and volatile. This means that confusion will not be changed by the program, but might itself be changed by some activity outside the bounds of the program. The pointer confusion_ptr, that points to confusion, is also const and volatile, meaning that the program will not change it either, but it, confusion_ptr, might be changed at any moment by something outside the program.

To further illustrate these concepts we have prepared a small program that contains both correct and incorrect statements. The comments on each line fully explain the definitions and assignment statements. Study the program, then experiment with these keywords until their full effect is clear.

```
/*
** const.c - Illustrates const Variables and Pointers
*/

#include <stdio.h>

int const a = 1;         /* a is a const */

const int b = 2;
const int * bptr = &b;   /* bptr is a pointer to a const int */

const int c = 3;
int const * cptr = &c;   /* cptr is also pointer to const int */

int d = 4;
int * const dptr = &d;   /* const pointer to int */

int e = 5;               /* a plain integer */

const int * const fptr;  /* const pointer to const int, uninitialized */

main()
{
    a     = 10;     /* error - can't modify a since it's const */
    *bptr = 11;     /* error - can't modify a const through a pointer */
    bptr  = &c;     /* okay  - bptr itself is not const */
    *cptr = 12;     /* error - can't modify a const through a pointer */
    cptr  = &d;     /* okay  - cptr itself is not const */
    *dptr = 13;     /* okay  - dptr does not point to a const */
    dptr  = &e;     /* error - can't modify dptr, it's a const itself */
    fptr  = &e;     /* error - can't modify fptr, it's a const itself */
}
```

Figure 10.10   Illustrates const Variables and Pointers—const.c

10.12 Complex Declarations

A frequent point of confusion for students of C (and experienced programmers too) is how to decipher complex declarations. For instance, what is the data item what_is_this in this declaration:

```
float (*(*what_is_this)[])();
```

Always keep two simple rules in mind when reading declarations that are not immediately obvious:

1. Start at the name of the item and work clockwise, from the inside out, initially moving to the right.

2. Always resolve all items within the parentheses before moving on.

These rules will not always identify incorrect declarations, but they will provide a handle for reading correct ones.

Further, a convention should be established for describing certain symbols. Here is a suggestion for the words with which to replace the symbols as they are being read. First the symbol will be shown, then the replacement phrase:

```
()    function returning
```

```
[]    array of
```

```
*     pointer to
```

Using these rules the declaration:

```
float (*(*what_is_this)[])();
```

can be described as "what_is_this is a pointer to an array of pointers to functions returning a float".

This declaration is invalid:

```
char *error_declare()[]
```

because it tries to make error_declare into a function returning an array of pointers, and functions cannot return arrays. This correction:

```
char *(error_declare())[]
```

does not help since the brackets still have precedence over the asterisk. The correct syntax is found in the declaration of this_too in Figure 10.11. Other complex declarations are also shown in program complex.c.

```
/*
**   complex.c - Complex Data Declarations
*/

float (*(*what_is_this)[])();     /* pointer to an array of pointers
                                     to functions returning a float */
```

```
int (*this_too())[];              /* function returning a pointer
                                     to an array of integers - note
                                     that arrays of functions and functions
                                     returning arrays are not allowed, so
                                     () and [] can never be adjacent
                                     without a parenthesis between them */

int (*and_this[5])();             /* array of 5 pointers to functions
                                     returning an integer */

char *ary[3];                     /* array of 3 pointers to characters */

main()
{
    printf("This program demonstrates some complex declarations\n");
}
```

Figure 10.11   Complex Data Declarations—complex.c

10.13 Self-Check

These statements are True or False. The answers are given at the end.

1. Pointer variable names must be formed by adding a leading p to an existing variable name.

2. A pointer contains the address of the object to which it points.

3. The & is only one of a number of operators that can initialize a pointer.

4. The * character, when defining or declaring a pointer, is read "pointer to."

5. The * character, when used to reference data, is read "contents of."

6. Any pointer can point at anything; the type specifier is merely used for documentation.

7. A pointer to a character is a pointer variable, while an array name is a pointer constant.

8. If msg is a character pointer, then msg = "A literal"; will copy the string literal "A literal" into the area pointed to by msg.

9. Pointers can be subscripted, just like array names.

10. All arithmetic done with pointers is scaled to the size of the object being pointed to.

11. Adding two pointers together is a quick way to create another pointer.

12. If a pointer variable is used as an actual argument when calling a function, then the compiler passes the address of where the pointer is located, not a copy of the pointer itself.

13. A far pointer allows us to access the entire 1Mb address space available to the 808x and above series of chips.

14. If two `*` characters are used when defining a variable, it is a pointer to another pointer.

15. A ragged-edge array of characters can sometimes be smaller than a square array containing the same amount of data.

16. The variable names `argc` and `argv` are reserved and can only be used with the `main()` function.

17. If `argc` is 3 then `argv[3]` must be a null character to represent the end of the list.

18. The type of the expression `(*++argv)[0]` is character.

19. If `ppx` points to `px` which points to `x`, then `px` is the same as `*ppx`.

20. Code that subscripts a pointer outside the defined boundaries of the array may compile, but logically be in error.

21. The symbols `()` mean "function returning," `[]` mean "array of," and `*` means "pointer to."

22. The definition `(*what_is_this())()` is that of a function returning a pointer to an array of integers.

Answers

1. F   2. T   3. F   4. T   5. T   6. F   7. T   8. F   9. T   10. T   11. F   12. F
13. T   14. T   15. T   16. F   17. T   18. T   19. T   20. T   21. T   22. F

10.14   Review Program—Sorting Arrays of Strings

Pointers present a flexible and fast means of accessing data. In this review program we will illustrate their use in sorting techniques applicable to arrays consisting of string elements. The algorithms we use can easily be adapted to arrays of different data types.

☐ *Design Specifications*

Our review program will consist of the implementation of a Shell sort algorithm applied to pointer arrays and will include a comparison function parameter represented by a pointer to a comparison function.

The Shell sort algorithm is relatively fast and not as hard to understand as faster algorithms such as Quicksort. The algorithm works by moving array elements that are greatly out of order into their approximate correct locations as quickly as possible. The list is divided into partitions with successive passes producing smaller and smaller partitions. Array elements are exchanged between adjacent partitions when necessary, depending on whether we wish ascending or descending sorted order of the final array.

Before we examine the Shell sort algorithm in detail, let's discuss a couple of approaches that can be used to exchange array elements. First, array elements may be exchanged directly, meaning that they are physically moved in memory. Second, they may be exchanged indirectly, which entails swapping pointers to the array elements. If the array consists of memory-sized elements only, then little or no speed gains are realized by using the pointer approach; however, if the array consists of larger than memory-sized elements, e.g., strings longer than, say, two bytes, then considerable speed gains can be realized by using the pointer approach. Furthermore, regardless of speed considerations, flexibility can be realized by using the pointer approach since the array can be viewed in logically different configurations, e.g., ascending or descending sort configurations. To illustrate the speed advantages to the pointer approach and how pointers can be used to generate different logical views of a string list, consider the following example:

POINTER VALUE	PHYSICAL STRING LIST	LOGICAL VIEW OF STRING LIST
100	String__003	String__003
101	String__001	String__001
102	String__004	String__004
103	String__005	String__005
104	String__002	String__002

An ascending view of this array using pointers would look like this:

POINTER VALUE	PHYSICAL STRING LIST	LOGICAL VIEW OF STRING LIST
101	String__003	String__001
104	String__001	String__002
100	String__004	String__003
102	String__005	String__004
103	String__002	String__005

The descending view looks like this:

POINTER VALUE	PHYSICAL STRING LIST	LOGICAL VIEW OF STRING LIST
103	String__003	String__005
102	String__001	String__004
100	String__004	String__003
104	String__005	String__002
101	String__002	String__001

Note that we have only moved the pointer values, not the actual strings themselves. As before, the pointer values represent physical memory locations and have been assigned arbitrary values. In practice, we will not concern ourselves with the actual value of a pointer, except at an abstract level using the normal C language conventions (the * and & operators).

The obvious question that arises from our illustration is this: Why use pointers? To answer this question let's look at the method used by the IBM-PC to access and store bytes (characters) of data. For the "near" memory model, each byte in memory has an associated address (pointer) consisting of a one-word value. Exchanging two pointers involves swapping these two one-word-length values. Exchanging two characters, in contrast, requires moving two byte-length values. If string elements consist of two characters each, then the time needed to swap strings is approximately the same as to exchange their pointers; however, as string elements become longer, the swap time required increases in proportion to the length of each string. On the other hand, the time needed to swap their associated pointers (memory addresses) always remains constant. Obviously, swapping pointers instead of physically moving the actual strings leads to a more efficient algorithm in the majority of cases. In our example, all the string elements are equal to 10 characters, which leads us to believe that a pointer-exchange algorithm will be at least five times as fast as a physical string swapping equivalent. This is indeed the case.

Note also that by using duplicate lists of pointers in lieu of the actual pointer list, we can produce different "views" of the string array without rearranging the "master" pointer list each time. This is precisely how modern data base systems produce index files used to access a data base. We will illustrate this technique in the example program.

□ *Program Design*

Now we will detail our sort algorithm, the Shell sort. As mentioned earlier, the Shell sort yields great speed advantages over more popular sorts like the bubble sort by moving elements into relative position very quickly. Instead of comparing adjacent elements of an array like the bubble sort, the Shell sort compares elements over an interval that decreases with each iteration of the sort routine itself. When an exchange of elements does occur, the Shell sort "backs up" to see if the exchange propagates back down the list. The pseudocode is as follows:

```
integer n                                    number of elements
integer distance                             distance of compare (interval size)
integer i , j                                work variables for iterations
integer limit                                limit for compare loop


begin shellsort(<array>)
    distance = n / 2                         integer division
    while (distance > 0)
        limit = n−distance                   compute ceiling
        j = 1
        while (j <= limit)
            if (<element_j > element_{j + distance}>)

                shellswap(<element_j, element_{j + distance}>, j)

            endif
            j = j + 1                         bump index
        endwhile
        distance = distance / 2              calculate new interval
    endwhile
end shellsort


begin shellswap(<two elements to be swapped>, j)
    xchg_flag = TRUE                         first swap always true
    while (xchg_flag)
        <swap element_j and element_{j + distance}>   swap the elements

        j = j − distance                     backup index
        if (j >= 1)
            if (element_j <= element_{j + distance})   is it propagating
                                             distance downward?
                xchg_flag = FALSE            end backup
            endif
        else
            xchg_flag = FALSE                end backup
        endif
    endwhile
    return
end shellswap
```

Note that we have named the exchange routine shellswap() instead of
simply swap() to indicate that the procedure does more than simply swap two
array elements; in fact, it may swap many elements depending on how the initial
exchange initiated by shellsort() propagates through the array. In our program
we will replace the comparison of two array elements with a pointer to a

comparison function, allowing us to write a generalized version of the Shell sort algorithm. This will allow `shellsort()` to produce ascending and descending views of the array. In our actual program, we will not write `shellswap()` as a separate function. We have only done so in the pseudocode to clarify the algorithms.

□ *Design Implementation*

```
/*-------------------------------------------------------------------
  shelsort.c
  Shell sort example using pointers
-----------------------------------------------------------------*/

#include <stdio.h>
#include <string.h>

#define TRUE 1                           /* defines for logical T/F */
#define FALSE 0

/*
  function prototypes
*/
void shellsort(char **, unsigned int, int (*)());
int ascending(char *, char *);
int descending(char *, char *);
void print_list(char **);

/*
  pointer array we're going to sort
*/
char *test_list[] = { "qrs",
                      "abc",
                      "wxy",
                      "z!@",
                      "hij",
                      "nop",
                      "def",
                      "tuv",
                      "klm",
                      NULL };              /* the null pointer used to mark */
                                           /* end of the array */
```

```
main()
{
   print_list(test_list);               /* print list "as is" */
/*
 perform ascending sort on list
*/
   printf("\nHit CR to do ascending sort...\n\n");
   getchar();                           /* dummy response */
   shellsort(test_list, sizeof(test_list) / sizeof(char *) - 1, ascending);
   print_list(test_list);               /* print ascending list */

/*
 perform descending sort on list
*/
   printf("\nHit CR to do descending sort...\n\n");
   getchar();                           /* dummy response */
   shellsort(test_list, sizeof(test_list) / sizeof(char *) - 1, descending);
   print_list(test_list);               /* print descending list */

   return;
}

/*-------------------------------------------------------------------
 void shellsort(list, n, compare)

     parm            type            desc
 ---------------!---------------!-------------------------------------
 list            char **         array of pointers to type character
 n               unsigned int    number of pointers in the array
 compare         int (*)()       pointer to comparison function


     ret value       type            desc
 ---------------!---------------!-------------------------------------
 ---             void
 ----------------------------------------------------------------*/
void shellsort(list, n, compare)
char **list;
unsigned int n;
int (* compare)();
{
   unsigned int gap, limit, j;          /* gap - interval gap size */
                                        /* limit - limit for compare */
                                        /* j - our loop variable and index */
```

(program continued on next page...)

```
    gap = n >> 1;                       /* same as n/2 only faster */
    while (gap)                         /* while gap exists */
        {
        limit = n - gap;               /* set upper limit */
        j = 0;                         /* start with first element */
        while (j < limit)              /* while not at limit */
            {
/*
 perform the compare as specified in "compare" function
*/
            if ((*compare)(*(list + j), *(list + j + gap)))
                {
                int i, xchg_flag;      /* i - temporary index */
                                       /* xchg_flag - backup flag */

                i = j;
                xchg_flag = TRUE;
                while (xchg_flag)      /* if swap has occurred */
                    {
                    char *temp;
/*
 swap the array elements
*/
                    temp = *(list + i);
                    *(list + i) = *(list + i + gap);
                    *(list + i + gap) = temp;
                    i -= gap;          /* backup to previous interval */
/*
 see if previous swap is propagating backwards in list
*/
                    if (i < 0 || (*compare)(*(list + i), *(list + i + gap)) == 0)
                        xchg_flag = FALSE;
                    }
                }
            ++j;
            }
        gap >>= 1;                      /* same as gap/2 only faster */
        }
    return;
}
```

```
/*-------------------------------------------------------------
  int ascending(s1, s2)

     parm           type            desc
  ---------------|---------------|-------------------------------
  s1              char *          string 1
  s2              char *          string 2

     ret value      type            desc
  ---------------|---------------|-------------------------------
  TRUE            int             string 1 > string 2
  FALSE           int             string 1 <= string 2
  ---------------------------------------------------------*/
int ascending(s1, s2)
char *s1, *s2;
{
   if (strcmp(s1, s2) > 0)              /* see if s1 > s2 */
      return(TRUE);
   return(FALSE);
}


/*-------------------------------------------------------------
  int descending(s1, s2)

     parm           type            desc
  ---------------|---------------|-------------------------------
  s1              char *          string 1
  s2              char *          string 2

     ret value      type            desc
  ---------------|---------------|-------------------------------
  TRUE            int             string 1 < string 2
  FALSE           int             string 1 >= string 2
  ---------------------------------------------------------*/
int descending(s1, s2)
char *s1, *s2;
{
   if (strcmp(s1, s2) < 0)              /* see if s1 < s2 */
      return(TRUE);
   return(FALSE);
}
```

(program continued on next page...)

```
/*---------------------------------------------------------------
void print_list(list)
Print a list of strings via a pointer array.  Pointer array must end
in an ascii null.

    parm            type            desc
----------------!---------------!-----------------------------------
 list            char **         an array of pointers to strings

    ret value       type            desc
----------------!---------------!-----------------------------------
 ---             void
-----------------------------------------------------------------*/
void print_list(list)
char **list;
{
    while (*list)                       /* look for null pointer */
        {
        printf("%s\n", *list);          /* print a string in the list */
        ++list;                         /* point to next array element */
        }
    printf("\n");
    return;
}
```

Although this program sorts a specific array defined outside of our main function, it can be used to sort any character array. The parameter `compare` allows
us to write a flexible function that can sort based on different comparison criteria.
Our function will also sort in a predictable time period regardless of the element
size in the array since we are using pointers. On the average, we expect that it will
also be considerably faster than a physical sort using the same algorithm.

You should note carefully how the indirection operator (*) is used in each of
the functions. Make sure you understand the difference in `list`, `*list` and
`**list` and the objects they represent.

Now, let's see a sample run from our program.

□ *Program Output*

```
qrs
abc
wxy
z!a
hij
nop
def
tuv
klm
```

```
Hit CR to do ascending sort...
```

```
abc
def
hij
klm
nop
qrs
tuv
wxy
z!a
```

```
Hit CR to do descending sort...
```

```
z!a
wxy
tuv
qrs
nop
klm
hij
def
abc
```

Points to Study

1. Use of the indirection operator, *. Study every occurrence of its use in the example program and make sure you understand the object it resolves.

2. Use of the parameter `compare` in `shellsort()`. Why don't we simply call the compare function directly?

3. How the array `list` is defined and initialized.

4. How the print function knows where the end of the list is. Do you suppose this is a common technique used to flag the end of a pointer list?

10.15 Exercises

1. Modify the review program to include the following features:
   a. Sorting of ragged-edge string arrays as well as arrays of strings of equal length.
   *b. Allowing `shellsort()` to sort any generic pointer array including `int **`, `char **`, `float **`, etc.
   (Hint: Use the type `void **` as a formal parameter instead of `char **`).
   c. Maintenance of different views of the list simultaneously without the need to resort the list every time a different view is needed.

2. A searching algorithm for sorted lists is the binary search. The algorithm goes as follows:
   a. Divide the sorted list into two halves.
   b. Compare the element searched for with the midpoint element.
   c. If the midpoint element is equal to the searched element, then we are finished. If not, determine which sublist the element should be in. This is the new "list" to search.
   d. Repeat steps a. through c. until the element is found or the searched list shrinks to zero, whichever occurs first.

   The binary search algorithm is fast since its time is proportional to $\log_2 n$ while a strictly linear search to n itself, where n is the number of elements in the array. Write a function to implement the binary search algorithm on an array. Include a "generic" comparison function, i.e., the function should be able to search a list in ascending order and descending order. As usual, write a test jig to demonstrate that your function works as required.

3. Write pointer versions of the string functions defined in Chapter 6, exercise 7.

4. Write a function that counts all the characters in a ragged-edge string array. The string array should end in a NULL pointer, allowing your function to work on any size array.

* 5. **Multiple levels of indirection are frequently encountered when using pointers, and do have practical applications. Consider an application designed to handle entries in a telephone book. We might represent a portion of the book like this:**

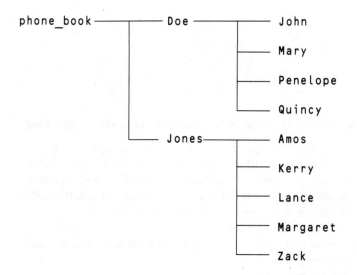

Devise a suitable representation for this structure using pointers. Write a program to initialize your representation with the data given below, then print the phone book.

Sample Data for Phone Book Problem

```
Doe, John
Doe, Mary
Doe, Penelope
Doe, Quincy

Jones, Amos
Jones, Kerry
Jones, Lance
Jones, Margaret
Jones, Zack

Mayhall, Berry
Mayhall, George
Mayhall, Jack

Newberry, Cathy
Newberry, Richard
Newberry, William
```

```
Smith, Gary
Smith, Gregory
Smith, Rosemary
Smith, Steven
Smith, Terry
Smith, Yvonne
```

* 6. Rewrite exercise 5, Chapter 6, using pointers instead of array subscripting.

7. The bubble sort algorithm, although one of the slower sorting methods, performs rather well on small (n < 100) arrays and arrays that are almost in order. As a matter of fact, you may have realized that our Shell sort algorithm degenerates into a modified version of the bubble sort (called a "shuttle sort") when the gap size becomes one. The algorithm goes as follows:

a. Start with the first two array elements.

b. Compare the elements and exchange them if the compare function indicates they should be swapped.

c. Bump up one element and repeat step b.

d. Continue until the end of the array is reached.

e. Repeat steps b. -> d. decreasing the upper limit on the array by one for each iteration of the loop. In other words, stop one element short of the previous iteration in the main loop.

f. End the sort if:

1. no exchanges occur during an iteration or,

2. the upper limit for the loop reaches one.

Implement the bubble sort algorithm using pointers on the following sample data:

```
char *zoo[] = { "TIGER",
                "BEAR",
                "AARDVARK",
                "PELICAN",
                "DOG",
                "PEACOCK",
                "ZEBRA",
                "RATTLESNAKE",
                "GIRAFFE",
                "TURKEY",
                "LION",
                "SEAL",
                "CAMEL",
                "DUCKBILL PLATYPUS",
                "LLAMA" };
```

Your program should print the unsorted list first, sort the list using a bubble sort, then print the sorted list.

*advanced exercises

10.16 Pretest

□ *Multiple Choice*

Circle ONE correct answer to each of the following:

1. Which one of the following declarations could be described as "a pointer to an array of pointers to integers"?
   a. `int *array[];`
   b. `int (*array)[];`
   c. `int *(array[]);`
   d. none of the above

2. Which pair of the following statements are equivalent?
   a. `*value[1];`
      `*(value + 1);`
   b. `**value;`
      `*value;`
   c. `*value[2];`
      `(*value++)++;`
   d. `*value;`
      `&value;`

3. The generic pointer `void *` is useful in functions that:
   a. Are being developed, but are not in production versions.
   b. Can possibly generate a null pointer.
   c. Are being designed in a general manner to return or receive more than one type of pointer.
   d. Cannot have a prototype due to a variable argument list.

4. What is wrong with the following code fragment?

```
char code[] = "This is a secret message...";

main()
{
    int checksum = 0;

    while (*code)
        {
        checksum += *code;
        ++code;
        }
```

   a. The array name "code" cannot be incremented.
   b. Characters cannot be added.
   c. The * operator cannot be used with a character array name.
   d. The loop will not terminate since a logical FALSE will never occur.

5. Consider the following code fragment:

```
char my_friends[] = { "Mike",
                      "Larry",
                      "Charles",
                      "Pamela",
                      "Phil" };

main()
{
   char *temp;

   temp = ++my_friends[2];
   printf("%s", temp);
         ...
```

What will the following statement do?

```
printf("%s", temp);
```

   a. Print "Pamela" on the display.
   b. Print "harles" on the display.
   c. Never ever execute since ++my_friends[2] will produce a compile error.
   d. Display nonsense since temp will be forced to point outside the array.

6. A null pointer can be described as:
   a. The same as void *.
   b. A "special" pointer that is typically used to flag an error or a termination indicator for arrays.
   c. A pointer that points to a binary zero in memory.
   d. Exactly the same as a logical FALSE value.

7. Given the variable definition below, which data type given below is not equivalent to type char *?

```
char a_story[] = "Once upon a time, there were three bears...
";
```

   a. "Once upon a time, there were three bears..."
   b. a_story
   c. a_story[3]
   d. &a_story[2]

8. A good application for using an array of pointers is when:
   a. The objects pointed to are different data types.
   b. One of the objects must be passed to a function.
   c. The design indicates indirect addressing of the objects pointed to.
   d. The objects are integers, which are always the same as pointers.

9. A function always receives a pointer when one of its parameters is a(n):
   a. local variable
   b. unsigned long integer
   c. floating point number
   d. array

10. When the variable `argv` is passed to `main()` it references:
    a. A string array.
    b. An array of pointers to the command line arguments (strings).
    c. Characters passed from the command line.
    d. All command line arguments beginning with the character '−'.

11

Structures

S tream I/O, which is oriented toward individual characters, forms the basis of C's interaction with files and devices. Record I/O, a common requirement of business data processing, is accomplished in C by using character I/O functions to fill a structure. A structure is the C data type that defines a record.

After studying this chapter, you will be able to do the following:

1. Define and recognize the parts of a structure.

2. Initialize a structure during and after definition.

3. Contrast structures with arrays.

4. Access structure members directly or through a pointer.

5. Show how structures can be linked together into lists.

6. Show how the #define directive or typedef command together with header files can be used to manage structures for multiple source modules.

11.1 Defining and Recognizing the Parts of a Structure

A *record* is an ordered sequence of named *members*. For instance, a very simple record might contain a name, address and telephone number all of which relate to one person. The data items name, address and telephone number are the members of the record. Each can be referenced separately or the entire record can be referenced as a single unit. Typically a record is a part of a larger body of information called a file. A *file* is composed of one or more records. Often the records are of the same type (i.e., they contain members that look alike, although the members in each record contain different data). In C a record can exist apart from a file (not so in all languages), but it does have the most utility when stored somewhere along with other record occurrences. Figure 11.1 shows how we might draw a picture of these terms.

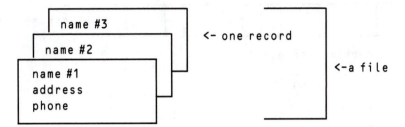

Figure 11.1   Records in a File

A *structure* is a record in C. Let's look at the simple structure definition in Figure 11.2 and discuss its components.

```
struct family {          /* structure tag appears before the braces */
    char lastname[20];   /* structure members follow inside the braces */
    int  numkids;
    long phone;
} Jones;                 /* optional structure variables after braces */
```

Figure 11.2   A Simple Structure

A structure definition begins with the keyword `struct`, followed by the structure *tag*. The tag in our example is `family`. It provides a name (which must be unique) by which the form of the structure can later be referenced. It is optional, but without it no reference can ever be made back to this particular structure without specifying the entire structure skeleton again. A set of matching braces follows. Inside the braces are coded the names of structure members. A *structure member* is a data item contained in the structure, like `lastname`, `numkids`, and `phone`.

You see that structures can contain data items of different types. For instance, the member `lastname` is an array of characters (therefore the name `lastname` is a character pointer constant), while the other two members are integer and long integer. Finally, after the closing brace is coded there appear one or more structure *variables* (or structure variable names), in this case the variable `Jones`. The structure variable names are the identifiers through which we reference the structure members; it is the structure variable names which actually reserve storage. The entire structure definition ends with a semicolon.

The structure can be illustrated with a diagram in Figure 11.3 (the size of the boxes are not meant to represent the size of different data items).

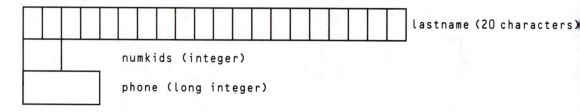

The structure `family`.

Figure 11.3   Diagram of a Structure

All the boxes together represent `Jones`, and each of the members is represented by a separate line of boxes.

The structure definition does not have to include the structure variable. The variables can be defined later, like this:

```
struct family {
    char lastname[20];
    int  numkids;
    long phone;
};
                            /* this combination works the same as above */
struct family Jones, Smith, Thompson;
```

Here the semicolon appears immediately after the closing brace that encloses the structure body. Because we are defining data, not code, the semicolon is required. This second form also illustrates that where one structure variable is defined, multiple variables can appear. The above code creates three separate instances of the structure `family`. Each instance will be referenced by a different structure variable name. It doesn't matter whether the variables appear immediately after the declaration of the structure or later. In this example the structure tag, `family`, is used when the structure variables are later defined so that it is clear which structure the variables are patterned after. It is not possible to create structure variables without designating the structure to be used for the pattern.

A structure cannot contain an instance of itself, i.e. structures cannot be defined recursively, for how would we know where to stop expanding the definition? A structure can, however, contain another type of structure, a pointer to another occurrence of itself or a pointer to another type of structure. Look at this example and the associated illustration in Figure 11.4.

```
struct added {
   char    address[20];
   int     year_moved;
};

struct family {
   char lastname[20];
   int  numkids;
   long phone;
   struct added    added_data;  /* added_data is a structure variable */
   struct family *next_family;  /* next_family is a structure pointer */
   struct added  *added_ptr;    /* added_ptr is a structure pointer too */
};
```

The revised structure family can be pictured like the diagram in Figure 11.4.

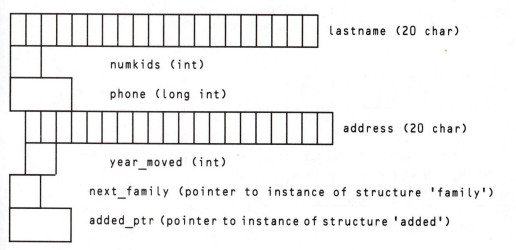

lastname (20 char)

numkids (int)

phone (long int)

address (20 char)

year_moved (int)

next_family (pointer to instance of structure 'family')

added_ptr (pointer to instance of structure 'added')

Figure 11.4   Revised Structure

In this example the member, struct added added_data, is an occurrence of the structure added. This structure occurs inside (is nested in) the structure family. We have tried to emphasize that fact by indenting the two members address and year_moved in the diagram. It is necessary that added be defined already (since we can't define a structure while inside another structure), but the other structure members like address and year_moved need have no previous definition. In fact, if there were already another data element with either of those names there would not be any conflict. The names of structure members must only be unique within the same structure. This is in contrast to early C compilers where a structure member name could only be used once throughout all structures.

The next to the last line is a pointer to another family structure. This means that there exists (or will exist) another area in the computer where the format of the data matches the family structure. That it points to another family structure is specified by the word family which appears between the word struct and the *. This pointer does not point to anything yet, but must be initialized with the address of a structure variable before it can be used. It is this type of member which allows structures to reference other structures of the same type (i.e., another family structure). While it is not possible to embed another structure of type family inside the family structure itself (if we did, where would it all end?) a pointer to an instance of the family structure can be included. That is the purpose served by the data item next_family.

The last line is a pointer to another added structure. Its status is identical to the family pointer on the previous line, and serves to illustrate that indeed structures can contain all varieties of references to other structures, including structures of the same and different types.

This new structure can be illustrated with the diagram in Figure 11.5 (again, the sizes of the boxes do not indicate anything in particular).

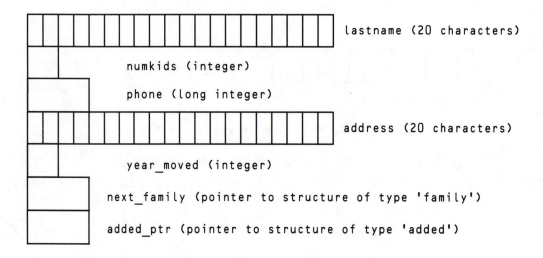

Figure 11.5   Expanded Structure

Quick Note 11.1   Structure Definitions

Structure tags do not reserve storage, but merely define the skeleton of the structure. Structure variables actually reserve the storage, and it is through them that we access the structure members. Structure member names must only be unique within the same structure. A structure may not contain another instance of itself, but may contain a pointer to another instance of itself.

11.2 Structures vs. Arrays

C language students are sometimes confused about the basic properties of structures and arrays. While the two may appear to be similar and possibly even interchangeable, they actually have very little in common. About the only property that applies to both is that the two are members of a group of data items called *aggregates*. This term accurately describes the two data types: both structures and arrays are a collection of other items which are associated with one another (unions also belong to this group). Table 11.1 compares some points about structures and arrays:

Basic Property	Structure	Array
1. The individual data items are called	members	elements
2. All items must be the same data type	no	yes
3. All items must be contiguous in memory	no	yes
4. As a function argument it is passed by	value	reference
5. In a function return it is passed back by	reference	reference
6. Items are referenced through which operator	dot	subscript

Table 11.1   Structures and Arrays Compared

We are going to illustrate most of these items in this chapter by showing various code fragments. The one item that is not as easily demonstrated is number 3: that array elements occupy contiguous memory locations, while structure members may or may not. The compiler is free to insert whatever filler is necessary between structure members. Filler may be needed between structure members since certain types of data used in the structure may have boundary alignment requirements which are dictated by the hardware. For instance, these two members appear right next to each other in the structure `family` above:

```
char    address[20];
int     year_moved;
```

If the machine on which we are writing the program requires that integers be aligned on a certain boundary, and if the integer `year_moved` does not align on that boundary automatically, then enough filler will be supplied by the compiler between the structure members `address` and `year_moved` to place `year_moved` on the necessary boundary.

Be careful not to make any assumptions about how much and where any filler space may be stored. This is especially true if structures are being read from or written to an external file. The same program that wrote the structures can certainly read them, but if another program tries to read the data, or if the program that wrote the structures is compiled again with another compiler or a newer version, there could be an incompatibility. A situation occurred once with an upgrade to the C compiler marketed by a well-known vendor. The newer compiler version inserted filler into structures differently from the older compiler version. When programs were recompiled and then used to access data structures that had been stored on disk files by programs compiled with previous compiler versions, problems quickly surfaced (even though the programmer had not changed the structure itself). Some compilers provide a switch that allows structures to be "packed," meaning that no filler space is inserted between members. This can slow down the resulting executable program when it runs, but it does avoid situations like the one just mentioned.

Therefore, do not count the size of the data items inside a structure, even if the structure only contains character data items. Use the `sizeof` operator to determine the size of the structure, either of the structure tag or a structure variable. This will be illustrated in the program `defstruc.c` below.

Antibugging Note 11.1   Be careful of filler space in structures

> Don't try to estimate the physical size of a structure, but rather use the `sizeof` operator. It is difficult to know whether filler space has been inserted between the members of the structure.

11.3 Initializing a Structure

A structure, like any other data item, must be initialized before it can be used. It can receive its initial value when it is created, or a value can be assigned to each member of the structure when the program executes. Naturally the members must be assigned a value before they can be legitimately referenced.

11.3.1 *Initializing a Structure When Defining It*

Using our two structures from above, we can provide some initialization data when they are defined, as shown in Figure 11.6.

```
/*
** defstruc.c - Sample Program to Define a Structure
*/

#include <stdio.h>

void main(void);

struct added {              /* no initialization data goes on this tag */
    char    address[20];
    int     year_moved;
} added_var;                /* we do have a variable found here */

struct family {             /* no initialization data on this tag either */
    char lastname[20];
    int  numkids;
    long phone;
    struct added    added_data;
    struct family *next_family;
    struct added  *added_ptr;
};

struct family family_var2, family_var = {"Jones", /* data found here */
                                         2,
                                         5551234,
                                         {"Apt. 3G", 1960},
                                         &family_var2,
                                         &added_var
                                        };

void main()
{
    printf("The sizeof struct family is %d\n", sizeof(struct family));
    printf("The sizeof family_var is also %d\n", sizeof(family_var));
    printf("The family_var structure variable contains:\n"
           "%s\n%d\n%ld\n%s\n%d\n", family_var.lastname,
                               family_var.numkids,
                               family_var.phone,
                               family_var.added_data.address,
                               family_var.added_data.year_moved);
}
```

Figure 11.6   Sample Program to Define a Structure—defstruc.c

This program will print out the following:

```
The sizeof struct family is 52
The sizeof family_var is also 52
The family_var structure variable contains:
Jones
2
5551234
Apt. 3G
1960
```

The program also illustrates some very important concepts about initializing structures. First, it is structure variables that are initialized, not structure tags. Remember that structure tags do not reserve any storage for the structure. Defining the structure tag family merely creates a skeleton for use in subsequent structure variable definitions, i.e., the definition of family_var. In our example the variable family_var2 receives no initializing data, while the variable family_var does. Second, initializing data can be coded any place where a structure variable is being defined, including when the variable appears after the definition of the structure body. The variables do not have to be defined in separate statements in order to use initializing data.

Third, the initialization data must appear inside matching braces, with the specific data value for each member appearing in order inside the braces. In our example the data items Jones, 2, etc. match the structure members lastname, numkids, and so on. The additional set of braces which contain Apt. 3G and 1960 match the structure variable added_data (of type added) which is contained inside the structure family_var (of type family). The address of operator, &, can be used to take the address of another structure variable in order to initialize a pointer to the same type of variable. In our example the address of family_var2 is stored in the member next_family of the structure variable family_var.

Do not use the address of operator with a structure tag. Remember, structure tags don't occupy memory, and consequently don't have an address. Structure tags only specify form.

Further, only constant values can be used to initialize a structure when the initialization occurs during the structure definition. Variables do not have value before the program executes (which is when the definition occurs), so there is no specific value to use for the initialization.

Finally, since structures are an aggregate data type (as are arrays) it used to be that they could be initialized during definition only if the definition of the structure was global and/or static. As we pointed out when discussing arrays this generated a double standard which the ANSI C standard (thankfully) eliminated. The ability to provide initialization data when defining aggregates of the automatic storage class is a feature that vendors will be adding to compilers as the compilers are updated to conform to the new standard.

11.3.2 *Initialization after Definition with the Dot Operator*

If a structure is not initialized when it is defined, explicit assignments can be used later to initialize the structure members. For instance, the first two members of the structure family_var could be initialized this way:

```
strcpy(family_var.lastname, "Jones");
family_var.numkids = 2;
```

The member name lastname is the name of a character array, and as we've already seen the assignment statement cannot be used to directly populate a character array. A function like strcpy() is needed to physically move the string into the array lastname. Of course, each element in the character array can be assigned individually, like this:

```
family_var.lastname[0] = 'J';
family_var.lastname[1] = 'o';
family_var.lastname[2] = 'n';
family_var.lastname[3] = 'e';
family_var.lastname[4] = 's';
family_var.lastname[5] = '\0';
```

Any structure member, including a structure within a structure, can be initialized in a similar manner. We would initialize a nested structure like this:

```
family_var.added_data.attr = 'b';
family_var.added_data.ftime = 4;
```

This new symbol which we have been using, the ., is the *dot operator*, also called the *structure member* or *member selection operator*. The name of a structure variable is coded on the left side of the dot, while a structure member is written on the right. The resulting expression can be used on either side of an assignment, i.e., it forms a valid lvalue. Do not use the structure tag name with the dot operator. Use only structure variable names, along with member names. Nor also does it matter how complicated the expression is that appears to the left of the dot. All that matters is that the expression denotes an occurrence of a structure.

The dot operator is an operator just like +, *, &&, and all others. As such it has precedence and must be considered along with all other operators in how parentheses are implicitly applied by the compiler as the expression is scanned. By design the dot operator has a very high precedence, meaning that if this is written:

```
x = family_var.numkids + 1;
```

or this:

```
family_var.numkids = x + 1;
```

then it is certain that this will not be created:

```
x = (family_var.(numkids + 1));
```

or this:

```
family_var.(numkids = (x + 1));
```

In other words, the dot operator "binds" more tightly to the surrounding operands than do most other operators. Refer back to the precedence table earlier in the book to review where these operators fit in relation to all other operators.

In executable code the entire structure cannot be assigned by using the matching braces technique such as we used when defining the structure. This is not valid:

```
family_var = {"Jones",
              2,
              5551234,
              {"Apt. 3G", 1960},
              &family_var2,
              &added_var
             };
```

Trying to do this will generate a syntax error because the opening brace cannot be used to surround data in the code portion of the program. Matching braces can only be used as a compound statement and occur wherever a single statement otherwise would appear. The use of matching braces to surround items of data must occur in a data-defining portion of the program. This does not mean that only the area outside of all functions is in a data-defining portion of the program. An automatic structure can be initialized immediately after the opening brace of a function, like this:

```
sub_func()
{
    static struct added added_var = {"123 Nine St.", 1947};
    printf("%s %d", added_var.address, added_var.year_moved);
}
```

Finally, the assignment operator can be used to copy an entire structure from one structure variable to another, providing the structure variables refer to structures of the same type. In our example above it would be correct to write this:

```
family_var2 = family_var;
```

because both family_var2 and family_var are structures of type family. It should be clear from this that structure variable names can appear on the left of the assignment statement because a structure variable name does not equate to a pointer constant, as in the case of an array. The structure variable name actually refers to the storage occupied by the structure.

11.4 Referencing Structure Members

We've given numerous examples of ways that structure members can be referenced directly. Let's summarize them before we demonstrate how structures can be accessed indirectly, or through pointers.

Quick Note 11.2   Structure Referencing

The dot, or structure member, operator is used to select a specific member from a structure. A structure variable, not a structure tag, is used along with the dot operator to reference the member. If structures are nested, a concatenated sequence of a structure variable name, dot, structure variable name, dot, etc. terminated by a structure member name will fully qualify a reference to a member in the innermost structure.

11.4.1   *Referencing Structures Through a Pointer*

A pointer can be used to access a structure, allowing programs to have dynamic, flexible methods of referencing structures. Consider these data definitions:

```
struct family {
    char lastname[20];
    int  numkids;
    long phone;
};

struct family family_one, family_two, family_three;        /* variables */
struct family *family_ptr_a, *family_ptr_b, *family_ptr_c; /* pointers */
```

This code creates the structure skeleton; the three structure variables, `family_one`, `family_two`, and `family_three`; and the three structure pointers, `family_ptr_a`, `family_ptr_b`, and `family_ptr_c`. We can initialize the pointers this way:

```
family_ptr_a = &family_one;
family_ptr_b = &family_two;
family_ptr_c = &family_three;
```

Then we can use the pointers to reference the structure variables like this:

```
family_ptr_a -> numkids = 1;
```

or like this:

```
x = family_ptr_a -> numkids;
```

This new operator, the -> or *structure pointer*, is formed by using both the hyphen and greater than symbols immediately adjacent to each other. The resulting expression, `family_ptr_a -> numkids`, is read "obtain the member numkids in the structure pointed to by `family_ptr_a`." A structure pointer can be set to point to any structure of the pointer's type. Like any other type of pointer a structure pointer can be changed while the program executes. Any structure member can be referenced through the structure pointer, including members which themselves are pointers to other structures, like this:

```
family_ptr_a -> next_family = family_ptr_b;
```

Here we've updated the member `next_family` in the structure pointed to by `family_ptr_a` and assigned to it the contents of what is in the field `family_ptr_b`. After this is done, `family_ptr_a` will point to the same structure as `family_ptr_b`. From these examples it should be evident that the structure pointer operator can be used on either side of an assignment. Figure 11.7 illustrates this situation.

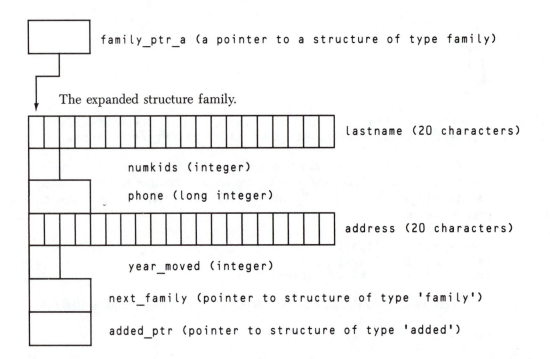

family_ptr_a (a pointer to a structure of type family)

The expanded structure family.

lastname (20 characters)

numkids (integer)

phone (long integer)

address (20 characters)

year_moved (integer)

next_family (pointer to structure of type 'family')

added_ptr (pointer to structure of type 'added')

Figure 11.7   Using the Structure Pointer Operator

We'll finish this explanation of structure pointers by mentioning that these two expressions are identical:

```
family_ptr_a -> next_family;
```

and

```
(*family_ptr_a).next_family;
```

The first is the normal structure pointer, while the second is the structure pointer used in combination with the . or member selection operator. The second example is read by evaluating the expression inside the parentheses, (*family_ptr_a). This expression is read "the contents of that to which family_ptr_a points." Since family_ptr_a points to a structure, this form of the expression is no different than using the structure variable name itself, except that with a structure pointer the name of the structure variable does not need to be known. In fact, we'll see shortly that when using dynamic memory allocation the structure variable name does not exist at all. The parentheses are necessary in our second expression because of the high precedence of the . operator. Without the parentheses the expression would be evaluated this way:

```
*(family_ptr_a.next_family);
```

which is not at all what we intended. This expression gives us a syntax error because we have tried to use a structure pointer, family_ptr_a, as a structure variable name. Were the structure pointer family_ptr_a replaced by a valid structure variable name, the resulting expression would describe the contents pointed to by the next_family pointer in the specified structure. This also indicates that

```
family_ptr_a.next_family
```

is not a correct expression, for the same reason. If the member selection operator, ., is to be used, the name to the left of any instance of . must be a structure variable name, not a structure pointer.

11.4.2   *Valid Operations on Structures*

Only certain operations can occur in conjunction with structures. These operations are:

1. Member selection using the . or -> operators.

2. Assignment of a structure to another structure of like type.

3. Passing the structure by value as a function argument.

4. Taking the address of a structure, either to initialize a pointer or to provide a return value from a function.

The member selection features were discussed above. Other structure operations will be illustrated with the program in Figure 11.8.

```c
/*
** funstruc.c - Structures as Arguments and Return Values
*/

#include <stdio.h>

#define EST struct example_struct_tag

EST {                       /* a structure that is passed and returned */
      int   intr;                   /* these members could be anything */
      float temp;
   } es_var = {1, 27.5};        /* initialize the members */

void main (void);       /* these are the function prototypes */
EST *sub_func(EST);     /* sub_func is a function with one */
                        /*    argument, a structure of type */
                        /*    example_struct_tag, and its return type is */
                        /*    a pointer to a structure of type */
                        /*    example_struct_tag */
void main()
{
   printf("a: %d %f\n", es_var.intr, es_var.temp);          /* before image */
   es_var = *(sub_func(es_var));           /* pass struct, return address */
   printf("b: %d %f\n", es_var.intr, es_var.temp);  /* print after image */
}

                        /* sub_func is the function name, EST * is */
                        /*    the return type, a pointer to a structure */
                        /*    of type example_struct_tag */
                        /* structure passed by value, returned by reference */
EST *sub_func(es_var1)
EST es_var1;        /* classic style parameter definitions */
{
   static EST es_auto_var;           /* static struct remains after exit */
   es_auto_var = es_var1;         /* can assign structures of like type */
                                            /* verify what was sent */
   printf("c: %d %f\n", es_var1.intr, es_var1.temp);
                                            /* verify what changed */
   printf("d: %d %f\n", es_auto_var.intr, es_auto_var.temp);
   es_auto_var.intr = 2;                         /* change the members */
   es_auto_var.temp = 11.1;
   return (&es_auto_var);         /* return the static structure address */
}
```

Figure 11.8 Structures as Arguments and Return Values—funstruc.c

This program prints out while executing:

```
a: 1 27.500000
c: 1 27.500000
d: 1 27.500000
b: 2 11.099999
```

The first line of the output comes from the `printf()` function, which was done before the function call. The second and third lines were done in the called function to insure that the entire structure was both passed and assigned correctly. `printf()` shows that the changes made in the called function can be seen from `main()` when the address of the changed structure is returned. The value `11.099999` illustrates that floating point arithmetic is not guaranteed to be as accurate as decimal arithmetic, since it was formed by assigning the value `11.1` to a float. Some compilers, however, may indeed return the value `11.100000`, because of differences in whether the floating point arithmetic is emulated or processed by a math coprocessor chip or circuitry.

A few of the lines from this program deserve further explanation. Consider this line:

```
es_var = *(sub_func(es_var));
```

What this line does is "invoke the function `sub_func()` using as an argument a copy of the entire structure `es_var` (a structure variable), then take the contents of that to which the return value points and assign it back into `es_var`." The function `sub_func()` receives as an argument a copy (passed by value) of a structure of type `example_struct_tag`, and returns a pointer to a structure of the same type. A copy of the entire structure is sent to the function, but only a pointer to the same type structure is returned.

The `static` keyword is used for the automatic variable `es_auto_var` defined inside the function `sub_func()`. This keyword is needed since automatic variables that are created inside a function but that are not `static` cease to exist after the control flow leaves a function. If `es_auto_var` no longer existed, a pointer to where it used to be would have absolutely no value. Although the `static` keyword also means that `es_auto_var` will not be initialized each time `sub_func()` is invoked, nevertheless it is necessary to use `static` in this case since we wanted to illustrate how to pass the address of a structure back as a return value.

Without `static`, `es_auto_var` officially disappears when the function `sub_func` terminates. If `static` is not used, the memory that `es_auto_var` occupied is released by the function `sub_func` when it returns to the portion of the program that invoked it. However, just because the memory is released does not mean that it will immediately be used again by either the program or the operating system. Therefore, it is entirely possible that the memory occupied by `es_auto_var` will still exist (unaltered) if `es_auto_var` is later referenced through the returned pointer, even if the `static` keyword was not used. This can be a difficult error to locate, like many errors involving pointers. Just because a pointer exists, and even though it once contained a valid address, does not mean that it still contains a valid address.

When the return value of the function (the address of `es_auto_var`) has the `*` or contents of operator applied to it, the result is the entire contents of the structure `es_auto_var`. This can be assigned into `es_var` because structure contents can be assigned from one structure into another if the structures are of like type. Since the return value of function `sub_func()` was defined to be a structure pointer, no type cast of the return value is needed.

Quick Note 11.3   Structures as Function Arguments

A common error of early C programmers was to use a copy of a structure as a function argument rather than using the address of the structure, and vice versa. While prototypes will help catch this error, be sure that you understand the difference between passing a structure by value and by reference.

11.5 Dynamic Structures

A dynamic structure is one whose size and location is not known until the program actually executes. If we know in advance that we only need five occurrences of a structure that is 20 bytes large, then we can explicitly create those five items when we write the program. For instance, we might have five separate structure variables, or the structure could be defined as an array element within an array with five elements. For either of these situations we would know when we write the program how much storage we need.

In many situations, though, we don't know the number of structures we will need, either because it is impossible to know in advance, or because by design we don't want to limit the capabilities of the program. A data-base management system, for example, allows a dynamic structure of significant size to be built. While there are limits placed on how large the entire structure can become, those limits are usually set quite high.

11.5.1 *Dynamic Memory Allocation*

In order to create a structure dynamically we must have a way to obtain more data storage "on the fly." The `malloc()` function will obtain a contiguous block of storage of requested size and return to the calling program the address of where the block is located. If the requested storage is not available, a null pointer is returned.

The format of `malloc()` is:

```
#include <stdlib.h>

char *cptr;
cptr = (char *) malloc(200);
```

The argument passed to `malloc()` is an integer which is the number of bytes of storage that is needed. If the storage is available, `malloc()` will return a `void *` which can be cast into whatever type pointer is desired. The concept of *void pointers* was introduced in the ANSI C standard and means a pointer of unknown type, or generic pointer. A void pointer cannot itself be used to reference anything (it doesn't point to any specific type of data), but it can contain a pointer of any other type. Therefore, any pointer can be converted into a void pointer and back without any loss of information.

In this example we need 200 characters, so we can explicitly use the number 200 since the size of a character is one byte. If we need storage space for 200 integers then we could say this:

```
int *iptr;
iptr = (int *) malloc(200 * sizeof(int));
```

or this:

```
int *iptr;
int inumber = 200;
iptr = (int *) malloc(inumber * sizeof(int));
```

Now `malloc()` will be told to obtain enough storage for "200 times the current size of an integer" (remember that integers are different sizes on different machines). We then cast the pointer `malloc()` returns into an integer pointer rather than a character pointer.

Antibugging Note 11.2   Don't assume dynamically allocated memory size

Don't assume the size of data items when dynamically allocating memory. Use the `sizeof` operator.

Each block of storage requested is entirely separate and distinct from all other blocks of storage. Absolutely no assumption can be made about where the blocks are located. Blocks are typically "tagged" with some sort of information that allows the operating system to manage the location and size of the block.

When the block is no longer needed it can be returned to the operating system this way:

```
free((void *) iptr);
```

This tells the operating system to return the block to which we are pointing to the pool of available storage. The operating system will use the pointer to find the block. Then the system will determine how to "rechain" this block back into the chain of other blocks available for allocation. The `(void *)` cast allows us to exactly match the argument type that `free()` is expecting.

Antibugging Note 11.3   Don't use an invalid value with `free()`

Don't use an invalid pointer with the `free()` function. Carefully check the program to make sure that the value passed to `free()` was obtained with `malloc()` or another similar function.

11.5.2   *Basic Linked List Terminology*

A *linked list* is the most fundamental of all dynamic data structures. The concept of a linked list begins by deciding to obtain storage "on the fly" as needed. As each piece of storage is obtained it is "linked" into a list so that all the pieces of storage can be traversed by navigating through the list. While it is possible to create a linked list by using explicitly defined variables or other storage items that are named in a program, the real utility of this approach is that:

1. Only exactly as much storage as needed is obtained.

2. The storage is not obtained until the moment when it is needed.

Figure 11.9 shows a diagram of a small but typical linked list.

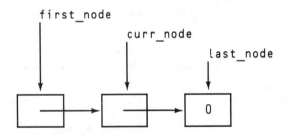

Figure 11.9   A Typical Linked List

Each box in the figure might be called a *node*; it represents one occurrence of a structure. This occurrence was created by a call to `malloc()`, and it resides somewhere in the memory from which `malloc()` obtains storage. The data item `first_node` is a pointer to the first node of the list, `curr_node` points to the node in the list that is currently being processed, and `last_node` points to the last node in the list. The definition of the 'node currently being processed is completely arbitrary and can change during the course of the program. The same is true of the concepts first and last in the list. Complete control can be exercised over how the list is organized.

Each node points to the next node in the list, and the pointer in the last node is null, i.e., contains a zero. This format creates a *single linked list* since the pointers only go in one direction, from the beginning to the end of the list. A *double linked list* is one with an additional pointer that points in the other direction, i.e., it allows the list to be walked from the end to the beginning. Adding this additional pointer can greatly simplify some applications.

The use of the `first_node`, `curr_node`, and `last_node` pointers is not required. For instance, it can be determined that the last node in the list is being processed when the pointer in that node is null or zero. By the same token a pointer to the `current node` may not be required. Not having at least one of these pointers makes using the list very difficult, though, so we recommend that the `first_node` pointer be retained at the very least.

11.5.3 *Single and Double Linked Lists*

As an example of how to create, walk, and delete nodes in a single linked list, let's look at the program in Figure 11.10.

```
/*
** linklist.c - A Linked List Example
**
** This program illustrates some simple concepts about dynamic memory
** allocation and how to create linked lists.  This code was written for
** clarity, not efficiency.  It is not bulletproof, but is to be used for
** example purposes only.  It manages a single linked list.
*/

#include <stdio.h>
#include <stdlib.h>            /* has the prototypes of the memory routines */

struct node
        {
            int  node_number;
            struct node *next_node;
        };              /* no variables needed, dynamic allocation used */

typedef struct node NODE;        /* allowed before structure is defined */

void main(void);                /* these are the prototypes for our functions */
NODE *create_node(void);
void delete_node(NODE *);
void insert_node(NODE *, NODE *);
void print_list(void);
void remove_node(NODE *);
```

(program continued on next page...)

```
NODE *first_node;                                       /* points to head of list */
NODE *last_node;                                         /* points to end of list */
NODE *curr_node;                                  /* points to active node in list */

void main(void)
{
                                                      /* create the first node */
    first_node = curr_node = last_node = create_node();
    curr_node -> node_number = 1;
    printf("\nAfter adding one node:\n");
    print_list();
                                      /* insert a second node after the first */
    insert_node(curr_node, create_node());      /* insert() calls create() */
    curr_node = curr_node -> next_node;            /* reset the current ptr */
    curr_node -> node_number = 2;
    printf("\nAfter adding a second node after the first:\n");
    print_list();
                                     /* insert a node at the head of the list */
    insert_node((NODE *)(0), create_node());     /* note the null pointer */
    first_node -> node_number = 3;
    curr_node = first_node;
    printf("\nAfter adding a third node at the head of the list:\n");
    print_list();
          /* remove the nodes in reverse order from how they were added */
    remove_node(curr_node);
    printf("\nAfter removing the most recently added node:\n");
    print_list();
    delete_node(curr_node);

    curr_node = last_node;        /* save pointer before removing last node */
    remove_node(last_node);
    printf("\nAfter removing the node which is last in the list:\n");
    print_list();
    delete_node(curr_node);
}

/*
** create_node()   Obtains dynamic memory for a node
*/
NODE *create_node(void)
{
    NODE *temp_ptr;
    temp_ptr = (NODE *) malloc (sizeof(NODE));            /* get the memory */
    temp_ptr -> next_node = '\0';                /* initialize the members */
    temp_ptr -> node_number = 0;
    return(temp_ptr);
}
```

```c
/*
** delete_node()  Frees and returns to the system a node's memory
*/
void delete_node(deleted_node_ptr)  /* this could be a macro */
NODE *deleted_node_ptr;
{
    free ((void *)deleted_node_ptr);                    /* return the memory */
}

/*
** insert_node()  Places a node into the list
**                Insert a node that has already been created
*/
void insert_node(after_node_ptr, inserted_node_ptr)
NODE *after_node_ptr, *inserted_node_ptr;
{
    if(after_node_ptr != NULL)          /* if it was NULL then it means */
    {                                   /* we're at the front of the list */
        inserted_node_ptr -> next_node = after_node_ptr -> next_node;
        after_node_ptr -> next_node = inserted_node_ptr;
    }
    else {                  /* here the request is for the front of list */
        inserted_node_ptr -> next_node = first_node;
        first_node = inserted_node_ptr;
    }
                                /* here we know we inserted the last node */
    if(inserted_node_ptr -> next_node == NULL) {
    last_node = inserted_node_ptr;
    }
}

/*
** remove_node()  Takes a node out of the list
*/
void remove_node(removed_node_ptr)
NODE *removed_node_ptr;
{
    NODE *temp_node_ptr;

    if(first_node == removed_node_ptr) {
        first_node = removed_node_ptr -> next_node;
        return;
    }
```

(program continued on next page...)

```
    /* at this point the node to be removed is not at the head of the list,
       which means that we must locate the previous node in the list so
       that we can correctly relink the nodes
    */

    temp_node_ptr = first_node;
    while(temp_node_ptr -> next_node != removed_node_ptr) {
        temp_node_ptr = temp_node_ptr -> next_node;
    }

    temp_node_ptr -> next_node = removed_node_ptr -> next_node;
}

/*
** print_list()  Print the linked list
*/
void print_list(void)
{
    int index;
    NODE *temp_ptr;

    for(index = 1, temp_ptr = first_node;        /* loop through the list */
        temp_ptr != NULL;
        index++, temp_ptr = temp_ptr -> next_node
       ) {
        printf("  Node %d is number %d\n", index, temp_ptr -> node_number);
    }
}
```

Figure 11.10   A Linked List Example—linklist.c

This link list example program will produce this output:

```
After adding one node:
  Node 1 is number 1

After adding a second node after the first:
  Node 1 is number 1
  Node 2 is number 2

After adding a third node at the head of the list:
  Node 1 is number 3
  Node 2 is number 1
  Node 3 is number 2

After removing the most recently added node:
  Node 1 is number 1
  Node 2 is number 2
```

```
After removing the node which is last in the list:
  Node 1 is number 1
```

Four basic functions are utilized in this example:

1. create_node()   Dynamically obtains storage for a new node, initializes the members, and then returns to the caller with the new node's address as the return value.

2. delete_node()   Frees the storage pointed to by the argument passed to the function. This returns the space occupied by the node to the heap.

3. insert_node()   Places a node into the list. One of the function arguments is a pointer to an existing node in the list, and the new inserted node is placed after this existing node.

4. remove_node()   Takes a node out of the list but does not free the storage occupied by the node.

A node is added to the list by calling create_node() and obtaining some storage for the node to occupy. Then, for all nodes except the first, insert_node() is called to link the two nodes together. When create_node() returns a NULL pointer it means that there is no more storage available for allocation. Typically the program would perform a test after calling create_node() to insure that the return value is not NULL, and would then perform some sort of error processing if NULL was returned. Our program example above has none of this error-trapping code. Also, many implementations of these functions would combine obtaining the storage with inserting the node in the list. There is only marginal use for a node that is not in a list.

The program has numerous examples of for loops that "run the list" from start to finish. Typically this is the technique used to process the list and change or access the information in each node. Our loops always began at the start of the list and ran until the end. The use of one or more curr_node pointers allows the list to be processed starting at any needed point and continuing until any other point is reached.

The function remove_node() is called to take a node out of the list; then delete_node() is used to return the storage occupied by the node to the operating system. As with the create/insert combination, the remove and delete functions are often combined because usually when a node is removed from the list it also needs to be deleted. Exceptions to this would be a more sophisticated implementation of linked lists, such as a full-scale database application.

A further expansion of the single list concept is a double linked list. The only enhancement needed to make a single linked list into a double one is to add another structure pointer to each node. This new pointer would point to the previous node rather than the next. Appropriate changes must be made to each function to initialize an additional structure member when the structure storage is obtained, to "hook" the node to the previous node too, and to "unhook" the node from both directions when the node is removed from the list. We'll leave as exercises the changes needed for the above functions in order to process a double linked list. Other changes could be added to implement a sorted list, separate lists that point to each other in various ways, and perform even more elaborate operations.

11.5.4   *Stacks and Queues*

Stacks and queues are special types of linked lists. A *stack* is a *LIFO* list (Last In-First Out), while a *queue* is a *FIFO* list (First In-First Out). Stacks are used whenever it is necessary to reverse the order of recent operations, or when it is important to retrace the steps that were just taken. A stack has items placed onto and removed from the list from the top. No access necessarily takes place against any other list member. For this reason only one pointer, the one to the head of the list, is required. In fact, if any other pointer is used to access the stack, there is a risk of corrupting the stack contents.

A queue is like a pipeline. It is used when things must be kept in order and not lost if they can't be handled or addressed at the time they are discovered. For example, hardware interrupts associated with communications processing must be queued up and handled later in the order in which they were received if they cannot be processed immediately. A queue needs at minimum two pointers, one to each end of the list. Typically queues are not as sensitive about having their contents altered as are stacks.

We will leave it as an exercise to alter the basic single linked list example above to create a stack or queue.

11.6 Header File Techniques, `typedef` vs. `#define`

It is a common technique to place structure definitions in header files so that the structure can be used in multiple source files. A *header file* typically has a filename extension of `.h`. Files like `stdio.h` which come with the compiler are header files, and it's possible to create personalized files with the `.h` extension and to place into them customized information. The definition of a structure is a common thing to place into a header file so that the structure definition exists in only one place. This definition is usually accompanied by a `typedef` command or `#define` directive so that one word can be used to reference the structure.

The `typedef` keyword allows new data types to be specified which are combinations of one or more existing types. It does not create fundamental data types, but rather provides a shorthand method of using types that already exist. Some people refer to these as *synonyms*. For instance, this typedef:

```
typedef struct family FAMILY;
```

creates a new type called FAMILY which can be substituted for the combination struct family. The typedef keyword is actually part of the language definition, so a semicolon is needed. The use of capitals is not required, but is often used to distinguish macros and typedef definitions from language keywords.

There is only a slight difference between using a typedef and a #define preprocessor directive. The #define would be written like this:

```
#define FAMILY struct family
```

Because the #define is not an actual C language keyword it does not form a statement. Therefore, a semicolon is not needed. If we happen to include a semicolon after struct family, the semicolon will appear everywhere that FAMILY is replaced. That would probably result in a syntax error at some point.

In older compilers one of the advantages of using #define rather than typedef was that a #define directive that used a structure tag name could be written before the structure was defined. Therefore, the name defined on the #define directive could be used inside the structure when creating a pointer to another instance of the same structure (i.e., a linked list). The typedef could not be used in the same way. To define a structure name using the #define we would write:

```
#define FAMILY struct family
FAMILY {
        char lastname[20];
        int  numkids;
        long phone;
        struct added   added_data;
        struct family *next_family;
        struct added  *added_ptr;
};
```

Some compilers allow typedef to be used in the same way as the #define directive, i.e., a typedef can be written before the structure is defined and then the word created with the typedef used inside the structure. When using a compiler that supports typedef in this manner the above example can be changed by replacing this line:

```
#define FAMILY struct family
```

with:

```
typedef struct family FAMILY;
```

It is a common technique to nest header files by placing #include directives in included files. This nesting can sometimes lead to duplicate definitions of structures or other data items because a header file might be included twice in a single source file. Including the file twice is no problem, but if the included file defines something then the second definition can result in a duplicate definition error. Some compilers are more forgiving about this than others, and can even ignore the error if the two definitions are exactly the same, even to the spacing used around the words and characters.

This problem can be solved by using preprocessor directives to shield the structure definition, like this:

```
#if !defined FAMILY_HEADER
#define FAMILY_HEADER
    struct family {
        char lastname[20];
        int numkids;
        long phone;
        struct added added_data;
        struct family *next_family;
        struct added *added_ptr;
    };
    typedef struct family FAMILY;
#endif
```

The `#if !defined` directive asks whether the identifier that follows has already been defined. If not, then the body of the `#if !defined` is performed. If the identifier has already been defined, then all source code between the `#if !defined` and the `#endif` is skipped. If the identifier has not been defined, then the body of code is passed to the compiler rather than skipped. Inside this code body we define the identifier `FAMILY_HEADER`, the same name being tested for by `#if !defined`. This means that the code body will be seen by the compiler only once during the compilation of any given source file, regardless of how the `#include` nesting is arranged. This technique can be used with any code definition in an included file.

Quick Note 11.4   Header File Techniques

If a structure is going to be used in more than one source file, put the structure definition into a header file. If a programming project utilizes multiple header files, shield definitions by using the `#if !defined`, `#define`, and `#endif` techniques.

11.7 Unions

A *union* is a structure in which each member has a *zero offset*, i.e. each member occupies space beginning at the start of the structure. These union members overlap, and only one of the members can occupy the union at any one time. There is nothing in C to keep track of which type of data is currently in the union. Each program must do that for itself. It is possible to place one type of data into the union and then reference the union as if it contained another type of data. The amount of storage reserved for the union is only as much as is needed for the largest member in the union. The following union is 12 characters large:

```
union u {
    int x;
    float y;
    double z;
    char cary[12];
};
```

This union:

```
union u {
    int x;
    float y;
    double z;
};
```

is the size of the `double` data type (probably eight bytes).

Unions are indispensable when we need to redefine data, i.e., when a data item is defined one way, but must be viewed as containing another type of data. If a type conversion is sufficient, a type cast can be performed. However, sometimes the bits themselves in the data item must be preserved and the bit pattern itself analyzed. For that reason unions are often associated with bit fields.

11.8   Bit Fields

A *bit field* is a data item whose size is specified by a number of bits rather than a particular data type. It is an expected feature of a language whose original purpose was to replace assembly language when writing the operating system for the PDP-11.

Bit fields can appear inside either structures or unions. They are defined like this:

```
union u {
    int x;
    float y;
    double z;
    char cary[12];
    int mybits : 5;             /* this is a signed bit field */
    unsigned mybits2 : 6;       /* this is an unsigned bit field */
};
```

The data item `mybits` consists of five bits stored inside an integer. Because an integer is considered to be signed the field `mybits` is also signed. The bit field acts as if it were a small integer. Any operation that can be performed on an integer can also be carried out on this bit field. The field `mybits2`, on the other hand, consists of six bits which will be treated as if they were unsigned.

Bit fields cannot "span" the unit of storage in which they are kept, although the ANSI C standard says that a compiler can allocate any type of storage large enough to hold the bit field. For instance, on computers that use two bytes to store an integer, a bit field can be from 1 to 16 bits. If successive bit fields are defined one after another, they will be stored within the same integer until the bits in the integer are exhausted; then the next integer will be used. In the above example only one word is needed because only 11 bits are defined.

Names are not required for bit fields, but it is not legal to do any of the following:

1. Take the address of a bit field.

2. Create a pointer to a bit field.

3. Make an array of bit fields.

These inconveniences are not too great since the structures and structure variables themselves can have all these operations performed on them.

11.9 Aggregate Combinations (Arrays of Structures of . . .)

Structures and arrays can be combined in a variety of ways to create any complex data structure imaginable. The basic combinations are these:

nested structures (structure of structures)
array of arrays (nested arrays)
structure of arrays
array of structures

Every other combination is merely an extension of these.

One of the first examples from the beginning of the chapter was something like this:

```c
struct added {
   char    address[20];
   int     year_moved;
};

struct family {
   char lastname[20];              /* an array inside a structure */
   int  numkids;
   long phone;
   struct added   added_data;      /* a nested structure */
   struct family *next_family;
   struct added  *added_ptr;
};
```

The member `added_data` is a structure within a structure, or a nested structure. We have already discussed how to reference a field in the innermost structure by writing something like `family_var.added_data.attr`. Structures can be nested as deeply as a compiler will allow.

An array of arrays is merely a multidimensional array, which was discussed in the chapter on arrays.

A structure of arrays is also shown in the example immediately above. The member `family_var.lastname` is an array inside the structure `family`. That it is a character array is immaterial. It could have been an array of any data type. To reference the first element of `lastname` we would write `family_var.lastname[0]`, and `family_var.lastname[19]` is the last character of the same array.

The one combination we have not yet seen is an array of structures. We can create one this way:

```
struct family {
    char lastname[20];
    int  numkids;
    long phone;
    struct added   added_data;
    struct family *next_family;
    struct added  *added_ptr;
}family_var_array[5];
```

The variable `family_var_array` is an array of five structures of type `family`. Perhaps it would be more clear if we wrote it this way:

```
struct  family  family_var_array[5];
```

Actually, this creates both an array of structures of arrays, and also an array of nested structures. Each array element is a structure, and there are both two arrays inside each array element, and also another structure.

To reference the first element of the structure member `lastname` which occurs in the second occurrence of `family_var_array` we would write

```
family_var_array[1].lastname[0]
```

The only limit to all this is the programmer's imagination and ability to understand the aggregate combinations that have been created. It is much easier to write the definitions than it is to navigate through the physical structures.

11.10 Self-Check

These statements are True or False. The answers are given at the end.

1. A structure does not need to contain objects that are of like type.

2. A semicolon is not needed after the closing brace of a structure definition.

3. The structure tag does not reserve storage for the structure, but instead gives a name to the structure skeleton.

4. A structure can contain other structures, including an instance of itself.

5. Aggregate data types include arrays, structures, and unions.

6. Structure members are always stored contiguously in memory.

7. Structures are passed by value when they are used as function arguments.

8. Structures can be returned by value from a function.

9. The dot operator requires a structure variable name or expression on the left side of the dot.

10. The structure pointer operator is a hyphen and greater than symbol pair coded without an intervening space.

11. Only structure variables, not structure tags, can be initialized.

12. If `sptr` is a structure pointer, then `(*sptr).` is an alternate way to reference a structure member.

13. Only constant values can be used to initialize structures when they are defined.

14. The value returned from `malloc()` is automatically cast to a pointer which points to the type of data the acquired storage will contain.

15. Structures that will be used in more than one source file should be placed into a header file.

16. A call to `malloc()` will return the value NULL if there is no more storage available to allocate dynamically.

17. Structures can be nested only four levels deep, a limitation that still allows the creation of complex data structures.

18. Any data item can be assigned to a structure variable.

19. Both the `typedef` and the `#define` command can be used to simplify the creation of structure variables apart from the initial definition of the structure.

20. A union is a structure in which every member begins at the front of the structure.

Answers

1. T   2. F   3. T   4. F   5. T   6. F   7. T   8. F   9. T   10. T
11. T   12. T   13. T   14. F   15. T   16. T   17. F   18. F   19. T   20. T

11.11 Review Program—Binary Trees and Abstract Data Types

☐ *Design Specifications*

We have already encountered the term *abstract data type* (ADT), which refers to objects possessing certain high-level properties. Examples of ADTs are tree nodes, records in a data base, stream files, and records in a queue. Each element in any data structure has similar properties that are common to each. The term ADT originated from a high-level description of these properties. For example, we have already looked at tree structures in previous chapters. A representative tree might appear as follows:

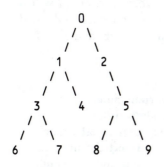

Here the nodes of our tree are labeled 0 through 9. Each node possesses certain properties:

1. A "parent" node, except for the "root," node 0.

2. An associated "value," which may consist of a simple or aggregate data type.

3. One or more "children," except for "terminal" nodes, which have no children.

It should be apparent by now that the ADT called "node" could be represented by a structure in the C language, since each of the node attributes may be different physical data types. In this review program we will look at a special tree structure, a binary tree, implemented using structures. Several important aspects of programming in C will be used, including pointers, recursion, functions, and structures.

☐ *Program Design*

A subset of tree structures in general is the binary tree which has the following properties:

1. Each node may have at most two children.

2. Given any arbitrary node in the tree, the value associated with the left child will be less than the parent, while the right child's value will always be greater than or equal to the parent's value.

3. A node may be added to or deleted from the tree, but the integrity of the structure must be restored after the operation has taken place.

Given such a data structure, you will see that it becomes a trivial matter to print the tree in sorted order and to search the tree for a particular node value. In our review program we will implement two node operations, insert and find. The insert operation allows us to add a node to the tree adhering to the rules of the binary tree structure. The algorithm is inherently recursive and involves stepping through the nodes in the tree until the proper insertion location is found. The insertion operation will always begin at the root node where a decision will be made to proceed to the left or right child. At some point in the recursion the node will be attached as the left or right child of the current node being examined. Now let's look at the pseudocode for this operation:

```
begin insert(cnode, inode)
ADT node cnode                              the current node
ADT node inode                              the node to insert
    if (<value of cnode> >= <value of inode>)   search left branch
        if (<left child of cnode> == NULL)      insert the node as
            <left child of cnode = inode>       left child of cnode
        else
            insert(<left child of cnode>, inode)    descend tree via
        endif                                       left child
    else                                        search right branch
        if (<right child of cnode> == NULL)     insert the node as
            <right child of cnode == inode>     right child of cnode
        else
            insert(<right child of cnode>, inode)   descend tree via
        endif                                       right child
    endif
    return
end insert
```

Note that we have not specified how the children and values of a node are resolved nor how parents are attached to their children. This will be identified in our structure definition for the ADT node.

The algorithm for find() is essentially a modified version of a binary search, with each node examined in the decision process "splitting" the subsequent subtree to be searched.

```
begin find(cnode, value)
ADT node cnode
string value
   if (<value of cnode  = =  to value> OR cnode  = =  NULL)
      return(cnode)
   else if (<value  > =  value of cnode>)
      return(find(<right child of cnode>, value))
   else
      return(find(<left child of cnode> , value))
end find
```

Note that the find operation is also recursive. It returns the current node examined if cnode is found or a NULL node if it is not found.

It should be evident by now that our binary tree can be built by repeatedly calling insert(). Each call passes one value to be incorporated into the tree structure. We will not concern ourselves at this point with where the data comes from, only that it is available in some suitable format in the C program. In reality, the data may come from an internal array, a disk file, or be entered by the user as required. Let's examine the pseudocode that will build our tree:

```
begin main
ADT node root                    the root node of the tree
ADT node inode                   a node to be inserted in the tree
   <set value of root  =  data 1>    set up the root node before building
                                    the rest of the tree

   <left child of root  =  NULL>
   <right child of root  =  NULL>

   while (<more data exists>)
      <left child of inode  =  NULL>    initialize children of node
      <right child of inode  =  NULL>   to insert
      <value of inode  =  next data value>   and value, also
      insert(root, inode)              insert the node
   endwhile
end main
```

Note that we "prime the pump" by initially creating the root node before building the rest of the tree. This is necessary since the insert() routine expects the tree to contain at least one node. Note also that the right and left children of the node to be inserted are initially set to NULL and its value is initialized before calling the insert() procedure.

After the tree is constructed, it becomes a trivial task to print the tree in sorted order. The algorithm used is known as an inorder listing. Two other useful tree algorithms are the preorder listing (which we saw in the maze searching exercise in Chapter 8) and a postorder listing. The inorder algorithm steps through the tree, always taking left branches, if possible. After stepping to the bottom of a leftmost branch, all nodes are listed as we travel back out of the branch. In order to visualize how the inorder algorithm works, consider the following binary tree:

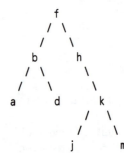

Using the inorder algorithm, the tree would be traversed as follows:

Current Node	List Node?	Nodes Listed Thus Far	Comments
f	No	——	Left branch to explore
b	No	——	Ditto
a	Yes	a	No left branches to explore
b	Yes	b	Ditto
d	Yes	d	Ditto
b	No	——	Node already listed
f	Yes	f	No left branches to explore
h	Yes	h	Ditto
k	No	——	Left branch to explore
j	Yes	j	No left branches to explore
k	Yes	k	Ditto
m	Yes	m	Ditto
k	No	——	Already listed
h	No	——	Ditto
f	No	——	Ditto

A little introspection will reveal that this will indeed print the tree in sorted order. The pseudocode is as follows:

ADT node cnode

begin inorder(cnode)
   if (< cnode is not equal to **NULL**>)
      inorder(< **left child of cnode**>)
      print (< **value of cnode**>)
      inorder(< **right child of cnode**>)
   endif
   return
end inorder

As before the function is recursive. As you may have realized, the binary tree is a recursive data structure, so it is natural that we use recursive algorithms.

Let's proceed now to implement our binary tree manipulation program in the C language.

□ *Design Implementation*

Before we begin to write code, we have a couple of design considerations. First, we must devise a suitable representation for the ADT node in C syntax. We have already decided that a structure should be our choice. Thus we code

```
struct node {
        <value>;                /* not valid syntax */
        struct node *left;      /* pointer to left child */
        struct node *right;     /* pointer to right child */
        };
```

Note that `<value>` is not valid C syntax. We must decide what data type value will represent. The choice depends on what type of item will be stored in the tree. For the sake of simplicity, we choose strings. Thus we write:

```
struct node {
        char *value;
        struct node *left;
        struct node *right;
        };
```

You should realize that `value` could have been chosen to be an array, integer, structure, pointer to function, and so forth; the choice is dictated by the application.

Second, now that we have chosen a data type for node value we must decide how it will be made available to our program. In the last chapter we saw how strings could be stored in the form:

```
char *value[] = { "string1",
                  "string2",
                  ...

                  "stringn" };
```

For the sake of comparison, we will use the same data set and format coded in the Chapter 10 review program. Let's proceed now to write the code for our review program.

```
/*----------------------------------------------------------------
 btree.c
 Binary tree manipulation using structures.
 ------------------------------------------------------------*/

#include <conio.h>
#include <stdio.h>
#include <stdlib.h>
#include <string.h>


                                     /* C version of abstract */
struct node {                        /*    data type node */
   char *value;                      /* the node value */
   struct node *left;                /* pointer to left child */
   struct node *right;               /* pointer to right child */
   };

typedef struct node BTREE_NODE;      /* convenient shorthand for node */

/*
 function prototypes
    note that main() has been prototyped, a technique which should eliminate
    all compiler warnings even at the highest level of checking
*/
void main(void);
void insert(BTREE_NODE *, BTREE_NODE *);
BTREE_NODE *find(BTREE_NODE *, char *);
void inorder(BTREE_NODE *);
```

```
/*
 our node values
*/
char *test_list[] = { "qrs",
                      "abc",
                      "wxy",
                      "z!@",
                      "hij",
                      "nop",
                      "def",
                      "tuv",
                      "klm",
                      NULL };          /* the null pointer used to mark */
                                       /* end of the array */
/*
 our list of values to search for to test the find() function
*/
char *search_list[] = { "z!@",
                        "agc",
                        "abc",
                        "def",
                        "yan",
                        "efh",
                        "tuv",
                        NULL };

void main()
{
    BTREE_NODE *root, *inode;         /* working nodes we need */
    char **str_ptr;                   /* work variable for value list */


/*
 initialize the root node in the binary tree
*/
    str_ptr = test_list;              /* point to value list */
    printf("Building binary tree structure with values...\n\n");
/*
 print the initial list of values
*/
    while(*str_ptr) {
        printf("%s\n", *str_ptr++);
    }
    printf("\n");
    str_ptr = test_list;              /* point to value list */
    if ((root = (BTREE_NODE *)malloc(sizeof(BTREE_NODE))) != NULL) {
        root->value = *str_ptr;       /* set root node's value */
        root->left = NULL;            /* no left child */
        root->right = NULL;           /* or right child */
```

(program continued on next page...)

```
/*
 now, build the tree starting at the root node
 space is allocated for each node using malloc()
*/
      while (
              ((inode = (BTREE_NODE *)malloc(sizeof(BTREE_NODE))) != NULL) &&
              *++str_ptr
            ) {
         inode->left = NULL;              /* no left child */
         inode->right = NULL;             /* no right child */
         inode->value = *str_ptr;         /* the node's value, a string */
         insert(root, inode);             /* insert node in tree */
      }
      printf("Press RETURN to print tree in order...\n\n");
      getchar();                          /* wait for user */
      inorder(root);                      /* do inorder listing of tree */
      printf("\n\n");
      printf("Press RETURN to test the find() function\n\n");
      getchar();
      str_ptr = search_list;   /* point to search list for find test */
      while (*str_ptr) {                  /* while more strings in search list */
         if (find(root, *str_ptr)) {   /* see if we can find it */
            printf("%s was found.\n", find(root, *str_ptr)->value);
         }
         else {
            printf("%s was NOT found.\n", *str_ptr);
         }
         ++str_ptr;
      }
   }
   else {
      printf("Memory allocation error. Exiting program...\n");
   }
}

/*-------------------------------------------------------------------
 void insert(cnode, inode)
 Insert a node into a binary tree structure.

    parm           type            desc
 ---------------!---------------!-------------------------------------
   cnode          BTREE_NODE *    pointer to a binary tree node
                                  usually the root note
   inode          BTREE_NODE *    ditto, the node to insert
    ret value     type            desc
 ---------------!---------------!-------------------------------------
    ---            void
 ---------------------------------------------------------------------*/
void insert(cnode, inode)
BTREE_NODE *cnode, *inode;
{
```

```
/*
 our if() construct determines which child branch to take
 strcmp() return value determines the left or right branch
*/
    if (strcmp(cnode->value, inode->value) >= 0) {
        if (cnode->left == NULL) {        /* if left child is empty */
            cnode->left = inode;          /* insert the node here */
        }
        else {
            insert(cnode->left, inode);   /* else keep searching */
        }
    }
    else {
        if (cnode->right == NULL) {       /* if right child is empty */
            cnode->right = inode;         /* insert node here */
        }
        else {
            insert(cnode->right, inode);  /* else keep searching */
        }
    }
    return;
}


/*-------------------------------------------------------------------
 void inorder(cnode)


    parm          type          desc
---------------!--------------!-------------------------------------
    cnode         BTREE_NODE *  pointer to beginning node in binary
                                tree, usually the root node
    ret value     type          desc
---------------!--------------!-------------------------------------
    ---           void
-------------------------------------------------------------------*/
void inorder(cnode)
BTREE_NODE *cnode;
{
    if (cnode) {
        inorder(cnode->left);             /* find bottom of left branch */
        printf("%s\n", cnode->value);     /* print node value */
        inorder(cnode->right);            /* find bottom of right branch */
    }
    return;
}
```

(program continued on next page...)

```
/*-------------------------------------------------------------------
 BTREE_NODE *find(cnode, value)

    parm            type            desc
 ---------------!---------------!-----------------------------------
    cnode           BTREE_NODE *    pointer to binary tree node to begin
                                    search from, usually the root node
    value           char *          node value we are searching for

    ret value       type            desc
 ---------------!---------------!-----------------------------------
    cnode           BTREE_NODE *    pointer to node found; if not found
                                    returns NULL pointer
 -----------------------------------------------------------------*/
BTREE_NODE *find(cnode, value)
BTREE_NODE *cnode;
char *value;
{
                            /*
                             if we've found the value or we're out of places
                                to search return the current node
                            */
    if (strcmp(value, cnode->value) == 0 || !cnode) {
        return(cnode);
    }
                                        /*
                                         else if value greater than current
                                            node search the right subtree
                                        */
    else {
        if (strcmp(value, cnode->value) > 0) {
            return(find(cnode->right, value));
        }
                                        /* else search the left subtree */
        else {
            return(find(cnode->left, value));
        }
    }
}
```

There are several important observations we should make regarding our review program. First, carefully study the structure definition for node. Note that struct node *left, which is a pointer to node, is NOT a recursive use of node, the structure itself. You should know how this pointer is initialized (via a NULL pointer) and how it is manipulated in the function insert(). Second, carefully examine the use of malloc() in the phrase

```
(inode = (BTREE *)malloc(sizeof(BTREE))) != NULL)
```

Note that we must type cast the return value of `malloc()`, normally type `void *`, to the desired `BTREE *`. Remember from Chapter 10 that `void *` is a generic pointer used to write generic code. The function `malloc()` can be used to allocate memory for any pointer type using the appropriate type cast. You should also realize that although we look for a return value of NULL from `malloc()`, indicating that the allocation failed, we have included no provisions to notify the user of the failure. In practice you should include such provisions in your production code.

Now, let's look at the output produced by our program.

☐ *Program Output*

```
Building binary tree structure with values...

qrs
abc
wxy
z!@
hij
nop
def
tuv
klm

Press RETURN to print tree in order...

abc
def
hij
klm
nop
qrs
tuv
wxy
z!@




Press RETURN to test the find() function

z!@ was found.
agc was NOT found.
abc was found.
def was found.
yan was NOT found.
efh was NOT found.
tuv was found.
```

The manner in which we structured our binary tree simulates a list sorted in ascending order. How could this be rewritten to produce a descending list?

Points to Study

1. The structure definition for node.

2. Use of `typedef` to produce `BTREE`.

3. Use of the library function `malloc()` to dynamically allocate memory for the nodes as they are inserted into the tree.

4. Function parameters and their return values, if any. How are the nodes passed to the functions? By value? By reference?

5. How recursion is implemented in each of the functions. Do you feel this is an appropriate application for recursive functions?

6. Why did we introduce the intermediate variable `str_ptr` instead of using `test_list` directly in our code?

7. How could the function `insert()` be rewritten to receive structure names as parameters instead of pointers? Is there any advantage between the two methods?

8. Carefully study the form of the expression `find(root, *str_ptr)->value` and how it reduces to a legal expression.

11.12 Exercises

1. Algorithms that can handle event scheduling have many applications in real-life situations. For instance, many retail stores require customers to take a number so that they may be assisted in order. Consider the following list of customer numbers:

Customer Number	Time In	Time Out	Day of Week
3	9:05	9:15	Saturday
4	9:10	9:16	Saturday
5	9:35	10:10	Saturday
6	10:07	10:42	Saturday

Note that the customers received their numbers at "Time In" and were assisted at "Time Out." Customers were served based on their number, the service order being from lowest to highest. In our example Customer 3 was first, 4 second, 5 third and 6 last. Each customer assistance can be viewed as an "event" with the following attributes:

1. a customer number
2. time in
3. time out
4. day of week

Such a system could be tracked effectively using a data structure known as a queue. The queue consists of events which are scheduled in a FIFO (First In-First Out) manner. As you might suspect, "event" could be viewed as an ADT with the previously referenced attributes.

Now for our program scenario. The "We Service 'Em Fast" retail outlet uses such a system to service its customers in an equitable manner. You, as a respected local software service company, have received a contract to computerize the customer queuing facilities. At the end of each day, the information from the system will be summarized to produce a report that looks like this:

Number of Customers Served	Average Waiting Period (Mins)	Day of Week
34	16	Saturday

Your program should allow customers to be entered into the queue dynamically (from the keyboard), assign a number (ranging from 1 to 10) and produce a summary report at the user's request. Devise your own sample set of data to demonstrate that your customer queuing system works correctly. It should include enough data to show that your system handles "wrap-around" situations (when the number exceeds 10). You may use military time to simplify time calculations. You must use a structure to represent each customer event.

2. Consider the following simple "road map":

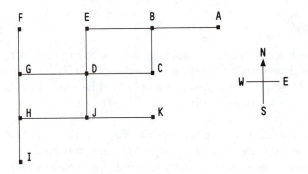

Junctions are labeled A, B, C,..., K and are connected by "roads" represented by the dashed lines. Each junction can be exited in various directions depending on the junction in question. For example, junction H has three possible exit directions—North, South, and East. Note also that three junctions are directly connected to junction H—G, J, and I. Each junction can be viewed as an ADT possessing the following attributes:

1. all possible exit directions
2. all directly connecting junctions

Note that each possible exit direction could be encoded as a logical value in a single data bit:

N: TRUE or FALSE
W: TRUE or FALSE
S: TRUE or FALSE
E: TRUE or FALSE

with TRUE indicating an exit path in the given direction and FALSE no exit path.

Write a program to perform the following:
a. Encode the road map using `malloc()` for each junction. Use a structure to represent the ADT junction. Use bit fields for each possible direction.
b. Allow the user to enter a junction.
c. Display all known information about the entered junction including all possible exit directions and all junctions directly connected.
d. Repeat b. and c. until the user wishes to exit.

3. Modify the review program to produce a descending view of the sample data coded in test_list, rather than an ascending view. Test the find() function to make sure it still works properly. If not, make the necessary revisions.

* 4. A stack is a data structure useful in tracking events that must be handled in a LIFO (Last In-First Out) manner. In Chapter 5 we alluded to error-handling methods that avoid problems associated with the use of the goto statement. Most program applications generate several classes of dynamic objects such as open files, allocated memory pointers, and others. These objects can cause problems if a nonfatal error occurs making recovery difficult. This is particularly true of recursive functions and deeply nested program logic. One way around this problem is to create an object stack that allows the application to keep track of these objects. In the event of a recoverable error, the application pops the objects off the stack and deals with them appropriately. Objects are pushed to the object stack in the order they are created. In effect, the object stack creates a "history" of the created objects so that the program can recover in the event of an error. As an example, consider the following pseudocode for a function called my_recursion().

```
begin my__recursion()
    file pointer fp1, fp2, fp3          pointers to type FILE
    memory pointer m1, m2               pointers to memory blocks
                                        pointer types may be different
    if (<end of recursion>)            termination condition for
                                        the recursion

        cleanup__the__mess()            release objects before exiting
        return
    endif
    push(<stack marker>)               mark stack for this level of
    <fp1 = open file #1>               recursion
    push(fp1)                          save fp1 to stack
    <fp2 = open file #2>
    push(fp2)                          save fp2 to stack
    <fp3 = open file #3>
    push(fp3)                          save fp3 to stack
    <m1 = allocate memory>
    push(m1)                           save m1 to stack
    <m2 = allocate memory #2>
    push(m2)                           save m2 to stack

    if (<an error has occurred>)
        cleanup__the__mess()           this function cleans up the
                                        environment before returning
                                        to the previous level

        return(error to previous level)
    else
        my__recursion()                if no error, do recursive call
end my__recursion
```

This function illustrates how an error is dealt with using an object stack. Object pointers are pushed to the stack as they are created. A stack marker marks the base of the object stack for the current recursive call. If an error occurs, a function called `cleanup_the_mess()` is called. This function pops the pointers off the stack, determines their type, and "destroys" them as appropriate. Thus our function `my_recursion()` can recover from a nonfatal error gracefully. Note that each object could be viewed as an ADT with the following properties:

1. a pointer to the object (file, memory, stack base, etc)
2. an object type (`FILE *`, `char *`, `struct xyz *`, stack, etc.)

Implement an error-recovery system based on the principles outlined above, using an object stack. Use a structure for the stack object. The structure should contain a union as one of its members to reference the object pointer itself. Use an array of such structures as the object stack. Write the function `cleanup_the_mess()` and demonstrate that it works by writing a test jig.

5. Write a simple dictionary program using the principles covered in the review program. Your program should allow the user to enter a word and its associated meaning. Also, at any time, the user should be allowed to enter a word to be looked up in the dictionary. If the word is found, the program should display its meaning; if not found, the user should be allowed to add the word and its meaning to the dictionary if so desired. The program should be menu driven and present a menu similar to this:

```
Dictionary Menu
---------------
<A>dd a word
<L>ook up a word
e<X>it program
```

```
Enter your choice [_]
```

Run the program, adding at least 10 words and meanings to demonstrate that your code works properly. Test both the add and look up functions thoroughly. Use a structure for the ADT dictionary entry and a tree data structure for the dictionary itself.

6. A double linked list consists of an array of elements possessing a value and pointers to the previous and subsequent list elements. This is in contrast to a single linked list where only one pointer is present. Double linked lists allow the list to be searched in forward and reverse directions. Modify the example program presented in the chapter to handle double linked instead of single linked lists. Run the program to demonstrate that your modifications produce the desired results.

* advanced exercise

11.13 Pretest

☐ *Multiple Choice*

Circle one correct answer to each of the following:

1. The term ADT (abstract data type) refers to:
   a. A data type not possible in the C language.
   b. A data type possessing high-level properties.
   c. A tree node only.
   d. A C structure only.

2. A union is used in C when:
   a. The code is very complicated.
   b. A single unit of storage is needed which may hold different data types, but not simultaneously.
   c. Writing code for low-level access routines only.
   d. A pointer to a structure won't work.

3. Every node in a tree structure possesses certain attributes. They are:
   a. A value, one or more children (except terminal nodes), and a parent (except the root).
   b. A value, pointers.
   c. A value, pointers, children, and parents.
   d. Pointers only.

4. The size of a structure (in bytes) depends on:
   a. The number of structure members, regardless of type.
   b. The compiler's implementation of the structure.
   c. The data types and numbers of each structure member.
   d. Where the structure is defined in the program itself.

5. Consider the following ADT:

```
customer_record          Example
   customer name         Jones, Bill
   previous payment      40.00
   account balance       545.75
   past due? (Y/N)       N
```

   Which structure definition below would best represent customer_record?
   a. struct customer_record {
   ```
           char *name;
           union {
              float previous_payment;
              float account_balance;
              };
           float past_due;
           };
   ```

```
b. struct customer_record {
          char *name;
          float previous_payment;
          float account_balance;
          float past_due;
          };
c. struct customer_record {
          char *name;
          float previous_payment;
          float account_balance;
          char past_due;
          };
d. struct customer_record {
          char *name;
          float previous_payment;
          float account_balance;
          int past_due:1;
          };
```

6. The -> structure operator is used to resolve
   a. A structure pointer and one of its members.
   b. A structure name and one of its members.
   c. A structure name and a pointer to one of its members.
   d. A structure pointer and a pointer to one of its members.

7. What is wrong with the following structure definition?

```
struct node {
   int node_number;
   char value1[20];
   char *value2;
   struct node left_child;
   struct node right_child;
   };
```

   a. An array may not be a structure member.
   b. A structure may not contain an instance of itself.
   c. node_number is not needed.
   d. The structure has no definite size, which it must have.

8. The library function malloc() is used to:
   a. Dynamically allocate memory for an object.
   b. Allocate system resources including memory, open files, and check port statuses.
   c. See if any memory is available to a program.
   d. Create structure definitions at runtime.

9. What does the following statement reference?

`my_struct[2].value`

    a. The third element of the array `value`.
    b. The second member of `my_struct` which is called `value`.
    c. The third structure in the structure array `my_struct` and its member `value`.
    d. None of the above.

10. Certain operations may not be performed on bit fields. Which operation below is legal?
    a. `sizeof`
    b. pointer to
    c. address of
    d. value of

Disk File and Record I/O

P erforming input and output on disk files is only slightly different from doing standard file I/O. This is because the C language views all files and devices as providers or receivers of characters. Therefore, all the concepts we've already discussed about stream and character I/O apply to disk file I/O, and some additional functions become available.

This chapter will have fewer sections and more code than most others. After studying this chapter, you will be able to do the following:

1. Reproduce and expand on techniques to analyze free-form disk files.

2. Contrast binary and text files.

3. Explain when binary file access is necessary.

4. Describe how to retrieve and update information randomly in files.

5. Show how to use structures in disk file input and output.

12.1 Reading Disk Files That Have Free-Form Format

In the chapter on standard I/O (Chapter 7) we illustrated how simple it was to access a standard file stream. No preparation is needed in the program to reference stdin or stdout. In fact, the very first statement in a program can be a reference to the getchar() or putchar() function.

In contrast to standard file I/O, programs that access disk files directly must perform certain activities before the file can be used. These activities can be summarized as follows:

1. Define a FILE pointer.

2. Open a file stream, initializing the FILE pointer.

3. Access the file stream using the FILE pointer.

4. Close the file stream using the FILE pointer.

In order to illustrate these requirements, we have prepared a set of program modules that are able to read a free-form disk file. Here is the disk file that will form the initial input test data for this chapter:

```
"Carol Cashout" "1620 Bankflower, Apt. #3G" "New Rich"   UM   54321   5556789
"Space Kadette","16 Star Trek Blvd.","Alpha Centauri",MW,99999,555????
"Sissy McClure", "123 Barbie Doll Lane", "Clownytown", CV, 77777, 5552642
"I. Q. Physics"    "149 E=MC Square"    "Science Town"   PS   78695   5554791
```

The first program in this chapter will simply read this file. Later we will place the data fields into an array of structures, and then perform disk file input and output on the structures. Although this chapter will illustrate how to perform I/O on structures (records), remember that all input and output in C is basically performed on characters. Record I/O is merely an extension of that concept, not an exception to it.

We're also going to practice some modular programming techniques by physically breaking up the program code into the various functions that will process the data. In later example programs we will be using functions from earlier programs, so it is easier if we keep the code in separate source files.

Because we're practicing more modular programming than previously done in this book, we need to employ more extensive header file techniques. Figure 12.1 shows the header file called parse.h which will be used throughout many of the program modules in this chapter. Note that some definitions and declarations appear in the header even though they are not used in the first example program. Because this header will be used throughout this chapter it contains everything needed for all programs in which it appears.

```
/*
** parse.h - Contains definitions common to various program modules.
**           The modules themselves illustrate disk file I/O techniques.
*/

#include <ctype.h>                  /* prototype for isspace() function */
#include <stdio.h>
#include <stdlib.h>
#include <string.h>
                                    /* function prototypes occur next */
int get_field(char * input_string, int max_size, FILE *input_file);

#define TRUE   1
#define FALSE  0
```

(program continued on next page...)

```
                                        /* define or declare variables depending */
                                        /* on where we are */
#if defined MAIN_PGM
    int end_of_file    = FALSE;
    int end_of_record  = FALSE;
    int found_an_error = FALSE;
#else
    extern int end_of_file;
    extern int end_of_record;
    extern int found_an_error;
#endif

struct personnel {                      /* holds converted free-form fields */
    char name[26];
    char addr[26];
    char city[21];
    char state[3];
    long zip;
    long phone;
};

typedef struct personnel PERSONNEL;
```

Figure 12.1   Header File—parse.h

For the first example program we will be maintaining the source code in two files, parsefld.c and getfield.c. They are compiled together using this command in UNIX:

```
cc parsefld.c getfield.c
```

Similar syntax is used in MS/PC-DOS for many C compilers. Often only the compiler name (cc) is changed, so consult the compiler documentation for specifics.

Remember, the purpose of these modules is to break down the test data into component parts. Only after the free-form input is analyzed can the resulting fields be placed into a structure. Examine the code, then read the explanation of the modules which follows.

```
/*
** parsefld.c - Program to Parse Free-Form Disk File Records
*/

#define MAIN_PGM

#include "parse.h"                /* has definitions for these routines */
```

```
main()
{
    FILE *file_ptr;
    char in_buffer[30];
    int  return_value;
    static char in_file[] = "subdir/parsetxt";

    if((file_ptr = fopen(in_file, "r")) != NULL)  /* NULL means not there */
    {
        while((return_value = get_field(in_buffer,
                                    (sizeof(in_buffer) -1),
                                    file_ptr)) != EOF)
        {
            printf("    size: %2d, end_of_record: %5s, field:%s\n",
                    return_value,
                    end_of_record ? "TRUE" : "FALSE",
                    in_buffer
                );
            end_of_record = FALSE;
        }
        fclose(file_ptr);                          /* close the opened file */
    }
    else {                                 /* do some error checking */
        fprintf(stderr, "An error occurred opening file %s\n", in_file);
    }
    if(found_an_error == TRUE) {
        fprintf(stderr, "An error occurred reading file %s\n", in_file);
    }
}

/*
** getfield.c - Gets the next free-form input field from a record.
**
**     Places the field in the specified string, with NULL added.
**     Leading blanks are dropped.
**     Returns - the string length if the input was valid, including the
**                 number of characters kept if the buffer overflowed
**             - EOF at end of file, even if input was valid
**     If the buffer overflows the function continues reading until the
**         end of the field is reached.
**     Fields can be ended by a comma, or any character that causes the
**         isspace() function to return TRUE.
**     A comma after a series of spaces will return an empty field
**         of length zero.
**     Imbedded isspace() characters require that double quotes
**         surround the string.
**     Double quote can start a field, but not end it.  So the
**         common practice of putting a comma after a closing quote will
**         work, the second quote merely turns off the flag that
**         allows imbedded blanks, etc. and then normal logic takes over.
```

(program continued on next page...)

```
**      Anything can be quoted, including numeric fields
**      A record is terminated by a newline character, and any open
**        quoted strings are also terminated.
**
**      input_string    is where the characters are placed
**      max_size        is the max number of valid characters to receive, so
**                      input_string should be at least one larger in size
**      input_file      is the stream pointer of the input file
*/

#define SUB_PGM

#include "parse.h"              /* has definitions for these routines */

int get_field(char * input_string, int max_size, FILE *input_file)
{
   int input_char;
   int index = 0;
   int quote_found  = FALSE;
   int value_found  = FALSE;
   int buffer_oflow = FALSE;

   if(!end_of_file) {                        /* this shields for reads past EOF */
      for(;;) {
         if(index >= max_size) {
            buffer_oflow = TRUE;
         }
         input_char = fgetc(input_file);        /* read one character */
         switch(input_char) {        /* check for end of file and record */
         case EOF:  end_of_file = TRUE;
                    if(ferror(input_file)) {
                        found_an_error = TRUE;
                    }          /* no break, EOF means end of record */
         case '\n': end_of_record = TRUE;
                    input_string[index] = '\0';
                    return(index);
                    break;            /* not required, but good habit */
         }
             /* having encountered a quote makes us less picky about */
                                        /* what's in the field */
         if(quote_found) {
            if(input_char == '\"') {      /* turn quote flag off so that */
               quote_found = FALSE;        /* normal end of field works */
            }
            else {                       /* keep all chars if inside a quote */
               if(!buffer_oflow) {
                  input_string[index++] = input_char;
               }
            }
         }
```

```
            else {  /* quote not found, so get picky about what's in field */
                          /* first see if field should be terminated */
             if((isspace(input_char) && value_found) !! input_char == ',') {
                input_string[index] = '\0';
                return(index);
             }
             else {

                                                        /* skip leading spaces */
                 if(!isspace(input_char)) {
                     if(input_char == '\"') {
                        quote_found = TRUE;
                     }
                     else {
                        if(!buffer_oflow) {             /* save char if room */
                           input_string[index++] = input_char;
                        }
                     }
                     value_found = TRUE;    /* stop skipping leading spaces */
                 }
             }
          }
      }
   }
   else {
      return(EOF);                          /* one exception to rtn length */
   }
}
```

Figure 12.2 Program to Parse Free-Form Disk File Records—`parsefld.c`

The module `parsefld.c` opens the input file, loops on each field returned from the module `getfield.c`, closes the file, and handles any error messages associated with the file access. The module `getfield.c` reads the input file until end of record, end of file, end of field, or an error occurs (an error causes `EOF` to be returned by the `fgetc()` function).

The data item `file_ptr` is defined as a `FILE` pointer, and the identifier `FILE` is defined in `stdio.h`. Each physical file and device (except standard files of course) used by a program must have an established `FILE` pointer. The pointers of standard files (`stdin`, `stdout`, `stderr`) are created by the prologue code (which is attached to the front end of each C program) in conjunction with the operating system. Other files must have a `FILE` pointer defined and initialized with the return value from the `fopen()` function. Here is how we might diagram this relationship:

```
file_ptr ———►   FILE ———►  external storage managed by operating system
```

The first i f statement test expression in parsefld.c not only opens the file whose name appears inside the string in_file, but also tests the return value of fopen(). If fopen() fails to open the file, a NULL value is returned, and the example shows how an error message can be sent to standard error to signal this condition. If fopen() succeeds it returns a value which is a pointer to a data item of type FILE, so the value is eligible to be assigned into a FILE pointer.

One error students occasionally make is trying to write this type of expression:

```
FILE *file_ptr = fopen(...
...
main()
```

This may look innocent enough, but note that fopen() is a standard library function, not a constant. Because it generates executable code it cannot appear outside a function in the program.

Antibugging Note 12.1   Using functions when initializing data

Be careful not to use executable functions to initialize global data items.

The second argument to the fopen() function is a file type or file mode which describes how we want to access the file. Our sample program opens the file to be read, but files can also be opened for writing and appending (adding onto the end). Table 12.1 gives a complete list of the text file modes supported by any ANSI standard compiler.

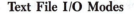

	Text File I/O Modes
r	Read only, file must exist
w	Write, create if needed
a	Append, open for writing at end, or create
r+	Update existing file, both read and write
w+	Create new file for update
a+	Open for update at end, or create

Table 12.1   Text File I/O Modes

If the fopen() function is successful, the file is eligible to be accessed by any stream input/output function that allows the stream to be explicitly identified. This means that getchar() cannot be used to access our file since the implied stream used by getchar() is stdin, the standard input stream. In our example we have used the function fgetc(), but other stream functions like getc(), fgets(), or `getw()` would also work because they require a `FILE` pointer as one of the arguments.

The header file `parse.h` is included in both program modules in order that the variable names be consistent, and because the same defined constants are needed when compiling both files. An interesting thing about this header file is that some variables, e.g., `end_of_file`, are either physically defined or else declared to be external to the module based on the presence or absence of a definition for `MAIN_PGM`. The storage class `extern` causes the module `getfield.c` to look elsewhere (i.e., back in `parsefld.c`) for the physical existence of `end_of_file`.

The module `getfield.c` examines the input stream and discards any leading space characters in each field. The character classification function `isspace()` is used to determine which characters can be discarded. Once a nonspace character is encountered in a field, space characters are no longer discarded, but serve to terminate the field (if double quotes are not used as delimiters), or are accepted as part of the input field (if double quotes are used). The flag `value_found` controls whether leading space characters are to be discarded or included in the field. The flag `quote_found` tells whether or not we're inside a quoted field.

A field ends when either the first space or comma is encountered, or if delimiting double quotes are used, when the first space or comma after the terminating double quote appears. The selected characters (minus any delimiting double quotes) are placed in the input buffer whose pointer is passed as the first argument to the function. During the entire process the size of the input buffer is taken into account so that a buffer overflow condition does not occur. The flag `buffer_oflow` makes sure that if this does occur the input stream is read until the end of the input file being processed. This insures that part of a field will not be left on the stream to appear as another field.

This routine does not handle trailing blanks in a field. The following:

```
"field number one" , fieldnumbertwo
```

will be interpreted as three fields. The first field is the double quote bounded string. The second is null because the space after the double quote and the comma both serve as field separator characters, which means that the final field is the word `fieldnumbertwo`.

Figure 12.3 shows the output of the `while` loop inside `parsefld.c`. Carefully examine this output and compare it to the input file shown above. Various combinations of double quotes, spaces, and commas were intentionally included to serve as field separators in order to provide a reasonable set of test data.

```
size: 13, end_of_record: FALSE, field:Carol Cashout
size: 25, end_of_record: FALSE, field:1620 Bankflower, Apt. #3G
size:  8, end_of_record: FALSE, field:New Rich
size:  2, end_of_record: FALSE, field:UM
size:  5, end_of_record: FALSE, field:54321
size:  7, end_of_record:  TRUE, field:5556789
size: 13, end_of_record: FALSE, field:Space Kadette
size: 18, end_of_record: FALSE, field:16 Star Trek Blvd.
size: 14, end_of_record: FALSE, field:Alpha Centauri
size:  2, end_of_record: FALSE, field:MW
size:  5, end_of_record: FALSE, field:99999
size:  7, end_of_record:  TRUE, field:555????
size: 13, end_of_record: FALSE, field:Sissy McClure
size: 20, end_of_record: FALSE, field:123 Barbie Doll Lane
size: 10, end_of_record: FALSE, field:Clownytown
size:  2, end_of_record: FALSE, field:CV
size:  5, end_of_record: FALSE, field:77777
size:  7, end_of_record:  TRUE, field:5552642
size: 13, end_of_record: FALSE, field:I. Q. Physics
size: 15, end_of_record: FALSE, field:149 E=MC Square
size: 12, end_of_record: FALSE, field:Science Town
size:  2, end_of_record: FALSE, field:PS
size:  5, end_of_record: FALSE, field:78695
size:  7, end_of_record:  TRUE, field:5554791
size:  0, end_of_record:  TRUE, field:
```

Figure 12.3   Output of the while Loop inside `parsefld.c`

When we are done with the input file we close it by using the `fclose()` function. In most cases the operating system will close any files that are still open when the program ends, but relying on that feature is sloppy programming practice. Leaving files open when the program ends is risky because some day an output file buffer may not be flushed or a final file update may not be performed, resulting in a loss of data. It also shows a lack of attention to detail.

A final point concerning this code is that the array `in_file` is initialized with a string that appears (on the surface) to be a valid UNIX path or file name, but not one which would work on an MS/PC-DOS system. However, later versions of MS/PC-DOS allow (internally) the forward slash to separate directories from other directories and file names. The more traditional way of writing the directory and file separator in MS/PC-DOS is to use the backslash character, and using it would require that our string look like this:

`"subdir\\parsetxt"`

The double backslashes are necessary for the string to be built correctly. A single backslash is used in C to designate an escape sequence or else to force the literal interpretation of a character. For instance, if a single backslash were used before the file name portion of the path name, and if the file name began with the letter t, then \t would be replaced in the string with the tab character, resulting in an incorrect file name. Again, UNIX does not have this problem since fully qualified file (path) names in UNIX use the forward slash to separate directories from other directories and file names.

12.2 Accessing Disk Files in Binary Mode

All the files (or *streams* as they are more appropriately called) that we have discussed in this book, including the standard files, are grouped together into a category known as *text files*. The other group into which files are assembled is that of *binary files*. The names imply the basic differences between the two groups.

Text files (or streams) contain sequences of characters which periodically include a newline or line feed character. C source programs are a good example of text files, as are the files that make up this book. In text files there is no requirement that individual characters remain unaltered as they are read into the computer or written back to a file. For example, the newline in ASCII is a single character whose value is a decimal 10. In hex it can be written as 0A and occupies eight bits; in a C program it is represented by the character constant '\n'. However, in disk files created under MS/PC-DOS (and many other operating systems) it physically is a carriage return-line feed (CRLF) sequence containing two characters, the carriage return (decimal 13) and a line feed (decimal 10). When a file is read the two character CRLF sequence is translated or mapped into the single newline character in the program; the reverse happens on output. A C program can actually test for the single newline character because inside the program there actually is only one character. If, however, you examine the file that was read or written, you will find a CRLF sequence in the file in the location corresponding to where you found the newline in the input or output stream. The CRLF sequence takes two bytes, while the newline only requires one.

On the other hand, none of the characters of a binary file ever changes when it is read or written. If a C program wants to read an executable file (on any machine, and any operating system) then the file should be read as a binary file. A file is specified as binary by including a b in the file mode when the file is opened. If the b is not present, the file is assumed to be a text file.

	Binary File I/O Modes
r b	Read only, file must exist
w b	Write, create if needed
a b	Append, open for writing at end, or create
r+b or rb+	Update existing file, both read and write
w+b or wb+	Create new file for update
a+b or ab+	Open for update at end, or create

Table 12.2   Binary File I/O Modes

This is an example of how an executable (binary) file on an MS/PC-DOS system would be opened for reading:

```
if((file_ptr = fopen("HELLO.EXE", "rb")) != NULL) /* read a binary file */
```

Files (like C program source files) created by text editors should be read and written in text mode. This will insure that the carriage return-line feed sequences are properly converted to single newline characters. Strictly data files, like master files, might best be read and written in binary mode. This will insure that no alteration of the data occurs except changes explicitly performed by the program.

Quick Note 12.1   Whether to Use Text or Binary File Access Mode

Many files can be accessed in text mode. Files that must appear to the program exactly as they exist in external storage should be accessed in binary mode. This would include executable files, data bases, and other master files.

12.3 Updating Characters in Place in a Disk File

Associated with an external file is an internal file pointer. This pointer must not be confused with a FILE pointer, which uniquely identifies the file. The *internal file pointer* keeps track of the position in the file, and many I/O functions alter its value. For instance, the fgetc() function moves the internal pointer ahead one character, while rewind() resets the pointer to the beginning of the file. The fseek() function can position the pointer to any desired place in the file.

Suppose that after creating our test data file we decide that Space Kadette's phone number should have zeroes in the last four digits rather than the question marks originally placed there. This is because we intend to store the phone number in a long integer field inside a structure, and question mark characters do not make very good numbers. While we could merely edit the test data and make the change, that certainly would be no challenge. So after deciding that a program is in order, we merely need to know how far into the file the four question marks are. Somehow we determine that they are 142 characters away from the start of the file, which means that we can use the SEEK_SET positioning operand of the fseek() function.

The fseek() function has three possible values for its third argument, which is the origin, or point of initial position, relative to which the second argument is applied. These possible values are:

1. SEEK_SET, beginning of file

2. SEEK_CUR, current position in file

3. SEEK_END, end of file

These values are defined in stdio.h. They should be written as shown in capitals.

The second argument of fseek() is used to position the internal file pointer relative to the third position. For example, this coding:

```
fseek(file pointer, (long) -20, SEEK_END);
```

sets the new position in the file to 20 characters before the end of the file. In the same way this example:

```
fseek(file pointer, (long) 50, SEEK_CUR);
```

moves the file pointer 50 characters further into the file. With that in mind, look at our program in Figure 12.4 to change the question marks to zeroes:

```
/*
**   fseek.c - Illustrates Updating in Place Characters in a File
*/

#include <stdio.h>

main()
{
    FILE *file_ptr;
    int input_char;
    static char in_file[] = "subdir/parsetxt";

    if((file_ptr = fopen(in_file, "r+")) != NULL) {    /* NULL means error*/
                /* position to where the phone number is question marks */
        if(fseek(file_ptr, (long) 142, SEEK_SET) == 0) {
            fputc('0', file_ptr);           /* replace the ???? phone number */
            fputc('0', file_ptr);           /* with zeroes */
            fputc('0', file_ptr);
            fputc('0', file_ptr);
                            /* demonstrate that we did what we tried to do */
            if(fseek(file_ptr, (long) 0, SEEK_SET) == 0) {
                while((input_char = fgetc(file_ptr)) != EOF) {
                    fputc(input_char, stdout);
                }
            }
        }
        else {
            perror("fseek to beginning of file failed");
        }
    }
```

(program continued on next page...)

```
        else {
            perror("fseek to find phone number failed");
        }
        fclose(file_ptr);                            /* clean up our act */
    }
    else {                                    /* do some error checking */
        perror("fopen failed");
        fprintf(stderr, "An error occurred opening %s\n", in_file);
    }
}
```

Figure 12.4   Illustrates Updating in Place Characters in a File—fseek.c

This program looks similar to `parsefld.c`, but with some important differences. First, note that the `r+` file mode caused the file to be opened in a manner that allows updating in place. This means that `fgetc()` and `fputc()` can both be used to access and update the file. Second, the first use of `fseek()` positioned the internal file pointer directly to the four question marks so that the next four calls to the `fputc()` function could place zeroes over the question marks. Then the next use of `fseek()` repositioned the internal file pointer to the beginning of the file so that the entire file could be read and written. The `rewind()` function will also reset the internal file pointer to the beginning of a file.

Third, and very important, the `perror()` function is used in this program. `perror()` should be used immediately after the failure of a standard library function. It prints a message to the `stderr` stream. It uses the system variable `errno` to determine what the error code from the failed library call was, so do not invoke any standard library functions between the failed call and the issuing of `perror()`. Most library functions will alter the value found in `errno`, so if it is not possible to call `perror()` immediately, save the contents of `errno` and then replace it before calling `perror()`.

The test data file now looks like this:

```
"Carol Cashout" "1620 Bankflower, Apt. #3G" "New Rich"  UM  54321  5556789
"Space Kadette","16 Star Trek Blvd.","Alpha Centauri",MW,99999,5550000
"Sissy McClure", "123 Barbie Doll Lane", "Clownytown", CV, 77777, 5552642
"I. Q. Physics"   "149 E=MC Square"  "Science Town"  PS   78695   5554791
```

12.4 Line Input Is Not Necessary

In the above programs we used the `fgetc()` function to perform all character input. The `fgets()` function might also be chosen to perform this same type of I/O. We don't recommend that, however, since to write truly safe programs we have to include code to handle the limitations of `fgets()`. These limitations are:

1. The fgets() function has as one of the arguments a maximum number of characters to read. This helps to make it a safer function since its input can be limited to the size of the buffer that is receiving the data. However, this also means that if the buffer is not large enough to hold the largest possible field being read, accommodations must be made to issue another fgets() function to get the rest of the input field.

2. Once the string is read into the program's buffer, the buffer must be scanned character by character anyway. This is no different than using fgetc() to receive the input data.

3. The fgets() function is oriented toward text files; it assumes a newline is present to terminate each line of input. This means that fgets() has difficulty with binary files. The carriage return-line feed sequence could easily appear (incorrectly) in a binary file since a two-byte integer with the decimal value 3338 is the same as the hex characters 0D0A, which is the newline sequence as it appears in an external file. fgets() would read this integer and think that it had come to the end of the line. If the file is opened as a binary file (which it should be) then the carriage return-newline translation is lost, eliminating a major reason for using fgets() in the first place.

It is true that filling a buffer by one call to fgets() is faster than repeatedly invoking the fgetc() function to get the same set of characters. However, if program speed is really an issue, the getc() function—which some compilers implement as a macro (and is consequently faster)—can be used to reduce the performance difference. Most business programs do not really have extreme performance requirements. The issues of programmer productivity, program maintainability, and so on, usually overshadow whether a particular program saves 10 seconds or $1 of the hardware resources each time it executes.

In summary, fgets() does not provide any significant features or power not already available with fgetc(). Further, it brings limitations that must be accounted for in the code if the program is to be bulletproof.

Antibugging Note 12.2   Be wary of fgets() in a production environment

Most programs that use fgets() make assumptions about the size of the input strings and do not account for handling buffer overflow. While fgets() might be acceptable for quick and dirty programs which don't need to be bulletproof, it is not a good choice for code that is to be used in a production environment.

12.5 Creating Structures on Disk Using `fwrite()`

Thus far in this chapter we have only manipulated text files and have performed all input and output on single characters. A large percentage of business data processing, however, is built around record I/O, i.e., operations on groups of characters. This section will demonstrate how to convert the free-form text input file previously described into an array of structures. We will then write that array, element by element, into a disk file.

Referring to our header file `parse.h`, the structure definition `PERSONNEL` can be used to create an array of structures like this:

```
PERSONNEL pers_rec[NBR_TEST_RCDS];
```

which creates an array `pers_rec`, with `NBR_TEST_RCDS` elements. The array is of type `PERSONNEL`, which is a struct of type `personnel`.

The program we will illustrate, `buildrec.c`, uses the file `getfield.c` which was developed above. We need the function `get_field()` to convert the free-form input text into strings and numeric values into internal numeric format. The program will call `get_field()` once for each input field, and will place the retrieved string either into the appropriate element of the array `pers_rec` (where each element is an occurrence of `PERSONNEL`), or into a temporary buffer from which it can be converted into the proper format and placed into the structure. Figure 12.5 presents the program, without the code for the function `get_field()` because we plan on using the same `get_field()` shown above. (Refer to the program `parsefld.c`).

```
/*
** buildrec.c - Builds Array of Structures from Free-Form Input
*/

#define MAIN_PGM

#include "parse.h"                    /* has definitions for these routines */

void read_records(FILE *file_ptr); /* our prototype */

#define NBR_TEST_RCDS  4


PERSONNEL pers_rec[NBR_TEST_RCDS];        /* holds the four test records */
```

```
main()
{
   FILE *file_ptr;
   static char in_file[] = "subdir/parsetxt";
   static char out_file[] = "subdir/dbstruc";

                                          /* do all the input next */
   if((file_ptr = fopen(in_file, "r")) != NULL)  /* NULL means not there */
   {
      read_records(file_ptr);
      fclose(file_ptr);                     /* close the opened file */
   }
   else {                                 /* do some error checking */
      fprintf(stderr, "This error occurred opening file \"%s\" : %s\n",
              in_file, strerror(errno));
   }
   if(found_an_error == TRUE) {
      fprintf(stderr, "An error occurred reading file %s\n", in_file);
   }


                                             /* now all the output */
   if((file_ptr = fopen(out_file, "wb")) != NULL)
   {
      fwrite(pers_rec, sizeof(pers_rec[0]), NBR_TEST_RCDS, file_ptr);
      if(ferror(file_ptr)) {
         fprintf(stderr, "An error occurred writing to file %s\n",
                 out_file);
      }
   }
   else {                                 /* do some error checking */
      fprintf(stderr, "This error occurred opening file \"%s\" : %s\n",
              out_file, strerror(errno));
   }
}

/*
**   read_records() - Called once to read all records
*/

void read_records(FILE *input_file)
{
   int counter;
   char temp_buffer[26];       /* holds strings before numeric conversion */
                                        /* loops once for each record */
   for(counter = 0; counter < NBR_TEST_RCDS; counter++) {
                                                /* get the name */
      get_field(pers_rec[counter].name,
                (sizeof(pers_rec[counter].name) - 1),
                input_file);
```

(program continued on next page...)

```
                                                       /* get the address */
    get_field(pers_rec[counter].addr,
              (sizeof(pers_rec[counter].addr) - 1),
              input_file);
                                                          /* get the city */
    get_field(pers_rec[counter].city,
              (sizeof(pers_rec[counter].city) - 1),
              input_file);
                                                         /* get the state */
    get_field(pers_rec[counter].state,
              (sizeof(pers_rec[counter].state) - 1),
              input_file);
                                            /* get and convert the zip code */
    get_field(temp_buffer, (sizeof(temp_buffer) - 1), input_file);
    pers_rec[counter].zip = atol(temp_buffer);
                                        /* get and convert the phone number */
    get_field(temp_buffer, (sizeof(temp_buffer) - 1), input_file);
    pers_rec[counter].phone = atol(temp_buffer);
                                /* see if end of file occurred unexpectedly */
    if (feof(input_file)) {
       printf("record #%d encountered unexpected EOF\n", counter + 1);
    }
                                /* see if an error occurred unexpectedly */
    if (ferror(input_file)) {
       printf("record #%d encountered unexpected error\n", counter + 1);
    }
  }
}
```

Figure 12.5   Builds an Array of Structures
from Free Form Input—buildrec.c

There are some important things to note in this program. First, the main()
function from buildrec.c has two primary sections, one each to do input and
output, and each is basically an if statement construct. If the input file is present, then the the array of structures pers_rec is built by one invocation of
read_records(), after which the input file is closed. The second section builds
the output file. If no records were read from the input file then the output file
will contain records filled with only binary zeroes. This is because the array of
structures, pers_rec, is defined as a global variable, and global variables are
initialized to binary zero by default.

Second, if the program is unable to open the input file, the strerror() function is used to develop an error message for output to stderr. The strerror()
function uses the system error message variable errno, which contains a value that
identifies the last error encountered by a standard library function (in this case the
fopen() function). Use strerror() to obtain from the system the message text
associated with this last (or any) error. Do not perform any standard library functions between the function that failed and the invocation of strerror() without

saving `errno` someplace where it can be used later. Note that `strerror()` is very similar to `perror()` which we discussed above.

Third, the output file is opened in binary mode. This is essential since opening the file in text mode actuates the carriage return-newline translation (and any other translations required by the computer being utilized). The problem is that since numeric values in internal format are in the records (structures), it is quite possible that one of the variables will have a value which will appear to be the newline character. This character would then be translated upon output. The same problem occurs when the file is later read back into the program.

Fourth, the functions `feof()` and `ferror()` are used to detect the end of file and error conditions, respectively. Note that they are invoked after an attempt has been made to read and convert all the data fields in the entire record. This does not trap an error that occurs on an individual field, but rather associates an error condition merely with a specific record. There are many ways in which error checking can be incorporated into programs. Usually a balance is required between frequent error checking (which would trap all errors immediately after the offending function invocation) and letting the program call an I/O function one or more times again after an error (which will merely return the same error again) until a common error-trapping portion of the code is reached. These compromises in no way alter our basic objective of writing bulletproof code.

Quick Note 12.2 Striving for bulletproof code

One of our basic programming objectives must be to write bulletproof code, which will handle (without aborting) all possible forms of input data. Do not hesitate to incorporate extensive edit checks and error traps into programs. Do not let the programmer be the main person who tests a program, because the programmer has the least incentive to find errors in the code.

Antibugging Note 12.3 Use binary mode I/O on master files

Always use binary mode I/O on any files that contain data items that cannot be translated into other data items by the operating system. Even if the structure (record) which is being read or written does not currently contain numeric values, it easily could in the future.

12.6 Reading and Using Structures from Disk Using `fread()`

We have deciphered free-form input files, converted the resulting strings to an internal format, and then written to disk copies of the structure that contained the input data. The remaining piece of the cycle is to use another program to read the disk file created by `recstruc.c` and verify that the data is stored on the file correctly.

The program `readstrk.c` in Figure 12.6 will do just that. It contains many of the same coding techniques used in earlier programs, but also introduces the function `ftell()` and includes further examples of `fseek()`. In order to make the program more interesting we have written it to access the records on the disk file in reverse order, i.e., the records will be read and displayed in the opposite order from how they are physically positioned on the file. Therefore, "Carol Cashout" will appear last and "I. Q. Physics" will be displayed first.

```
/*
** readstrk.c - Reading structures from a disk file
*/

#define MAIN_PGM

#include "parse.h"                      /* has definitions for these routines */

void read_record(FILE *file_ptr);   /* our prototype */

#define NBR_TEST_RCDS  4

PERSONNEL pers_rec;                                  /* holds one test record */

main()
{
    FILE *file_ptr;
    unsigned long file_size;
    int nbr_rcds;
    static char in_file[] = "subdir/dbstruc";

                                                      /* do all the input next */
    if((file_ptr = fopen(in_file, "rb")) != NULL) /* NULL means not there */
    {
        fseek(file_ptr, (long) 0, SEEK_END);      /* position to end of file */
                                      /* compute number of records in the file */
        nbr_rcds = ftell(file_ptr) / sizeof(pers_rec);
        while(nbr_rcds--) {
                        /* position to start of record, working backwards */
            fseek(file_ptr, (long) (nbr_rcds * sizeof(pers_rec)), SEEK_SET);
            read_record(file_ptr);
            if (feof(file_ptr)) {
                fprintf(stderr, "record #%d had unexpected EOF\n",
                        nbr_rcds + 1);
            }
                                      /* see if an error occurred unexpectedly */
            if (ferror(file_ptr)) {
                fprintf(stderr, "record #%d had unexpected error\n",
                        nbr_rcds + 1);
            }
        }
```

```
      fclose(file_ptr);                              /* close the opened file */
   }
   else {                                            /* do some error checking */
      fprintf(stderr, "This error occurred opening file \"%s\" : %s\n",
            in_file, strerror(errno));
   }
}

/*
**   read_record() - Called once for each record on the disk file
*/

void read_record(FILE *input_file)
{
                                                     /* read the record */
   fread(&pers_rec, sizeof(pers_rec), 1, input_file);
   printf("Name  : %s\nAddr  : %s\nCity  : %s\nState : %s\nZip    : %ld\n"
          "Phone : %ld\n\n", pers_rec.name,
                             pers_rec.addr,
                             pers_rec.city,
                             pers_rec.state,
                             pers_rec.zip,
                             pers_rec.phone);
}
```

Figure 12.6   Reading Structures from a Disk File—readstrk.c

The program down through this statement

```
fseek(file_ptr, (long) 0, SEEK_END);
```

is similar to the others in this chapter. This line, however, is positioning the file to its very end, and enables this expression from the next statement:

```
ftell(file_ptr)
```

to return the number of bytes in the file. By dividing that size by the size of an individual record we can determine the number of records in the file, a value kept in the variable nbr_rcds. We used nbr_rcds to drive a loop that reads the records, and within the loop we computed the starting location of each record by multiplying the relative record number by the size of an individual record. Once position in the file was obtained, the FILE pointer, file_ptr, was passed to the function that actually reads the file. Although the records were written to the file from an array of structures, they are read one at a time. The function read_record() reads only one record at a time. It then displays each field of the record to verify that the data was accessed correctly.

Here is the output of the program `readstrk.c`:

```
Name  : I. Q. Physics
Addr  : 149 E=MC Square
City  : Science Town
State : PS
Zip   : 78695
Phone : 5554791

Name  : Sissy McClure
Addr  : 123 Barbie Doll Lane
City  : Clownytown
State : CV
Zip   : 77777
Phone : 5552642

Name  : Space Kadette
Addr  : 16 Star Trek Blvd.
City  : Alpha Centauri
State : MW
Zip   : 99999
Phone : 5550000

Name  : Carol Cashout
Addr  : 1620 Bankflower, Apt. #3G
City  : New Rich
State : UM
Zip   : 54321
Phone : 5556789
```

12.7 Self-Check

These statements are True or False. The answers are given at the end.

1. Standard files are always present and do not need to be opened or closed.

2. The FILE pointer for standard file names can always be used on the left side of an assignment.

3. The fopen() function returns a NULL if there is a problem opening the file.

4. After opening a file there is an internal file pointer which represents the position within the file where the input or output is being performed.

5. Two backslashes are needed inside strings (to represent one backslash) because one backslash merely indicates that the following character is to be taken literally.

6. The ftell() function serves double duty, both positioning and reporting position within a file.

7. The ANSI standard defines only three standard file handles: input, output, and error.

8. The `extern` keyword is used to provide access to variables defined in another source file.

9. Line input and record input are the same thing in C.

10. In binary files any carriage returns that appear before a line feed are dropped.

11. The internal file pointer can be positioned relative to the first, end or current location in the file.

12. `SEEK_SET` is a value passed to the `ftell()` function.

13. When reading binary files no changes are automatically made to the characters that are read.

14. The function `fopen()` returns a NULL if the requested file cannot be opened.

15. Line input is not convenient since the input lines can be split across two buffers.

16. If a binary file is read as a text file, an integer may appear as a carriage return-line feed sequence.

17. The `sizeof` operator should be used when reading data to fill a structure.

Answers

1. T	2. F	3. T	4. T	5. T	6. F	7. T	8. T	9. F
10. F	11. T	12. F	13. T	14. T	15. T	16. T	17. T	

12.8 Review Program—An Indexed Data Base with Views

As you have learned in this chapter, disk files can be accessed in sequential and random modes. We will illustrate both of these techniques in this review program in addition to other basic file manipulations. We have also included rudimentary error trapping for each file access function call. You should examine these code sections carefully.

In order to write a complete program, we will utilize functions we have coded in previous review programs, notably the following:

Function	Chapter Reference	Description
shellsort()	10	Shell sort routine
ascending()	10	ascending compare
get_input_field()	7	user input routine
cls()	7	clear screen routine

Of the four, only `shellsort()` has been modified to fit our specific application.

☐ *Design Specifications*

In Chapter 10 we coded a Shell sort function designed to sort an array of pointers to strings. We saw how a pointer array could be used to produce different views of the string array itself. Our shellsort() function did not modify the physical arrangement of the strings themselves, only the pointers.

A similar design, using disk files, can be accomplished as follows:

1. Create a master data base file consisting of records each containing the sort compare value. In our example, each record will consist of a three-character string.

2. Create a second file, the index file, consisting of records that contain the record number of each corresponding data file record. Records in the index file effectively map or image the organization of the database file itself.

3. To create different views (ascending, descending, etc.) of the data base file, sort the index file records as pointers to the data base file records. This is precisely analogous to sorting a pointer array, as we did in Chapter 10.

Perhaps an illustration will clarify our file-mapping scheme. Consider two files, datafile and indexfile whose record contents are as follows:

INDEXFILE	POINTS TO	DATAFILE
0	qrs	qrs
1	abc	abc
2	hij	hij

As with our pointer example, we can produce an ascending view of datafile by rearranging indexfile's records as follows:

INDEXFILE	POINTS TO	DATAFILE
1	abc	qrs
2	hij	abc
0	qrs	hij

Accessing the record values in indexfile sequentially and printing the record value pointed to in datafile will produce the desired result.

Applying these principles in this program, we will build a menu-driven application that allows two basic functions:

1. Appending records to the database file.

2. Printing an ascending list of the records in this file.

The first menu function will consist of opening the datafile, allowing entry of record values (three-character strings), writing the records sequentially, and closing the file. Our second menu function will be slightly more complicated. First, both datafile and indexfile will be opened and their respective number of records determined. If they are not equal, it is assumed that the index file is no longed valid and will be rebuilt. After being sorted (using a modified `shellsort()` function) the indexes will be resident in memory for fast access. The records in datafile will be printed in order by referencing this array sequentially. Only one record at a time will be memory-resident from datafile. After the datafile records are printed, both files will be closed.

Error-trapping routines will be coded for some of the file access functions. It will be left as an exercise to fully develop the program by including error traps in all necessary locations.

□ *Program Design*

Now, let's look at pseudocode for `append()` and `list_file_ascending()`:

```
function append(datafile)
string datafile                          path name of database file

    print(<function title>)
    if (<open(datafile) okay>)
       <inform user how to exit this function>
       while (<user wishes to enter more data>)
          <get data for datafile record>
          if (<write record to datafile not okay>)
             print(<error message>)
          end if
       end while
    else
       print(<error message>)
    end if
    close(datafile)
    return
end function



function list_file_ascending(datafile, indexfile)
string datafile                  path name to database file
string indexfile                 path name to index file
```

(program continued on next page...)

```
        if (<open(datafile) not okay>)
            print(<error message>)
            return
        end if
        if (<open(indexfile) not okay>)
            print(<error message>)
            return
        end if
        <index file routine goes here>

        if (<# records in datafile does not equal # records in indexfile>)
            if (<allocate memory for index array not okay>)
                print(<error message>)
                return
            end if
            <initialize index array with 0—> record count in datafile>
            <shellsort index array>
            rewind(indexfile)
            <write sorted index array to indexfile>
        end if

        rewind(indexfile)
        print(<report heading>)
        read(<1st indexfile record>)
        while (<not end of indexfile>)
            seek(<record in datafile per indexfile value>)
            read(<datafile record>)
            print(<datafile record value>)
            read(<next indexfile record>)
        while end

        close(indexfile)
        close(datafile)
        return
    end function
```

Note that append() simply writes records sequentially to datafile as input by the user. A function we coded in an earlier review program, get_field_input(), is used to retrieve the user's entries. Our ascending list function, list_file_ascending(), is more complicated. First, both files are opened and their length, in number of records, is compared. If they are not equal, the index file entries are rebuilt by Shell sorting an index array. Next the record values stored in datafile are listed according to the record pointers stored in indexfile. We have not included the pseudocode for our modified shellsort() since the algorithm has not changed. Only slight modifications are necessary to allow the function to work on disk files rather than arrays.

☐ *Design Implementation*

```
/*-------------------------------------------------------------------
  dbview.c
  Example data and index file manipulation using high-level file
  I/O function calls.  Index file contains an image (record mapping)
  of the data file records sorted in ascending order.
-------------------------------------------------------------------*/
#include <stdio.h>
#include <stdlib.h>
#include <string.h>

#define LINES 25                        /* # display lines for cls() */

#define TRUE 1                          /* logical true */
#define FALSE 0                         /* logical false */

#define DATABASE "dbview.dat"           /* data base file */
#define INDEX "dbview.ndx"              /* data base index file */

#define IN_CHAR '#'                     /* input character for mask */
/*
  function prototypes
*/
int  get_field_input(char *, char *, char *);
void shellsort(unsigned long *, unsigned long, int (*)(), FILE *);
int  ascending(char *, char *);
void append(char *);
void list_file_ascending(char *, char *);
void cls(void);
int  get_chars_safely(int, char *);

struct template1 {                      /* image for data records */
    char value[4];
    };

typedef struct template1 DATA_RECORD;

struct template2 {                      /* image for index records */
    long rec_num;
    };

typedef struct template2 INDEX_RECORD;
```

(program continued on next page...)

```
/*
 menu list to display
*/
char menu[] = { "\n\
CHAPTER 12 REVIEW PROGRAM MAIN MENU\n\n\
<A>ppend database\n\
<L>ist file ascending\n\
e<X>it program\n\n" };



main()
{
    char choice;
    do {
        cls();                          /* clear screen */
        printf("%s", menu);             /* print the menu */
        printf("Enter your choice - ");
        choice = toupper(getchar());    /* get user's choice */
        while(getchar() != '\n') {      /* flush the buffer */
            ;
        }
        switch (choice)                 /* get user's choice */
           {
           case 'A':                    /* append datafile choice */
              {
              cls();                     /* clear screen */
/*
 append records to data file
*/
              append(DATABASE);
              break;
              }
           case 'L':                    /* list file choice */
              {
              cls();                     /* clear screen */
/*
 shellsort via index file and print the results
*/
              list_file_ascending(DATABASE, INDEX);
              printf("\nPress RETURN to continue...\n");
              while(getchar() != '\n') { /* wait for user, flush the buffer */
                 ;
              }
              break;
              }
```

```
         case 'X':                            /* exit program choice */
             {
             break;
             }
         default :                            /* invalid choice */
             {
             cls();
             printf("Invalid menu choice.  Press RETURN to continue.\n\n");
             while(getchar() != '\n') { /* wait on user, flush the buffer */
                 ;
             }
             break;
             }
         }
     }
   while (choice != 'X');                      /* cycle menu if not exit */

   return;
}

/*-------------------------------------------------------------------
 int append(datafile)
 Append records to datafile.  Records are appended sequentially.
--------------------------------------------------------------------*/
void append(datafile)
char *datafile;
{
   FILE *dat;                          /* file pointer to datafile */
   DATA_RECORD drec;                   /* data record image */

   printf("Append File Function\n");
   printf("--------------------\n\n");
   if (dat = fopen(datafile, "a + b")) {        /* if open is good */
/*
 read data from user and write to file until user wishes to quit
*/
       printf("HIT <RETURN> ON BLANK FIELD TO EXIT.\n\n");
       while (get_field_input("Data ", "###", drec.value) && !ferror(dat)) {
           printf("\n");
           if (fwrite((DATA_RECORD *)&drec, sizeof(drec), 1, dat) != 1) {
               perror("Error writing datafile\n");
           }
       }
   }
   else {
       perror("Error opening datafile\n");
   }
   fclose(dat);
   return;
}
```

(program continued on next page...)

```
/*-------------------------------------------------------------------
 void list_file_ascending(datafile, indexfile)
 Prints the records contained in datafile in ascending order.
 Records stored in indexfile point to the records in datafile.
 Function calls a modified version of shellsort() which sorts the
 indexfile records.
 -----------------------------------------------------------------*/
void list_file_ascending(datafile, indexfile)
char *datafile, *indexfile;
{
    FILE *dat, *ndx;                     /* file pointers for data and */
                                         /* index files */
    DATA_RECORD drec;                    /* data record image */
    INDEX_RECORD irec;                   /* index record image */
    unsigned long dsize, isize, j;       /* some variables we need */
    unsigned long *index;

/*
 open datafile and indexfiles
 include error traps for open errors
*/
    if (!(dat = fopen(datafile, "rb"))) {
        perror("Error opening datafile");
        return;
    }
    if (!(ndx = fopen(indexfile, "rb"))) {
/*
 if file doesn't exist, try to create it, otherwise exit with error
*/
        if (!(ndx = fopen(indexfile, "w+b"))) {
            perror("Error opening indexfile");
            return;
        }
    }

    fseek(dat, (long) 0, SEEK_END);    /* set pointer to end of each file */
    fseek(ndx, (long) 0, SEEK_END);

    dsize = ftell(dat) / sizeof(drec); /* compute #  records in each file */
    isize = ftell(ndx) / sizeof(irec);

    if (dsize != isize) {                /* if not equal, make updated index */
        j = dsize;
        fclose(ndx);                     /* close indexfile */
/*
 reopen indexfile for reading, writing, destroying previous contents
*/
        if (!(ndx = fopen(indexfile, "w+b"))) {
            perror("Error opening indexfile");
            return;
        }
```

```
/*
 make room for the index array and check for memory allocation error
*/
     if (!(index = (unsigned long *)malloc(dsize * sizeof(long)))) {
         printf("Error allocating memory for indexfile array.\n");
         return;
     }

/*
 load the index array in memory with sequential numbers from 0 to dsize - 1
*/
     while (j--) {
         index[j] = j;
     }
/*
 now, sort the array with our modified Shell sort
*/
     shellsort(index, dsize, ascending, dat);

     rewind(ndx);                       /* rewind to start of indexfile */
     for (j = 0; j < dsize; ++j) {      /* write the sorted indexes */
         fwrite((long *)&index[j], sizeof(long), 1, ndx);
     }
   }
/*
 read in indexfile records in one large chunk
*/
   rewind(ndx);
   fread((unsigned long *)index, dsize * sizeof(unsigned long), 1, ndx);

   printf("Record\tValue\n");
   printf("------\t-----\n");
/*
 now, list the datafile using the indexfile record values
*/
   for (j = 0; j < dsize; ++j) {
/*
 move pointer in datafile according to index record value (a record #)
 this sets us up for a random read
*/
     fseek(dat, index[j] * sizeof(drec), SEEK_SET);
/*
 read, randomly, the datafile value (a string) into d
*/
     fread((DATA_RECORD *)&drec, sizeof(drec), 1, dat);
```

(program continued on next page...)

```
/*
 print it out
*/
      printf("%ld\t%s\n", index[j], drec.value);
   }

   fclose(ndx);                              /* close both files */
   fclose(dat);
   free(index);                             /* free index array memory */
   return;
}
/*-------------------------------------------------------------------
 void shellsort(list, n, compare, datafile)

    parm              type             desc
---------------:---------------:-----------------------------------
   list            unsigned         array of unsigned long integers
                   long *
   n               unsigned int     number of pointers in the array
   compare         int (*)()        pointer to comparison function



    ret value       type             desc
---------------:---------------:-----------------------------------------
   ---             void
-------------------------------------------------------------------*/
void shellsort(list, n, compare, dat)
unsigned long *list;
unsigned long n;
int (* compare)();
FILE *dat;
{
   DATA_RECORD drec1, drec2;
   unsigned int gap, limit, j;          /* gap - interval gap size */
                                        /* limit - limit for compare */
                                        /* j - our loop variable and index */
   gap = n >> 1;                        /* same as n/2 only faster */
   while (gap) {                        /* while gap exists */
      limit = n - gap;                  /* set upper limit */
      j = 0;                            /* start with first element */
      while (j < limit) {               /* while not at limit */
/*
 perform the compare as specified in compare function
*/
         fseek(dat, list[j] * sizeof(drec1), SEEK_SET);
         fread((DATA_RECORD *)&drec1, sizeof(drec1), 1, dat);

         fseek(dat, list[j + gap] * sizeof(drec2), SEEK_SET);
         fread((DATA_RECORD *)&drec2, sizeof(drec2), 1, dat);
```

```
              if ((*compare)(drec1.value, drec2.value)) {
                  int i, xchg_flag;              /* i - temporary index */
                                                 /* xchg_flag - backup flag */

                  i = j;
                  xchg_flag = TRUE;
                  while (xchg_flag) {            /* if swap has occurred */
                      unsigned long temp;
/*
 swap the array elements (record indexes)
*/
                      temp = list[i];
                      list[i] = list[i + gap];
                      list[i + gap] = temp;
                      i -= gap;                  /* back up to previous interval */
/*
 see if previous swap is propagating backwards in list
*/
                      fseek(dat, list[i] * sizeof(drec1), SEEK_SET);
                      fread((DATA_RECORD *)&drec1, sizeof(drec1), 1, dat);

                      fseek(dat, list[i + gap] * sizeof(drec2), SEEK_SET);
                      fread((DATA_RECORD *)&drec2, sizeof(drec2), 1, dat);

                      if (i < 0 || (*compare)(drec1.value, drec2.value) == 0) {
                          xchg_flag = FALSE;
                      }
                  }
              }
          ++j;
          }
      gap >>= 1;                                 /* same as gap/2 only faster */
   }
   return;
}

/*-------------------------------------------------------------------
 int ascending(s1, s2)

    parm            type            desc
---------------!---------------!------------------------------------
 s1               char *          string 1
 s2               char *          string 2

    ret value       type            desc
---------------!---------------!------------------------------------
 TRUE             int             string 1 > string 2
 FALSE            int             string 1 <= string 2
-----------------------------------------------------------------*/
```

(program continued on next page...)

```
int ascending(s1, s2)
char *s1, *s2;
{
   if (strcmp(s1, s2) > 0) {              /* see if s1 > s2 */
      return(TRUE);
   }
   return(FALSE);
}




/*-------------------------------------------------------------------
  int get_field_input(prompt, edit_mask, dest_buffer)

  Generate a maskable entry field and store input as a string into
  the destination buffer. The edit mask is used as a template only
  and is not included in the returned input string.  This function is
  portable across all environments supporting the C language.

  The user input is terminated by pressing the <Return> (or <Enter>)
  key.  No validation checking is performed on the input.

  parm           type           description
  ...................................................................
  prompt         char[]         the user prompt
  edit_mask      char[]         the edit mask, a string consisting of
                                characters & input characters;
                                the input characters are defined in the
                                macro IN_CHAR
  dest_buffer    char[]         buffer where input retrieved is stored; will
                                contain the actual characters input not
                                including the edit_mask string; should be
                                dimensioned at least field_length + 1 to
                                accommodate null character appended to
                                characters retrieved

  return         type           description
  ...................................................................
  ---            int            the actual number of characters retrieved
                                which will be <= edit_mask
-------------------------------------------------------------------*/
int get_field_input(prompt, edit_mask, dest_buffer)
char prompt[], edit_mask[], dest_buffer[];
{
   int spaces_over;                       /* used to position cursor for input */
   int field_length;                      /* # of spaces in edit_mask */
   char temp_buffer[80];                  /* temporary buffer for user input */
```

```
   printf("%s", prompt);              /* print user prompt */
   printf("%s", edit_mask);           /* print edit mask string */
   printf("\n");                      /* move down to next display row */
/*
 calculate cursor positioning
*/
   spaces_over = strlen(prompt);   /* first half of spacing adjustment */
   {
   int i = 0;                      /* find first valid position in mask */
   while(edit_mask[i] != '\0' && edit_mask[i] != IN_CHAR)
      {
      ++i;
      }
   spaces_over += i;               /* second half of spacing adjustment */
   }
/*
 space over to proper position on display under the edit mask
*/
   {
   int i = spaces_over;
   while(i--)
      {
      putchar(' ');
      }
   }
/*
 get the user input
*/
   get_chars_safely(strlen(edit_mask), temp_buffer);
   {
   int i = 0, j = 0;
/*
 move user input to destination buffer stripping out mask characters
*/
   while(edit_mask[i] != '\0' && temp_buffer[i] != '\0')
      {
      if(edit_mask[i] == IN_CHAR)
         {
         dest_buffer[j++] = temp_buffer[i];
         }
      ++i;
      }
   dest_buffer[j] = '\0';                  /* tack on null terminator */
   }
   return(strlen(dest_buffer));            /* send back the input length */
}
```

(program continued on next page...)

```
/*---------------------------------------------------------------
    get_chars_safely()
        This function accepts characters from standard input until one of
        three conditions is met:
            1. As many characters as max_num_chars have been entered.
            2. End of file on standard input has been reached.
            3. A newline is received on standard input.
        You must define where_chars_go at least as big as max_num_chars + 1.
        A \0 is placed in where_chars_go after the last character received.
        The newline, if received, is not placed into the string.
        The function returns the actual number of characters in the string
            without counting the terminating null.
        No characters are left on the input stream.
        The defined constant EOF is located in <stdio.h>.
    ---------------------------------------------------------------*/
int  get_chars_safely (max_num_chars, where_chars_go)
int  max_num_chars;
char where_chars_go[];
{
    int input_char, index = 0;          /* initialize the subscript to zero */
    while (index < max_num_chars &&
            (input_char = getchar()) != EOF &&
            input_char != '\n'
        ) {
        where_chars_go[index] = input_char;      /* put character in array */
        index++;
    }
    where_chars_go[index] = '\0';  /* the terminating null makes a string */
    while (input_char != EOF && input_char != '\n') {
        input_char = getchar();                     /* flush the input stream */
    }
    return (index);
}


/*---------------------------------------------------------------
  void cls()
  clear the screen
  (print LINES newlines)
  ---------------------------------------------------------------*/
void cls()
{
    int i;

    for (i = 0; i < LINES; ++i) {
        printf("\n");
    }
    return;
}
```

In this review program we have used most of the major file-pointer disk access functions. `append()` uses sequential access while `list_file_ascending()` uses both sequential and random modes. Error traps are included in several file access function calls although it will be left as an exercise to add all the necessary error traps. This is an often overlooked aspect of programming to which you should pay close attention.

☐ *Program Output*

```
CHAPTER 12 REVIEW PROGRAM MAIN MENU

<A>ppend database
<L>ist file ascending
e<X>it program

Enter your choice - l


[screen cleared]


Error opening datafile: No such file or directory

Press RETURN to continue...


[screen cleared]


CHAPTER 12 REVIEW PROGRAM MAIN MENU

<A>ppend database
<L>ist file ascending
e<X>it program

Enter your choice - a


[screen cleared]
```

(program continued on next page...)

```
Append File Function
--------------------

HIT <RETURN> ON BLANK FIELD TO EXIT.


Data ###
     qrs

Data ###
     abc

Data ###
     wxy

Data ###
     z!a

Data ###
     hij

Data ###
     nop

Data ###
     def

Data ###
     tuv

Data ###
     klm

Data ###



[screen cleared]


CHAPTER 12 REVIEW PROGRAM MAIN MENU

<A>ppend database
<L>ist file ascending
e<X>it program

Enter your choice - l


[screen cleared]
```

```
Record   Value
------   -----
1        abc
6        def
4        hij
8        klm
5        nop
0        qrs
7        tuv
2        wxy
3        z!@

Press RETURN to continue...

[screen cleared]



CHAPTER 12 REVIEW PROGRAM MAIN MENU

<A>ppend database
<L>ist file ascending
e<X>it program

Enter your choice - x
```

Our first menu selection, l (List file ascending), causes an error to be generated. Note how the error message is constructed automatically by the `perror()` library function. Part of the error message is ours and the other part "looked up" by `perror()`. Refer to the documentation of the compiler being used for specifics. Our second menu choice, a (Append database), allows us to append data to our simple database. We have chosen to enter the sample string list defined in the Chapter 10 review program. Note the file access mode used in `append()` and the coding of `fwrite()`. Our third choice, l, works this go-around since datafile now exists. Carefully study all aspects of both `append()` and the modified Shell sort routine.

This is certainly a review program that you should actually type in, compile, link, and run. It is difficult to acquire a real appreciation for disk access techniques without actually seeing the disk drive light blink in response to your code (assuming that such a light is present and visible.)

Points to Study

1. Methods of file access used, both sequential and random.

2. Error-trapping routines incorporated and where they are absent.

3. Method used in `list_file_ascending()` to indirectly retrieve the proper records from datafile.

4. Modifications necessary in `shellsort()` to act on disk files rather than arrays.

12.9 Exercises

1. Modify the review program to include error-trapping routines for all file access function calls. Listed below are return codes for all functions that were used in the program and require monitoring for a possible error.

| FUNCTION | RETURN | |
	SUCCESS	FAILURE
fopen	FILE *	NULL
fclose	0	EOF
fread	# items to read	short count
fwrite	same as fread	same as fread
fseek	current position of file pointer	-1L
rewind	0	nonzero number

* 2. Write a program similar to the review program, but use binary tree techniques instead of applying a Shell sort algorithm to an index array. Design the append() function to automatically update the index file. This will be in contrast to our review program that maintains the index file in list_file_ascending(). Include provisions to print the data base data in at least two views, ascending and descending order.

3. Write a program to perform the following:
   a. Request a filename from the user.
   b. Open the file for reading.
   c. Read the file and perform a file compression algorithm (given below).
   d. Print the compressed file, inserting flags in the printout to indicate where compression has been applied.

The following compression algorithm should be used:

Compress "whitespace" (spaces, tabs, etc.) where appropriate. For example, if four spaces in a row were encountered, the sequence could be represented in two bytes of storage, rather than four. In hexadecimal notation we would encode:

    20 20 20 20 = 20 04
    (4 spaces) (1 space, 4 times)

You may modify this basic compression scheme in any manner of your choosing as long as the resulting file conforms to the requirements.

4. "Pretty printer" is a general term used to describe a class of utility programs that produce formatted printer listings of C source files. Most of these programs paginate the listing and include page numbers, source code line numbers, and a simple page heading. Write a "pretty printer" with the following features:

   a. Allow the source file to be specified as a command-line argument.
   b. Print the file properly paginated and with source code line numbers.
   c. Include statistics at the end of the printed listing including the number of source code lines and a list of functions defined in the source itself.

* 5. Modify the mailing list program in Chapter 7, exercise 4, to include the following features:

   a. Storage of the mailing list to a disk file.
   b. Ability to print the mailing list in order by last/first name or zip code.

   Your program should maintain the file entirely from disk including additions and deletions of mailing list records. You may use separate index files to produce different printed views of the mailing list records if you so desire.

6. Write a utility program that searches a file for a specific string pattern specified by the user. The string to be located may be retrieved as a command line argument or under dynamic program control via an input field. Your program should report all instances of the string and print the entire "sentence" where the string is used in the file. This will entail locating carriage return-line feed "boundaries" in the file that confine the string itself. For example, suppose the file to be searched looks as follows:

   Mary had a little lamb.
   Its fleece was white as snow.
   Everywhere that Mary went
   Her lamb was sure to go.

   Now suppose our string search utility is called `findit`. Typing

   `findit Mary`   `(MS-DOS environment)`

   or,

   `findit.out Mary`   `(UNIX environment)`

   would produce the output:

   Mary had a little lamb.
   Everywhere that Mary went

7. Discuss the relative difficulty, advantages, and disadvantages of changing the module `getfield.c` so that it would accept, and optionally discard trailing space characters in a field. What changes would have to be made to the code? What other functions, if any, would have to be sacrificed? What additional features would be gained by making such a change?

* 8. Using the code presented in this chapter as a base, produce a functional replacement for the `fscanf()` function.

* 9. Add logic to the module `recstruc.c` to check for a situation in which no more input fields are expected, yet end of record has not yet occurred. This could happen if delimiting double quotes were not placed around a text field, and the text field contained a space or comma.

* advanced exercises

12.10 Pretest

□ *Multiple Choice*

Circle one correct answer to each of the following:

1. What is wrong with the following code fragment?

```
char filename[] = "testfile";

fopen(filename, "rb");
```

     a. `"testfile"` is not a valid pathname.
     b. `fopen()` is not used with character strings.
     c. A file pointer has not been specified.
     d. The correct syntax should be `filename = fopen(filename, "rb");`.

2. Which function listed below does not return an error code?
     a. `putchar`
     b. `fopen`
     c. `fclose`
     d. `rewind`

3. To accomplish file pointer, random-read access of a file's data, you could use which set of functions listed below?
     a. `open, lseek, fread, rewind`
     b. `fopen, fseek, fread, rewind`
     c. `fopen, fread, rewind, lseek`
     d. `rewind, open, fseek, read`

4. Upon encountering an error, fopen() returns:
   a. EOF
   b. 0
   c. -1L
   d. NULL

5. To locate a given record in a random-access file, which formula below would apply relative to the beginning of the file?
   a. record number * byte offset of the record
   b. record number * size of each record in bytes
   c. (record number * size of each record in bytes) / file size
   d. none of the above

6. Why should the code returned by fseek() be checked for an error?
   a. The file may not be open.
   b. There may be a hardware failure.
   c. The requested pointer move may extend past EOF.
   d. All of the above.
   e. a. and b.

7. If an open file is not closed, what could result, depending on the particular application?
   a. The number of open files could exceed the limit of the operating system.
   b. The file could be "lost".
   c. The next fopen() statement to the same file could cause a system "crash".
   d. Nothing.

8. A "pathname" consists of:
   a. a filename.
   b. a directory path and a filename.
   c. a directory path only.
   d. a string eight characters long.

9. The rewind() function can be replaced by:
   a. ftell()
   b. fopen()
   c. fseek()
   d. fflush()

10. The extern keyword is used to:
    a. Identify a source file which is held in a separate location.
    b. Name a data file which will be accessed at a later time.
    c. Address a data item which is defined outside this source file.
    d. Define a pointer to a system variable.

13

The Preprocessor

T he preprocessor is the part of the C compiler that first sees the source code. By using directives that serve as a language in their own right it acts as a smart text editor and processes the file before passing the altered file on to the rest of the compiler. Understanding and using the preprocessor features can bring an additional dimension of power and flexibility to C programming.

After studying this chapter, you will be able to do the following:

1. Explain when the preprocessor phases of the compiler take place.

2. Show how to perform simple text substitutions with the `#define` directive.

3. Demonstrate how to create preprocessor macros.

4. Describe the concept of conditional compilation.

5. Use the preprocessor to process files without compiling a program.

13.1 Preprocessor Concepts

A preprocessor has always been a part of most C compilers. The original features of the preprocessor were present in UNIX, while the ANSI C standard provides additional features which enhance and facilitate good programming practices.

Available to the programmer as part of the preprocessor are certain directives and operators which are very different from commands like `while`, `for`, and `if`. These directives and operators all begin with a `#` sign and their evaluation by the preprocessor and effect on the resulting program are very different from the processing of commands like `while`, `for`, and `if`.

The ANSI C standard requires that the translation from C source to executable code take place in a phased manner. The first few phases of the compiler involve changing the source program text into *tokens* which the compiler can better understand. A good example of this type of process is seen when the MS/PC-DOS TYPE command is used on a BASIC program which has not been stored in ASCII format. The BASIC program has been stored as tokens, which is a form more easily understood by a machine and consequently less easily understood by people.

The evaluation of preprocessing directives occurs in the early phases of translation. Specifically it occurs before those phases that are thought of as being the compiler. By the time commands like `while` are evaluated all preprocessing directives will have been fully examined and their effect expressed in the source code. Although it is not technically precise we can think of the preprocessor as a smart text editor. This comes from the fact that most of the things the preprocessor does could be accomplished by actually using a text editor.

Below is a list of the ANSI standard preprocessing directives. We'll describe each of these, give examples of their use, and show how the preprocessor can help C programmers be more productive.

```
#include
#define
#undef
#if
#ifdef
#ifndef
#else
#elif
#endif
#line
#error
#pragma
##
#
defined
```

Quick Note 13.1 The Preprocessor

The preprocessor is merely a smart text editor and has absolutely no regard for the C code it creates. Whether the resulting code can be compiled correctly is of no concern to the preprocessor. It assumes no responsibility to create syntactically correct code.

13.2 Macros and the #define Directive

The #define directive creates macros, and these macros can be of two forms. They can be used to perform simple replacements for source program text (called *object-like* macros in the ANSI C standard), or they can be full featured, complete with arguments and parameters (called *function-like* macros). Macros expand into *in-line code*, which is faster than a function call but can increase the size of the program more than a function call if the macro is used many times.

Simple replacement (using object-like macros) is performed whenever the identifier named in a #define is found outside of a string literal or other name in the C source code. This means that:

```
#define ONE 1                /* this defines ONE as 1 */
```

will replace the ONE in this statement:

```
printf("The number is %d\n", ONE);
```

but not the ONE found here inside a string:

```
char msg[] = "This is ONE of a kind";
```

and also not the ONE found here inside the name DONE:

```
int DONE = 1;    /* uppercase not recommended for variables */
```

The fact that macro names are no longer replaced (expanded) if they occur inside strings is a significant change to the language.

If the defined identifier name appears inside its own definition it is not replaced again during the macro expansion. This means that

```
#define ONE ONE 1         /* this is legal, and expands once */
```

does not continue expanding indefinitely. Rather, ONE is replaced by ONE 1, and the net effect is that the macro name is left in the program. Note that comments can be placed on the same line as the macro without any effect on the macro expansion or resulting definition. Comments are removed from the source file before any analysis of preprocessing directives takes place.

An existing macro name can also be used in the definition of another macro, like this:

```
#define ONE   1
#define TWO   (ONE + ONE)
```

which causes TWO to become 1 + 1. If these two directives were reversed an error would occur because ONE would be used before it was defined. Here's another example:

```
#define NESTMAC(x) ((x) + 1)
...
NESTMAC(NESTMAC(4));
```

will generate this statement:

```
((((4) + 1)) + 1);
```

The NESTMAC macro works, even though some of the above examples did not, since the name NESTMAC does not appear inside its own body. That it does appear inside its own argument list when the macro is used is not the same thing as using a macro name in its own body.

Macros can also have parameters, just like functions. When a function-like macro is coded arguments are provided to replace the parameters as the macro expands. The list of identifiers, operators, literals, and other macro names that can be coded after the macro name is called the *macro body*. The parameters are included in this list.

Unlike those in a function the parameters in a macro body do not have a particular data type, i.e., there are no integer parameters, float parameters, and so on. Parameters are replaced by the argument of the same name when the parameter name is found as a token in the macro body. We won't try to fully explain the concept of tokens. Rather, a few examples will demonstrate what is and isn't a token. If we create these macros:

```
#define ONE 1
#define MAC1(x)   ((x) + (x) + myx + ONE)
```

then there are only two x tokens, not three. The x in myx is not a token and is not replaced by whatever argument is supplied when the macro is invoked. The macro MAC1 also illustrates that macros, arguments, and other items can be used together in a macro body.

Likewise,

```
#define MAC2(x)   printf("The value of x is %d\n", (x));
```

has only one token, not two. The x inside the string literal is not replaced by the value of the supplied argument. This means that macro parameters as well as macro names are not replaced if they occur inside string literals. Therefore, the expansion of MAC2(hours) would be:

```
printf("The value of x is %d\n", (hours));
```

Parentheses should be used liberally in the body of a macro. This helps insure that no unintended grouping of operands occurs, as would happen in this case:

```
#define DOUBLE(x)   (x * 2)
DOUBLE(y + y);
```

The expression DOUBLE creates is:

```
(y + y * 2);
```

which is certainly not the ((y + y) * 2) that we intended. Rather, DOUBLE should be defined like this:

```
#define DOUBLE(x)   ((x) * 2)
```

Antibugging Note 13.1   Use parentheses around macro arguments

Whenever possible in the body of a macro, use parentheses around each
macro argument. Also place parentheses around all arithmetic expressions,
including the entire macro body if it is an arithmetic expression.

One common use of #define is to give a name to literal strings so that it is
more convenient to use them multiple times in a program. If the string is too long,
it can be extended to a second line, like this:

```
#define LONG "first part of very long string, which is continued with a "
             "second part on the next line"
```

By definition a #define directive terminates when the end of the line (i.e.
newline) is reached, in contrast to normal C syntax which ignores characters like
newlines, form feeds, tabs and so on. This means that macros cannot normally
"span" lines. The ANSI C standard specifies, however, that adjacent literal strings
are to be concatenated into one string. We count on that fact here since we enclosed
both parts of the string in double quotes. The resulting definition of LONG is as
if we had coded both string parts as one string in the first place.

One reason for this new feature of concatenating adjacent literal strings was
to reduce the need for the backslash at the end of the line when creating long
literals. The backslash is still needed, however, in those circumstances where the
body of the #define must be continued across multiple lines. When used to continue a #define definition onto a second line the backslash must be the very last
character on the line, i.e., it must immediately precede the newline character that
terminates the line of source code. This signals the compiler to include in the definition the line that follows, as if there had been no intervening newline. See the
program macro.c in this chapter for an example of a macro that requires more
than one line to define.

In all these examples macro names have been capitalized to distinguish them
from variable names. This is traditional, although it is becoming common that safe
macros (those which do not evaluate any argument more than once, and therefore do not generate any side effects) have lowercase names.

Also, remember that no semicolon is needed at the end of any directive since
"the preprocessor doesn't know C." If a semicolon is included, it will also be
included in the expanded code. This can make both object- and function-like
macros less flexible, since if they contain a semicolon at the end they cannot be
used in places where a semicolon would cause an error (for example, inside the
test expression of a while statement.

**Antibugging Note 13.2 Don't end #define directives
with a semicolon**

Do not include a semicolon when defining any type of macro. Provide
the semicolon when the macro is coded in the program. This approach
is more flexible and subject to fewer errors.

13.3 Other Preprocessor Directives

The preprocessor directives can be categorized into two groups: those directives
which have been present on most compilers since the early days of the language,
and the recently added directives which have been sanctioned because of their
inclusion in the ANSI C standard. #include, #define, #undef, and the #if
directives have existed for many years, while #line, #error, #pragma, and the
and ## operators, along with the predefined macros, are fairly recent additions
to most compilers.

13.3.1   #undef

If it is necessary to reuse a macro name by specifying it in another #define directive, #undef should be used to "clear" the first definition. These three directives:

```
#define ONE 1
#undef   ONE
#define ONE '1'
```

allow ONE to be redefined without any warning or error messages. We don't recommend redefining identifiers, but if it is necessary then use #undef.

Antibugging Note 13.3   Don't 're-use' macro names

Defining a macro name twice causes the meaning of the name to depend
on the placement of the macro definitions in the program. This introduces
confusion into the code since the name no longer means one and only
one thing throughout the entire source file.

13.3.2   #if *and Conditional Compilation*

A number of directives allow the creation of almost any kind of conditional check
using defined values. We'll discuss these directives together because they must be
used two at a time. We can call these the #if family of directives. They control
whether lines of the source program are passed to or seen by the compiler. This

concept is called *conditional compilation*. It is a very powerful tool to use when writing programs.

There are two ways to determine whether or not an identifier is currently defined. If it is not known whether the identifier `DEBUG` has been defined, then this directive:

```
#ifdef DEBUG
```

will be logically true if `DEBUG` has been defined. So also will this directive:

```
#if defined DEBUG
```

If possible, use the `#if defined` form rather than `#ifdef` since that is the stated direction of the language. Also, `#if defined` allows for multiple tests on one line, while `#ifdef` does not. See the program `ifdirect.c` below for an example of this.

What the identifier has been initialized to is completely unimportant to either of these directives; it matters only that `DEBUG` is or isn't defined. `#ifdef` is like `#ifndef`, `#if`, `#elif`, and `#else` in that they all require a corresponding `#endif` to follow somewhere. In contrast, `#ifndef` tests for the absence of a definition and is considered to be true when the identifier is not defined. `#if !defined` tests the same condition.

`#ifdef`, `#ifndef`, `#if defined`, and `#if !defined` all require only that an identifier appear after the directive and an intervening space. In all of these cases, if the test is true then the lines of code appearing between the test and the corresponding `#endif` will be included in the compilation. They will not be included if the result of the test is false.

`#if`, `#else`, and `#endif` can form the traditional "if-then-else" sequence of tests. The multiple test situations (analogous to the `switch` statement) can be coded using the `#elif`, which stands for "else-if". `#if` also requires that constant values be used in the test expression. Constants are necessary because these preprocessor directives are evaluated before the program is compiled, and variables do not exist during that time. However, values created with the `#define` directive can be used in `if` statements. Any sort of relational test can be coded, such as testing for less than, equal to, or greater than a constant. The effect of using `#if` is the same as using `#ifdef` in that the source file lines appearing between the `#if` and the corresponding `#endif` are only compiled if the test is true.

The `#if` group of directives can also be nested, as we demonstrate below. The same basic rules apply as for the C statement `if`, i.e., that `#else`, `#elif`, and `#endif` will all be matched to the nearest associated directive regardless of indentation.

It might also seem possible to use the `sizeof` operator within the `#if` preprocessor directive, like this:

```
int index;
...
#if sizeof(index) == 2
```

However, this doesn't work, and for a very good reason. Remember that sizeof is an actual compiler operator (like *, +, etc.) while #if is a directive to the preprocessor. The expressions tested by the #if directive must be constant values, and the only way sizeof(index) could be a constant is if the preprocessor ran after the compiler. It would be possible, however, to place sizeof in a #define directive since all that #define does is perform a temporary text substitution in the program.

Let's use all these identifiers in an example (Figure 13.1) which has been constructed to show a number of different combinations of preprocessor directives. The intent is to illustrate each directive and to demonstrate how multiple test situations and the nesting of #if related directives would be handled. Note that directives do not have to begin in column 1 of a line, an asset that can be used to make the program much easier to read. We've also included a block of code to show that any number of source file lines can appear shielded by the #if or related directive.

```
/*
** ifdirect.c    Examples of #if and Related Directives
*/

#include <stdio.h>

#define DEBUG 3
#define EXTRA_DEBUG 4

main()
{
   #if defined (DEBUG)                    /* see if DEBUG is defined */
      {
      printf("DEBUG was defined\n");
      printf("and blocks of code are allowed\n");
      }
   #endif


                  /* see if both DEBUG and EXTRA_DEBUG are defined */
   #if defined (DEBUG) && defined (EXTRA_DEBUG)
      {
      printf("Both DEBUG and EXTRA_DEBUG were defined\n");
      }
   #endif

   #if !defined (DEBUG)                   /* see if DEBUG is not defined */
      printf("DEBUG was not defined\n");    /* this comment goes too */
   #endif
```

(program continued on next page...)

```
    #if defined (DEBUG)                    /* see if DEBUG is defined */
      #if   DEBUG == 1                     /* compare DEBUG to the number 1 */
        printf("DEBUG was a 1\n");
      #elif DEBUG == 2
        printf("DEBUG was a 2\n");
      #else
        #if DEBUG < 10
          printf("DEBUG is less than 10\n");
        #else
          printf("DEBUG is not less than 10");
        #endif
      #endif
    #endif
}
```

Figure 13.1 Example of #if and Related Directives—ifdirect.c

This is the code generated when DEBUG is defined to be 3 and EXTRA_DEBUG is 4:

```
main()
{
    {
    printf("DEBUG was defined\n");
    printf("and blocks of code are allowed\n");
    }
    {
    printf("Both DEBUG and EXTRA_DEBUG were defined\n");
    }
        printf("DEBUG is less than 10\n");
}
```

This output was produced when the program executed:

```
DEBUG was defined
and blocks of code are allowed
Both DEBUG and EXTRA_DEBUG were defined
DEBUG is less than 10
```

Here is the program when `DEBUG` is defined as 1 and `EXTRA_DEBUG` is 4:

```
main()
{
    {
    printf("DEBUG was defined\n");
    printf("and blocks of code are allowed\n");
    }
    {
    printf("Both DEBUG and EXTRA_DEBUG were defined\n");
    }
    printf("DEBUG was a 1\n");
}
```

When `DEBUG` is defined as 12 and `EXTRA_DEBUG` is not defined:

```
main()
{
    {
    printf("DEBUG was defined\n");
    printf("and blocks of code are allowed\n");
    }
        printf("DEBUG is not less than 10");
}
```

When both `DEBUG` and `EXTRA_DEBUG` are not defined at all:

```
main()
{
    printf("DEBUG was not defined\n");
}
```

Note that in the above examples the comments do not appear in the output of the preprocessor (unless specifically requested when the compilation occurs). Also, comments were specifically included on lines that both were and were not going to be passed to the compiler by the preprocessor. This was done to illustrate how to "comment out" comments themselves. It is not possible to nest comments because the comments will match up in a way that leaves one or more */ sequences unmatched, like this:

```
/*          <- start of comment
    /*
    **
    */      <- end of comment
*/      <- error!
```

Quick Note 13.2   Commenting out code that contains comments

#if is the only way to comment out a section of code that contains comments. The directive #if 0 can be used to eliminate a section of code from the program.

Smart programmers include debugging code in programs so that the program's performance can be analyzed while it is executing. The code can display or write to a log file any type of information, including (but certainly not limited to):

values of particular variables
intermediate results of complex calculations
execution paths through the functions
number of times certain iterations/recursions are performed

There are two basic techniques available to C programmers for including this code in a program. The first technique uses the #if directive, the second the if statement. Both can be used to manage the debugging code.

A section of code shielded with the #if directive might look like this (this code can be written in a number of ways):

```
#if defined (DEBUG)
  ...
#endif
```

The if approach might look like this:

```
if (DEBUG) {
  ...
}
```

In the first case, using the #if directive, all that is required to cause the shielded code to be included is to define the constant DEBUG (remember the value to which it is defined is immaterial). In the second case the constant DEBUG must be defined to something other than zero in order for the test to be true. Both of these techniques have their advantages and disadvantages, as explained in Table 13.1.

`#if`	`if`
No extra code left in program during execution, so size is smaller and program slightly faster.	Debugging code always available during execution, with slight size and performance penalty.
No editing of file needed to add code back in before compiling again, but another compilation is necessary.	No compilation necessary because code is always present.
No run-time diagnostics available if code was not compiled into executing module.	Run-time diagnostics are always available, and can be turned on or off while the program executes.

Table 13.1   Using `#if` vs. `if` for debugging

Perhaps a judicious approach is to combine the two techniques, like this:

```
#if (DEBUG_PREPROCESS)
   if (DEBUG_RUNTIME == 1) {
      ...
   }
#endif
```

Now there are two defined constants which must be managed, one for the compile time inclusion/exclusion of the code, and one for the run-time environment. But certainly this solution provides additional flexibility over using either technique separately.

Antibugging Note 13.4   `#if` and `if` as debugging tools

Liberally sprinkle programs with `#if` directives and/or `if` statements to facilitate debugging. Carefully examine programs to determine which variables are the most informative and which execution paths are the most likely. Set traps on these variables and along these paths to help determine the health of a program.

Quick Note 13.3   Conditional Compilation

Conditional compilation allows the use of the same base source code so
that a program can be used in a variety of target environments and in
a variety of situations.

13.3.3   #, *the Stringizing Operator*

When a single # precedes a parameter in a macro definition the parameter is surrounded by double quotes as it is replaced during macro expansion. The result is
that the parameter becomes a string literal both in the macro and ultimately in
the program. This operator is necessary because parameters are not replaced if they
occur inside string literals that are explicitly coded in a macro. Figure 13.2 shows
an example.

```
/*
**   stringer.c    Illustrates #, the Stringizing Operator
*/

#include <stdio.h>

#define PRINT(f,v)  printf(#v " is %" #f "\n", v)
#define STRING(x)   # x " is a string literal"

main()
{
    PRINT(d, 5);
    PRINT(f, 15.0);
    printf("%s\n", STRING('one two three'));
}
```

Figure 13.2   Example of #, the Stringizing Operator—stringer.c

Note how the PRINT macro provides a terse way to print a data item with
a specified format code. Here we have used to our advantage the requirement that
adjacent string literals are concatenated into one string. The expansion of PRINT
(d, 5) is:

```
PRINT(d, 5)
printf(#5 " is %" #d "\n", 5);
printf("5" " is %" "d" "\n", 5);
printf("5 is %d\n", 5);
```

Further proof that the single # operator generates a string is evidenced by the
fact that we only used one %s conversion character in the printf() function that
utilizes the STRING macro. The expansion of STRING is:

```
printf("%s\n", STRING('one two three'));
printf("%s\n", # 'one two three' " is a string literal");
printf("%s\n", "'one two three'" " is a string literal");
printf("%s\n", "'one two three' is a string literal");
```

The output of the entire program is:

```
5 is 5
15.0 is 15.000000
'one two three' is a string literal
```

13.3.4 ##, *the Concatenation Operator*

It is possible to build macro and variable names dynamically by using the ## operator. When ## appears in a macro it is processed after the macro parameters are substituted and before the macro is examined again to see whether there are any remaining macros that must be further processed. It causes the items on either side of the ## to be "pasted" together as if they had been typed together in the first place.

For instance, this macro:

```
#define MACR(a, b)   ab
```

might appear to build a concatenation of the two macro arguments, a and b. However, the name ab is left in the program after the macro MACR is used, regardless of which arguments are coded along with MACR. This is because neither a nor b exist as a separate item in the macro body. The correct way to code this macro is:

```
#define MACR(a, b)   a ## b
```

The program in Figure 13.3 builds both a macro and a variable name. The CONCATA macro, when used with the argument value of 1, builds the macro name MAC1. MAC1 is then further replaced by the string literal it represents. CONCATB, when used with a 2, creates the variable name not_a_macro2.

```
/*
**   concat.c   Illustrates ##, the Concatenation Operator
*/

#include <stdio.h>

#define MAC1        "macro #1"        /* this is the final name */
#define CONCATA(n)  MAC ## n          /* this builds a macro name */
#define CONCATB(x)  not_a_macro ## x  /* this builds a variable name */

int not_a_macro2  = 123;
```

(program continued on next page...)

```
main()
{
    printf("%s\n", CONCATA(1));
    printf("%d\n", CONCATB(2));
}
```

Figure 13.3   Example of ##, the Concatenation Operator—`concat.c`

The expansion of these macros occurs like this:

```
CONCATA(1)
MAC ## 1
MAC1
macro #1
```

and

```
CONCATB(2)
not_a_macro ## 2
not_a_macro2
```

This program then prints this output:

```
macro #1
123
```

13.3.5   *Predefined Macros*

Certain macros have been predefined by the ANSI C standard. These macros are primarily used in debugging, and are especially helpful when using numerous nested include files:

```
__LINE__
__FILE__
__DATE__
__TIME__
__STDC__
```

All of these names are formed by writing two underscores both before and after the letters. The macros __LINE__ and __FILE__ are replaced by the current line number and file name when they are expanded, while __DATE__ and __TIME__ become the date and time of when the compilation takes place. The __DATE__ and __TIME__ macros can be used to initialize variables in the program; then the variables can be used to provide additional debugging information when the program executes. Often it is important to know when a program was compiled, in order to match it to a source program listing or library entry. The

__STDC__ macro will be a 1 (one) if the current compilation is operating under conditions that are strictly compatible with the ANSI C standard. If such conditions are not present, this macro value will not be 1, and may be undefined.

The program in Figure 13.4 illustrates what is printed when some of these macros are expanded and displayed:

```
/*
**   predefin.c - Printing the Predefined Macros
*/

#include <stdio.h>

main()
{
    printf("__LINE__ is %d\n", __LINE__);   /* source file line number */
    printf("__FILE__ is %s\n", __FILE__);   /* source file name */
    printf("__DATE__ is %s\n", __DATE__);   /* current Mmm dd yyyy */
    printf("__TIME__ is %s\n", __TIME__);   /* current hh:mm:ss */
}
```

Figure 13.4   Printing the Predefined Macros—predefin.c

Running this program results in the following information being displayed:

```
__LINE__ is 9
__FILE__ is C:\TC\PREDEFIN.C
__DATE__ is Jul 24 1987
__TIME__ is 21:10:02
```

By using the __DATE__ and __TIME__ macros the date and time of compilation can be stored in the program so that it can be used in a report header or other situation. Often it is invaluable to know when a particular program was compiled, not just when it executed.

13.3.6   #line, #error and #pragma

These directives are new to the language, having been included by the ANSI C standard. #line can alter the values found in __LINE__ and __FILE__, as we see from the program in Figure 13.5.

```
/*
** othermac.c - Changing the Predefined Macros
*/

#include <stdio.h>

main()
{
   printf("__LINE__ is %d\n", __LINE__);   /* see line number */
   printf("__FILE__ is %s\n", __FILE__);   /* see file name */
   #line 200 "newfile"                      /* change line and file */
   printf("__LINE__ is %d\n", __LINE__);   /* see line number */
   printf("__FILE__ is %s\n", __FILE__);   /* see file name */
}
```

Figure 13.5   **Changing the Predefined Macros**—othermac.c

This program creates this output:

```
__LINE__ is 9
__FILE__ is C:\TC\OTHERMAC.C
__LINE__ is 200
__FILE__ is newfile
```

The new filename supplied for #line is optional, but if it is present then the line number must also be coded.

#error is a directive that immediately terminates the compilation. Typically it would be used in conjunction with one or more #if related directives and would be invoked if a condition was detected which merited aborting a long-running compile. Such a condition might be a defined value outside an acceptable range, or a value that was not defined at all. Before the #error directive was available programmers had to invent all sorts of creative preprocessor statements to halt the compile.

#pragma is strictly an implementation-dependent directive which allows a compiler vendor to add extensions to the standard preprocessor directives.

13.4 Macro Debugging

We normally don't see the output of the preprocessor because it is passed directly into the compiler. Therefore, sometimes it can be very difficult to determine whether a defined constant, with or without arguments, is being replaced correctly. This is especially true when expressions are passed as macro arguments. If parentheses are not used to shield the arguments, unexpected groupings of operands can occur. Further, because the content of the macro is hidden when looking at the source code, it may not be readily apparent that the use of a particular macro is causing a problem.

For example, this code fragment:

```
#define  Z    1
int x;
...
x += Z++;
```

will not work. It expands to:

```
x += 1++;
```

which indicates that we tried to increment a constant, since the expression x += 1++; is the same as:

```
x = x + (1 = 1 + 1);
```

If the capital Z did not alert us to the fact that we were trying to increment a defined constant, the compiler certainly will because the resulting code will not compile.

Unfortunately, most problems with macros are not as obvious as trying to increment a constant. Take for example the program in Figure 13.6. Imagine how difficult it might be to discover the error in the IF_ISPUNCT macro at 2 a.m., after staring at a computer screen for hours.

```
/*
** macro.c - Macro Debugging Problems
**           This program has an error in the IF_ISPUNCT macro and will
**           not compile unless the error is fixed.
*/

#include <ctype.h>
#include <stdio.h>

#define IF_ISPUNCT(digit) if(!(((digit) == '\x7F') || \
                              ((digit) <= '\x20') || \
                              (((digit) >= '0') && ((digit) <= '9') || \
                              ((digit) >= 'a') && ((digit) <= 'z') || \
                              ((digit) >= 'A') && ((digit) <= 'Z')))
```

(program continued on next page...)

```
main()
{
    int digit;

    for (digit = 0; digit <= 127; digit++) {
        IF_ISPUNCT(digit) {
            printf("\'%c\', value %3d, is a punctuation character,"
                    " and ispunct %s\n",
                    digit, digit, ispunct(digit) ? "agrees" : "disagrees");
        }
    }
}
```

Figure 13.6   Macro Debugging Problems—macro.c

A top-quality C compiler will accurately identify the error as having to do with a missing right parenthesis where IF_ISPUNCT is used. A poor-quality compiler could miss the real problem entirely. The difficulty with a macro like IF_ISPUNCT is that the missing right parenthesis can sometimes cause many lines of source code to be included in the macro expansion. One of the authors experienced a similar problem once. The error message the author received indicated that the compiler had run out of macro space, which was interesting since there were only a few macros in the program. Worse yet, the line on which the compile failed was 60 lines away from where the problem macro was used, and was also a line that had been in error in the previous compile. Needless to say, the root problem was not immediately obvious.

Most C compilers provide a way to create a file that holds the output of the preprocessor. The output is sent to the file instead of to the compiler. Usually the request to create this file comes from a switch on the command line (so consult the documentation for the compiler being used to see how this is done). This is the technique used by the author mentioned above to diagnose his problem macro. Once the preprocessor output was examined it quickly became clear that the problem was the "drawing in" of subsequent lines of source code after the macro, and from there it was a quick connection to the missing right parenthesis.

Antibugging Note 13.5   Avoid elaborate macros

Avoid elaborate macros. Stick to simple, straightforward macros, using two separate ones even if they could have been combined into one extensive macro.

Quick Note 13.4   Saving the Preprocessor output

When encountering difficulty debugging macros, use the compiler switch, which creates a file containing the output of the preprocessor. Examine that file for additional hints about where the macro is failing.

13.5   Self-Check

These statements are True or False. The answers are given at the end.

1. The preprocessor has been a part of C from the inception of the language.

2. Preprocessing directives are evaluated before C language keywords like `while`, `for`, or `if`.

3. It is appropriate to think of the preprocessor as a smart text editor.

4. One macro cannot be used to help define another.

5. The `#define` directive is used to create both simple replacement and function-like macros.

6. Macro parameters have data types, just like function parameters.

7. Every macro parameter occurrence in the macro body should be surrounded by parentheses.

8. The backslash is needed to continue the definition of a macro to another line.

9. It is required that macro names be in uppercase.

10. `#undef` should be used to redefine a macro.

11. The `#if defined` directive requires that the identifier being examined not only be defined, but also have at least a space for a value.

12. The `#if` and related directives can be nested.

13. The `#` operator creates a character pointer whose name is that of the macro argument.

14. The concatenation operator can be used to dynamically build both macro and variable names.

15. The preprocessor helps you debug your C syntax.

16. All macros must be defined in your program.

17. Conditional compilation can help you move your program to new environments while retaining one set of base code.

18. Assigning a macro name to string literals make changing your program easier.

19. If a compiler already has a macro called `min`, we would have problems creating a `MIN` macro to be used together with `min`.

20. Arithmetic expressions in a macro should be surrounded by parentheses, even if that means enclosing the entire macro body.

Answers

1. T   2. T   3. T   4. F   5. T   6. F   7. T   8. T   9. F   10. T
11. F   12. T   13. F   14. T   15. F   16. F   17. T   18. T   19. F   20. T

13.6   Review Program—Program Maintenance and Macros

In this review program we will revisit a review program presented earlier, `area.c`, making some strategic changes to speed the program execution. To do this we will substitute macro definitions for the area calculation functions `rect()`, `tria()`, and `trap()`. These are prime candidates for macros instead of functions since their code contains only simple mathematics and no looping constructs. We will also place the area calculation macros in our own include file, `my_math.h` to demonstrate file inclusion using the preprocessor. This is common practice in a development environment. As a matter of fact, you will find that as your own personal array of generic functions and macros grows, it will be advantageous to build customized libraries and include files. Last, just for fun, we will demonstrate the stringizing preprocessor directive to build a macro that displays menu choices.

□ *Program Specifications*

This is one of the only review programs for which it will not be necessary to write pseudocode. Instead we will discuss utilization of macros in lieu of functions for algorithm implementation.

It is important first to make a clear distinction between a macro call and a function call. As we have studied earlier, use of a macro causes the preprocessor to substitute code, in-line, directly in your source at the point of invocation. On the other hand, a function call causes the compiler to generate code to make a call to the referenced function. You should realize that a function call takes time to process by the CPU; the macro does not generate any function call code, hence it is generally faster. Macros do, in general, lengthen the resulting executable code since each macro invocation generates ALL the code each time it is invoked. Our area calculation routines can be rewritten as macros with a definite advantage because their equivalent functions are short and involve simple math. Now let's see how each could be coded as macros.

Function:

```
/*-------------------------------------------------------------------
 calculate area of rectangle
-----------------------------------------------------------------*/
float rect(l,h)
float l, h;
{
   return(l * h);
}
```

Written as a macro:

```
#define AREA_RECT(l, h)     ((l) * (h))
```

Function:

```
/*-------------------------------------------------------------------
 calculate area of right triangle
-----------------------------------------------------------------*/
float tria(side1,side2)
float side1,side2;
{
   return(rect(side1,side2) / 2);
}
```

Written as a macro:

```
#define AREA_TRIA(a, b)     ((AREA_RECT(a, b)) / (2))
```

Function:

```
/*-------------------------------------------------------------------
 calculate area of trapezoid
-----------------------------------------------------------------*/
float trap(top,bottom,height)
float top,bottom,height;
{
   return(((top + bottom) / 2) * height);
}
```

Written as a macro:

```
#define AREA_TRAP(b1, b2, h)  (((b1) + (b2)) / (2 * (h)))
```

You should note how we have included parentheses liberally in our macros to avoid side-effect problems that might arise in their expansion within the code. Although in our review program no problems would arise, remember that we are writing macros for use in any program, not just an isolated case.

All that is left now is to create a file, my_math.h, which consists of these macros for inclusion in our program

```
/*-------------------------------------------------------------------
 my_math.h
 Fast math routines using macros.
 --------------------------------------------------------------*/
#define AREA_RECT(l, h)      ((l) * (h))
#define AREA_TRIA(a, b)      ((AREA_RECT(a, b)) / (2))
#define AREA_TRAP(b1, b2, h)  (((b1) + (b2)) / (2 * (h)))
```

And, of course, the following changes in our program:

Old statement:

```
printf("Area is %f\n\n", rect(l,h));
```

New statement:

```
printf("Area is %f\n\n", AREA_RECT(l,h));
```

Old statement:

```
printf("Area is %f\n\n", tria(a,b));
```

New statement:

```
printf("Area is %f\n\n", AREA_TRIA(a,b));
```

Old statement:

```
printf("Area is %f\n\n", trap(b1,b2,h));
```

New statement:

```
printf("Area is %f\n\n", AREA_TRAP(b1,b2,h));
```

Now, let's look at our modified review program.

□ *Design Implementation*

```
/*-------------------------------------------------------------------
  areamac.c
  This program allows the user to calculate the area of several
  geometric objects via a simple menu interface.

  This is the same program as area.c with macros used
  for the area calculations for faster speed.
------------------------------------------------------------------*/
#include <stdio.h>
#include "my_math.h"                       /* our include file with */
                                           /* macros for area calculations */


#define LINES 25

/*
  just for fun, we try out the stringize directive
*/
#define MENU_CHOICE(choice)    printf("%s\n", # choice)

char rectangle[] = "\n\n\
    ---------- \n\
^ !          !\n\
h !          !\n\
v !          !\n\
    ---------- \n\
  <--  l   --> \n\n";

char triangle[] = "\n\n\
 ^ !\\           \n\
 ! ! \\          \n\
   !  \\          \n\
 a !  \\         \n\
   !   \\        \n\
 ! !    \\      \n\
 v !     \\     \n\
   ------- \n\
   <--b--> \n\n";
                        /* the trapezoid is developed with the new ANSI */
                        /* C capability of concatenating literal strings */
char trapezoid[] = "\n\n"
"     <- b1 ->     \n"
"     --------     \n"
"    /    ^   \\\\   \n"
"   /     h    \\\\  \n"
"  /      v     \\\\ \n"
"  --------------- \n"
"  <---  b2  ----> \n\n";
```

(program continued on next page...)

```
main()
{
   char selection;
   do {
      cls();                              /* clear the screen */
      printf("Area Calculation Program\n");
      printf("------------------------\n");
      MENU_CHOICE(<R>ectangle);
      MENU_CHOICE(<T>riangle);
      MENU_CHOICE(Trape<Z>oid);
      MENU_CHOICE(e<X>it program);
      printf("\n\n");
      printf("Select object: ");
      scanf(" %1c", &selection);
      cls();
      switch (selection = toupper(selection))   /* make selection uppercase */
         {
         case 'R':                      /* selected rectangle */
            {
            float l, h;

            printf("%s\n\n", rectangle);
            printf("l ? ");
            scanf("%f", &l);
            printf("h ? ");
            scanf("%f", &h);
            printf("Area is %f\n\n", AREA_RECT(l, h));
            break;
            }
         case 'T':                      /* selected triangle */
            {
            float a, b;

            printf("%s", triangle);
            printf("Side a ? ");
            scanf("%f", &a);
            printf("Side b ? ");
            scanf("%f", &b);
            printf("Area is %f\n\n", AREA_TRIA(a, b));
            break;
            }
```

```
        case 'Z':                        /* selected trapezoid */
            {
            float b1, b2, h;

            printf("%s", trapezoid);
            printf("Side b1 ? ");
            scanf("%f", &b1);
            printf("Side b2 ? ");
            scanf("%f", &b2);
            printf("h ? ");
            scanf("%f", &h);
            printf("Area is %f\n\n", AREA_TRAP(b1, b2, h));
            break;
            }
        case 'X':                        /* exit program */
            break;
        default:                         /* bad choice */
            {
            printf("\nInvalid menu choice. Reenter your selection.\n\n");
            }
        }
    if (selection == 'X') {
        continue;
    }
    else {
        printf("\n\nEnter X to exit, any other letter to continue...\n");
        scanf(" %1c", &selection);
        selection = toupper(selection);
    }
   } while (selection != 'X');
}

/*-------------------------------------------------------------------
 clear the screen
 (print LINES newlines)
 -----------------------------------------------------------------*/
cls()
{
    int index;

    for (index = 0; index < LINES; ++index)
        printf("\n");
    return;
}
```

To see the effect of these changes, let's look at the preprocessed version of the affected program lines:

Before preprocessing:

```
printf("Area is %f\n\n", AREA_RECT(l,h));
```

After preprocessing:

```
printf("Area is %f\n\n", ((l) * (h)));
```

Before preprocessing:

```
printf("Area is %f\n\n", AREA_TRIA(a,b));
```

After preprocessing:

```
printf("Area is %f\n\n", ((((a) * (b))) / (2)));
```

Before preprocessing:

```
printf("Area is %f\n\n", AREA_TRAP(b1,b2,h));
```

After preprocessing:

```
printf("Area is %f\n\n", (((b1) + (b2)) / (2 * (h))));
```

Before preprocessing:

```
MENU_CHOICE(<R>ectangle);
MENU_CHOICE(<T>riangle);
MENU_CHOICE(Trape<Z>oid);
MENU_CHOICE(e<X>it program);
```

After preprocessing:

```
printf("%s\n", "<R>ectangle");
printf("%s\n", "<T>riangle");
printf("%s\n", "Trape<Z>oid");
printf("%s\n", "e<X>it program");
```

Before preprocessing:

```
for (i = 0; i < LINES; ++i)
```

After preprocessing:

```
for (i = 0; i < 25; ++i)
```

Points to Study

1. Transformations necessary to rewrite the area calculation functions as macros. Why didn't we rewrite `cls()` as a macro?

2. Use of the stringize `#` operator in `MENU_CHOICE()`. What advantages does the macro offer us in this application?

13.7   Review Program—N-dimensional Tic-Tac-Toe

Our final review program will illustrate how C provides the ability to implement an elegant solution to a moderately complex problem. You should study this program carefully, not so much for the algorithms used, but rather to see how well C handles them. The program includes nearly every major strength of the language, including extensibility, pointer manipulation, recursion, prototyping, modularity, and conciseness. Although the review program does not effectively illustrate the majority of the concepts presented in this chapter, the exercises will. You should attempt to work this problem even if you don't fully understand the review program. It has been carefully designed to reinforce practically every concept presented in the chapter in the best manner possible—by doing.

☐ *Design Specifications*

Our goal for this program can be simply stated:

Develop a program that can determine if a win has occurred in a game of tic-tac-toe. Further, the program must be able to handle games in any dimensional space.

Now for our refresher course in tic-tac-toe. Recall that a win in this rather simple game is determined by the first player to form a straight line consisting of a set number of that player's respective game token, X or O. The game is normally played by two players who alternately place an X or O token on a grid consisting of a square matrix of cells. For example, suppose the following sequence of plays occur in a two-dimensional game:

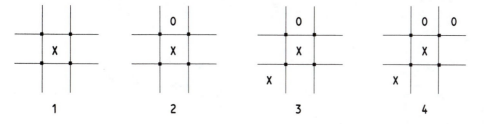

(program continued on next page...)

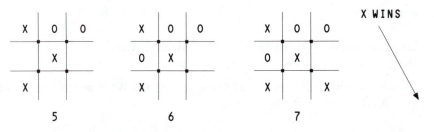

Here X wins along the left-to-right diagonal with three X's in a straight line. Developing a win-determination algorithm for only the two-dimensional version would be quite simple and could be done using a "brute-force" method—check all rows, columns and the two corner-to-corner diagonals. Our algorithm, however, must be flexible enough to handle n-dimensional versions of this classic game.

Before attacking this problem it would be appropriate at this point to define a win in more precise and general terms. First, the game space itself can be conveniently viewed using a Cartesian coordinate system. For example, the two-dimensional game space can be viewed as:

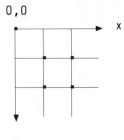

A three-dimensional version might be viewed as:

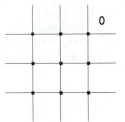

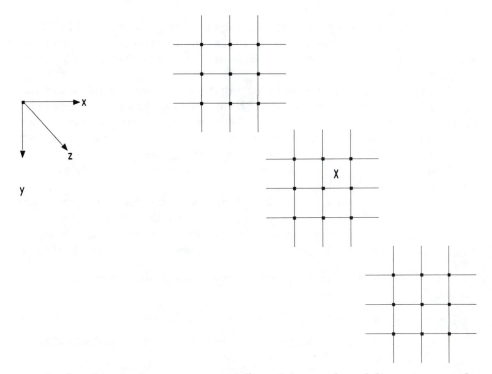

Each cell in the game space, regardless of the number of dimensions, can be assigned a set of coordinates. In the diagram above, X would have coordinates x = 2, y = 1, z = 2, or simply 2,1,2 where O has coordinates 3,0,0.

Next, we must place a restriction on the axes themselves. Each must be of equal length. In simpler terms, the game space must be square. A win in n-dimensional tic-tac-toe consists of a straight line of n, like tokens where n is the length of one side in the game space. For example, in our two-dimensional game n is equal to three and in the three-dimensional version, four.

Last, a straight line means that the coordinates of each token must lie exactly on the imaginary line drawn through its endpoints. For example, consider the following situation:

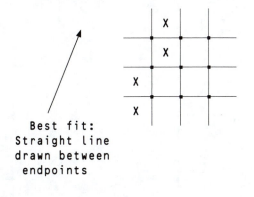

Best fit:
Straight line
drawn between
endpoints

Although four like tokens lie on an imaginary straight line (best fit!), two of them (the middle two) do not lie exactly on the line. Therefore, this particular situation does not constitute a win and the imaginary line is not a straight line by our definition.

It may be intuitively obvious by now that the only way a straight line can be formed is with lines parallel to one of the coordinate axes or along the corner-to-corner diagonals in the game space. Straight lines can be formed by varying only one axis coordinate, while holding all others constant, or by varying two or more axis coordinates equally while holding the remaining ones constant.

Now that we have defined win in precise terms we can formulate a general win-determination algorithm.

First, since we will use real-world coordinates, each point in the game space will have associated point coordinates, i.e., x for one-dimensional, x,y for two-dimensional, x,y,z for three-dimensional, x,y,z,w for four-dimensional, and so on. Next, to determine if a win exists in the game space we will follow these steps:

1. Start with the origin point (point with each coordinate at zero) in the game space.

2. Look to see if a valid token, X or O, exists in the cell.

3. If so, step along each valid straight line beginning with the point looking for n tokens in a row. If found, a win exists.

4. Repeat for each point in the address space until a win has been found or all points have been examined, whichever comes first.

This rather systematic algorithm satisfies the required level of generality necessary to perform an exhaustive win search of the n-dimensional game space. We will refer to each straight line examined as a vector since it possesses both length and direction.

To visualize how the algorithm works, let's trace through it using a two-dimensional, n = 3 game space:

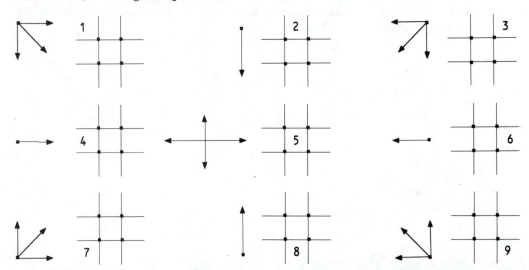

Here we have labeled each iteration of the algorithm with numbered squares and the valid vectors (straight lines) from that point with arrows. Although it should be evident that there is redundancy in our algorithm, we won't press our luck, and cloud the issue, by further optimization efforts. Let's proceed to write pseudocode for win(), our win-determination algorithm:

□ *Program Design*

Global variables we need:

integer array coord[]	array used to hold coordinates of current point to be examined
integer array step[]	step values used to generate vectors from current point
integer array temp[]	temporary array to hold current point coordinates
integer D	number of dimensions
integer S	size of game space (length of an axis)

```
function win(tok, d, s, gs)
character tok              the token, X or O
integer d                 the number of dimensions in the game space
integer s                 the size of the game space (length of an axis)
character array gs         array that holds game space itself

   if (d > 0)             this stops the recursion
      d = d-1
      for (i = 0 to s step 1)
         coord[d] = i    this sets up the point coordinates of the current
                         point we're looking at
         if (win(tok, d, s, gs))      make the recursive call; note that
                                      only d varies with each recursive
                                      call—tok, s, and gb remain constant
            return(TRUE)              return a TRUE (win found) if a
                                      subsequent recursive call returns
                                      a TRUE
         endif
         if (d = 0 AND <point contains tok>
             AND <one of the vectors from the current point is a win>)
            return(TRUE)
         endif
      endfor
   endif
   return(FALSE)
end win
```

Our function win() performs the scan of each point looking for tokens that match tok which has been passed to it as an argument. Recursive calls are made until the bottom dimension is reached; then valid vectors from that point are examined for a win situation. When a win is found, win() returns a logical true to all previous levels, terminating the recursion for good. Note that win() is a generalized version of a nested loop written recursively to accommodate an arbitrary number of dimensions. One aspect of this function needs to be resolved before we write the actual code. First, the generalizations "<point contains tok>" and "<one of the vectors from the current point is a win>" need their own pseudocode. The rest of the pseudocode for win() will translate quite easily into C code. First, let's write pseudocode for "<point contains tok>":

```
function point__is__token(tok, gb, i)
character tok            the token, X or O
character array gs       the game space itself
integer i                index into gs, the game space; this is a linear
                         index, not the actual point coordinates


    if (gs[i] == tok)
        return(TRUE)
    endif
    return(FALSE)
end point__is__token
```

Well, that was painless! Unfortunately, we are not so lucky with "<one of the vectors from the current point is a win>." As you may have suspected, this function will perform most of the work to determine if a win has occurred:

```
function vectors(tok, d, s, gs)
character tok            the token, X or O
integer d               the number of dimensions in the game space
integer s               the size of the game space (length of an axis)
character array gs       array that holds game space itself

    integer i, j, k      some loop variables we'll need
    BOOLEAN win          a Boolean (TRUE/FALSE) variable

    if (d > 0)           starts out just like win(); as in win(), this
                         terminates the recursion
        for (i =−1 to 1 step 1)
            if (win != TRUE)
                step[d] = i
                if (vectors(tok, d, s, gs)   same as for win(), the recursive
                                             call
                    return(TRUE)
                endif
```

```
    if (d == 0)                 if we're at the bottom of the recursion
        <save the current coordinates in a temporary place>
    win = TRUE
    for (j = 0 to S - 1)        loop from 0 to S - 1 since we
                                already know the current point
                                is the token or we wouldn't have
                                gotten this far

        if (win == TRUE)
            for (k = 0 to D)
                coord[k] = coord[k] + step[k]    update each coordinate
                                                 according to the
                                                 current step values

            endfor
            if (<point is within game space> AND
                point_is_token(tok, gs, <linear index based on D and S>)
                win = TRUE              this must occur S times for this
                                        condition to stick
            else
                win = FALSE
            endif
            if (<the points we've been looking at all have the same
                coordinates>)          vectors() looks at all possible vectors
                win = FALSE            including the zero vector
            endif
        endif
        <restore coord[] to its previous values>
    endfor
    endif
    return(win)                          send back our verdict, win or no win
end vectors
```

This is the most complicated function we will need in this program. `vectors()` attempts to look in all directions from the current point and contains traps to rule out invalid vectors (vectors whose coordinates lie outside the current game space). The generalization "**<point is within game space>**" must be better defined. Its pseudocode turns out to be trivial:

```
function point_ok()
    integer i

    for (i = 0 to D)
        if (coord[i] < 0 OR coord[i] >= S)
            return(FALSE)
        endif
    endfor
    return(TRUE)
end point_ok
```

In addition, we must clarify "<the points we've been looking at have the same coordinates>." This additional piece of logic is necessary because the loop-generating vectors includes the possibility that the step values are all zero. In this situation, vectors() would return a false win. At any rate, the code is quite simple:

```
function chk__if__same__pt(d)          (check if same point)
integer d                              number of dimensions

    integer status  =  TRUE

    while (d > 0)
       if (coord[i] != temp[d])
           status  =  FALSE
       endif
    endwhile
    return(status)
end chk__if__same__pt
```

Note that chk_if_same_pt() starts by assuming that the two points in question are indeed the same. The if test changes that assumption if it is not true.

The last generalization to clarify is "<linear index based on D and S>." It will become evident, after we start coding our program, that the game space itself will have to be stored in a linear array to maintain dimensional independence. This means that to access a point in the game space using real-world coordinates, a mapping function will have to be used to transform these coordinates to a linear index into gs[]. We have already developed such a function, point_index(), in the review program in Chapter 9, ndindex.c.

Now that we have all the necessary tools to write our program, let's look at the code.

□ *Design Implementation*

```
/*-------------------------------------------------------------------
win.c
This program determines if a win has occurred in a game of n-dimensional
tic-tac-toe.  The defined constants NBR_DIM and AXIS_SIZE may be changed and
the program recompiled/linked for other dimensions.
-------------------------------------------------------------------*/
#include <stdio.h>

#define NBR_DIM 2                      /* vector space dimensions */
                                       /* (2-D space) */
#define AXIS_SIZE 3                    /* vector space size */
                                       /* (each axis is 3 units long) */
#define TRUE 1
#define FALSE 0
```

```
typedef int BOOLEAN;
                                        /* function prototypes, classic style */
BOOLEAN win(char, int, int, char *);
BOOLEAN vectors(char, int, int, char *);
BOOLEAN point_is_tok(char, char *, int);
BOOLEAN point_ok();
BOOLEAN chk_if_same_pt(int);
int     point_index(int, int, int *);
int     ipow(int, int);

/*
 The following arrays hold point coordinate values and step increments.
 They are global and are used by many of the supporting functions
 in this program.
*/
int temp_coord_pt[NBR_DIM];                 /* temporary coordinate array */
int coord_cur_pt[NBR_DIM];                  /* array to hold current point */
int step_value[NBR_DIM];                    /* array to hold step values */

main()
{
    char *token;                      /* temporary pointer for token list */
    char **test_game;                 /* ditto for test game spaces */

    static char token_list[] = "XO"; /* valid tokens for tic-tac-toe */

    static char *game_spaces[] = {
      "XXX"
      "   "
      "O O",

      "X  "
      "X O"
      "X O",

      "X O"
      " XO"
      "OOX",

      "XXO"
      "OOO"
      "OOX",

      NULL };

    test_game = game_spaces;          /* point to list of test game spaces */
```

(program continued on next page...)

```
    while (*test_game) {                    /* while more games to examine */
                                   /* print the game space one row at a time */
        printf("Game space array:\n");
        {
            int index = 0;
            int inner_loop;
            int max_nbr_squares;
            max_nbr_squares = ipow (AXIS_SIZE, NBR_DIM);
            while (index < max_nbr_squares) {
                putchar('\t');
                for (inner_loop = 0;
                     inner_loop < AXIS_SIZE;
                     inner_loop++, index++) {
                    putchar((*test_game)[index]);
                }
                putchar('\n');
            }
        }
        token = token_list;              /* point to the list of valid tokens */

        while (*token) {                 /* while there are more tokens */
                                         /* to examine */
                                         /* see if the current token has a win */
            if (win(*token, NBR_DIM, AXIS_SIZE, *test_game)) {
                printf("%c has a winning combination!\n", *token);
            }
            else {
                printf("%c does NOT have a winning combination.\n", *token);
            }
            ++token;
        }
        printf("\n");
        ++test_game;
    }
    exit(0);
}


/*-----------------------------------------------------------------------
BOOLEAN win(tok, nbr_dim, dim_siz, game_sp)
This function checks for a win (AXIS_SIZE tokens in a row) in n-dimensional
tic-tac-toe. win()  searches the vector space (game space) systematically by
examining each point in the space.  It first looks to see if the point
being examined is the token passed to it (either X or O).  It then calls
vectors() whose job is described below.  win()  makes recursive calls
until the first dimension is reached.  Upon careful examination, you will
see that both  win()  and  vectors()  simulate a nested loop by using
recursion.  This is precisely how they achieve dimensional independence.
```

```
parameter       type            description
-----------+-----------+-------------------------------------------------
tok             char            token to compare against
nbr_dim         int             number of dimensions
dim_siz         int             dimensional size
game_sp         char *          game space to examine

return          type            description
-----------+-----------+-------------------------------------------------
TRUE            int             win for token found in vector space
FALSE           int             win not found
--------------------------------------------------------------------*/
BOOLEAN win(tok, nbr_dim, dim_siz, game_sp)
char tok;                               /* the token to examine */
int nbr_dim, dim_siz;                   /* game space dimensions and size */
char *game_sp;                          /* the game space */
{
   register int i;

   if (nbr_dim--) {                     /* start with bottom dimension */
      for (i = 0; i < dim_siz; ++i) {   /* cover all dim_siz */
         coord_cur_pt[nbr_dim] = i;
                                        /* make the recursive call */
         if (win(tok, nbr_dim, dim_siz, game_sp)) {
            return(TRUE);
         }
         if (!nbr_dim &&
             point_is_tok(tok,
                          game_sp,
                          point_index(NBR_DIM, AXIS_SIZE, coord_cur_pt)
                         ) &&
             vectors(tok, NBR_DIM, AXIS_SIZE, game_sp)
            ) {
            return(TRUE);
         }
      }
   }
   return(FALSE);
}

/*-------------------------------------------------------------------
 BOOLEAN vectors(tok, nbr_dim, dim_siz, game_sp)
 This function is called by win() after a valid token is found at a given
 point.  vectors() then looks in all valid directions searching for the
 same token.  If it finds AXIS_SIZE tokens in a row, a win has been found.
 The information is returned to win() which then terminates and returns the
 win to the calling code.
 vectors()  searches diagonals by varying each axis equally.  The values
 stored in the global array  step_value[]  hold these values for each
 iteration.  As with  win(),  vectors()  achieves dimensional independence by
 simulating a nested loop of indeterminate depth by using recursion.
```

(program continued on next page...)

```
---------------------------------------------------------------------*/
BOOLEAN vectors(tok, nbr_dim, dim_siz, game_sp)
char tok;
int nbr_dim, dim_siz;
char *game_sp;
{
    register int i, j, k;                /* temporary counters for loops */
    int win;

    win = FALSE;                         /* set initial value for win */
    if (nbr_dim--) {
        for (i = -1; i <= 1 && !win; i += 1) {
            step_value[nbr_dim] = i;
                                              /* make the recursive call */
            if (vectors(tok, nbr_dim, dim_siz, game_sp)) {
                return(TRUE);
            }
            if (!nbr_dim) {
                for (k = 0; k < NBR_DIM; ++k) {
                                              /* save the coords; we'll need them */
                    temp_coord_pt[k] = coord_cur_pt[k];
                }
                win = TRUE;                /* on the next iteration */
                for (j = 0; j < AXIS_SIZE - 1 && win; ++j) {
/*
 vary the coordinate according to the step values
*/
                    for (k = 0; k < NBR_DIM; ++k) {
                        coord_cur_pt[k] += step_value[k];
                    }
/*
 if point is in vector space and point value is the token, then...
*/
                    if (point_ok() &&
                        point_is_tok(tok,
                                 game_sp,
                                 point_index(NBR_DIM, AXIS_SIZE, coord_cur_pt)
                                 )
                        ) {
                        win = TRUE;        /* must occur dim_siz times for this */
                    }
                    else {                 /* to stick */
                        win = FALSE;
                    }
                    if (chk_if_same_pt(NBR_DIM)) {  /* can't be the same point */
                        win = FALSE;                /* we're looking at! */
                    }
```

```
            }
            for (k = 0; k < NBR_DIM; ++k) {
                coord_cur_pt[k] = temp_coord_pt[k];
            }
        }
    }
}
    return(win);                        /* send back our verdict */
}

/*-------------------------------------------------------------------
 BOOLEAN point_is_token(tok, game_sp, i)
 This function checks to see if the object at the point game_sp[i]
 is the token we're looking for.
 ------------------------------------------------------------------*/
BOOLEAN point_is_tok(tok, game_sp, i)
char tok;
char *game_sp;
register int i;
{
    if (game_sp[i] == tok) {
        return(TRUE);
    }
    return(FALSE);
}

/*-------------------------------------------------------------------
 BOOLEAN point_ok()
 This function checks a point whose coordinates are stored in the global
 array  coord[]  to see if the specified point is on the game space.  Certain
 step values will cause  vectors()  to look at points that don't exist.
 ------------------------------------------------------------------*/
BOOLEAN point_ok()
{
    register int i;
    for (i = 0; i < NBR_DIM; ++i) {
        if (coord_cur_pt[i] < 0 !! coord_cur_pt[i] >= AXIS_SIZE) {
            return(FALSE);              /* point is out of address space */
        }
    }
    return(TRUE);                       /* point is okay */
}
```

(program continued on next page...)

```
/*-------------------------------------------------------------------------
  BOOLEAN chk_if_same_pt()
  Check if same point.  This function is only called by  vectors().  It is
  used to determine if the step values are all zero, which would mean that
  vectors() is analyzing the same point repetitively; this would
  cause vectors() to return a logical TRUE at an inappropriate time.
  chk_if_same_pt()  basically keeps  vectors()  from doing something stupid.
  -------------------------------------------------------------------------*/
BOOLEAN chk_if_same_pt(nbr_dim)
register int nbr_dim;
{
   int status = TRUE;

   while (nbr_dim--) {
      if (coord_cur_pt[nbr_dim] != temp_coord_pt[nbr_dim]) {
         status = FALSE;
      }
   }
   return(status);
}


/*-------------------------------------------------------------------------
  point_index()
  This function performs a mapping function from n-dimensional coordinates
  to a linear array that stores the actual point values contained within
  the n-dimensional address space. The array  c[]  contains the
  n-dimensional coordinates of the point, which are used to calculate the
  linear index. The following formula is used:
```

$$i = (s_d^{d-1} * c_d) + (s_{d-1}^{d-2} * c_{d-1}) + \ldots + (s_1^{d-d} * c_1)$$

```
  where,

        i : linear index into linear mapping (one-dimensional array)
        s : length of dimensional axes (must be equal!)
        d : number of dimensions
        c : coordinate of point for axis n

  The variable names used in this function match the above formula.
  -------------------------------------------------------------------------*/
int point_index(d, s, c)
int d, s, c[];
```

```
{
    int i = 0;

    while (d--) {                       /* start at highest dimension and */
        i += ipow(s, d) * c[d];         /* work down */
    }
    return(i);                          /* return linear array index */
}

/*-----------------------------------------------------------------
 int ipow()                    y
 This function calculates x  where x and y are integers.
 -----------------------------------------------------------------*/
int ipow(x, y)
register int x, y;
{
    int result = 1;

    while (y--) {
        result *= x;
    }
    return(result);
}
```

Note that main(), our test jig, feeds test game spaces to win() and reports the results. Also, functions that return TRUE/FALSE values have been defined as returning type BOOLEAN using a typedef. This more accurately reflects their true state.

For the sake of brevity, we have only tested two-dimensional game spaces although win() will handle any dimension. Since one-dimensional game spaces are rather uninteresting and four-dimensional game spaces and higher are difficult to visualize, you should recompile and link the program with D = 3 and S = 4 feeding win() three-dimensional test game spaces. Try using the following board position:

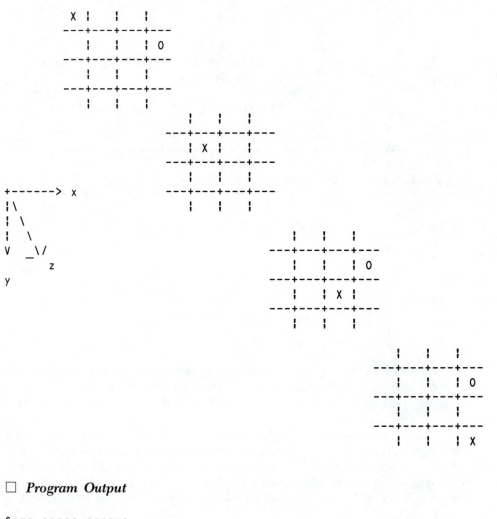

□ *Program Output*

```
Game space array:
     XXX


     O O
X has a winning combination!
O does NOT have a winning combination.

Game space array:
     X
     X O
     X O
X has a winning combination!
O does NOT have a winning combination.
```

```
Game space array:
        X O
         XO
         OOX
X has a winning combination!
O does NOT have a winning combination.

Game space array:
        XXO
        OOO
        OOX
X does NOT have a winning combination.
O has a winning combination!
```

Note that the test jig prints the array `game_spaces` one row at a time. This displays a two-dimensional array in a very readable fashion.

Points to Study

1. Which variables are treated as local and which as global, and why? Do you suppose the program could be written using only variables of local scope? With variables of only global scope?

2. Why were recursive versus nonrecursive functions used? Do you suppose that recursive functions depend rather intimately on locality of variables?

3. How a `typedef`, BOOLEAN, was used to enhance readability.

4. How register storage class variables were used to advantage. Do you suppose that the compiler honors these as register variables even though the functions are recursive?

5. The data type of `game_spaces` and the number of elements it contains. Note how the string literals were coded on separate lines to enhance readability.

13.8 Exercises

1. Write a set of macros for inclusion in `my_math.h` for the following math operations:
   a. square of a number, x
   b. cube of a number, x
   c. maximum of two numbers, x and y
   d. minimum of two numbers, x and y
   e. x multiplied by y, where y is a power of two
   f. x divided by y, where y is a power of two

2. Write a set of macros to perform the following English-metric conversions:

Temperature:
— degrees Fahrenheit to degrees Celsius
— degrees Celsius to degrees Fahrenheit

Distance:
— centimeters to inches
— inches to centimeters
— meters to feet
— feet to meters
— miles to kilometers
— kilometers to miles

Weight:
— ounces to grams
— grams to ounces
— pounds to kilograms
— kilograms to pounds

Volume:
— fluid ounces to milliliters
— milliliters to fluid ounces
— gallons to liters
— liters to gallons

3. One aspect that introduces art into programming is the balance of speed versus portability in applications development. Functions designed to manipulate the display device are notorious in this respect. Very fast routines are almost certainly tied closely to a specific piece of hardware for which the application is designed. One partial solution to this problem is to introduce conditional compilation statements into the application source code and recompile for different environments. For example, clearing the screen is a frequently used routine in most applications. Our `cls()` function, which uses `printf()`, is very portable but very slow. This implementation should run on any machine that supports the C language. A faster `cls()` can be coded using ANSI escape sequences but would be limited to machines using the MS/PC-DOS operating system (with an ANSI.SYS driver, of course!). An even faster one, possibly the fastest, would utilize direct video RAM writes and be restricted to IBM machines and close compatibles. It should be possible to code several versions of `cls()` provided in the same source file and use conditional compilation to include the version needed at the moment. Write a file for inclusion in your programs that accomplishes this goal. The completed code should include the three versions as outlined above.

4. Write a macro that determines if its argument is a leap year. The macro should evaluate to a positive integer if the argument is a leap year, otherwise to a zero. For example, the invocation

```
if (IS_LEAP_YEAR(1987))
```

should be FALSE. Write a test jig to test your macro and demonstrate that it evaluates properly.

5. The assembly language instruction rotate is supported by most processing environments and usually includes a right and left version. The instruction is used to rotate the bits in an integer argument by a fixed or variable number of bit positions. For example, consider the binary number given below:

```
11010100
```

Applying the operation ROL(11010100) would produce:

```
10101001
```

as a result. Obviously, the ROL operation is dependent on the integer size of the machine in question. Write two macros, ROL() and ROR() designed to overcome the problem of integer size on a particular machine.

6. Functions that utilize printer control codes are notoriously non-portable from environment to environment. One solution to this problem is to place printer-specific control codes in a header file and define appropriate switches to allow compilation of the application for different environments. The printer functions, taken as a whole, can then be included as a driver along with the main application code. Write a set of printer driver functions that perform the following:
   a. Reset the printer to a known state.
   b. Place the printer in compressed print mode.
   c. Activate a form feed.
   d. Activate a line feed.
   e. Sound the bell.

   You may use the control codes for whatever printer type you have available. Make sure your driver will easily accommodate other printer types.

* 7. Modify the review program to include the following features:
   a. Allow the number of dimensions and size of each dimension to be input as command line arguments when the program is invoked. You will have to use argc and argv for this purpose.
   b. Include provisions for the game space array to be stored and retrieved from a disk file. In addition, allow the disk file name to be specified as a command line argument.

* indicates advanced exercises

13.9 Pretest

☐ *Multiple Choice*

Circle one correct answer for each of the following:

1. A macro, compared to its equivalent function implementation, is generally:
   a. More complicated.
   b. Faster in execution speed.
   c. Coded from a different algorithm.
   d. None of the above.
   e. All of the above.

2. What is wrong with the following macro?

```
#define TRUE 1
#define FALSE 0
#define TEST(bin, bit) bin & bit ? TRUE : FALSE
```

   (Assume that `bin` is a binary number and `bit` is the bit to be tested.)
   a. The type `bin` is not valid in C.
   b. The macro will always return TRUE.
   c. Side effects may arise in the expansion.
   d. TRUE and FALSE will not be expanded in TEST.

3. One use for the `#ifdef` preprocessor directive could be:
   a. Building applications that can be used in different operating system environments.
   b. Nesting one function within another.
   c. Dynamic memory allocation within a macro.
   d. None of the above.

4. What is wrong with the code fragment given below?

```
#define SQUARE(x)   ((x) * (x))
        ...
/* produce a table of squares from 1 to 10 */

int i = 0;

while (i <= 10)
   printf("%d squared = %d\n", SQUARE(++i));
        ...
```

   a. The loop will not terminate because `++i` will not be evaluated in the macro expansion.
   b. The macro expansion will introduce side effects, resulting in an incorrect table of squares.

c. The increment operator cannot be used in a macro.

d. The macro argument x cannot be used more than once in the macro definition. A compile error will be the result.

5. Which statement is not true when applied to the #if family of preprocessor directives?

a. They can be nested.

b. They can be used as functionally equivalent to the C construct if/else.

c. They are always evaluated before compilation takes place.

d. The #else, if present, is always associated with the closest preceding #if directive.

6. The predefined macros __DATE__ and __TIME__ are useful because

a. They can be used to reset the system date and/or time.

b. They are difficult (impossible?) to retrieve by other methods.

c. They can be used to dynamically retrieve the current date/time at runtime.

d. None of the above.

7. What is wrong with the following code fragment?

```
#define IBM
#if defined(IBM)
   #define MAX_INT 16
#elif defined(MACINTOSH)
   #define MAX_INT 32
#else defined(ATARI800)
   #define MAX-INT 8

      ...

printf("Maximum integer is %d\n", MAX_INT);
```

a. There is no #endif directive.

b. IBM has no value.

c. The #define directives cannot be indented.

d. MAX_INT would be undefined, which would produce a compile error.

e. All of the above.

f. None of the above.

Appendix A
Using the Turbo C Compiler

A.1 The Necessary Hardware and Software

The Turbo C compiler (version 1.0) runs on any IBM-PC/XT/AT/PS-2 or true compatible with at least 384Kb (version 2.0 needs 448kb) of memory and MS/PC-DOS 2.0 or above. An 80-column monitor is needed, and while it will run on a machine with only one floppy drive, two floppy drives and/or a hard disk are recommended.

The following configurations illustrate the files needed for writing programs using Turbo C 1.0. The `install` program of Turbo C 2.0 will create for you either the floppy or hard disk arrangement.

The files listed below are present on different Turbo C distribution disks. If an entry is preceded by a backslash (\), it is the name of a subdirectory which must be present, and created if necessary. The files that should be placed in the subdirectory are indented below the subdirectory name.

A.1.1 One Floppy Drive

To use Turbo C on a system that has one floppy disk of at least 360Kb, the files should be organized in this manner:

Integrated Environment Version

```
Program Disk
   tc.exe
   tchelp.tch

Work Disk
   \include subdirectory
      all .h files except mcalc.h
      \sys subdirectory
         stat.h
   \lib subdirectory
      c0s.obj
      cs.lib
      emu.lib
      fp87.lib
      maths.lib
```

Command Line Version

Borland recommends that the Command Line version of Turbo C not be used if there is only one disk drive. The Integrated Environment version works much more smoothly.

When using the Integrated Environment version, remove the Program disk after invoking the `tc` program. Replace it with the Work disk for the remainder of the edit/compile session. The root directory should be the current directory on the work disk. Use the Options menu to set the `include` and `lib` subdirectories.

A.1.2   *Two Floppy Drives*

To use Turbo C on a system that has two floppy disks, each with at least 360Kb, the files should be organized in this manner:

Integrated Environment Version

> Program Disk
>   `tc.exe`
>   `tchelp.tch`
>
> Work Disk
>   `\include` subdirectory
>   all `.h` files except `mcalc.h`
>   `\sys` subdirectory
>   `stat.h`
>   `\lib` subdirectory
>   `c0s.obj`
>   `cs.lib`
>   `emu.lib`
>   `fp87.lib`
>   `maths.lib`

Command Line Version

> Program Disk
>   `tcc.exe`
>   `tlink.exe`
>   `\include` subdirectory
>   all `.h` files except `mcalc.h`
>   `\sys` subdirectory
>   `stat.h`
>   `\lib` subdirectory
>   `c0s.obj`
>   `cs.lib`
>   `emu.lib`
>   `fp87.lib`
>   `maths.lib`

> Work Disk
>   Contains only `.c`, `.obj`, and `.exe` files.

Place the Program disk in drive `A:` and the Work disk in drive `B:`. The root directory should be the current directory on drive `B:`. The root directory of the `A:` drive should be present in the MS/PC-DOS PATH statement.

The first time the Integrated Environment version is used the Options menu must be used to set the `include` and `lib` subdirectories. Then the Options menu should also be used to specify the location of the help files. Save these settings to disk after they have been entered.

A.1.3   *Turbo C on a Hard Disk*
To use Turbo C on a system that has a hard disk, the files should be organized in this manner:

```
\turboc
   tc.exe
   tchelp.tch
   tcc.exe
   tlink.exe
   \include subdirectory
       all .h files except mcalc.h
       \sys subdirectory
           stat.h
   \lib subdirectory
       c0s.obj
       cs.lib
       emu.lib
       fp87.lib
       maths.lib
```

The `turboc` directory of the hard drive must be the current directory when invoking the Integrated Environment version. The first time this version is used the Options menu must be used to set the `include` and `lib` subdirectories. Then the Options menu should also be used to specify the location of the help files. Save these settings to disk after they have been entered.

A.2   The Turbo C Integrated Development Environment Editor
The Turbo C editor is very similar to the editors found in other Borland products. The command structure is also a derivative of the commands used in WordStar. The editor allows lines to have a maximum of 248 characters. Lines longer than 77 characters cause the screen to scroll as they are entered or edited. There is no automatic word-wrap.

A.2.1   *Cursor Movement Commands*
A few of the commands shown in Table A.1 deserve special comment. First, the `word right` and `word left` commands are oriented somewhat toward C language syntax. A word is any series of characters delimited by any of the following characters on each side (the characters on either side do not have to be the same):

```
space < > , ; . ( ) [ ] ^ ' * + - / $
```

Second, the commands to move to the beginning and end of blocks work whether the block is visible or not (see Section A.2.2 for how to make blocks hidden or visible). And finally, the `last position of cursor` command (`Ctrl-q p`) restores the cursor to the position it occupied before the last command.

Cursor Movement	Control Keys	Extended Keys
Character left	Ctrl-s	Left Arrow
Character right	Ctrl-d	Right Arrow
Word left	Ctrl-a	Ctrl-LA
Word right	Ctrl-f	Ctrl-RA
Line up	Ctrl-e	Up
Line down	Ctrl-x	Down
Scroll screen up one line	Ctrl-w	
Scroll screen down one line	Ctrl-z	
Page up one full screen	Ctrl-r	PgUp
Page down one full screen	Ctrl-c	PgDn
Beginning of line (to col 1)	Ctrl-q s	Home
End of line (to last char)	Ctrl-q d	End
Top of window/screen	Ctrl-q e	
Bottom of window/screen	Ctrl-q x	
Top of file	Ctrl-q r	
End of file	Ctrl-q c	
Beginning of block	Ctrl-q b	
End of block	Ctrl-q k	
Last position of cursor	Ctrl-q p	

Table A.1   Summary of Turbo C Cursor Movement Commands

A.2.2   *Insert, Delete and Block Commands*

These commands are listed in Table A.2. Characters are inserted into the file and existing text moved to the right when in the Insert mode (which is the default mode when the editor begins). Pressing the Ins key toggles the editor into Overwrite mode. The Overwrite mode does not cause text to move to the right as characters are typed, but rather causes the existing characters to be lost as new characters are typed.

The backspace and del commands perform similar actions on different characters. The backspace key deletes the character to the left of the cursor, while the del key deletes the character under the cursor. Pressing the backspace key while on position 1 will delete the carriage return-line feed character combination which separates lines. This will cause the line on which the cursor is positioned to "jump up" and be appended to the end of the previous line. The del key will do exactly the same thing if the cursor is positioned at the end of the previous line. There is no way to restore deleted lines and blocks, so delete with care.

Only one block can exist at any given time. When a block is copied the marking is removed from the "from" block and applied to the new "to" block. Blocks can also be made "invisible" by hiding their marking. An invisible block has not gone away, but the move, copy, delete, and write block commands do \not work while the block is hidden. The commands to jump to the beginning and end of the block work whether the block is displayed or not.

Finally, the mark single word command marks the word on which the cursor is located, or the first word to the left if the command is invoked while the cursor is between two words.

Text Management Operation	Control Keys	Extended Keys
Insert mode on/off	Ctrl-v	Ins
Insert line	Ctrl-n	
Delete line	Ctrl-y	
Delete to end of line	Ctrl-q y	
Delete character left of cursor	Ctrl-h	Backspace
Delete character under cursor	Ctrl-g	Del
Delete word right of cursor	Ctrl-t	
Mark beginning of block	Ctrl-k b	
Mark end of block	Ctrl-k k	
Mark single word	Ctrl-k t	
Copy block	Ctrl-k c	
Delete block	Ctrl-k y	
Hide/display block	Ctrl-k h	
Move block	Ctrl-k v	
Read block (file) from disk	Ctrl-k r	
Write block to disk	Ctrl-k w	
Print block	Ctrl-k p	

Table A.2   Summary of Turbo C Insert, Delete and Block Commands

A.2.3   *Miscellaneous Editing Commands*

These commands are listed in Table A.3. The autoindent on/off feature causes the cursor to position itself under the first nonblank character of the previous line rather than in column 1. This is very helpful when trying to align statements, especially since the tab settings are fixed at eight characters and cannot be altered to the traditional three spaces per tab, the normal C convention. Also, the set and find place marker commands allow up to four place markers (Ctrl-k 0, Ctrl-k 1, etc.) to be entered, which can then be jumped back to with Ctrl-q 0, Ctrl-q 1, etc.

The find and replace commands can search for a string up to 30 characters long, and replace it with another string also not longer than 30 characters. When the Find command is invoked with Ctrl-q a a prompt appears for the find string. At that point the previous find string can be retrieved with the word right command. When building the find string, Ctrl-a is a wild card that matches any one character; Ctrl-m j matches the end of line character.

When the string to be found has been entered a prompt for the Find options to use will appear. These options are shown in Table A.4. They can be combined, such as using BU to search backward and also ignore case. The W option will allow a search string of day to match day but not the letters day in the string mayday. When building a replace string, two additional options can be used: N replaces without asking and n allows entry of a number that specifies the next n number of replacements to make.

Anytime a prompt for input appears the entire command can be aborted by using the Ctrl-u command. In the same way any changes made to any one line can be deleted by using the Ctrl-q l command as long as the cursor has not left the line.

Miscellaneous Command	Control Keys	Extended Keys
Abort operation	Ctrl-u	
Autoindent on/off	Ctrl-o i	
Compile		alt-F9
Compile menu		alt-C
Control character prefix	Ctrl-p	
Debug menu		alt-D
Edit		alt-E
Exit Turbo C		alt-X
File menu		alt-F
Find	Ctrl-q f	
Find and replace	Ctrl-q a	
Find place marker	Ctrl-q (0,1,2,3)	
Help (context sensitive)		F1
Help (last screen seen)		alt-F1
Invoke main menu		F10
Load file		F3
Make a program		F9
Next error		F8
Options menu		alt-O
Pick from a file list		alt-F3
Previous error		F7
Project menu		alt-P
Quit edit, no save	Ctrl-k d or Ctrl-k q	
Repeat last find	Ctrl-l	
Restore line	Ctrl-q l	
Run (compile if needed)		alt-R
Save and continue editing	Ctrl-k s	F2
Set place marker	Ctrl-k (0,1,2,3)	
Switch to active window		F6
Tab	Ctrl-i	Tab
Tab mode	Ctrl-o t	
Version number display		alt-F10
Zoom/unzoom (full/split screen toggle)		F5

Table A.3   Summary of Turbo C Miscellaneous Editing Commands

Option	Meaning
B	Search backward
G	Search global (start at top)
L	Local search in marked blocks
N	Find next (start here)
n	Find nth occurrence
U	Ignore upper/lowercase
W	Search whole words only

Table A.4   Turbo C Find Command Options

A.3   The Turbo C Command Line Environment

The Command Line version of Turbo C, the tcc program, provides a quick way to compile a program that has already been written with an editor other than the one provided in the Integrated Development Environment. The tcc program operates in a similar manner to the UNIX cc command in that tcc will both compile and link source (.C) and object (.OBJ) files at the same time. Turbo C's tcc command will also let assembly language modules be named on the command line, and will allow a specific library to be used at link time in addition to naming the directory where library files are to be found.

A.3.1   A Quick Turbo C Batch Compile Session

We have described how to use the Integrated Development Environment to load and compile the hello.c program, which is distributed with the Turbo C distribution disks. The following command will both compile and link the same program from MS/PC-DOS:

```
tcc -Iinclude -Llib hello.c
```

To run the hello program after it has been compiled and linked, enter the following at the MS/PC-DOS prompt:

```
hello
```

This will execute the program and then display the MS/PC-DOS prompt again. When a program is compiled, linked, and run in this manner the "Press any key to return to Turbo C . . ." message does not appear (Turbo C version 1.0).

A.3.2   Compiler and Linker Options

In the section above we saw the -Iinclude and -Llib sequence of characters appear on the line after the program name tcc. These character sequences, which begin with a dash, are called command line switches and are used to pass information to the Turbo C batch compile program tcc. More than one switch can appear in conjunction with a command.

The first character that appears after the dash is the switch itself, and this switch must be entered in the correct case. For instance, the -A switch cannot be entered as a lowercase -a because there is already another switch with the name -a which means something entirely different. Also, a space must be left before the dash because some switches use trailing dashes to designate an inverse or toggled value.

Table A.5 gives a partial list of the command line switches that are available in Turbo C. Consult the Turbo C documentation for a complete list.

Switch	Meaning
-A	Allow ANSI keywords only
-a-	Alignment of byte
-c	Compile only, no link
-Dname	Defines name to a single space character
-Dname=string	Defines name to specified string
-d	Duplicate strings are merged
-efilename	Name the executable file filename.exe
-f	Floating point uses 8087 if present, uses emulation if 8087 is not present
-f-	Floating point routines are not included
-f87	Floating point requires 8087 to be present
-Ipathname	Location of directories containing .h files (searches all if multiple −I switches are used)
-K-	Characters are signed by default
-k	Use a standard stack frame (useful for debugging)
-Lpathname	Location of directories with .lib files (uses last one if multiple −I switches are used)
-ms	Small model used
-N	Test for stack overflow
-npathname	Output directory
-p-	Use C calling conventions (not Pascal)
-r	Use register variables
-1	Generate 80186/80286 code
-1-	Generate 8088/8086 code

Table A.5 Turbo C Command Line Switches (partial list)

A.3.3 *Example Command Lines*
Here are some sample batch compile command lines:

1. tcc -c -IC:\tc\include -LC:\tc\lib hello.c
   Valid. Only compile and do not link (-c option) the file hello.c, look for the .h files in the directory C:\tc\include (-I option), and look for the .lib files in the directory C:\tc\lib (-L option).

2. `tcc -f87 -Iinc -LC:\tc\lib hello.c`

   Valid. Force the use of 8087 instructions only and do not include code to emulate the 8087 if it is not there, look for the `.h` files in the subdirectory `inc` which must be within the current directory (`-I` option), and look for the `.lib` files in the directory `C:\tc\lib` (`-L` option).

3. `tcc -1 -Iinc -Iinc2 -Llib -Llib2 hello.c`

   Valid, but questionable. Force the use of 80186 instructions, look for the `.h` files in both the `inc` and `inc2` subdirectories which must be within the current directory (`-I` option), and look for the `.lib` files in only the directory `lib2` (`-L` option). Note that the directory `lib` is not searched for libraries.

4. `tcc -efinal mysub.obj hello.c`

   Valid. Compile and link `hello.c` and link in the file `mysub.obj` at link time. Name the resulting executable file `final.exe` (`-e` option) rather than using the name of the first source or object module name that appears on the command line (i.e. `mysub`). The `.h` include files and the `.lib` library files are assumed to be in the current directory since the `-I` and `-L` switches were not used.

5. `tcc -5 hello.c`

   Invalid. `-5` is not a valid switch. The compilation is immediately terminated with an error message.

A.3.4   *The TURBOC.CFG File*

If the `tcc` version of Turbo C is used, some very long command lines will be needed unless all include and library files are in the current directory. We recommend putting all these files into subdirectories so that the only files in the current directory are the `.c`, `.obj` and `.exe` files that are created. Then the `-I` and `-L` switches would be used on the command line.

A permanent copy of these frequently used command line switches can be made by placing them into a file called `turboc.cfg`. This file can be created by any ASCII editor (including Turbo C's built-in editor) and is read by the `tcc` program when `tcc` first begins to execute.

The `tcc` program first processes any switches it finds in the `turboc.cfg` file; then it processes any command line switches which were also supplied for this compile session. Command line switches override the same options specified in `turboc.cfg`. This is a valuable concept which allows minor adjustments to be made to command line switches without editing or creating multiple `turboc.cfg` files.

The options can appear on separate lines in the `turboc.cfg` file, or multiple options can be placed on the same line. A `turboc.cfg` file for the second example command line in section A.3.3 above might look like this:

```
-f87 -Iinc
-LC:\tc\lib
```

Note that two options were placed on one line, and one on a second line. Be sure to save the turboc.cfg file in a place where it can be used again.

A.4   The Turbo C Preprocessor

The Turbo C preprocessor is not only incorporated into the tc and tcc programs, but is also provided as a separate program called cpp. All switches that can be specified for tcc can also be specified for cpp, and any switch that does not apply to the preprocessor function will be ignored (e.g., −1, −f, etc.). In addition, the switches in Table A.6 are also recognized by cpp.

Switch	Meaning
−P	Prefix lines with file names and line numbers
−P−	Do not include file names and line numbers (needed if output file is to be compiled)

Table A.6   Turbo C Preprocessor Switches

Usually the −I switch is needed when using the preprocessor because the included files (those ending in .h) are incorporated into C programs through a preprocessor directive, #include. The cpp program creates a file with the same name as the source program, but with the file extension .i. The .i file is created in the current directory unless the −n switch is used.

For example, if the Turbo C include files are located in the directory c:\tc\include, this command will preprocess the program hello.c, creating the file hello.i in the current directory:

```
cpp -IC:\tc\include hello.c
```

Each line in the file hello.i will be prefaced with the file name and line number of where that line originated.

Appendix B
Using the Quick C Compiler

B.1 The Necessary Hardware and Software

Quick C is fully compatible with the Microsoft C Optimizing Compiler. It runs on any IBM PC/XT/AT or true compatible with at least 448Kb of memory, MS/PC-DOS 2.1 or above, two double-sided floppy-disk drives or one floppy drive and a hard disk. While Quick C will run on a machine with just two 360Kb floppy disk drives, there is a certain awkwardness about the process which is eliminated if larger floppy disk drives, or a hard disk, are used.

The following configurations illustrate the files needed for compiling programs with Quick C 1.0. The medium memory model is the default for the Quick C programming environment which combines the editor and compiler (the qc command), while the small model is the default when Quick C is run in batch mode (the qcl command). If the Quick C 2.0 version is used, then follow the instructions given by the setup program.

Most of the files listed below are present on one of the Quick C distribution disks. The library files (files with a .lib extension), however, must be created from the component libraries, which are on the distribution disks. The setup program will build all required libraries for all selected memory models, and the libbuild program can be used to create additional libraries after setup is completed (the /L switch is used with Quick C 2.0).

In the lists below, if an entry is preceded by a backslash (\), it is the name of a subdirectory that must be present (created if necessary). The files that should be placed in the subdirectory are indented below the subdirectory name.

B.1.1 *Compiling In Memory from Floppy Disks*

Quick C 1.0 is distributed in two different forms. When bundled with the Microsoft C compiler it is packaged without the overlay file, qc.ovl. When packaged as a separate product the overlay file is included. For either situation we can create a set of disks which allow Quick C to be used on computers which do not have a hard disk. At least two floppy disks, each with at least 360Kb, are required.

If the overlay file, qc.ovl, is not available, the files should be organized in this manner:

☐ *Program Disk*

```
qc.exe
\include subdirectory
    conio.h
    ctype.h
    fcntl.h
    malloc.h
    memory.h
    process.h
    search.h
    stdarg.h
    stddef.h
    stdio.h
```

stdlib.h
string.h

Work Disk
qc.hlp (optional)
qc.ini (created by qc to hold options that were last selected)
all .c, .obj and .exe files

Environment Variables
INCLUDE=A:\INCLUDE
PATH=A:\;B:\
TMP=B:\

Place the Program disk in drive A: and the Work disk in drive B:. The B: drive should be the current drive, and its root directory should be the current directory. The environment variables are created by using the SET command at the MS/PC-DOS prompt. For example,

SET TMP=B:\

To start Quick C enter the following command at the MS/PC-DOS prompt:

qc [pgm.c]

where pgm.c is optional, needed only if an existing file is being edited and compiled. If pgm.c is not entered, use the File Menu/Open... Command to select the file to be processed.

Notice that not all include files are present in the subdirectory \INCLUDE on drive A:. This is because there is not enough space on the Program disk for all the include files, so those shown above are merely a representative sample. If other include files are needed, they can be substituted for those that are not needed, or the entire \INCLUDE subdirectory can be placed on the Work disk. The latter would require that the Environment variable INCLUDE be changed to INCLUDE= B:\INCLUDE. The file qc.hlp is optional, but without it the Help function within Quick C is not available.

This arrangement leaves a large amount of free disk space available on the Work disk. It does not allow any .exe files to be created, either through the qcl program or by checking the Output option of Exe in the Compile Dialog box. Note that even though a file with the .exe extension may be left on the Work disk, that file cannot be executed outside of Quick C. The library routines included in that .exe program require the qc shell to execute properly.

If the overlay file, qc.ovl, is present, the files should be organized in this manner:

Program Disk #1
```
qc.exe
```

Program Disk #2
```
qc.hlp
qc.ovl
link.exe (see text)
\include subdirectory (with all distribution disk files)
\include\sys subdirectory (with all distribution disk files)
```

Work Disk
```
all .c, .obj and .exe files
```

Environment Variables
```
INCLUDE=A:\INCLUDE;A:\INCLUDE\SYS
LIB=A:\;B:\
PATH=A:\;B:\
TMP=B:\
```

Place Program Disk #1 in drive A: and the Work disk in drive B:. The B: drive should be the current drive, and its root directory should be the current directory. The environment variables are created by using the SET command at the MS/PC-DOS prompt. For example,

```
SET TMP=B:\
```

To start Quick C enter the following command at the MS/PC-DOS prompt:

```
qc [pgm.c]
```

where pgm.c is optional, needed only if an existing file is being edited and compiled. If pgm.c is not entered, use the File Menu/Open... Command to select the file to be processed.

After Quick C begins, remove Program Disk #1 from drive A: and replace it with Program Disk #2. When needed, the overlay file, qc.ovl, will be used by Quick C rather than the main executable file itself.

This arrangement, like the one described immediately above, leaves a large amount of free space available on the Work disk. It also makes the help files available. It does not allow any .exe files to be created, either through the qcl program or by checking the Output option of Exe in the Compile Dialog box. Note that even though a file with the .exe extension may be left on the Work disk, that file cannot be executed outside of Quick C. The library routines included in that .exe program require the qc shell to execute properly.

This arrangement does, however, have the advantage that all include files are available to Quick C, rather than just a subset. Also, since the overlay file, qc.ovl, is smaller than qc.exe Quick C runs faster since the overlay file loads more quickly than does the executable file.

Both arrangements require that other library files be placed on the Work Disk before creating an .exe file which will be executed outside of Quick C. The library files will use much of the space on the Work Disk, so we recommend using the arrangement described in section B.1.2 if .exe files are needed. If no .exe files will be created then the file link.exe is not needed for either arrangement.

B.1.2   Batch Execution and .exe File Creation from a Floppy

To create .exe files while using qc.exe, or to use qcl, the batch version of qc, the files of Quick C 1.0 can be organized in this manner:

Program Disk
qc.exe
qcl.exe

Work Disk
link.exe
\include subdirectory
   conio.h
   ctype.h
   fcntl.h
   malloc.h
   memory.h
   process.h
   search.h
   stdarg.h
   stddef.h
   stdio.h
   stdlib.h
   string.h
   other .h files as needed
\lib subdirectory
   mlibce.lib (medium memory model library)
qc.ini (created by qc to hold options that were last selected)
all .c, .obj and .exe files

Environment Variables
INCLUDE=B:\INCLUDE
LIB=B:\LIB
PATH=A:\;B:\
TMP=B:\

Place the Program disk in drive A: and the Work disk in drive B:. The B: drive should be the current drive, and its root directory should be the current directory. The environment variables are created by using the SET command at the MS/PC-DOS prompt. For example,

```
SET TMP=B:\
```

To start the Quick C programming environment (combined editor and compiler) enter the following command at the MS/PC-DOS prompt:

```
qc [pgm.c]
```

where pgm.c is optional, needed only if an existing file is being edited and compiled. If pgm.c is not entered, use the File Menu/Open... Command in Quick C to select the file to be processed, or begin entering the program source code from scratch. To run Quick C as a batch program (no editor), use this command:

```
qcl /AM  pgm.c
```

where pgm.c is not optional because the name of the file to be compiled must be explicitly provided to qcl.

Notice that not all include files are present in the subdirectory \INCLUDE on drive B:. This is because the above configuration leaves the Work disk with only 50-60Kb free space, severely limiting the size of the program that can be developed. If other include files are needed, they can be added at the expense of Work disk space. A good rule of thumb is to double the size of the program to indicate how much free Work disk space is needed when compiling the program. Note also that this arrangement leaves no room for the help files, qc.hlp and qcl.hlp.

It is possible to create stand-alone .exe files with this configuration, however, either through the qcl program or by checking the Output Option of Exe in the Compile Dialog box. This capability is provided at the expense of free space on the Work disk. The .exe files are medium memory model programs, which require that the /AM command switch be used when compiling in a batch mode. That is necessary to override the small memory model format normally used by the qcl program.

B.1.3   *Quick C on a Hard Disk*

The setup program provided with Quick C will perform the installation quickly and easily on a hard disk. If there is enough disk space both the small and medium memory models should be created. The small memory model is the default used by the qcl program, while the medium model is the default for qc.

The setup program will use or create these subdirectories in the root directory of the disk specified in the setup invocation:

\BIN	executable (.exe) files of the compiler, linker, etc.
\INCLUDE	include (.h) files
\LIB	library (.lib) files
\TMP	temporary work space needed by the compiler, linker, etc.

If the hard disk is named `C:`, these are the environment variable settings needed to access all the files installed by the `setup` program:

```
INCLUDE=C:\INCLUDE
LIB=C:\LIB
PATH=C:\BIN
TMP=C:\TMP
```

To start the Quick C programming environment (combined editor and compiler) enter the following command at the MS/PC-DOS prompt:

```
qc [pgm.c]
```

where `pgm.c` is optional, needed only if an existing file is being edited and compiled. If `pgm.c` is not entered, use the `File Menu/Open... Command` in Quick C to select the file to be processed. To run Quick C as a batch program (no editor), use this command:

```
qcl pgm.c
```

where `pgm.c` is not optional because the name of the file to be compiled must be explicitly provided to `qcl`.

All include and help files will be available, and the size of the programs that can be compiled is limited only by the amount of free space left on the hard disk.

B.2   The Quick C Programming Environment

The Quick C Programming Environment features an integrated editor, compiler, and debugger. The Quick C editor supports a maximum line length of 255 characters per line, and has a set of basic commands, which are very similar to those found in WordStar(R) by MicroPro. Most of these commands have two key sequences, the WordStar key sequence and an alternate sequence provided by Microsoft. Additional commands control the compiling and debugging portions of the environment. The friendly, window-style display uses a single-line menu bar. The look and feel is the same as QuickBASIC, and Microsoft promises that it also will be very similar to the OS/2 Presentation Manager.

B.2.1   Cursor Movement Commands

Table B.1 describes the Quick C cursor movement commands. Of special note, the `word right` and `word left` commands are oriented toward C language syntax. A word is any series of characters delimited by any of the following characters on each side (the characters on either side do not have to be the same):

```
space < > , ; . ( ) [ ] ^ ' * + - / $
```

Cursor Movement	WordStar Keys	Quick C Keys
Character left	Ctrl-s	Left Arrow(LA)
Character right	Ctrl-d	Right Arrow(RA)
Word left	Ctrl-a	Ctrl-LA
Word right	Ctrl-f	Ctrl-RA
Line up	Ctrl-e	Up
Line down	Ctrl-x	Down
Page up one full screen	Ctrl-r	PgUp
Page down one full screen	Ctrl-c	PgDn
Page left one full screen		Ctrl-PgUp
Page right one full screen		Ctrl-PgDn
Beginning of line (to col 1)	Ctrl-q s	Home
End of line (to last char)	Ctrl-q d	End
Top of window/screen	Ctrl-q e	
Bottom of window/screen	Ctrl-q x	
Top of file	Ctrl-q r	Ctrl-Home
End of file	Ctrl-q c	Ctrl-End

Table B.1   Summary of Quick C Cursor Movement Commands

B.2.2   *Insert, Delete and Block Commands*

These commands are listed in Table B.2. Characters are inserted into the file and existing text moved to the right when in the Insert mode (which is the default mode when the editor begins). Pressing the Ins key toggles the editor into Overwrite mode. The Overwrite mode does not cause text to move to the right as characters are typed, but rather causes the existing characters to be lost as new characters are typed.

The backspace and del commands perform similar actions on different characters. The backspace key deletes the character to the left of the cursor, while the del key deletes the character under the cursor. Pressing the backspace key while on position 1 will delete the carriage return-line feed character combination, which separates lines. This will cause the line on which the cursor is positioned to "jump up" and be appended to the end of the previous line. The del key will do exactly the same thing if the cursor is positioned at the end of the previous line.

Text is marked, or selected, by using one of the select commands. The selected text can be identified by the highlighted characters, normally shown in reverse video. Once selected, the text can be deleted, or cut or copied to the clipboard. Be careful using certain keys while text is selected. For instance, pressing the Del key while text is selected deletes the entire selected text rather than just the character under the cursor. To unselect text press any arrow key by itself.

Text Management Operation	WordStar Keys	Quick C Keys
Insert mode on/off	Ctrl-v	Ins
Insert line above	Ctrl-n	
Insert line below		Enter
Insert line deleted with Ctrl-y		Shift-Ins
Insert tab	Ctrl-i	Tab
Delete line	Ctrl-y	
Delete to end of line	Ctrl-q y	Ctrl-q y
Delete character left of cursor	Ctrl-h	Backspace
Delete character under cursor	Ctrl-g	Del
Delete word right of cursor	Ctrl-t	
Select character left		Shift-left
Select character right		Shift-right
Select word left		Shift-Ctrl-left
Select word right		Shift-Ctrl-right
Select screen up		Shift-PgUp
Select screen down		Shift-PgDn
Select to beginning of file		Shift-Ctrl-Home
Select to end of file		Shift-Ctrl-End
Deleted selected text		Del
Cut selected text to clipboard		Shift-Del
Copy selected text to clipboard		Ctrl-Ins
Paste clipboard text		Shift-Ins
Unselect text		any arrow key

Table B.2   Summary of Quick C Insert, Delete and Block Commands

B.2.3   *Miscellaneous Editing Commands*

These commands are listed in Table B.3. The set and find place marker commands allow up to three place markers (Ctrl-k 0, Ctrl-k 1, etc.) to be entered, which can then be jumped back to with Ctrl-q 0, Ctrl-q 1, etc.

The Find and Replace commands can search for a string up to 36 characters long, and replace it with another string also not longer than 36 characters.

Any command can be aborted by using the Esc key. In the same way changes made to any line can be reversed or backed out by using the Ctrl-q l or alt-backspace commands as long as the cursor has not left the line.

Miscellaneous Commands	Control Keys	Extended Keys
Debug menu		alt-D
Edit		alt-E
File menu		alt-F
Set program list		alt-F L
Load file		alt-F O
Save and continue editing		alt-F S
Exit Quick C		alt-F X
Run/compile menu		alt-R
Next error		Shift-F3
Previous error		Shift-F4
Help (context sensitive)		F1
Open last file		F2
Delete last watch		Shift-F2
Repeat last find		F3
Display output screen		F4
Execute to next breakpoint (continue)		F5
Start (compile if necessary)		Shift-F5
Execute to current cursor		F7
Execute next statement, trace through function		F8
Set breakpoint		F9
Execute next statement, trace around function		F10
Find	Ctrl-q f	Ctrl-\ Ctrl-l
Find and replace	Ctrl-q a	
Find matching {}[] < > ()		Ctrl-]
Find place marker	Ctrl-q n	
Set place marker	Ctrl-k n	
Tab	Ctrl-i	Tab
Abort operation		Esc
Undo changes to current line		Alt-backspace

Table B.3   Summary of Quick C Miscellaneous Editing Commands

Regular expression characters can be used with the FIND command and offer a very flexible environment for manipulating the source file. See the Quick C Programmer's Guide for additional details.

Character	Meaning
.	Match any single character
^	Match beginning of line When used inside [] means to match all except those characters specified
$	Match end of line
*	Match zero or more repetitions of previous character
[]	Match sets of characters
\	Next character treated literally

Table B.4   Quick C Regular Expression Special Characters

B.2.4   *Compiling and Debugging*

Quick C provides a fully integrated debugging environment, which allows single-stepping, breakpoint setting, and watchpoint settings for monitoring the state of variables as the program executes. In addition, a screen-swapping facility allows the programmer to toggle back and forth between the screen generated by the program and the debug display.

B.2.4.1   *General Debugging Instructions*

Following are the necessary steps needed to turn the debugging features on:

1. Enable the debug option before compiling the program.

2. Turn on debugging features (breakpoints, watchpoints, etc.).

3. Compile and run the program.

After determining the source of errors within the program, correct the errors and repeat the above steps.

B.2.4.2   *Adding Watchpoints*

Watchpoints allow the programmer to view the state of variables within the program while it is executing. Quick C allows watchpoints to be set for:

1. simple variables (`char`, `int`, `float`, etc.)

2. composite variable types (`struct`, `arrays`, etc.)

Arithmetic operators should not be included in watchpoint expressions.

To add program watchpoints, use the `Debug` menu. Quick C will then open a dialog window in which the watch expression should be entered. More than one watchpoint may be entered by separating each expression with a semicolon.

B.2.4.3   *Setting Breakpoints*

Breakpoints cause the debugging to stop program execution at the line where a breakpoint is enabled. Multiple breakpoints can be set in a program. Breakpoints are particularly useful when used in conjunction with watchpoints, allowing the programmer to view the state of variables at specific places within the program, while not having to resort to a single-stepping mode.

To set a breakpoint, move the cursor to the line in the program and press F9. After the breakpoint has been set, it may be removed by pressing F9 when the cursor is again on the same line. Individual breakpoints may be toggled by using F9 where desired. To remove all breakpoints, use the Debug menu.

B.3   The Quick C Command Line Environment

The Command Line version of Quick C, the qcl program, provides a quick way to compile a program that has already been written, either previously with Quick C or with an editor other than the one provided in the Quick C Programming Environment. The qcl program operates in a similar manner to the UNIX cc command and the Microsoft C compiler cl command in that qcl will both compile and link source (.C) and object (.OBJ) files at the same time.

B.3.1   *A Simple Quick C Batch Compile Session*

We have described how to use the Quick C Programming Environment to load and compile the program called hello.c (which consists of nothing more than a display of the message "Hello World"). The following command will both compile and link the program hello.c:

```
qcl hello.c
```

To run the hello program after it has been compiled and linked, enter the following at the DOS prompt:

```
hello
```

This will execute the program and then display the DOS prompt again. When a program is compiled, linked and run in this manner the message Program returned ( ). Press any key message does not appear.

B.3.2   *Compiler and Linker Options*

In the section above we saw the /AM sequence of characters appear on the line after the program name qcl. Character sequences like these, which begin with a slash, are called command line switches and are used to pass information to the Quick C batch compile program qcl. More than one switch can appear in conjunction with a command. For compiler options both a slash / and a dash - can identify an option. The dash is the same character used to identify switches in both UNIX and Turbo C.

The characters that appear after the slash (or dash) constitute the switch itself, and this switch must be entered in the correct case. For instance, the /C switch cannot be entered as a lowercase /c because there is already another switch with the name /c, which means something entirely different.

All switch options are compatible with the Microsoft C Optimizing Compiler. Any switches that do not apply to Quick C are simply ignored.

Table B.5 gives a partial list of the command line switches that are available in Quick C. Consult the Quick C documentation for a complete list, or produce the latest list by using this command:

```
qcl /help
```

Switch	Meaning
/AC	compact model
/AL	large model
/AM	medium model (default for qc)
/AS	small model (default for qcl)
/C	don't strip comments (valid only with /E, /EP or /P option)
/c	compile only, no link
/D<name>[=text]	define macro
/E	preprocess to stdout
/EP	same as /E but without line #'s
/Fefilename	executable filename
/Fmfilename	map filename
/Fofilename	object filename
/FPi	inline with emulator (default)
/FPi87	inline with 8087
/G0	8086 instructions (default)
/G2	286 instructions
/Gc	Pascal style function calls
/Gs	no stack checking
/Od	disable optimizations
/Ol	enable loop optimizations
/Ot	enable optimization
/P	preprocess to .i file
/U<name>	remove predefined macro
/u	remove all predefined macros
/Za	disable Microsoft extensions
/Zd	line number information
/Ze	enable extensions (default)
/Zi	symbolic debugging information
/Zq	enable debug interrupts
/Zr	enable pointer checking
/Zs	syntax check only
/W<number>	warning level (0 lowest, 3 highest)
/link [linker_options_and_libraries]	

Table B.5   Quick C Compiler Command Line Switches

Table B.6 is a partial list of the command line switches that are available in the Microsoft Linker. Consult the Linker documentation for a complete list, or produce the latest list by using this command:

```
link /help
```

The linker does not accept a dash - in addition to a slash / to indicate a linker switch.

Linker options can be supplied on the command line when compiling a program. First use the /link option immediately after the name of the program being compiled, and then follow /link with any other linker switches needed. See the second sample command line below for an example.

/BA	do not prompt if library not found
/CO	prepare Codeview debugging data
/E	pack executable files
/F	optimize far calls (use with /PAC)
/INF	display linking process information
/M	create a map file
/NOI	preserve case sensitivity
/PAC	pack segments (use with /F)
/PAU	pause before writing .exe file
/ST\<number>	stack size, bytes (2Kb default)

Table B.6   Linker Command Line Switches

B.3.3   *Example Command Lines*

1. qcl /c hello.c
   Valid. Compile only and do not link (/c option) the file hello.c.

2. qcl hello.c /link /ST:8000
   Valid. Compile and link the program, passing to the linker the /ST:8000 command, which specifies that the stack size is to be 8000 (decimal) bytes rather than the default 2048 (decimal) bytes.

3. qcl /G2 /FPi87 hello.c
   Valid. Compile and link hello.c, enabling the use of 80286 instructions when the program is compiled. Also handle floating point math operations by generating instructions for an 8087 or 80287 math coprocessor. The resulting .exe program cannot be executed on a machine that has the 8088 or 8086 processor and that does not have a math coprocessor.

4. `qcl /Fefinal hello.c`
   Valid. Compile and link `hello.c` and name the resulting executable file `final.exe` (`/Fe` option), rather than using the name of the first source or object module name that appears on the command line (i.e., `hello`).

5. `qcl /5 hello.c`
   Invalid. /5 is not a valid switch. It is ignored, and the compilation takes place as if no switches had been provided on the command line.

B.3.4   *Permanent Batch Compile Options*

When using the `qc` program all options selected during the session are saved in the file `qc.ini` when the session is terminated. The `qcl` (batch) version of Quick C provides a similar feature by allowing frequently used options to be stored in an environment variable. For instance, suppose that (1) stack checking code is not to be included in any compiled program (/Gs option), (2) null and invalid pointer checking code should always be included (/Zr option), (3) the most stringent level of warning messages is always to be used (/W3 option), and (4) all Microsoft extensions to the language are always to be disabled (/Za option). This MS/PC-DOS SET command would create that environment:

```
SET CL=/Gs /Zr /W3 /Za
```

Since options identified in the `CL` environment variable are read by the `qcl` program before options given on the `qcl` command line, use this command to compile the source file `pgm.c` and optimize in favor of execution time over code size (/Ot option):

```
qcl /Ot pgm.c
```

It will be interpreted as if this had been entered:

```
qcl /Gs /Zr /W3 /Za /Ot pgm.c
```

We suggest that the `CL` environment variable be set in the `autoexec.bat` file, which also contains other instructions needed each time the computer is powered on.

Appendix C—Trigraphs

The efforts to standardize the C language recognized the fact that C is becoming very popular on machines that do not use the ASCII character set. In particular, some terminals in the IBM 3270 family do not have the [or] symbols. Also, in Europe, some computers use the ISO-646 character set, which is a subset of ASCII; consequently not all characters are available.

The ANSI C standard committee realized that a truly portable language needed standard symbol sequences to represent those characters that were not always available. Trigraphs were created for the purpose of representing those characters. A trigraph is a sequence of three characters, with the first two always being ??. Each third character was chosen because it resembled to some degree the character it represented. Trigraphs are recognized by ANSI standard C compilers and can be used anywhere in a C program to replace the characters they represent. They are listed in Table C.1.

Trigraph	Character in C
??=	#
??(	[
??/	\
??)	]
??'	^
??<	{
??!	¦
??>	}
??–	~

Table C.1 Trigraphs

The following code illustrates how trigraphs would look in a program:

```
#include <stdio.h>

void with_trigraphs(void);
void with_out_trigraphs(void);

int i;
int array[5] = {10, 20, 30, 40, 50};

main()
{
    with_out_trigraphs();
    with_trigraphs();
}
```

(program continued on next page...)

```
void with_out_trigraphs()
{
   for (i = 0; i <= 4; i++)
     printf("element %d has the value %d\n", i, array[i]);
}

void with_trigraphs()
??<
   for (i = 0; i <= 4; i++)
     printf("element %d has the value %d??/n", i, array??(i??));
??>
```

Appendix D—Standard Headers

This appendix lists in alphabetical order all identifiers that should be defined in ANSI C standard header files. This list will assist you in finding which header file is needed for which identifier. For instance, to find which header file contains the prototype for the function `abort()`, look down the middle column of the list and find `abort(void)`, then note that `stdlib` is the header file named on the right.

The header files for some compilers will closely match the list, while others will contain significant differences. For instance, a common addition to the `stdio.h` header file is the definition of `NULL`. This allows `NULL` to be available when `stdio.h` has been included without also requiring `stddef.h`.

The header files required by the ANSI C standard are shown in Table D.1.

HEADER FILE	PURPOSE
assert.h	Diagnostics
ctype.h	Character handling and conversion
float.h	Floating point support
limits.h	Maximum and minimum limits
locale.h	International support
math.h	Mathematics
setjmp.h	Jumps
signal.h	Signal handling
stdarg.h	Variable number of arguments
stddef.h	Standard definitions
stdio.h	Input and output support
stdlib.h	General definitions and utilities
string.h	String handling
time.h	Time and date support

Table D.1   Header Files Required by the ANSI C Standard

Table D.2 gives the alphabetical list of identifiers. Remember that `void *` can be cast to a pointer of any type, and that for most purposes the term `size_t` can be replaced by `int`.

TYPE	IDENTIFIER	HEADER
	_IOFBF	stdio
	_IOLBF	stdio
	_IONBF	stdio
void	abort(void);	stdlib
int	abs(int j);	stdlib
double	acos(double x);	math
char *	asctime(struct tm *timeptr);	time
double	asin(double x);	math
void	assert(int expression);	assert
double	atan(double x);	math
double	atan2(double y, double x);	math

(table continued on next page...)

TYPE	IDENTIFIER	HEADER
int	atexit(void (*func)(void));	stdlib
double	atof(char *nptr);	stdlib
int	atoi(char *nptr);	stdlib
long	atol(char *nptr);	stdlib
void *	bsearch(void *key, void *base, size_t nbr, size_t size,	
	int (*compar)(void *, void *));	stdlib
	BUFSIZ	stdio
void *	calloc(size_t nbr, size_t size);	stdlib
double	ceil(double x);	math
void	clearerr(FILE *stream);	stdio
	CLK_TCK	time
clock_t	clock(void);	time
	clock_t	time
double	cos(double x);	math
double	cosh(double x);	math
char *	ctime(time_t *timer);	time
double	difftime(time_t time1, time_t time0);	time
div_t	div(int numer, int denom);	stdlib
	div_t	stdlib
	EDOM	math
	EOF	stdio
	ERANGE	math
	ERANGE	stdlib
	errno	stddef
void	exit(int status);	stdlib
double	exp(double x);	math
double	fabs(double x);	math
int	fclose(FILE *stream);	stdio
int	feof(FILE *stream);	stdio
int	ferror(FILE *stream);	stdio
int	fflush(FILE *stream);	stdio
int	fgetc(FILE *stream);	stdio
int	fgetpos(FILE *stream, fpos_t *pos);	stdio
char *	fgets(char *s, int n, FILE *stream);	stdio
	FILE	stdio
double	floor(double x);	math
double	fmod(double x, double y);	math
FILE *	fopen(char *filename, char *mode);	stdio
	fpos_t	stdio
int	fprintf(FILE *stream, char *format, ...);	stdio
int	fputc(int c, FILE *stream);	stdio
int	fputs(char *s, FILE *stream);	stdio
size_t	fread(void *ptr, size_t size, size_t nbr, FILE *stream);	stdio
void	free(void *ptr);	stdlib
FILE *	freopen(char *filename, char *mode, FILE *stream);	stdio
double	frexp(double value, int *exp);	math

TYPE	IDENTIFIER	HEADER
int	fscanf(FILE *stream, char *format, ...);	stdio
int	fseek(FILE *stream, long offset, int whence);	stdio
int	fsetpos(FILE *stream, fpos_t *pos);	stdio
long	ftell(FILE *stream);	stdio
size_t	fwrite(void *ptr, size_t size, size_t nbr, FILE *stream);	stdio
int	getc(FILE *stream);	stdio
int	getchar(void);	stdio
char *	getenv(char *name);	stdlib
char *	gets(char *s);	stdio
struct tm *	gmtime(time_t *timer);	time
	HUGE_VAL	math
	HUGE_VAL	stdlib
int	isalnum(int c);	ctype
int	isalpha(int c);	ctype
int	iscntrl(int c);	ctype
int	isdigit(int c);	ctype
int	isgraph(int c);	ctype
int	islower(int c);	ctype
int	isprint(int c);	ctype
int	ispunct(int c);	ctype
int	isspace(int c);	ctype
int	isupper(int c);	ctype
int	isxdigit(int c);	ctype
	jmp_buf	setjmp
	L_tmpnam	stdio
long	labs(long j);	stdlib
double	ldexp(double x, int exp);	math
ldiv_t	ldiv(long numer, long denom);	stdlib
	ldiv_t	stdlib
struct tm *	localtime(time_t *timer);	time
double	log(double x);	math
double	log10(double x);	math
void	longjmp(jmp_buf env, int val);	setjmp
void *	malloc(size_t size);	stdlib
void *	memchr(void *s, int c, size_t n);	stdlib
int	memcmp(void *s1, void *s2, size_t n);	stdlib
void *	memcpy(void *s1, void *s2, size_t nbr);	stdlib
void *	memmove(void *s1, void *s2, size_t nbr);	stdlib
void *	memset(void *s, int c, size_t n);	stdlib
time_t	mktime(struct tm *timeptr);	time
double	modf(double value, double *iptr);	math
	NDEBUG	assert
	NULL	stddef

(table continued on next page...)

TYPE	IDENTIFIER	HEADER
	offsetof(structure, member)	stddef
	OPEN_MAX	stdio
int	perror(char *s);	stdio
double	pow(double x, double y);	math
int	printf(char *format, ...);	stdio
	ptrdiff_t	stddef
int	putc(int c, FILE *stream);	stdio
int	putchar(int c);	stdio
int	puts(char *s);	stdio
void	qsort(void *base, size_t nbr, size_t size,	
	int (*compar)(void *, void *));	stdlib
int	raise(int sig);	signal
int	rand(void);	stdlib
	RAND_MAX	stdlib
void *	realloc(void *ptr, size_t size);	stdlib
int	remove(char *filename);	stdio
int	rename(char *oldfname, char *newfname);	stdio
void	rewind(FILE *stream);	stdio
int	scanf(char *format, ...);	stdio
	SEEK_CUR	stdio
	SEEK_END	stdio
	SEEK_SET	stdio
void	setbuf(FILE *stream, char *buf);	stdio
int	setjmp(jmp_buf env);	setjmp
char *	setlocale(int category, char *locale)	locale
int	setvbuf(FILE *stream, char *buf, int mode, size_t size);	stdio
	sig_atomic_t	signal
	SIG_DFL	signal
	SIG_ERR	signal
	SIG_IGN	signal
	SIGABRT	signal
	SIGFPE	signal
	SIGILL	signal
	SIGINT	signal
void	(*signal(int sig, void(*func)(int)))(int);	signal
	SIGSEGV	signal
	SIGTERM	signal
double	sin(double x);	math
double	sinh(double x);	math
	size_t	stddef
int	sprintf(char *s, char *format, ...);	stdio
double	sqrt(double x);	math
void	srand(unsigned seed);	stdlib
int	sscanf(char *s, char *format, ...);	stdio
	stderr	stdio

TYPE	IDENTIFIER	HEADER
	stdin	stdio
	stdout	stdio
char *	strcat(char *s1, char *s2);	stdlib
char *	strchr(char *s, int c);	stdlib
int	strcmp(char *s1, char *s2);	stdlib
size_t	strcoll(char *to, size_t maxsize, char *from);	stdlib
char *	strcpy(char *s1, char *s2);	stdlib
size_t	strcspn(char *s1, char *s2);	stdlib
char *	strerror(int errnum);	stdlib
size_t	strftime(char *s, size_t maxsize, char *format, struct tm *timeptr);	time
size_t	strlen(char *s);	stdlib
char *	strncat(char *s1, char *s2, size_t n);	stdlib
int	strncmp(char *s1, char *s2, size_t n);	stdlib
char *	strncpy(char *s1, char *s2, size_t n);	stdlib
char *	strpbrk(char *s1, char *s2);	stdlib
char *	strrchr(char *s1, int c);	stdlib
size_t	strspn(char *s1, char *s2);	stdlib
char *	strstr(char *s1, char *s2);	stdlib
double	strtod(char *nptr, char **endptr);	stdlib
char *	strtok(char *s1, char *s2);	stdlib
long	strtol(char *nptr, char **endptr, int base);	stdlib
unsigned long	strtoul(char *nptr, char **endptr, int base);	stdlib
int	system(char *string);	stdlib
double	tan(double x);	math
double	tanh(double x);	math
time_t	time(time_t *timer);	time
	time_t	time
struct	tm	time
	TMP_MAX	stdio
FILE *	tmpfile(void);	stdio
char *	tmpnam(char *s);	stdio
int	tolower(int c);	ctype
int	toupper(int c);	ctype
int	ungetc(int c, FILE *stream);	stdio
type	va_arg(va_list ap, type);	stdarg
void	va_end(va_list ap);	stdarg
	va_list	stdarg
void	va_start(va_list ap, parmN);	stdarg
int	vfprintf(FILE *stream, char *format, va_list arg);	stdio
int	vprintf(char *format, va_list arg);	stdio
int	vsprintf(char *s, char *format, va_list arg);	stdio

Table D.2   Standard Header File Identifiers

Appendix E
ASCII/EBCDIC Character Codes

ASCII CHARACTER CODES

Dec	Hex	Char	Dec	Hex	Char	Dec	Hex	Char	Dec	Hex	Char
000	00	^@	032	20	SP	064	40	@	096	60	`
001	01	^A	033	21	!	065	41	A	097	61	a
002	02	^B	034	22	"	066	42	B	098	62	b
003	03	^C	035	23	#	067	43	C	099	63	c
004	04	^D	036	24	$	068	44	D	100	64	d
005	05	^E	037	25	%	069	45	E	101	65	e
006	06	^F	038	26	&	070	46	F	102	66	f
007	07	^G	039	27	'	071	47	G	103	67	g
008	08	^H	040	28	(	072	48	H	104	68	h
009	09	^I	041	29	)	073	49	I	105	69	i
010	0a	^J	042	2a	*	074	4a	J	106	6a	j
011	0b	^K	043	2b	+	075	4b	K	107	6b	k
012	0c	^L	044	2c	,	076	4c	L	108	6c	l
013	0d	^M	045	2d	−	077	4d	M	109	6d	m
014	0e	^N	046	2e	.	078	4e	N	110	6e	n
015	0f	^O	047	2f	/	079	4f	O	111	6f	o
016	10	^P	048	30	0	080	50	P	112	70	p
017	11	^Q	049	31	1	081	51	Q	113	71	q
018	12	^R	050	32	2	082	52	R	114	72	r
019	13	^S	051	33	3	083	53	S	115	73	s
020	14	^T	052	34	4	084	54	T	116	74	t
021	15	^U	053	35	5	085	55	U	117	75	u
022	16	^V	054	36	6	086	56	V	118	76	v
023	17	^W	055	37	7	087	57	W	119	77	w
024	18	^X	056	38	8	088	58	X	120	78	x
025	19	^Y	057	39	9	089	59	Y	121	79	y
026	1a	^Z	058	3a	:	090	5a	Z	122	7a	z
027	1b	ESC	059	3b	;	091	5b	[	123	7b	{
028	1c		060	3c	<	092	5c	\	124	7c	¦
029	1d		061	3d	=	093	5d	]	125	7d	}
030	1e		062	3e	>	094	5e	^	126	7e	~
031	1f		063	3f	?	095	5f	_	127	7f	

ASCII CHARACTER CODES

Dec	Hex	Char	Dec	Hex	Char	Dec	Hex	Char	Dec	Hex	Char
128	80	Ç	160	a0	á	192	c0	L	224	e0	α
129	81	ü	161	a1	í	193	c1	⊥	225	e1	β
130	82	é	162	a2	ó	194	c2		226	e2	Γ
131	83	â	163	a3	ú	195	c3	⊢	227	e3	π
132	84	ä	164	a4	ñ	196	c4	—	228	e4	Σ
133	85	à	165	a5	Ñ	197	c5	+	229	e5	σ
134	86	å	166	a6	ª	198	c6	⊨	230	e6	μ
135	87	ç	167	a7	º	199	c7	⊩	231	e7	τ
136	88	ê	168	a8	¿	200	c8	⊾	232	e8	Φ
137	89	ë	169	a9	⌐	201	c9		233	e9	Θ
138	8a	è	170	aa	¬	202	ca	⊫	234	ea	Ω
139	8b	ï	171	ab	½	203	cb		235	eb	δ
140	8c	î	172	ac	¼	204	cc	⊩	236	ec	∞
141	8d	ì	173	ad	¡	205	cd	=	237	ed	φ
142	8e	Ä	174	ae	«	206	ce		238	ee	ε
143	8f	Å	175	af	»	207	cf	⊥	239	ef	∩
144	90	É	176	b0	▒	208	d0	⊔	240	f0	≡
145	91	æ	177	b1	▓	209	d1	⊤	241	f1	±
146	92	Æ	178	b2	▓	210	d2	⊤	242	f2	≥
147	93	ô	179	b3	│	211	d3	⊔	243	f3	≤
148	94	ö	180	b4	┤	212	d4	⊾	244	f4	⌠
149	95	ò	181	b5	╡	213	d5	F	245	f5	⌡
150	96	û	182	b6	╢	214	d6		246	f6	÷
151	97	ù	183	b7	╖	215	d7	┼	247	f7	≈
152	98	ÿ	184	b8	╕	216	d8	╪	248	f8	°
153	99	Ö	185	b9	╣	217	d9		249	f9	•
154	9a	Ü	186	ba	║	218	da	┌	250	fa	·
155	9b	¢	187	bb	╗	219	db	█	251	fb	√
156	9c	£	188	bc	╝	220	dc	▄	252	fc	η
157	9d	¥	189	bd	╜	221	dd	▌	253	fd	²
158	9e	₧	190	be	╛	222	de	▐	254	fe	▪
159	9f	ƒ	191	bf	┐	223	df	▀	255	ff	

EBCDIC CHARACTER CODES

Dec	Hex	Char	Dec	Hex	Char	Dec	Hex	Char	Dec	Hex	Char
000	00	NUL	032	20	DS	064	40	SP	096	60	
001	01	SOH	033	21	SOS	065	41		097	61	/
002	02	STX	034	22	FS	066	42		098	62	
003	03	ETX	035	23		067	43		099	63	
004	04	PF	036	24	BYP	068	44		100	64	
005	05	HT	037	25	LF	069	45		101	65	
006	06	LC	038	26	ETB	070	46		102	66	
007	07	DEL	039	27	ESC	071	47		103	67	
008	08		040	28		072	48		104	68	
009	09		041	29		073	49		105	69	
010	0a	SMM	042	2a	SM	074	4a		106	6a	
011	0b	VT	043	2b	CU2	075	4b	.	107	6b	,
012	0c	FF	044	2c		076	4c	<	108	6c	%
013	0d	CR	045	2d	ENQ	077	4d	(	109	6d	–
014	0e	SO	046	2e	ACK	078	4e	+	110	6e	>
015	0f	SI	047	2f	BEL	079	4f	|	111	6f	?
016	10	DLE	048	30		080	50	&	112	70	
017	11	DC1	049	31		081	51		113	71	
018	12	DC2	050	32	SYN	082	52		114	72	
019	13	TM	051	33		083	53		115	73	
020	14	RES	052	34	PN	084	54		116	74	
021	15	NL	053	35	RS	085	55		117	75	
022	16	BS	054	36	UC	086	56		118	76	
023	17	IL	055	37	EOT	087	57		119	77	
024	18	CAN	056	38		088	58		120	78	
025	19	EM	057	39		089	59		121	79	
026	1a	CC	058	3a		090	5a	!	122	7a	:
027	1b	CU1	059	3b	CU3	091	5b	$	123	7b	#
028	1c	IFS	060	3c	DC4	092	5c	*	124	7c	@
029	1d	IGS	061	3d	NAK	093	5d	)	125	7d	'
030	1e	IRS	062	3e		094	5e	;	126	7e	=
031	1f	IUS	063	3f	SUB	095	5f	¬	127	7f	"

EBCDIC CHARACTER CODES

Dec	Hex	Char	Dec	Hex	Char	Dec	Hex	Char	Dec	Hex	Char
128	80		160	a0		192	c0		224	e0	
129	81	a	161	a1		193	c1	A	225	e1	
130	82	b	162	a2	s	194	c2	B	226	e2	S
131	83	c	163	a3	t	195	c3	C	227	e3	T
132	84	d	164	a4	u	196	c4	D	228	e4	U
133	85	e	165	a5	v	197	c5	E	229	e5	V
134	86	f	166	a6	w	198	c6	F	230	e6	W
135	87	g	167	a7	x	199	c7	G	231	e7	X
136	88	h	168	a8	y	200	c8	H	232	e8	Y
137	89	i	169	a9	z	201	c9	I	233	e9	Z
138	8a		170	aa		202	ca		234	ea	
139	8b		171	ab		203	cb		235	eb	
140	8c		172	ac		204	cc		236	ec	
141	8d		173	ad		205	cd		237	ed	
142	8e		174	ae		206	ce		238	ee	
143	8f		175	af		207	cf		239	ef	
144	90		176	b0		208	d0		240	f0	0
145	91	j	177	b1		209	d1	J	241	f1	1
146	92	k	178	b2		210	d2	K	242	f2	2
147	93	l	179	b3		211	d3	L	243	f3	3
148	94	m	180	b4		212	d4	M	244	f4	4
149	95	n	181	b5		213	d5	N	245	f5	5
150	96	o	182	b6		214	d6	O	246	f6	6
151	97	p	183	b7		215	d7	P	247	f7	7
152	98	q	184	b8		216	d8	Q	248	f8	8
153	99	r	185	b9		217	d9	R	249	f9	9
154	9a		186	ba		218	da		250	fa	
155	9b		187	bb		219	db		251	fb	
156	9c		188	bc		220	dc		252	fc	
157	9d		189	bd		221	dd		253	fd	
158	9e		190	be		222	de		254	fe	
159	9f		191	bf		223	df		255	ff	

Appendix F
MS/PC-DOS Operating System Specifics

The MS/PC-DOS operating system was originally developed by the Microsoft Corporation for use on the IBM-PC/XT/AT series of personal computer systems. MS/PC-DOS is a single-user, nonmultitasking operating system. PC-DOS refers to the operating system as supplied specifically for the IBM-PC/XT/AT with MS-DOS referring to the generic system that runs on the popular compatibles. All material in this appendix will apply to both the generic and IBM operating system versions, unless otherwise stated.

F.1   Process Control

Since MS/PC-DOS is a single-tasking operating system, process control under its environment encompasses the following:

1. Invocation of processes.

2. Message passing from the calling process to the invoked process and vice versa.

F.1.1   *Invoking Processes—*spawn() *and* exec()

A process can be best described as an executing program. One process can invoke another under MS/PC-DOS using two basic schemes:

1. A parent (calling) process invokes a child (called) process and is overlaid by the child. When the child "dies", control passes to the process that invoked the parent (usually MS/PC-DOS).

2. A parent process invokes a child process and waits for the child to terminate. After the child "dies," the parent process resumes execution.

The exec() family of system calls can be used to invoke processes using scheme (1). The following example illustrates their use, utilizing execl():

```
┌─────────────────────────────┐
│  PARENT PROCESS CODE        │
└─────────────────────────────┘

    /*
     parent.c
     Example parent/child process invocation using execl()
    */
    #include <stdio.h>
    #include <process.h>

    main()
    {
        printf("Greetings from the PARENT process!\n");
        printf("---------------------------------\n");
        printf("I will now invoke a CHILD process using execl().\n\n");
```

```
/*
 Up to this point, only the PARENT exists
*/
    execl("\\msc\\workfile\\child.exe", "child.exe", "test_arg1",
                                        "test_arg2", NULL);
/*
 If CHILD is successfully created, this will never print
*/
    printf("There was an error creating the CHILD process.\n");
    exit(1);
}
```

┌─────────────────────┐
│ CHILD PROCESS CODE │
└─────────────────────┘

```
/*
 child.c
 The child process invoked by parent.exe
*/
#include <stdio.h>
#include <process.h>

main(argc, argv)
int argc;
char **argv;
{
    int arg_no = 0;

    printf("Greetings from the CHILD process!\n");
    printf("----------------------------------\n");
    printf("The %d args passed to me from the parent are:\n\n", argc);

    while(*argv)
        {
        printf("Argument #%d is %s\n", arg_no, *argv);
        ++argv;
        ++arg_no;
        }
    exit(0);
}
```

Running the program parent.exe produces the following output:

```
Greetings from the PARENT process!
----------------------------------
I will now invoke a CHILD process using execl().
```

(program continued on next page...)

```
Greetings from the CHILD process!
---------------------------------
The 3 args passed to me from the parent are:

Argument #0 is \msc\workfile\child.exe
Argument #1 is test_arg1
Argument #2 is test_arg2
```

In this example, the parent process runs the program child.exe passing to it the command line arguments child.exe, test_arg1 and test_arg2. If the child (child.exe) is successfully spawned, control will never return to the parent. When the child terminates, control will return to the process that invoked the parent (in this case, command.com, the MS/PC-DOS command-line processor).

In a similar manner, scheme (2) can be implemented using the spawn() family of system calls. An example, using spawnl(), is as follows:

```
┌─────────────────────────────┐
│ PARENT PROCESS CODE         │
└─────────────────────────────┘
```

```c
/*
 parent2.c
 Example parent/child process invocation using spawnl()
*/
#include <stdio.h>
#include <process.h>

main()
{
    printf("Greetings from the PARENT process!\n");
    printf("----------------------------------\n");
    printf("I will now invoke a CHILD process using spawnl().\n\n");
/*
 Up to this point, only the PARENT exists
*/
    if (spawnl(P_WAIT, "\\msc\\workfile\\child.exe", "child.exe",
               "test_arg1", "test_arg2", NULL) >= 0)
/*
 This will print after control is returned from the child process
*/
        {
        printf("\nGreetings again from the PARENT process!\n");
        }
    else
        {
        printf("\nThere was an error spawning the CHILD process.\n");
        }
    exit(1);
```

```
┌─────────────────────┐
│ CHILD PROCESS CODE  │
└─────────────────────┘
```

```c
/*
 child.c
 The child process invoked by parent.exe
*/
#include <stdio.h>
#include <process.h>

main(argc, argv)
int argc;
char **argv;
{
    int arg_no = 0;

    printf("Greetings from the CHILD process!\n");
    printf("---------------------------------\n");
    printf("The %d args passed to me from the parent are:\n\n", argc);

    while(*argv)
        {
        printf("Argument #%d is %s\n", arg_no, *argv);
        ++argv;
        ++arg_no;
        }
    exit(0);
}
```

Running the program `parent2.exe` produces the following output:

```
Greetings from the PARENT process!
-----------------------------------
I will now invoke a CHILD process using spawnl().

Greetings from the CHILD process!
---------------------------------
The 3 args passed to me from the parent are:

Argument #0 is \msc\workfile\child.exe
Argument #1 is test_arg1
Argument #2 is test_arg2

Greetings again from the PARENT process!
```

Note that in this example, the parent process spawns the child, waits, then receives control again after the child process dies. The macro `P_WAIT` is defined in the header file `process.h`. It specified that the parent is to wait for termination of the child process. If the spawn call fails, a value of -1 is returned; otherwise, the exit code of the child is returned (greater than or equal to zero).

F.1.2   *Exiting a Process*—`exit()`

All processes should use the system call `exit()` to terminate. The syntax of `exit()` is:

```
exit(status)
```

where `status` is an integer value. By convention, an exit status of 0 indicates that the process executed successfully and that no error (that is, no error that the parent should be aware of) occurred. A status greater than zero indicates that an error occurred.

The exit status of a child process can be examined by the parent by retrieving the return value from a `spawn()` call, as in the following code fragment:

```
     .
     .
     .
int status;
     .
     .
     .
/*
 Here a child process is spawned successfully using spawnl().
*/
status = spawnl("child.exe", "child.exe", NULL);

/*
 After the child process terminates, its status is examined.
*/

if (status == 0)
    {
    printf("Child process indicates no error occurred.\n);
    }
else if (status > 0)
    {
    printf("Child process indicates that an error occurred.\n");
    }
else
    {
    printf("Child could NOT be spawned.\n");
    }
     .
     .
     .
```

F.2   Screen Control

The IBM-PC and other microcomputers provide methods of using the hardware which many programmers who have worked on minicomputers and mainframes have never seen. There are three ways to get information from a program onto the CRT when using the IBM-PC. These are, from fastest to slowest:

1. Write directly to the memory locations that are associated (mapped) to the CRT. Characters will instantly appear on the screen.

2. Use the BIOS (Basic Input/Output System) which is present in the ROM (Read-Only Memory) chips inside the PC's system unit. All PC's, including clones, have this BIOS.

3. Use MS/PC-DOS to write the characters to the desired file or device. (Note that using ANSI.SYS requires this third technique.)

When writing directly to the memory locations or ports the programmer has complete control over the entire I/O operation. This also requires that the programmer know about hardware locations, device status codes, error checking, and so forth. Using the BIOS is slightly easier since there are routines built into the BIOS to facilitate device access. One of the most widely used BIOS routines is the video I/O interrupt, 10H, which gives access to the CRT(s) and display adapter(s).

These first two display techniques, although faster, have various liabilities. They are not always portable, require more programmer training and debugging effort, and are subject to change with different hardware configurations. Using MS/PC-DOS to manage the I/O (the third technique) removes from the programmer much of the responsibility for status checking, knowing device names or locations, or even knowing which BIOS routines are present on a particular machine. Although it is the slowest approach, it is also the most portable.

F.2.1   ANSI Screen Control Concepts

Computer manufacturers have for years provided a fairly portable convention for controlling CRT screen cursor location, cursor movement, and screen color. This convention, using ANSI standard terminal control sequences, is available in an abbreviated form for the PC. While the actual codes used on the PC may not exactly match those used on other computers, the concept is the same and the technique just as easy to use. The approach consists of sending special sequences of characters to the CRT screen. These characters are merely part of the display output stream, which is continuously examined by a device driver program (ANSI.SYS). This program resides in the computer's memory at all times, having been placed there when the operating system loaded itself at boot time. The character sequence that actuates the device driver contains special control codes, which are never used as part of normal screen display data. This means that a programmer must intentionally request that the device driver take action; no unintended action should ever take place.

F.2.2   *Installing ANSI.SYS*

ANSI.SYS is a device driver program that must be "installed" in the computer. This means that the file ANSI.SYS must be identified to MS/PC-DOS at the time the computer is either turned on (cold boot) or reset with the Ctrl-Alt-Del key sequence.

If a hard disk system is being used, there is probably a file called CONFIG.SYS in the root directory of the hard drive. If the file ANSI.SYS is in the root directory, the following line should be added to CONFIG.SYS:

```
DEVICE=C:\ANSI.SYS
```

If the file ANSI.SYS is put in the subdirectory named DOS the line added to CONFIG.SYS should look like this:

```
DEVICE=C:\DOS\ANSI.SYS
```

If the file CONFIG.SYS does not already exist, create one with a text editor and add the appropriate line. After CONFIG.SYS has been created or modified, the machine must be rebooted to invoke ANSI.SYS. If the installation was successful, then setting the MS/PC-DOS prompt to this:

```
PROMPT $e[37;44m
```

will result in the subsequent display showing white letters on a blue background. The left square bracket symbol should not be visible. If the monitor being used is monochrome rather than color, use this prompt:

```
PROMPT $e[0;7m$p$g $e[0m
```

which will turn all attributes off, display the current drive, path and a space in reverse video, and then reset the attributes to normal white on black.

F.2.3   *Clearing the Screen*

The remaining sections of this appendix will demonstrate how to control the screen by using the `printf()` function, by sending character sequences that cause the ANSI.SYS device driver to change the screen.

The ANSI.SYS control sequences all start with the escape character. This is an ASCII defined code, which has the numerical value of 27. When ANSI.SYS sees an escape character, it begins to take special note of the characters that immediately follow. If they match a defined sequence, an action can take place. For instance, if the characters

```
[2J
```

follow an escape character then the screen is cleared. After the screen clears the cursor is placed in the upper left corner of the screen. The square left bracket is the same character that C uses for array subscripting. The J must be capitalized; a lowercase j will not work. The case of letters is important for all the ANSI.SYS control sequences.

To use this character sequence any one of the following printf() statements could be written:

```
printf("\x1b[2J");                /* use only one of these */
printf("\033[2J");
printf("\033[%dJ", 2);
```

The \x1b is the way that the decimal number 27 is written in hex. To write the same number in octal (base 8), use \033.

The #define directive can also add clarity to the program in this way:

```
#define  CLEAR_SCREEN  printf("\x1b[2J")
```

allowing this to be written later in the program

```
CLEAR_SCREEN;
```

whenever the screen needs to be cleared. Notice that we did not include the semi-colon in the definition of CLEAR_SCREEN. We provided it when we actually used the definition. This adds flexibility to our programming because we can use CLEAR_SCREEN in places where a semicolon would cause an error (e.g., we can follow CLEAR_SCREEN with a comma if necessary).

If "funny characters" appear on the screen from the printf() statement described above, like a left arrow followed by the square bracket, then it means that ANSI.SYS was not installed. Double-check all the changes that were made, especially the entry in CONFIG.SYS. One of the authors had a problem getting ANSI.SYS to work when writing this book. The problem turned out to be a supplemental library which the author used when compiling programs. This library redefined the printf() function to write directly to the video I/O memory rather than to go through MS/PC-DOS. Obviously the ANSI.SYS driver can't translate a command if it never sees it!

F.2.4 *Moving the Cursor*

The escape sequence to move the cursor to a particular row and column location is:

```
ESC[#;#H
```

where ESC designates the escape character 27 and the # symbols indicate the need for a row and column number, in that order. Both the row and column numbers are required. The upper left corner of the screen is row 1, column 1. The H that terminates the sequence must be in uppercase, and the semicolon that separates the numbers is required.

For example, to move the cursor to row 10, column 13 we can write

```
printf("\x1b[%d;%dH", 10, 13);
```

The 10 and 13 could also be hard coded in the command this way:

```
printf("\x1b[10;13H");
```

If invalid row and column locations are sent to ANSI.SYS, e.g., row 200, column 300 on a 25-line 80-column monitor, ANSI.SYS merely does nothing.

A macro that would implement this ANSI.SYS command might look like this:

```
#define  POSITION_CURSOR(row, col)  printf("\x1b[%d;%dH", row, col)
```

allowing this to be written later:

```
POSITION_CURSOR(10, 13);
```

It would accomplish the same thing as the explicit version above.

F.2.5   *Determining the Cursor Position*

Occasionally it may be necessary to determine the current location of the cursor. Such situations typically arise when the application must restore the cursor to a previous position or perform cursor positioning relative to dynamic row/column settings. The ANSI escape sequence to accomplish this task is:

```
ESC[6n
```

where ESC designates the escape character 27. The ANSI driver places the result (current row and column settings) on the stdin input stream, embedded in another escape sequence according to the template:

```
ESC[##;##R
```

where # represents a digit of the row or column returned, with the row value given first, immediately following the [character. To extract the row/column settings from the escape sequence the following steps must be performed:

1. Retrieve the first two characters, ESC and [, using a stdin function such as getch() and ignore the result.

2. Retrieve (and save) the next two characters. These collectively represent the current row setting.

3. Retrieve and ignore the next character, ;.

4. Retrieve (and save) the next two characters. These collectively represent the current column setting.

5. Discard all remaining characters (flush out the stdin input stream). A suitable code fragment to accomplish this is:

```
while(getch() != '\r') {
    ;
}
```

An example of how to use this ANSI.SYS command will be found in the example program, ginpansi.c, in Figure F.2 at the end of this appendix.

F.2.6   *Setting the Attributes*

The escape sequence to set the screen attributes is

```
ESC[#;...;#m
```

where ESC is still the escape character 27 and the # symbols designate one or more screen attribute characteristics. The m that terminates the sequence must be in lowercase, and the semicolons that separate the numbers are required.

The valid parameters that can be used for this ANSI.SYS command are listed in Tables F.1 and F.2.

Value	Effect
0	All attributes off—normal white on black
1	Bold (high intensity)
4	Underscore on (monochrome only)
5	Blink on
7	Reverse video on
8	Invisible on (background == foreground)

Figure F.1   ANSI.SYS General Screen Attribute Values

Foreground	Color	Background
30	Black	40
31	Red	41
32	Green	42
33	Yellow	43
34	Blue	44
35	Magenta (reddish-purple)	45
36	Cyan (greenish-blue)	46
37	White	47

Figure F.2   ANSI.SYS Screen Color Values

Once the screen colors have been changed, all subsequent output that uses ANSI.SYS (i.e., all output through MS/PC-DOS) will appear with the new characteristics. For example, to set the screen attributes to bold, blinking white foreground on blue background, we could do the following:

```
printf("\x1b[%d;%d;%d;%dm", 37, 44, 1, 5);
```

A macro can be written to simplify this task:

```
#define  SET_ATTRIBUTE(attr)  printf("\x1b[%dm", attr)
```

The macro would be used like this to accomplish the same net effect as the `printf()` statement above:

```
SET_ATTRIBUTE(37);
SET_ATTRIBUTE(44);
SET_ATTRIBUTE(1);
SET_ATTRIBUTE(5);
```

Although we wanted to set four attributes at the same time in this particular situation, it is unlikely that we would always want to set four attributes at the same time. While the technique of setting one attribute at a time is less efficient, it is more practical and much easier to use.

The screen effects set with ANSI.SYS last until some subsequent request changes the screen colors again. If the screen is set blinking and then the program is terminated, MS/PC-DOS will continue to produce blinking output even after the program ends. It might be wise, then, to set the MS/PC-DOS prompt so that it will turn off all the attributes, like this:

```
PROMPT $e[0m$p$g
```

The program in Figure F.1 uses the macros and `printf()` statements defined above. It clears the screen, sets the cursor, then puts out a message in reverse video. Notice that by using macros and preprocessor directives the program is almost self-documenting.

```
/*
**   Illustration of ANSI.SYS Screen Control - ansi_sys.c
*/

#include <stdio.h>

#define  CLEAR_SCREEN              printf("\x1b[2J")
#define  POSITION_CURSOR(row, col) printf("\x1b[%d;%dH", row, col)
#define  SET_ATTRIBUTE(attr)       printf("\x1b[%dm", attr)
```

```
main()
{
    CLEAR_SCREEN;
    POSITION_CURSOR(10,10);
    SET_ATTRIBUTE(7);                          /* reverse video */
    printf("This should appear in reverse video\n");
}
```

Figure F.3 An Illustration of ANSI.SYS **Screen Control—**ansi_sys.c

Using ANSI screen control, a fancier version of the getinput() routine
(Chapter 7 review program) can be developed. This version uses the cursor-
positioning facilities of ANSI to allow user-input within, instead of underneath,
the edit mask. Notice that using getch() allows get_field_input() to "skip
over" the mask characters retrieving only the IN__CHAR portions of the edit field.
The program in Figure F.2 was run under PC-DOS version 3.3 on an IBM-PC.

```
/*-------------------------------------------------------------------
 ginpansi.c
 Maskable inputs using ANSI.SYS cursor control and getch()
 The  main()  function is simply a driver to test the function
 get_field_input()
---------------------------------------------------------------*/
#include <conio.h>                           /* for getch() prototype */
#include <stdio.h>

void locate_cursor(int, int);                /* declaration and argument type */
                                             /* checking for locate_cursor() */
void get_cursor_location(int *, int *);
int get_field_input(char *, char *, int, char *);

main()
{
    int in_buf_length;                       /* length of input retrieved */
    char in_buffer[80];                      /* buffer where input is placed */
/*
 get date from user and print what's returned with its length
*/
    in_buf_length = get_field_input("Enter date :", "[  /  / ]", 6, in_buffer);
    printf("\nin_buffer = %s, in_buf_length = %d\n", in_buffer, in_buf_length);
```

(program continued on next page...)

```
/*
 get user's initials and print what's returned with its length
*/
   in_buf_length = get_field_input("Enter your initials (first,middle,last) :",
                              "[ , , ]", 3, in_buffer);
   printf("\nin_buffer = %s, in_buf_length = %d\n", in_buffer, in_buf_length);
/*
 get user's height in feet/inches and print what's returned with its length
*/
   in_buf_length = get_field_input("Enter height :", "[ ' \"]", 3, in_buffer);
   printf("\nin_buffer = %s, in_buf_length = %d\n", in_buffer, in_buf_length);
}


/*-------------------------------------------------------------------
 int get_field_input(prompt, edit_mask, field_length, dest_buffer)
```

MS-DOS/ANSI.SYS VERSION
Generate a maskable entry field and store input as a string into the
destination buffer. The edit mask is used as a template only and is not
included in the returned input string.

```
    entry:
    parm           type        description
    ..............................................................
    prompt         char[]      the user prompt
    edit_mask      char[]      the edit mask, a string consisting of
                               characters and spaces; spaces represent the
                               actual field characters to retrieve
    field_length   int         the number of characters to retrieve; should
                               equal the number of spaces in edit_mask
    dest_buffer    char[]      buffer where input retrieved is stored; will
                               contain the actual characters input, not
                               including the edit_mask string; should be
                               dimensioned at least field_length + 1 to
                               accommodate ASCII NULL appended to
                               characters retrieved

    exit:
    variable       type        description
    ..............................................................
    j              int         the actual number of characters retrieved
                               which will be <= field_length
-------------------------------------------------------------------*/
int get_field_input(prompt, edit_mask, field_length, dest_buffer)
char prompt[], edit_mask[], dest_buffer[];
int field_length;
```

```
{
    int current_row, current_col;       /* storage for current cursor */
                                        /* row and column */
    int i, j;                           /* array indexes, i for edit_mask */
                                        /* and j for dest_buffer */
    char c;                             /* variable to hold character */
                                        /* inputs from user */
    printf("%s", prompt);               /* print user prompt */
/*
 get current cursor location, both row and column
*/
    get_cursor_location(&current_row, &current_col);
    i = 0;                              /* initialize edit mask index */
    printf("%s", edit_mask);            /* print edit mask string */
    while (edit_mask[i] != ' ') {       /* determine start location within */
        ++i;                            /* edit mask itself */
    }
/*
 put cursor on screen within start of edit_mask
*/
    locate_cursor(current_row, current_col + i);
    j = 0;                              /* initialize input buffer index */
    dest_buffer[j] = '\0';              /* zero first position in case */
                                        /* user inputs nothing */
/*
 get characters from stdin until user hits return
*/
    while ((c = getch()) != '\r')
        {
        switch (c)
            {
            case '\b':                  /* if backspace */
                {
                if (j != 0)             /* if not first field position, */
                    {
                    --j;                /* backup dest_buffer index */
/*
 if it's not the last field position, then back up up to previous
 edit mask location and clear the character that's there
    else
 just backspace and clear the character that's there
*/
```

(program continued on next page...)

```
                        if (j < field_length - 1)
                           {
                           while (edit_mask[--i] != ' ')
                               ;
                           locate_cursor(current_row, current_col + i);
                           putchar(' ');
                           putchar(c);
                           }
                        else
                           {
                           putchar(c);
                           putchar(' ');
                           putchar(c);
                           }
                        }
                     break;
                     }
                default:
                   {
                   if (j < field_length)              /* if we're not at end of field */
                      {
                      putchar(c);                      /* display the character */
                      dest_buffer[j] = c;              /* and put in dest_buffer */
                      ++j;                             /* then bump the index */
/*
 if still not at the end of the field, find the next field
 position and put the cursor there
*/
                      if (j < field_length)
                         {
                         while (edit_mask[++i] != ' ')
                             ;
                         locate_cursor(current_row, current_col + i);
                         }
                      }
                   break;
                   }
                }
             fflush(stdin);
             }

      dest_buffer[j] = '\0';                           /* tack on the NULL character */
      return(j);                                       /* and return the input length */
}
```

```
/*-----------------------------------------------------------------
  void locate_cursor(row, column)

MS-DOS/ANSI.SYS VERSION

Locate the cursor using the ANSI escape sequence ESC[#;#H

 parm           type           description
...................................................................
 row            int            cursor row
 column         int            cursor column

 return         type           description
...................................................................
 ---            void
-------------------------------------------------------------*/
void locate_cursor(row, column)
int row, column;
{
/*
 NOTE: MS-DOS/ANSI.SYS SPECIFIC CODE FOLLOWS
*/
    printf("\x1b[%d;%dH", row, column);
    return;
}


/*-----------------------------------------------------------------
  void get_cursor_location(row, column)

MS-DOS/ANSI.SYS VERSION

Locate the cursor using the ANSI escape sequence ESC[#;#H

 parm           type           description
...................................................................
 row            int *          pointer to row variable
 column         int *          pointer to column variable

 return         type           description
...................................................................
 ---            void
-------------------------------------------------------------*/
void get_cursor_location(row, column)
int *row, *column;
{

    printf("\x1b[6n");                    /* get cursor coordinates to stdin */
```

(program continued on next page...)

```
/*
 Now, extract cursor coordinates from stdin.
 String to operate on will have the form ESC[##;##R.
*/
    getch();                              /* throw away ESC character */
    getch();                              /* and [ character */
    *row = (getch() - '0') * 10;          /* the first row digit */
    *row += getch() - '0';                /* the second row digit */
    getch();                              /* discard ; character */
    *column = (getch() - '0') * 10;       /* first column digit */
    *column += getch() - '0';             /* second column digit */
    while(getch() != '\r') {              /* discard the rest */
        ;
    }
    return;
}
```

Figure F.4   An Ansi Version of get_field_input()—ginpansi.c

Here is the output of the above program:

```
Enter date :[01/10/88]
in_buffer = 011088, in_buf_length = 6
Enter your initials (first,middle,last) :[R,R,S]
in_buffer = RRS, in_buf_length = 3
Enter height :[5'11"]
in_buffer = 511, in_buf_length = 3
```

Figure F.5   ginpansi.c Program Output

Note that the get_field_input() function depends intimately on the ANSI.SYS driver and the unbuffered nature of the standard library function getch().

Appendix G
UNIX Operating System Specifics

UNIX is a multiuser, multitasking operating system developed at Bell Laboratories in 1969. Since that time there have been several versions of UNIX.

UNIX System III
UNIX Version 7
Berkley UNIX
Xenix
UNIX Version V

In 1985, a document called AT&T System V Interface Definition (SVID) was published to help standardize the operating system across different environments. The information in this appendix conforms to this standard.

G.1 Process Control

Loosely speaking, a process can be thought of as an executing program. A process is usually invoked by another process, normally the shell or parent process. Although UNIX provides a rich set of process-control system calls, only a limited, but useful, set will be covered here.

In a multitasking environment, three primary concerns of process control are:

1. Invocation of processes.

2. Synchronization of processes.

3. Interprocess communication.

UNIX provides the `fork()` and `exec()` system calls to handle invocation of processes and the `wait()` system call for synchronization of processes. The only call we will considered for interprocess communication will be the `exit()` system call. Be aware, however, that UNIX provides a wide and thorough array of facilities to handle interprocess communication. An extensive discussion of this subject is beyond the scope of an appendix.

G.1.1 *Invoking Processes*—`fork()`, `exec()` *and* `wait()`

A couple of important system calls are `fork()` and `exec()`. The `fork()` system call is used to invoke a second copy of the caller's executing code. In essence, `fork()` produces two identical programs that are executing simultaneously. The program the initially invokes the `fork()` call is known as the parent process; the duplicate process is known as the child process.

To illustrate, consider the following program fragment:

```
main()
{
   int pid = 0;                  /* pROCESS idENTIFICATION */

/*
 Only one process exists at this point, the PARENT process.
*/
   printf("Hi, I am the PARENT process.\n");
   printf("Now, I will create a CHILD process using fork()...\n");

   pid = fork();

/*
 Assuming fork() is successful, two processes are now executing
 simultaneously.
*/

   if (pid == 0)              /* if 0, CHILD process */
      {
      printf("Hi, I'm the CHILD process.\n");
      }
   else if (pid > 0)         /* if positive, PARENT process */
      {
      printf("Hi, I'm the PARENT process. \n");
      }
   else
      {
      printf("CHILD process could not be spawned.\n");
      printf("PARENT process is exiting...\n);
      exit(1);
      }
/*
 If we get this far in the code, the CHILD process has been
 spawned.

 wait() is used by the PARENT process to wait for the CHILD process
 to terminate ("die" in classic UNIX terminology).
*/
   if (wait(NULL) < 0)
      {
      printf("I am the CHILD and am exiting...\n");
      exit(0);
      }
   else
      {
      printf("I am the PARENT and this code will execute\
              after my CHILD exits.\n");
      }
```

The situation that fork() produces can best be illustrated as shown in Figure G.1.

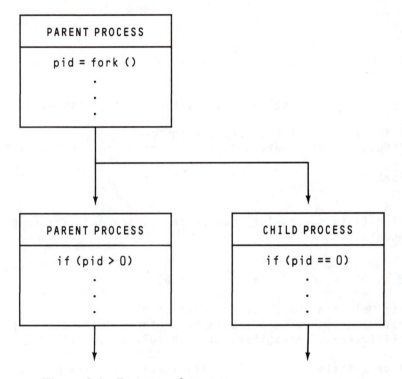

Figure G.1   Diagram of fork()

In the first section of the program, the fork() system call is used to "spawn" a child process. The child is, for all practical purposes, an exact duplicate of the calling process. The variable pid is assigned the return value of the fork() call. If the fork() call is successful, the parent will possess the process identification (pid) of the child process. If pid == 0, then the process is the child; if pid > 0, then the process is the parent; else the fork() call failed. Note that the child process begins execution immediately after the fork() call.

In the second section of the code, a wait() system call is used to release the child process after it dies. Note that wait() returns a −1 value if no child process exists, which would be true for the child process in this example. wait() normally returns the process identification of the child process, which can be used to identify which child terminates in multiple invocations of the fork() call. The wait() system call can also take a pointer to a status variable (integer) and will return the exit code of the child process. In our example we simply used a NULL pointer, which signals wait() to ignore returning the child exit status.

Since fork() produces a copy of the parent process, another system call, exec(), is useful for invoking processes that differ from the parent process.

Actually, `exec()` exists as a family of related system calls that can be applied in different situations. To illustrate, consider the following code fragment using the `execl()` call:

```c
main()
{
    int pid = 0;              /* pROCESS idENTIFICATION */

/*
 Only one process exists at this point, the PARENT process.
*/
    printf("Hi, I am the PARENT process.\n");
    printf("Now, I will create a CHILD process using fork()...\n");

    pid = fork();

/*
 Assuming fork() is successful, two processes are now executing
 simultaneously.
*/

    if (pid == 0)             /* if 0, CHILD1 process */
        {
        printf("Hi, I'm the CHILD 1 process.\n");
        printf("I will now be overlaid by another program...\n");
        execl("/usr/student/child2.out","child2.out", NULL);
/*
 if exec() call fails, then CHILD 1 still exists, therefore...
*/
        printf("Message from CHILD 1:\
                Child 2 could not be spawned.\n");
        }
    else if (pid > 0)         /* if positive, PARENT process */
        {
        printf("Hi, I'm the PARENT process. \n");
        }
    else
        {
        printf("CHILD1 process could not be spawned.\n");
        printf("PARENT process is exiting...\n);
        exit(1);
        }
/*
 If we get this far in the code, then the CHILD process has been
 spawned.

 wait() is used by the PARENT process to wait for the CHILD process
 to terminate ("die" in classic UNIX terminology).
*/
```

```
    if (wait(NULL) < 0)
        {
/*
 This will not print if CHILD 2 is spawned successfully. Why?
*/
        printf("I am CHILD 1 and am exiting...\n");
        exit(0);
        }
    else
        {
        printf("I am the PARENT and this code will execute\
                after my CHILD exits.\n");
        }
```

A diagram of this process is shown in Figure G.2.

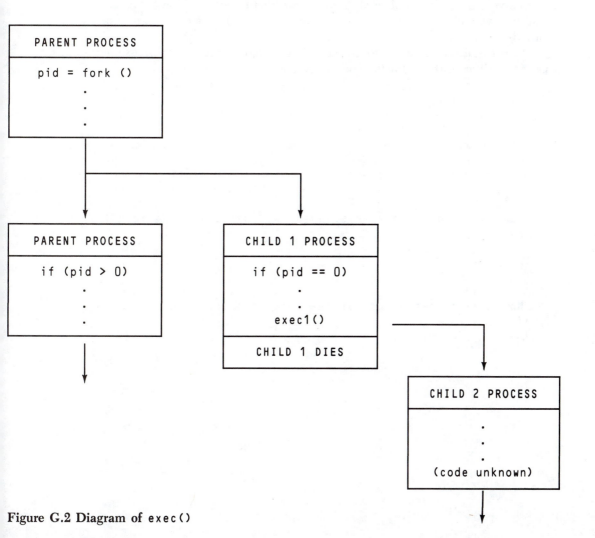

Figure G.2 Diagram of exec()

First the fork() system call is used to invoke a child process, which is essentially a duplicate of the parent. If successful, execl() is used to run a program called child2.out from the directory /usr/student. Note that if successful, child process #1 is destroyed (overlaid) by child process #2. Note also that the parent process does not know which child process is executing since both children will possess the same process identification.

G.1.2   *Exiting a Process*—exit()

All processes should use the system call exit() to terminate. The syntax of exit() is:

```
exit(status)
```

where status is an integer value. By convention, an exit status of 0 indicates that the process executed successfully and that no error (that is, no error that the parent should be aware of) occurred. A status greater than zero indicates that an error occurred.

The exit status of a child process can be examined by the parent by issuing a wait() call as in the following code fragment:

```
        .
        .
        .
    int status;
        .
        .
        .
    /*
      Here a child process is spawned successfully using fork().
    */
        .
        .
        .
    /*
      Now, the parent waits for the child process to die.
    */
```

```
wait(&status);

/*
 After the child process terminates, its status is examined.
*/

if (status != 0)
    {
    printf("Child process indicates that an error occurred.\n);
    printf("Error code is %d.\n", status);
    }
else
    {
    printf("Child process was successful with no errors.\n");
    }
       .
       .
       .
```

G.2   Screen Control Using `<curses.h>` for UNIX and VAX/VMS

The most portable way to accomplish screen control in the UNIX environment is to use the `<curses.h>` package. Unfortunately there is not yet a standard for the names and implementation of the functions used in `<curses.h>`. Each C compiler vendor seems to provide a slightly different set of functions, and often the techniques that are used are specific to a particular type of hardware.

The `<curses.h>` package includes windows, has a rich set of functions and macros which can be used to manipulate all aspects of terminal appearance and cursor movement, and is in general very easy to use. Using `<curses.h>` in a C program in the UNIX environment will require some, but possibly only slight, modification when the program is compiled with another vendor's compiler.

The example program in Figure G.3 was run under the VAX/VMS environment, version V4.5, using version 2.3 of VAX C. While VAX/VMS is not UNIX, this particular version of the C compiler incorporates most of the current ANSI standard features and includes a `<curses.h>` package. Fortunately most of the `<curses.h>` statements are almost self-documenting, so we'll merely place the explanation of the program in comments in the code itself. By no means is this an exhaustive use of `<curses.h>`. Further information is provided in the documentation by the vendor of the compiler being used.

```
/*
** An illustration of Curses Screen Control - curses.c
*/

#include "curses.h"
```

(program continued on next page...)

```
main()
{
   char a_string[24];

   initscr();        /* initscr opens a window called stdscr */

   clear();          /* clear the window stdscr */

   move(5, 13);      /* move positions the cursor */

                     /* setattr sets the screen attributes */
                     /*   notice how they are OR'd together */
   setattr(_BLINK | _BOLD | _REVERSE | _UNDERLINE);

                     /* printw uses the window stdscr, not standard output */
                     /*   the output occurs at the current cursor location */
   printw("BLINK and BOLD and REVERSE and UNDERLINED");

    /* clrattr clears specified attribute settings, leaving the rest set */
   clrattr(_BLINK | _BOLD);  /* REVERSE and UNDERLINE are left set */

                     /* mvaddstr combines move and printw */
   mvaddstr(3, 5, "Please enter a string");

        /* mvgetstr does NO checking about the length of the input string */
   mvgetstr(3, 30, a_string);

   endwin();        /* a window is ended with endwin */
}
```

Figure G.3   An Illustration of `<curses.h>` Screen Control—`curses.c`

Using curses screen control, a fancier version of the `getinput()` (Chapter 7 review program) can be developed (see Figure G.4). This version uses the cursor-positioning and windowing facilities of curses to allow user-input within, instead of underneath, the edit mask. In addition, the function `raw()` is called to allow `get_field_input()` to regain control after every keystroke instead of after a newline is encountered. Notice that this facility allows the function to "skip over" the mask characters, retrieving only the IN_CHAR portions of the edit field. The program was run under ULTRIX on a DEC-PDP 11/73 and compiled with the command line "`cc ginpunix.c -lcurses -ltermlib`"

```
/*---------------------------------------------------------------------
ginpunix.c
Maskable inputs using "curses" cursor control under UNIX.
The 'main()' function is simply a 'driver' to test the function
'getfinp()'.
---------------------------------------------------------------------*/
```

```
#include <stdio.h>
#include <curses.h>                      /* curses header file */

#define IN_CHAR ' '                      /* the edit_mask field entry char */
/*
 raw keystroke definitions
 NOTE: TERMINAL DEPENDENT!
*/
#define RETURN -115                      /* 'return' key */
#define BKSPACE -120                     /* 'backspace' key */




main()
{
   int in_buf_length;                    /* length of input retrieved */
   char in_buffer[80];                   /* buffer where input is placed */
/*
 open standard screen facilities and set mode
*/
   savetty();                            /* save terminal state */
   initscr();                            /* open "stdscr" */
   refresh();                            /* clear display */

/*
 get date from user and print what's returned with its length
*/
   in_buf_length = getfinp("Enter date :", "[  /  /  ]", 6, in_buffer);
   printw("\nin_buffer = %s, in_buf_length = %d\n", in_buffer, in_buf_length);
   refresh();
/*
 get user's initials and print what's returned with its length
*/
   in_buf_length = getfinp("Enter your initials (first,middle,last) :",
                           "[ , , ]", 3, in_buffer);
   printw("\nin_buffer = %s, in_buf_length = %d\n", in_buffer, in_buf_length);
   refresh();
/*
 get user's height in feet/inches and print what's returned with its length
*/
   in_buf_length = getfinp("Enter height :", "[ ' \"]", 3, in_buffer);
   printw("\nin_buffer = %s, in_buf_length = %d\n", in_buffer, in_buf_length);
   refresh();

   endwin();                             /* close window */
   resetty();                            /* restore terminal state */
}
```

(program continued on next page...)

```
/*-------------------------------------------------------------------
 int getfinp(prompt, edit_mask, field_length, dest_buffer)

UNIX/CURSES VERSION

Generate a maskable entry field and store input as a string into
the destination buffer. The edit mask is used as a template only
and is not included in the returned input string.

entry:
parm            type        description
...............................................................
prompt          char[]      the user prompt
edit_mask       char[]      the edit mask, a string consisting of
                            characters & spaces; spaces represent the
                            actual field characters to retrieve
field_length    int         the number of characters to retrieve; should
                            equal the number of spaces in edit_mask
dest_buffer     char[]      buffer where input retrieved is stored; will
                            contain the actual characters input not
                            including the edit_mask string; should be
                            dimensioned at least field_length + 1 to
                            accommodate ascii nul appended to
                            characters retrieved

exit:
variable        type        description
...............................................................
j               int         the actual number of characters retrieved
                            which will be <= field_length
--------------------------------------------------------------------*/
int getfinp(prompt, edit_mask, field_length, dest_buffer)
char prompt[], edit_mask[], dest_buffer[];
int field_length;
{
   int row, col;                            /* storage for current cursor */
                                            /* row and column */
   int i, j;                                /* array indexes, i for edit_mask */
                                            /* and j for dest_buffer */
   int c;                                   /* variable to hold character */
                                            /* inputs from user */
   printw("%s", prompt);                    /* print user prompt */
/*
 get current cursor position, both row and column
*/
   getyx(stdscr, row, col);                 /* get current cursor coordinates */
   i = 0;                                   /* initialize edit mask index */
   printw("%s", edit_mask);                 /* print edit mask string */
   while (edit_mask[i] != IN_CHAR)          /* determine start location within */
      ++i;                                  /* edit mask itself */
```

```
/*
put cursor on screen within start of edit_mask
*/
   move(row, col + i);                  /* move cursor */
   refresh();                           /* refresh stdscr display */
   raw();                               /* get raw keystrokes from keyboard */
   noecho();                            /* and don't echo to display */

   j = 0;                               /* initialize input buffer index */
   dest_buffer[j] = '\0';               /* zero first position in case */
                                        /* user inputs nothing */
/*
get characters from stdin until user hits RETURN
*/
   while ((c = getch()) != RETURN)      /* get keystrokes until user hits */
      {                                 /* 'return' key */
      switch (c)
         {
         case BKSPACE:                  /* if backspace */
            {
            if (j != 0)                 /* if not first field position, */
               {
               --j;                     /* backup dest_buffer index */
/*
if it's not the last field position, then backup up to previous
edit mask location and clear the character that's there
   else
just backspace and clear the character that's there
*/
               if (j < field_length - 1)  /* if not end of field */
                  {
                  while (edit_mask[--i] != IN_CHAR)
                     ;
                  }
               move(row, col + i);
               addch(IN_CHAR);
               move(row, col + i);
               }
            break;
            }
         default:
            {
            if (j < field_length)       /* if we're not at end of field */
               {
               addch(c);                /* display the character */
               dest_buffer[j] = c;      /* and put in dest_buffer */
               ++j;                     /* then bump the index */
```

(program continued on next page...)

```
/*
 if still not at the end of the field, find the next field
 position and put the cursor there
*/
             if (j < field_length)
                {
                while (edit_mask[++i] != IN_CHAR)
                   ;
                move(row, col + i);
                }
             }
          break;
          }
       }
    refresh();                         /* update the display */
    }
    dest_buffer[j] = '\0';             /* tack on the nul character */
    noraw();                           /* turn off raw keystroke gathering */
    return(j);                         /* and return the input length */
}
```

Figure G.4   A Curses Version of `get_field_input()`—`ginpunix.c`

Figure G.5 shows the output from the program `ginpunix.c`:

```
Enter date :[01/10/88]
in_buffer = 011088, in_buf_length = 6
Enter your initials (first,middle,last) :[R,R,S]
in_buffer = RRS, in_buf_length = 3
Enter height :[5'11"]
in_buffer = 511, in_buf_length = 3
```

Figure G.5   `ginpunix.c` Program Output

The curses function `initscr()` is used to open a window called `stdscr`. This is the default window device, much as `stdout` is the default display device. Other windows can be opened using `WINDOW *` in a similar fashion as with other devices (i.e., stream access using `FILE *`).

Two important facilities used in the function `getfinp()` are `raw()` and `noecho()`. Since the function `getch()` is normally buffered and echoed, `raw()` is used to retrieve the user keystroke in an unbuffered, low-level manner, while `noecho()` allows the function to examine the user keystrokes before they are echoed to `stdscr`. The `raw()` function causes all subsequent input to be terminal dependent, which means that the values returned by the `getch()` function will be different for each different type of terminal. For instance, a VT200 terminal will return different codes than will a DCMII, and programs written to expect codes from one terminal type will not work when used from a terminal of a different type.

It is important to remember that display manipulation is almost always nonportable. Functions written that manipulate the display in a sophisticated manner (such as getfinp()) will most certainly have to be modified if ported to a different machine environment.

Index